Military-Civilian Interactions

NEW MILLENNIUM BOOKS
IN INTERNATIONAL STUDIES

Deborah J. Gerner, University of Kansas, *Series Editor*

New Millennium Books issue out of the unique position of the global system at the end of the Cold War, the end of the 20th century, and the beginning of a new millennium in which our understandings about war, peace, identity, sovereignty, security, and sustainability—whether economic, environmental, or ethical—are likely to be challenged. In the new millennium of international relations, new theories, new actors, new policies and processes are all bound to be engaged. Books in the series will be of three types: compact core texts, supplementary texts, and "hypertexts."

Editorial Board

Mark Boyer University of Connecticut	**Ole Holsti** Duke University	**Anne Sisson Runyan** Wright State University
Maryann Cusimano Catholic University of America	**Barry Hughes** University of Denver	**Gerald Schneider** University of Konstanz, Germany
John Freeman University of Minnesota	**George Irani** University of Balamand, Lebanon	**Philip Schrodt** University of Kansas
Nils Petter Gleditsch International Peace Research Institute	**Christopher Joyner** Georgetown University	**Eric Selbin** Southwestern University
Joshua Goldstein American University	**Margaret Karns** University of Dayton	**Tim Shaw** Dalhousie University
Vicki Golich California State University—San Marcos	**Audie Klotz** University of Illinois—Chicago	**Thomas Weiss** City University of New York
Ted Robert Gurr University of Maryland	**Marc Levy** Columbia University	**Eugene Wittkopf** Louisiana State University
	Laura Neack Miami University	**Michael Zuern** Bremen University

Forthcoming

NEGOTIATING A COMPLEX WORLD: AN INTRODUCTION TO INTERNATIONAL NEGOTIATION
By Brigid Starkey, Mark A. Boyer, and Jonathan Wilkenfeld

Military-Civilian Interactions

Intervening in Humanitarian Crises

Thomas G. Weiss

ROWMAN & LITTLEFIELD PUBLISHERS, INC.
Lanham • Boulder • New York • Oxford

ROWMAN & LITTLEFIELD PUBLISHERS, INC.

Published in the United States of America
by Rowman & Littlefield Publishers, Inc.
4720 Boston Way, Lanham, Maryland 20706

12 Hid's Copse Road
Cumnor Hill, Oxford OX2 9JJ, England

Copyright © 1999 by Rowman & Littlefield Publishers, Inc.

All rights reserved. No part of this publication may be reproduced, stored in a retrieval system, or transmitted in any form or by any means, electronic, mechanical, photocopying, recording, or otherwise, without prior permission of the publisher.

British Library Cataloguing in Publication Information Available

Library of Congress Cataloging-in-Publication Data

Weiss, Thomas George.
   Military-civilian interactions : intervening in humanitarian crises / Thomas G. Weiss.
   p.   cm.
   Includes bibliographical references and index.
   ISBN 0-8476-8745-7 (alk. paper).—ISBN 0-8476-8746-5 (alk. paper)
   1. Intervention (International law)   2. Civil-military relations.
3. Armed Forces—Civic action.   I. Title.
JZ6369.W45   1999
341.5'84'09045—dc21   98-27504
                                                                      CIP

Printed in the United States of America

∞ ™ The paper used in this publication meets the minimum requirements of American National Standard for Information Sciences—Permanence of Paper for Printed Library Materials, ANSI Z39.48—1984.

For Rebeccah, Hannah, and Priscilla

Contents

List of Illustrations	ix
Foreword, *Brian Urquhart*	xi
Preface	xiii
List of Abbreviations	xvii
Introduction	1
1 Armed Forces and Humanitarian Action: Past and Present	7
2 Framework for Estimating Military Costs and Civilian Benefits from Intervention	31
3 Northern Iraq, 1991–1996: A Difficult Act to Follow?	43
4 Somalia, 1992–1995: The Death of Pollyannaish Humanitarianism?	69
5 Bosnia, 1992–1995: Convoluted Charity?	97
6 Rwanda, 1994–1995: Better Late than Never?	137
7 Haiti, 1991–1996: Why Wait So Long?	167
8 Humanitarian Intervention: Costs, Benefits, Quandaries	193
Notes	221
Selected Bibliography of the 1990s	257
Index	269
About the Author	281

Illustrations

Maps

3.1	Iraq	44
4.1	Somalia	70
5.1	Former Yugoslavia	98
6.1	Rwanda	138
7.1	Haiti	168

Tables

2.1	Estimating Military Costs (for Troop-Contributing Countries) and Civilian Benefits (for Targeted Country) from Intervention	32
3.1	Northern Iraq: Military Costs and Civilian Benefits from Intervention, April–July 1991	65
3.2	Northern Iraq: Military Costs and Civilian Benefits from Continued Intervention, August 1991–1996	66
4.1	Somalia: Military Costs and Civilian Benefits from Intervention, 1992–1995	92
5.1	Bosnia and Herzegovina: Military Costs and Civilian Benefits from Intervention, 1992–1995	131
6.1	Rwanda: Military Costs and Civilian Benefits from Intervention, 1994–1995	160
7.1	Haiti: Military Costs and Civilian Benefits from Intervention, 1991–1996	188
8.1	Depicting Military Costs and Civilian Benefits across Cases	194

Photos

Food being distributed to displaced persons	16
UNITAF soldier shares light moment with Somalis	22
A boy speaks to a French UNPROFOR soldier in the besieged capital city of Sarajevo	27
Transporting relief items in Sarajevo	36
Medical personnel carry an Iraqi refugee into a camp near Safwan	39
British army medical officer	55
UNHCR in northern Iraq distributes shelter and roofing materials	63
UNITAF soldiers ride in back of an auto on a Somali street	79
A French United Nations soldier stands guard at a street corner in Mogadishu	89
UNPROFOR soldiers in Stari Vitez, Yugoslavia	106
Relief supplies arrive in Sarajevo	110
UN APCs at British Battalion in Stari Vitez	123
Bosnian Muslims wait at a checkpoint	129
A UN soldier from Russia plays with a baby in a camp at Ruhengeri	145
Two girls receive vaccinations from health workers in Goma	153
A French soldier protecting a camp in Gikongoro	164
Haitians celebrate the election of Father Aristide in Port-au-Prince	173
A Canadian MP, part of UNMIH, talks with local youth while patrolling Port-au-Prince	184
Local police train new policemen in Cap-Haïten; Canadian Civil Police observe the training	190
A child in Bosnia surveys the destruction in a war-torn city	196
Food is distributed to Rwandan children who lost their parents in recent massacres	205
A UNMIH peacekeeping soldier from Canada greets a young Haitian boy on the streets of Port-au-Prince	213

Foreword

The five cases studied in this book—northern Iraq, Somalia, Bosnia, Rwanda, and Haiti—already seem to belong to another era, and soon they will be part of another century. Even now it is hard to recall those heady and euphoric days of the early post–Cold War period, when nothing seemed impossible and when the United Nations Security Council could agree on just about anything. The sky seemed to be the limit, and the mood, briefly at any rate, that of President John F. Kennedy's inaugural address. A "new world order" and "assertive multilateralism" were the policies not of do-gooders and starry-eyed internationalists, but of the United States government. No problem was so daunting that the Security Council would not resolve to pitchfork the UN into yet another complex intrastate operation, and if the worst came to the worst, the troops would be there in support. All of this was less than seven years ago.

Of course it did not last. Failure and expense took their toll. Casualties in Somalia produced a U-turn in U.S. policy on UN peacekeeping operations. After some seventeen new operations in the early 1990s, it is now almost impossible to get U.S. agreement to the smallest and simplest UN peacekeeping operation. The talk is all of "reluctant sheriffs," "coalitions of the willing," and regional responses to disaster.

And yet there has been no moratorium on humanitarian disasters, and it seems likely that the world will continue to face a fairly steady succession of intolerable threats to very large groups of human beings. Even if governments do not necessarily feel a moral obligation to do something about all of them, experience shows that it is in the general interest to try to forestall such tragedies, or failing that, to cope with them as soon as possible. They cannot be ignored. It is therefore essential to work out the most effective and economical way for the world community—international organizations, governments, and nongovernmental organizations alike—to meet these situations in the future.

The trouble with the euphoric period of international humanitarian intervention of the early 1990s was that little effort was made, before taking action, to think out the significance of the changed nature of international involvement, to devise new mandates and arrangements for essentially new situations, and to decide who was to do what. The result was that the military very often drifted into the humanitarian field without much prior thought or planning, and the dreaded phrase "mission creep" was born.

The military is often the only organization with the necessary equipment and capacity for immediate action to be able to cope with a humanitarian emergency. On the other hand, this is *not* the main role of the military, and other priority military functions will inevitably get in the way. Far more thought needs to be given to the relative roles of the military and civilian sectors, and to the basic objectives of international humanitarian action, if we are to be able to meet humanitarian responsibilities in the future both with the maximum efficiency and without provoking the kind of backlash that recent experiences have caused.

Only a very courageous author would lead the first reconnaissance patrol into this murky and booby-trapped territory. This is what Thomas Weiss has done in this book. His work provides a very useful starting point from which governments and others can begin to devise better ways to meet humanitarian emergencies in the future.

> Brian Urquhart,
> Former undersecretary-general
> of the United Nations

Preface

At the end of the 1980s and beginning of the 1990s, the obligatory first sentence of most foreign policy analyses pointed to the sea change in international relations resulting from the Communist bloc's collapse and then the implosion of the Soviet Union. The disappearance of the other superpower did, in fact, alter substantially strategic calculations in the Pentagon and the North Atlantic Treaty Organization (NATO). At the same time, the initial euphoria about the shape of the new world order was clearly misplaced. State interests remain the basis for the international system, and peace has hardly broken out. As the French would say, *"Plus ça change, plus ç'est la même chose."*

That being said, substantial upheavals have occurred. One of the most important new dynamics of the post–Cold War period has been downsizing the armed forces and simultaneously assigning them new roles in a host of tragedies. The result of military-civilian interactions have, however, received a black eye from the so-called Somalia and Bosnia syndromes. The exchange of polemics continues between proponents and critics of external military involvement in troubled spots around the planet. There is great uncertainty about key functions (logistics and security), as well as the presence of contradictory and incomplete data. Nowhere are these characterizations more apt than in the United States.

I began to investigate this subject because of the confusion that reigned during numerous lectures, seminars, and conferences. More invective than coherent arguments and data were exchanged. I had originally been persuaded of the potential for expanded military involvement in what are now called "complex humanitarian emergencies" when I was executive director of the International Peace Academy in New York and began investigating the possibilities for United

Nations peacekeeping in regional conflicts as perestroika and glasnost permeated Mikhail Gorbachev's Soviet Union. Observing the occasional use of traditional peacekeepers to foster humanitarian values in such conflicts as those in Lebanon and Cyprus, I asked myself straightforwardly, "Why not elsewhere?"

As someone whose own revulsion with U.S. activities in Vietnam had led him to dismiss cavalierly the role of the armed forces, I found over the years that the military and the use of force were essential variables in the equations for wars, as well as for conflict management. Somewhat paradoxically then, this former conscientious objector was less keen about a "peace divided" than many observers; rather, I was intrigued about the possible uses of outside military forces to foster international peace and security. For me, the most likely and desirable peace dividend would be the application of military might and expertise to dampen violence and help victims under the auspices of a strengthened United Nations. As I remind my students, military teeth were supposed to distinguish the UN from its defunct predecessor, the League of Nations.

I should also indicate at the outset that there is an emphasis upon the United States in the following pages. This represents a conscious and substantive decision on my part rather than any unwitting parochialism. The United States finances 40 percent of NATO's bills and, until recently, over 30 percent of UN military expenditures. More importantly, as the remaining major (if not super-) power, multilateral military initiatives to respond to large-scale crises are virtually infeasible without Washington's concurrence and support. My non-American colleagues and friends will have to live with this political reality, and my emphasis, for some time.

Like many people in this business, my own thinking was dramatically influenced by the late Fred Cuny, who was murdered while on a humanitarian mission in Chechnya in April 1995. He first urged me in 1986 to pursue my notion of the expanded use of peacekeepers and other external military forces in the context of warming relations between Washington, D.C., and Moscow that would soon facilitate the growth of UN operations. He pressed me to organize a conference that resulted in one of the first critical investigations into this arena—my edited volume *Humanitarian Emergencies and Military Help in Africa* (London: Macmillan, 1990). He later contributed a thoughtful essay to *Soldiers, Peacekeepers, and Disasters* (London: Macmillan, 1991), which I had the pleasure to edit with my mentor, Leon Gordenker. Cuny was a brash Texan who taught me much. In particular, there is no reason to accept cowardice, unresponsiveness, and incompetence in the world's governments and the intergovernmental institutions charged with doing something about tragedies. We all miss him.

The judicious mixture of military might and expertise within the context of the civil wars of the 1990s continued to preoccupy me within the Humanitarianism and War Project at Brown University's Watson Institute. I have had the pleasure to codirect this effort with Larry Minear since 1990. While he is routinely more skeptical about the advantages of the armed forces than I, his constant prodding to "break new ground" has been crucial and very much appreciated. I could not have asked for a better or more stimulating close collaborator. I thus also owe a debt to the forty or so supporters of this project since its inception—governments, UN organizations, nongovernmental organizations (NGOs), and foundations have provided a vote of confidence and the means to pursue an important topic.

The present book grew from a challenge to spell out my thinking from Joanna Macrae, one of the editors of *Disasters: The Journal of Disaster Studies, Policy, and Management*. In June 1997, and after helpful comments from anonymous referees, "A Research Note about Military-Civilian Humanitarianism: More Questions than Answers" was published (*Disasters* 21, no. 2 [June 1997]: 95–117). I am grateful for the republication of parts of that argument here.

Also, I am thankful that Jennifer Knerr, the political science editor at Rowman & Littlefield, urged me to tackle this ambitious task and pursue the argument sketched in the article. This is my fourth book that she has commissioned, and it is harder to imagine a more agreeable editor. The present volume has, hopefully, a few more answers but has hardly exhausted the subject matter. I have endeavored to make distinctions and present available data so that believers and critics (of military intervention or of the text) will be able to identify clearly with what they are in either agreement or disagreement. There is little political will at present, but evidence here suggests how multilateral military operations could expand or contract in the future to the benefit or peril of war victims.

I have benefited from close readings of the draft manuscript by several colleagues: Jarat Chopra, a specialist in public international law as an assistant professor at Brown University and a friend and collaborator since the beginning of this decade; S. Neil MacFarlane, Lester B. Pearson Professor of International Relations at Oxford University and a colleague whose friendship and collaboration goes back to the mid-1980s; Anthony McDermott, coeditor of *Security Dialogue* and senior researcher at the International Peace Research Institute in Oslo and former journalist with the *Financial Times*; Giles Whitcomb, a consultant and former UN official whose comments on several publications have been invaluable; and two anonymous and very knowledgeable readers from Rowman & Littlefield. Errors were reduced and subtleties introduced as a result of their commentaries, queries, and suggestions. In expressing appreciation to such colleagues, I am once again reminded how thankful I am to be in this business.

I also wish to acknowledge my debt to a rare undergraduate research assistant, Michael Bhatia (Brown University, class of 1999). Mike worked tirelessly during the summers of 1996 and 1997 to dig up the information that forms the heart of the five case studies. He also helped to push out my own understanding of these issues by asking the kind of probing questions that the very best of one's students do. I wish him well as he launches what will no doubt be a productive and successful career in international affairs.

It would have been impossible to have found someone more knowledgeable and experienced to write a foreword for a volume on civilian-military interactions than Sir Brian Urquhart. Known widely not only for his contribution to international conflict management as the "father of peacekeeping," but also for his own elegant prose and insightful books, I am honored indeed that he agreed to grace this book with a few introductory words. Having admired from afar his work as the paragon of integrity as an international civil servant, I subsequently have encountered him in numerous professional contexts—as a board member at the International Peace Academy, in a variety of conferences, and as an overseer at the Watson Institute. Few persons have done more to merit the title of "gentleman and scholar."

The Watson Institute provided funding for research assistance, as well as a congenial base from which to draft the manuscript. I am thus grateful to my colleague Tom Biersteker for having made this possible. I am particularly grateful to Laura Sadovnikoff and Fred Fullerton for their assistance in the production of this volume and to Melissa Phillips for her help in the selection of photographs. Without their help, this book would have been slower to appear and considerably less well presented.

This book is dedicated to my family, to whom my debt is beyond measure. To quote political scientists Maurice Chevalier and Louisa May Alcott, "Thank heaven for little girls and women."

Notwithstanding the many individuals who helped make this book possible, I alone am responsible for any remaining errors of fact or interpretation.

T. G. W.
Providence, Rhode Island

Abbreviations

ACUNS	Academic Council on the United Nations System
AIDS	acquired immunodeficiency syndrome
AOR	Area of Responsibility
CARE	Cooperative for Assistance and Relief Everywhere
CDC	Centers for Disease Control
CDR	Coalition pour la Défence de la République [Rwanda]
CIA	Central Intelligence Agency
CMOC	Civil-Military Operations Center
CMR	crude mortality rate
CNN	Cable News Network
CSCE	Conference on Security and Cooperation in Europe
DART	Disaster Assistance Response Team [U.S.]
DHA	Department of Humanitarian Affairs [UN]
DOD	Department of Defense [U.S.]
DOS	Department of State [U.S.]
EC	European Community
ECHO	European Community Humanitarian Office
EMMIR	Elément Médical Militaire d'Intervention Rapide
EU	European Union
FAdH	Forces Armées d'Haiti (Haitian Armed Forces)
FAO	Food and Agriculture Organization [UN]
FAR	Rwandan Armed Forces
FRAFBATT	French-speaking African Battalion
FRAPH	Front Révolutionnaire pour l'Avancement et le Progrès en Haïti (Front for Haitian Advancement and Progress, later the Armed Front of the Haitian People)
FRY	Federal Republic of Yugoslavia [Serbia and Montenegro]

Abbreviations

GAO	General Accounting Office [U.S.]
GDP	gross domestic product
GNP	gross national product
HOC	Humanitarian Operation Center
HRS	Humanitarian Relief Sector
HVO	Croatian Army
ICRC	International Committee of the Red Cross
IDP	internally displaced person
IFOR	Implementation Force [in the former Yugoslavia]
IFRC	International Federation of Red Cross and Red Crescent Societies
IGO	intergovernmental organization
IPSF	Interim Public Security Force [Haiti]
IRC	International Rescue Committee
JNA	Yugoslav National Army
JTF	Joint Task Force
KDP	Kurdish Democratic Party
MEF	Marine Expeditionary Force [U.S.]
MICIVIH	Mission Civile Internationale en Haiti (International Civilian Mission in Haiti)
MIST	Military Information Support Team [U.S.]
MNF	Multinational Force
MP	military police
MRND	Mouvement Révolutionnaire National pour le Développement [Rwanda]
MSF	Médecins sans Frontières [Doctors without Borders]
NATO	North Atlantic Treaty Organization
NCCNI	NGO Coordination Committee for Northern Iraq
NGO	nongovernmental organization
OAS	Organization of American States
OAU	Organization of African Unity
OCHA	Office for the Coordination of Humanitarian Affairs [UN]
ODF	Operation Deny Flight
OECD	Organization for Economic Cooperation and Development
OEOA	Office of Emergency Operations in Africa [UN]
OFDA	Office of Foreign Disaster Assistance [U.S.]
OPC	Operation Provide Comfort [U.S.]
ORH	Operation Restore Hope
OPR	Operation Provide Relief [U.S.]
OSCE	Organization on Security and Cooperation in Europe (formerly CSCE)

OSH	Operation Support Hope [U.S.]
PAHO	Pan-American Health Organization
PDD	Presidential Decision Directive
PKK	Kurdistan Workers' Party
PUK	Patriotic Union of Kurdistan
PSYOP	psychological operations [U.S.]
ROEs	rules of engagement
RPF	Rwandan Patriotic Front
RPG	Refugee Policy Group
SF	Special Forces [U.S.]
SFOR	Stabilization Force [in the former Yugoslavia]
SIPRI	Stockholm International Peace Research Institute
SNA	Somali National Army [pre–civil war Somalia]; Somali National Alliance [post-Barre]
SNM	Somali National Movement
SRSG	special representative of the secretary-general [UN]
SSDF	Somali Salvation Democratic Front
TDF	Territorial Defence Forces (of the former Yugoslavia)
TNC	Transitional National Council
UNAMIR	UN Assistance Mission in Rwanda
UNCRO	UN Confidence Restoration Operation [in Croatia]
UNDP	UN Development Programme
UNDRO	UN Disaster Relief Office
UNGCI	UN Guards Contingent in Iraq
UNHCR	UN High Commissioner for Refugees
UNICEF	UN Children's Fund
UNIDIR	UN Institute for Disarmament Research
UNIKOM	UN Iraq-Kuwait Observer Mission
UNITAF	Unified Task Force [U.S.]
UNMIH	UN Mission in Haiti
UNOMUR	UN Observer Mission in Uganda-Rwanda
UNOSOM	UN Operation in Somalia
UNPA	UN Protected Area
UNPROFOR	UN Protection Force [in the former Yugoslavia]
UNREO	UN Rwanda Emergency Office
UNSCOM	UN Special Commission
USAID	United States Agency for International Development
USC	United Somali Congress
WFP	World Food Programme
WHO	World Health Organization
ZHS	Zone Humanitaire Sure (Humanitarian Safe Zone)

Introduction

Decisionmakers and humanitarians continued to fumble in late 1996 and 1997 in the Great Lakes region of Africa (Rwanda, Burundi, and eastern Zaire, now the Democratic Republic of the Congo). Humanitarian delivery and protection continue as experiments in world politics.

The end of East-West tensions, the erosion of sovereignty, the evolution of norms, genuine altruism, domestic politics, media coverage, and the desire to contain refugee flows provide partial explanations for why the West is sometimes willing to intervene. The humanitarian impulse has been unleashed in the last half decade, with outside military forces in the avant-garde. Whether or not we actually are in Raimo Väyrynen's "age of humanitarian emergencies,"[1] ensuring better access to and treatment of victims clearly preoccupies policymakers, pundits, parliamentarians, and the public.

That almost 1 percent of the world's population is displaced by war, and probably an equal number have remained behind with totally disrupted lives,[2] is one motivation to improve third-party military responses in war zones. Another is the oft-cited trend from military toward civilian war fatalities, who now often constitute 90 percent of the victims. Earlier in the twentieth century, the statistic was closer to 10 percent. Although there is considerable doubt about the existence of sufficient political will to deploy multilateral military forces in future humanitarian crises, the logic seems compelling on the face of it. This book explores the extent to which the prima facie case holds up to analysis of experiments in the 1990s.

It is humbling to recall how quickly optimism vanished at the end of the Cold War. George Bush's "new world order" and Bill Clinton's "assertive multilateralism" ceded quickly to more somber views, if not a catchy slogan.[3] The new Western shibboleths of democratization and liberalization have spread, but so has the plague of micronationalism, fragmentation, and massive human displacement. The demise of East-West tensions did not result in the peaceful triumph of Western liberal democracy and Francis Fukuyama's "end of history."[4] Rather, this latest in a series of inaccurate forecasts actually ushered in a painful epoch with record numbers of refugees, internally displaced persons (IDPs), and other victims.

Some observers point to integration as the dominant analytical paradigm for contemporary international relations, with globalization of trade, finance, and communications as part of the international political economy. So too are complex emergencies, but they point to fragmentation. Placing them together within the same theoretical framework is an intellectual challenge. As such, James Rosenau's adjective "turbulent" accurately describes both world politics and the status of contemporary international relations theory.[5]

The onset of the post–Cold War era initially reinvigorated the United Nations, where collegiality existed among the Security Council's permanent members (Britain, China, France, Russia, and the United States). The framers of the UN Charter had originally planned on such collaboration among the great powers as the basis for a new security regime, but it had never materialized because of East-West tensions. There remain inveterate optimists and visionaries—how else do we explain *Our Global Neighbourhood*,[6] the title of the report from yet another eminent international commission, which was published in the middle of the turbulent 1990s?

However, pessimism has supplanted bullishness. The initial flurry of new peacekeeping operations in the late 1980s and the enforcement action to roll back Iraqi aggression against Kuwait in 1991 were followed by well-publicized UN shortcomings or outright failures in Bosnia, Croatia, Somalia, Haiti, and Rwanda, along with less visible ones in Angola, Afghanistan, and the Sudan.

Much of the criticism confuses the "two United Nations"—the first, where governments meet and make decisions, and the second, comprising the various secretariats, officials, and soldiers who implement these decisions.[7] Although both have been at fault, the old adage should be repeated here that the latter mainly can do what the former permits. Social scientists employ the terms "independent" and "dependent" variables to describe this phenomenon, but a simpler approach to avoid the harmful confusion is sensible. Prescriptions to build upon successes or avoid failures must specify whether it is the behavior, attitudes, and policies of states or rather of their national and international civil servants and soldiers that is responsible.

Whatever the apportionment of blame, a new reality emerged in

1993 with the label of the "Somalia syndrome."[8] Facile notions about intervening militarily to help sustain civilians trapped in war zones have been replaced by more realistic estimates about the limits of such undertakings. Former U.S. Assistant Secretary of State Richard Holbrooke, the architect of the Dayton Accords to curtail the war in the former Yugoslavia, suggests that "the damage that Bosnia did to the U.N. was incalculable."[9] Whichever of the two United Nations is most at fault and whichever debacle wins first prize, the conventional wisdom in policy circles is now to refrain from robust involvement by the military in humanitarian crises. Then UN Secretary-General Boutros Boutros-Ghali codified the rhetorical retreat from his bullish 1992 *An Agenda for Peace* in his far more cautious 1995 *Supplement to "An Agenda for Peace."*[10] This tentativeness has continued under Kofi Annan, whose heralded but lackluster statement about reform in July 1997 reflects a somber vision of UN possibilities.[11]

In spite of a widespread tendency among both analysts and practitioners to generalize, "military-civilian humanitarianism" (or the coming together of military forces and civilian agencies to deal with the human suffering from complex emergencies) has actually taken a variety of forms.[12] This book focuses on those among external intervenors—outside military forces and outside aid and protection institutions. There are obviously numerous "interactions" between outsiders and insiders—both military and civilian—that are relevant throughout the analysis, but it is those among external intervenors that preoccupy us in these pages.

Whatever the variations, however, enchantment has definitively evaporated for what the editor of *Foreign Affairs* had described somewhat prematurely as the "springtime for interventionism."[13] There has been a backlash—by civilian humanitarians and the military, parliaments and editorial boards—in spite of success in northern Iraq and Haiti, as well as, arguably, valuable contributions in Rwanda and, more arguably still, in Somalia and Bosnia. The growing conventional wisdom is that humanitarian intervention—or coercive measures by outside military forces to ensure access to civilians or the protection of rights without the consent of local political authorities—is infeasible and unsustainable.[14] Moreover, many civilian humanitarians argue that military force complicates their work because, in the short run, it works against the impartiality, neutrality, and consent that have traditionally underpinned their work; and in the long run, it addresses none of the structural problems or root causes that had led to the eruption of violence. In fact, the increasing number of attacks on NGO and International Committee of the Red Cross (ICRC) staff indicate that even without military forces the traditional principles of humanitarian aid workers are no shield against violence and even death.[15]

Benevolence is never adequate, but the provision of military support thus seems to have caused more problems than it has solved. Or has it? Leslie Gelb's "wars of national debilitation" can thwart rational thought and induce nihilism,[16] but they can also push us to ask: Is it possible and worthwhile to use the military in conjunction with humanitarian action in order to thwart violence and mitigate civilian suffering? Admittedly there is little political will at present, and humanitarian interventions may become less prevalent than in the early 1990s—with gallows humor, more than one military officer and civilian humanitarian has voiced nostalgia for the 1991–1994 period when crisis piled upon crisis.

Yet, the point of departure here is a continual and unfruitful exchange of polemics between proponents and critics. Confusion concerns the functions of logistics and of security, as well as the presence of contradictory and incomplete data. This book distinguishes and presents data so that readers will be able to agree or disagree with the content. Evidence in the first half of the post–Cold War era suggests how multilateral military operations could expand or contract to the benefit or peril of war victims.

Chapter 1 begins with an overview of the armed forces and humanitarianism, of military-civilian interactions, and of the range of possible military contributions to humanitarian action; there follows an overview of recent developments in wars and in the deployments of outside military forces. A framework in Chapter 2 assesses the effectiveness of military-civilian humanitarianism. The heart of the book follows in Chapters 3 to 7: case studies of the experience from five crucial cases of military interactions after the end of the Cold War—in northern Iraq, Somalia, Bosnia, Rwanda, and Haiti. Each contains a brief narrative of the background to the humanitarian crisis of the 1990s and discussions of post–Cold War international responses along with their costs and benefits. The historical narratives can be skipped by the seasoned observer because the compilation of military-civilian information is new, but the histories are not.

These cases of multilateral military operations and humanitarian action in war zones lay the groundwork for making use of the framework to assess the effectiveness of military-civilian interactions. This book develops and then fleshes out a schema to juxtapose the nature of outside military involvement and the accompanying costs for intervening countries with the magnitude of a humanitarian tragedy in a targeted country and of the postintervention impact on civilians in it. The concluding chapter pulls together the various strands of the analysis in order to discuss the costs, benefits, and quandaries associated with military-civilian interactions. To get ahead of the story of intervening in humanitarian crises in the 1990s, there is much room for reflection in a subject so fraught with ambiguity in the post–Cold War era. Contextualizing such efforts and developing situational ethics for the present generation of wars is a daunting task for analysts, decisionmakers, and the educated public.

For the reader, "truth in packaging" at the outset would be useful. One of the colleagues who reviewed this manuscript initially commented that I was "not as assertive as in other writings." But he was also quick to acknowledge and appreciate the preliminary and tentative nature of the comparative exercise attempted in these pages.

At the risk of repeating here what exists in greater detail in the second and concluding chapters, it is worth stressing straightforwardly the limits of this volume. Rather than refusing to draw lessons from five different cases with the predictable sui generis defense of an academic, I have run the risk of trying to compare what are for the moment largely incomparable cases. The ground of humanitarian intervention has been much trampled by a host of analysts pursuing individual case studies. The challenge, indeed the crying policy need, is to begin to see the forest for all of these trees.

The referee is correct that the prose in the following chapters is tinted with tentativeness. The framework, the cases, and the conclusions are not as clear as I would like, but they aim to advance debate. The actual statistics themselves provide a poor basis for judgment—they hardly convey the crispness and objectivity of baseball or cricket data. The statistics about military-civilian interactions are incomplete at best and inconsistent or absent at worst. Moreover, they should be tempered by events on the ground in the country in crisis, and by their origins. It is easier to quantify the costs of the intervenor than of the intervenee. Furthermore, the difficulty of assigning values to things and people cannot be overemphasized: What is the value of a life? How does one place a value on a displaced person or the means to un-displace her?

I am persuaded that the effort is worthwhile, although the conclusions will be somewhat easy to criticize. There can probably never be any definitive measurement. However, the reader should now have a foretaste of the deliberately reserved conclusions and quandaries. This is a good-faith effort to come up with the best assessments possible at this stage for interventions in humanitarian crises.

Finally, there is a fundamental voluntarist assertion driving this book: that human beings can control their destinies, that they are as strong as the administrative and political structures that they create.

As the late economist Kenneth Boulding quipped, "We are as we are because we got that way."[17] The structures that circumscribe humanitarian action in war zones—including outside armed forces and civilian humanitarian organizations—are only as permanent and helpful as we make them. These human constructs are subject to manipulation.

In trying to understand the morality behind and the ambiguity of humanitarian intervention in the 1990s, Michael Ignatieff writes, "There is nothing in the emergence of this global conscience that gives us reason to be complacent. But there is also nothing that justifies disillusion."[18] Worthwhile change is never easy, but to think it impossible is to reject the evidence of history.

1

Armed Forces and Humanitarian Action: Past and Present

The end of the Cold War has not altered the fundamental nature of state-interest decisionmaking. Humanitarian impulses abound, but they are not the fundamental characteristics of international relations. At the same time, the types of civil wars, as well as international responses to them, are different from their predecessors of this century and certainly those of the Cold War period. The present context for the use of outside military forces under UN auspices and the historical precedents for military-civilian humanitarianism are an essential part of the background necessary to evaluate more precisely the costs and benefits of military intervention in five recent humanitarian tragedies. Before exploring the contemporary context, a brief introduction to humanitarian actors and a historical interpretation of military-civilian interactions are in order.

Humanitarian Actors

Simply listing the contemporary cast of characters on the international humanitarian stage, along with the strengths and weaknesses displayed in their respective roles, can be confusing even to a knowledgeable critic. It would thus be useful to describe the most important humanitarian actors in some detail.[1]

Seven major institutional actors make up the existing system of international assistance and protection, or what is called "humanitarian

7

action." Three sets of actors are based within conflict areas: host governments and military forces; insurgent political and military forces; and national and local private organizations. The focus here is on external actors who dominate the delivery of emergency assistance and the protection of human rights. This book is about the interactions between external intervening military forces and external aid and protection agencies. However, the fact that locals are outnumbered by external counterparts should not obscure the importance of the former. Local actors obviously play pivotal roles in the conduct of the wars to which outsiders are reacting, and local actors also set the terms within which external actors function and humanitarian activities take place. A host of "interactions" between outsiders and insiders is present throughout this text, but here the goal is to introduce the external actors.

Three sets of civilian organizations are based outside contemporary theaters of armed conflict and figure in this analysis most directly: donor governments; intergovernmental organizations (IGOs); and private agencies, both nongovernmental organizations and the International Committee of the Red Cross. A fourth set of outside actors is constituted by military forces. Straightforward details about each would perhaps be useful; shortcomings for each set of actors do not appear here but, rather, throughout subsequent analyses. The following sections could be skipped by knowledgeable readers.

Donor Governments

In addition to their financial support for both IGOs and NGOs, governments are major actors in their own right. Clearly the foreign policies of major and minor powers address matters like trade and commerce with countries experiencing conflict, and sometimes foreign policies directly concern armed conflicts themselves. In this way, for example, the Washington-based United States Agency for International Development (USAID) and the London-based Department for International Development have their own direct humanitarian assistance programs in many of the conflicts under review, just as they have development assistance projects throughout the world. The kinds of relationships and the resources employed by the major powers with Rwanda or Somalia are different from those government-to-government ones of the Netherlands or Canada.

Historical diplomatic, economic, and political relationships of a government within a region may also make it more or less welcome as a partner when emergency strikes. Because of its traditions and resources, the United States usually plays a major role (oftentimes financing a third of the bills). But Washington is also more suspect than smaller neutral countries like Austria and Switzerland or such Nordic countries as Sweden and Finland. Former colonial powers, especially France and Britain, have historical links that affect their proclivity to intervene in a region and their acceptability—both in positive and negative ways. Over time, more and more bilateral resources are being channeled to IGOs and NGOs by bilateral aid agencies, but the latter still control the bulk of the resources and the leverage.

Intergovernmental Organizations

Prominent among outside humanitarian organizations are IGOs. In principle, the fact that their membership is composed of states means that initiatives by intergovernmental organizations are more acceptable than when they are sponsored by only a single or a few governments. Complicating rapid and robust decisionmaking, of course, is the presence of states with differing perspectives and interests.

Outside the UN system, the main intergovernmental actor is the European Community Humanitarian Office (ECHO). Initially, the role of the former European Community (EC) and now European Union (EU) was relatively small, serving mainly as a channel for contributions to other European organizations by member states. However, since its creation in 1992, ECHO has developed its own programs, posted its own staff, and asserted an important financial role in complex emergencies (now approaching $1 billion annually).

The main intergovernmental actors are from the United Nations system: the Office for the Coordination of Humanitarian Affairs (OCHA); the UN High Commissioner for Refugees (UNHCR); the UN Children's Fund (UNICEF); the World Food Programme (WFP); and the UN Development Programme (UNDP). At the outset it should be noted that the term "system" or "family" is somewhat of a misnomer when applied to the entities of the United Nations. The secretary-general is not really the chief executive officer of anything except the UN Secretariat itself in New York. The executive heads of the other agencies are responsible for their own programs; they raise funds that are comparable to those controlled by the secretary-general himself (not yet herself) and report to autonomous governing boards.

OCHA is a recent acronym, dating from January 1998. The Department of Humanitarian Affairs (DHA) was its predecessor, from 1992 to 1997, and was established in response to donor dissatisfaction with the inability of the UN system and international NGOs to coordinate their activities in the Gulf crises. The UN Disaster Relief Office (UNDRO) had been established in 1971 to help in natural catastrophes and was subsumed in the DHA. The major functions of OCHA are consolidated appeals and information sharing, along with humanitarian diplomacy in New York. Part of the "cabinet" of the UN secretary-general, OCHA is not operational.

From its new headquarters on the Place des Nations in Geneva, the UNHCR is guardian of the 1951 Convention Relating to the Status of Refugees and the 1967 Protocol. Its responsibilities include the protection of refugees, their resettlement into a country of first asylum or elsewhere, and their repatriation to their country of origin when possible. Increasingly, the organization has also been charged with "persons in refugee-like situations" but who have not fled across an international border—namely, internally displaced persons and war victims who have not moved at all. Other UN agencies and especially NGOs contract with the UNHCR to implement programs. The UNHCR's budget grew dramatically in the 1990s, peaking in 1994–1995 at some $1.3 billion, with about $500 million for the former Yugoslavia and $300 million for Rwanda.

Headquartered across First Avenue in New York from the UN itself, UNICEF provides material assistance such as food, clothing, and medical supplies in relief operations while keeping its eye turned toward longer-term development for women and children. Established in 1946 to provide immediate relief to child victims of World War II, UNICEF receives the bulk of its resources from governments, but about 30 percent comes from private fund-raising (unusual for an IGO). During the Cold War, UNICEF was unlike other organizations of the UN system and able to deal with insurgent authorities because of its unusual role in helping the most vulnerable victims, women and children. About a quarter of UNICEF's annual $1 billion budget is devoted to emergency assistance.

Food insecurity after World War II led to founding the Food and Agricultural Organization (FAO) in Rome; but the main humanitarian actor operating from that city is the WFP, which was established as a food surplus disposal organization following the World Food Conference of 1974. Part of the WFP's $1 billion annual budget comes from the FAO's International Food Emergency Reserve, but most comes from voluntary contributions in cash or in kind from bilateral donors. The WFP began with a development orientation, but it now devotes about 80 percent of its efforts to emergencies. It coordinates food shipments with other UN agencies and NGOs; it has become the logistics specialist within the UN system.

Also across First Avenue in New York are the headquarters for the UNDP, which was established as the central source of funding for technical assistance and prefeasibility projects within the UN system. With an annual budget of about $1 billion, the senior UNDP official in recipient countries (the resident representative) normally acts as the resident coordinator for all UN activities. When war erupts, this official may remain to coordinate humanitarian aid; but often he or she is replaced by someone with a greater expertise in emergencies and political negotiations, the special representative of the secretary-general (SRSG). After violence has settled down, the UNDP's top official returns to replace the secretary-general's personal envoy and to assume overall responsibilities for reconstruction, rehabilitation, and development.

Private Organizations: NGOs and the ICRC

The third major category of external civilian actors consists of nongovernmental organization. These include such familiar associations as the Cooperative for Assistance and Relief Everywhere (CARE), Oxfam, Save the Children, World Vision, Médecins sans Frontières (MSF; translated as Doctors without Borders), and Catholic Relief Services; lesser-known but important ones like the International Rescue Committee (IRC); and largely unknown ones like Mercy Corps International. The delivery of emergency relief is dominated by about fifteen to twenty major international NGOs or federations of national NGOs that have annual budgets of at least $75–100 million and work in at least eight to ten countries around the world.

Extreme heterogeneity, in terms of the size of their operations and their approach to issues, makes generalizations about NGOs problematic. Across-the-board characterizations are difficult between giants like CARE (with a $500 million annual budget) and much smaller operations; between those that carry out operations themselves mainly with expatriate staff and those that work mainly through local counterparts within crises; and between those that accept no funds from governments to underscore their autonomy and those that are essentially entirely financed by public resources.

Nonetheless, it is fair to say that the hallmark of NGOs is their link to the grass roots and their action orientation. They are normally reputed to be more nonbureaucratic, flexible, and creative than their governmental or intergovernmental counterparts; and they are certainly less constrained by legal formalities and diplomatic niceties. NGOs have assumed an increasing importance in the last decade and can no longer be dismissed as "do-gooders." They receive a growing proportion of resources as part of the privatization of international relations, and they are endeavoring to improve their professionalism. There are national and international professional associations—for example, the

Washington-based InterAction is a consortium of 160 American private agencies, and the Steering Committee for Humanitarian Response draws together several of the largest international NGOs that respond to complex emergencies.

A very special private organization is the International Committee of the Red Cross, so special that it is often considered in a category by itself. A private organization with a board of governors of prominent Swiss citizens, the ICRC is like NGOs in that it receives both private and public contributions (governments typically provide 90 percent of its annual budget, which in the mid-1990s approached $1 billion). However, the ICRC is distinct in that it has a specific recognition in international humanitarian law, for which it is designated the custodian. It enjoys, for example, observer status in the UN General Assembly, and its chief delegate in New York meets monthly with the president of the Security Council. The ICRC has unique missions under international humanitarian law—such as monitoring the treatment of prisoners of war and detainees, and promoting family reunification.

The ICRC, along with the International Federation (formerly League) of Red Cross and Red Crescent Societies (IFRC) and its national chapters in some 165 countries, constitute the "Red Cross movement." Founded in 1864 by a businessman of the time, Henri Dunant, following his revulsion to the bloody battle of Solferino, the ICRC has its headquarters in Geneva and is staffed in key international posts largely by Swiss nationals. For specific assignments, it accepts the services of persons from national societies. Its location in a neutral country and its staffing underscore its mandate under the Geneva Convention of 1949 and the Additional Protocols of 1977 that effectiveness in the humanitarian arena depends on strict neutrality and impartiality. It is the oldest and largest international humanitarian organization outside of the UN system.

Unlike most other humanitarian agencies, the ICRC has clear and carefully elaborated principles, and its disciplined staff abides by them. This provides consistency to its approach in activities in about fifty countries. Unlike most other NGOs and IGOs that mount a range of activities from relief to reconstruction and development, the ICRC works only in war zones—both international ones like Iraq-Kuwait or civil wars (which the ICRC prefers to label "noninternational wars") like Somalia and Rwanda.

Outside Military Forces, Especially UN Peacekeepers and Enforcers

The fourth set of external actors comprises military forces. In spite of provisions in several articles of the UN Charter and fear in many conservative hearts within the United States, there is no United Nations military capacity. The soldiers who serve in UN operations—called "blue helmets" because of their distinctive headgear—are part of the armed forces of their own countries. However, they conduct themselves differently from the soldiers who conduct unilateral interventions—for example, Americans in Panama in 1989, or the Brits in the Falklands in 1982, or the Vietnamese in Cambodia in 1978. Because all of the humanitarian interventions under analysis in this volume were under UN auspices, it would be sensible to introduce briefly the nature of UN military operations and the peculiar evolution of UN operations during the Cold War.

The five permanent and ten rotating members of the Security Council rarely addressed humanitarian concerns during the Cold War, although they have become something of a mantra since—the word "humanitarian" appeared eighteen times in the resolution authorizing the intervention in Somalia. Although the narrowest interpretations of nonintervention in the domestic affairs of states had been the rule, especially with regard to outside military forces, many decisions of the 1990s regard the egregious violation of human rights or the denial of access to starving populations as evidence that a state has lost its entitlement to sovereignty.

The effective projection of military power in such circumstances was supposed to distinguish the UN from its defunct predecessor, the League of Nations. But the onset of East-West tensions made this impossible because one of the permanent members (most often the Soviet Union and frequently the United States) vetoed the idea of backing militarily international decisions. Consequently, a new means for maintaining the peace was required, one that would permit the UN to act when the major powers agreed or at least acquiesced.

UN peacekeeping became that method. Although it is not mentioned in the UN Charter, it became the world organization's primary activity in the field of international peace and security. The use of blue helmets is widely recognized to have begun during the 1956 crisis in Suez. Contemporary accounts credit Canada's Secretary of State of External Affairs and later Prime Minister Lester B. Pearson with proposing that Secretary-General Dag Hammarskjöld organize a force that resembled more police than warriors. Close to half a million served during the Cold War, and 700 lost their lives. In 1988, UN peacekeepers received the Nobel Prize.

Hammarskjöld coined the expression "chapter six-and-a-half" to describe something that was between the pacific settlement of disputes (spelled out in Chapter VI of the Charter) and coercion (Chapter VII). Peacekeepers usually observed the peace (that is, monitored and reported on the status of agreed cease-fires) or kept the peace (that is, acted as a buffer between belligerents who wished them to be there). Blue helmets were normally troops from small or nonaligned states, with permanent members of the Security Council and other major powers making troop contributions only under exceptional circumstances. They were lightly armed troops who were more symbols than soldiers because they had the consent of the warring parties, and they rarely used force except in self-defense. Effectiveness reflected cooperation from belligerents mixed with the moral weight of the United Nations.

Thirteen operations took place before 1978, and then there were none until 1988 in spite of the proliferation of regional conflicts. Mikhail Gorbachev's ascension to power changed the face of the former Soviet Union and also of UN military efforts. In 1987, Moscow vowed to repay its UN debts and, in 1988, called for the application of his "new thinking" to the management of international conflicts. In the last year of his presidency in 1988, Ronald Reagan abruptly altered the UN bashing that had characterized his administration. In particular, he responded to the Soviet leader's overture and agreed that the UN was central to the management and resolution of regional conflicts. President George Bush, a former UN ambassador, maintained the momentum that resulted in a veritable revitalization of the United Nations. After a ten-year hiatus, five new operations were launched in 1988. Although there were several new twists (for example, election monitoring), these operations were essentially extensions of the time-honored recipe for UN peacekeeping—in particular, all enjoyed the consent of warring parties and relied upon defensive concepts of minimal force by lightly armed soldiers.

Iraq's invasion of Kuwait in August 1990 and the UN's subsequent reactions (with Chapter VII economic and then military sanctions) suggested the extent to which changing world politics created new opportunities for outside military forces. The international response also set the stage for the first of the cases in the volume, on behalf of the Kurds in northern Iraq, which represents a bellwether for military-civilian interactions in other humanitarian crises.

Historical Overview of Military-Civilian Interactions

The military performs two sets of functions in the humanitarian arena: logistics (relief activities and support for civilian relief agencies) and security. Inevitably, physical succor to victims jumps to the imagination in thinking about the impact of fulfilling both logistics and security functions; but the armed forces also protect the human rights of victims. Indeed, observers point to difficulties in distinguishing between delivery and protection—these two components of humanitarian "action"—because they are so linked.[2] Nonetheless, it is easier to quantify the former than the latter, which is why so much attention is normally paid to the volume and value of goods and personnel devoted to the delivery of food, medicines, and shelter when war is raging. "Protection" certainly amounts to more than the total number of human rights monitors or UNHCR legal protection officers, but it is harder to measure than metric tonnage.

Hidden protection issues can be gleaned from many examples. For instance, NATO member states were unwilling to interpret the mandates for the Implementation Force (IFOR) and the Stabilization Force (SFOR) to include vigorously pursuing indicted war criminals in the former Yugoslavia. But the physical presence alone of troops there and elsewhere can sometimes halt or slow down abuses. The protection of human rights includes safeguarding the well-being of victims by ensuring that they have access to material assistance. Protection minimizes the damaging impact of violence and can also facilitate respect for international norms by belligerents and political authorities. Operationally, protection can result from the insertion of soldiers or aid personnel between victims and combatants. Although such forces almost always could have done more—which has been criticism made by Human Rights Watch of regular UN peacekeeping operations[3]—their mere presence almost certainly reduced abuses. These factors should be kept in mind during the case studies of Iraq, Somalia, Bosnia, Rwanda, and Haiti.

The more routine involvement by third-party military forces in humanitarian efforts is a phenomenon of the post–Cold War era, but the use of military forces for such purposes is not new.[4] In fact, there is an almost automatic association in most of the public's minds between the military and disaster relief, often with the expectation that the armed forces will assist civilian populations after emergency strikes. The earliest recorded instances predate Alexander the Great. They continued in Europe through the Napoleonic Wars and into the twentieth century. Sometimes assistance was seen as a humane gesture to the vanquished, usually mixed with the desire to help secure loyalty from newly subject populations. Variations of this theme were played out by colonial armies who orchestrated assistance to the civil authority.

A quantum expansion of the military into the humanitarian arena took place after World War II. The task of occupying Germany and Japan, as well as reconstructing as quickly as possible Europe's economic base, required new types of personnel within the armed forces: administrators, planners, developmentalists, and logisticians. At that time, there were relatively few international NGOs, and the UN's humanitarian delivery mechanisms were just beginning to function. UNICEF was established in 1946 as a temporary (or "emergency") agency, while the other two contemporary main players, the UN High Commissioner for Refugees and the World Food Programme, were not established until 1950 and 1961, respectively.

The aftermath of World War II witnessed such an expansion of the armed forces in civil affairs that the influence on both military doctrine and the international civilian response system should not be underestimated. When thinking about the ambitious agenda for peacebuilding in a country like postgenocide Rwanda, for example, analysts should not forget the enormity of challenges in postwar Europe. Virtually an entire continent was administered while the vestiges of a regime responsible for the Holocaust were eradicated. Populations were re-

Food being distributed to displaced persons.
Credit: UNRRA/5918 from United Nations Archives

united or resettled, war criminals rounded up and prosecuted, economies revived, the rule of law reestablished, administration restructured, and the fabric of society reknit.

In expanding the military's role as never before, its integration into the conduct of civil affairs and in humanitarian operations was remarkable. The military had resources and controlled logistics. The association in the eyes of the public and parliaments was natural. Many of today's strategies and approaches build naturally upon the experience of postwar collaboration in Europe.

Indeed, over the last half century, military assistance in natural disasters has become a routine extension of civil defense. In recent memory, the U.S. military, for instance, has rushed to the scene of Hurricane Andrew in Florida, helped Bangladesh when monsoons struck (troops happened to be in the area on the way back from Somalia), and aided the Philippines (where there was a U.S. base) when a volcano erupted. Media treatment of these events has become commonplace since the dramatic involvement in humanitarian relief with the Berlin airlift of 1947, when an entire city was supplied by air. As Fred Cuny wrote: "More than any other event, the images of those planes delivering everything from food to coal fostered acceptance of the link between armed forces and humanitarian assistance and, more importantly, acceptance of the costs incurred."[5]

Armed forces often possess an abundance of precisely those resources that are in the shortest supply when disaster strikes: transport, fuel, communications, commodities, building equipment, medicines, and large stockpiles of off-the-shelf provisions. In addition, the military's "can-do" mentality, self-supporting character, and rapid response capabilities, as well as its hierarchical discipline, are essential assets within the turmoil of acute tragedies. The same capacities that are relevant for help in domestic disasters can also be applied to international crises. Because both relief agencies and the public understand that the military has resources and know-how, it is reasonable that political authorities think about calling upon its forces for a resource-poor country whose local capacities have been overwhelmed by a disaster.

The end of the Cold War removed the raison d'être for the bulk of military spending in the West, which in turn provided an occasion for the military to become more heavily engaged in humanitarian action than at any time since the late 1940s. This development has coincided with the renaissance of sorts in UN conflict management. Western publics demanded downsizing military establishments. Military expenditures dropped even if the much-vaunted peace dividend did not really materialize; the availability of military help for humanitarian tasks seemed to be a "dividend" of sorts.

The successful allied mobilization for the Gulf War and the subsequent use of the armed forces in support of humanitarianism in northern Iraq—along with substantial if sometimes less popular versions in Somalia, Bosnia, Rwanda, and Haiti—have provided a means for militaries to fend off pressures to reduce further their infrastructure and personnel.[6] These cases are examined in depth later, but it is worth noting here the judgment of Larry Minear and Philippe Guillot after examining the role of outside military forces in Rwanda in 1994:

> An ethos is evolving in which the contribution of military resources to major humanitarian crises is coming to represent a key element in the exercise of global stewardship. The commitment of troops is becoming the new "currency of the realm." . . . Governments who in earlier years provided humanitarian assistance now offer military assets. . . . Governments that had previously welcomed the established aid agencies now receive foreign troops as well.[7]

Proposals and conferences have been sponsored by virtually all Western militaries. "Operations other than war" is the preferred term in Washington and one acceptable to most militaries,[8] the essence of which should increasingly be the integration of political, military, and humanitarian missions.[9] As one observer quipped about the American military but with more general applicability: "For the near future our military is more likely to participate in humanitarian interventions and in peacekeeping than it is to participate in war or in peace enforcement."[10]

Although too infrequently distinguished in both eulogies and critiques, the humanitarian advantages—or disadvantages, depending on one's point of view—of using the armed forces in war zones are twofold. The first benefit is the logistics cornucopia—some cynics argue that such aid frequently amounts to military surplus disposal—through the provision of direct assistance to people in need and also to support the work of civilian organizations. Military engagements of this type have taken place with a rapidity and regularity as well as on a scale unknown since the 1940s, including burying bodies, digging latrines, purifying water, and conducting large-scale inoculations.

The appropriateness of using military resources—that is, determining when and where they are useful, when and where they are wasteful—is the essence of the analysis in the rest of this book. The adequacy of funds for civilian humanitarian agencies should be kept in mind when determining whether military humanitarianism is an add-on or a replacement for civilian efforts. The public perception is that the costs of military participation in such exercises are borne by respective military establishments. But in many, perhaps most, countries, defense ministries are reimbursed totally or in part by foreign ministries or aid departments. Even when the military is not reimbursed, developing an overall program to address a particular emergency normally reflects conscious choices between military and civilian entities competing for limited funds, rather than preordained preferences.

The second benefit, or shortcoming, results from the military's direct exercise of security capacities, related to its primary function of war fighting and using superior force to overwhelm an enemy. These capacities should be distinguished from military deployments after natural disasters or as a fringe benefit of traditional peacekeeping forces in the Congo, Cyprus, and Lebanon. Deployments involving limited point relief during active conflicts, large-scale intervention, and cross-border operations involve the direct use of military capacities for which there is no civilian substitute.

Such forces can gain access to suffering civilians, when insecurity makes it impossible or highly dangerous, and foster a secure enough environment to permit succor and protection for civilians. Sympathizers and critics alike have commented severely about the security function because "humanitarian intervention" and "humanitarian war" often are viewed as oxymorons.[11] Moreover, in the absence of leadership from the major powers, the potential political costs of body bags or of involvement in a quagmire have led to something akin to a zero-casualty foreign policy, an obvious constraint for the exercise of this second capacity.

The Post–Cold War Context for Military Operations under UN Auspices

I have discussed UN military operations elsewhere, and part of the following discussion may even seem commonplace at this juncture.[12] However, because UN operations circumscribe the analysis of military-civilian interactions in humanitarian emergencies, it is worth summarizing briefly at the outset three characteristics circumscribing international responses to post–Cold War crises: the prevalence of civil wars and civilian deaths; the increased demand for UN soldiers and the world organization's overextension; and subcontracting to regional and nongovernmental organizations.

Civil Wars and Civilian Deaths

Because their trades are based on sovereignty and noninterference in domestic matters, diplomats and international lawyers have pointed out the most significant feature of international responses in the 1990s: the growing willingness to address, rather than ignore, emergencies within the borders of war-torn states. In its annual *Human Development Report* on the fifth anniversary of the collapse of the Berlin Wall, for example, the United Nations Development Programme emphasized that eighty-two armed conflicts had broken out since 9 November 1989 and that seventy-nine were intrastate wars; in fact, two of the three remaining ones (Nagorno-Karabakh and Bosnia) also could legitimately be categorized as civil wars.[13]

Virtually all of the thirty or so wars with more than 1,000 deaths each (the conventional analytical cutoff for "major armed conflicts") per year in the mid-1990s were within states rather than between them. Ted Robert Gurr and Will H. Moore examined 1995 data and saw fifty-eight under way, of which forty-nine were civil wars over ethnic politics, secession, and autonomy. Indeed, only one was a "traditional" interstate conflict (the border dispute between Ecuador and Peru).[14]

In the five years between the early 1990s and mid-decade, the humanitarian costs of these wars was reflected in the massive expansion of overseas development assistance and the proportion devoted to relief—from a few percent on average to over 10 percent, some $10–12 billion. Moreover, natural disasters accounted for almost none of these allocations, with war-generated emergencies dominating allocations. For instance, some 97 percent of allocations by the European Commission were for war-related emergencies, and the WFP allotted only $19 million for natural disasters and some $1.5 billion to conflict-related emergencies.[15]

Although security specialists can argue that wars on the periphery of Europe threaten Western interests, none of these peripheral conflicts really qualifies as a threat to global order. What they do, however, is lead to spiraling assistance costs for Western taxpayers and the existence of what has entered the public policy lexicon as "complex emergencies." Although there is still no agreed definition for the UN system as a whole, the working one is: "a humanitarian crisis in a country, region or society where there is a total or considerable breakdown of authority resulting from internal or external conflict and which requires an international response that goes beyond the mandate or capacity of any single agency and/or the ongoing UN country programme."[16]

Complex emergencies refer almost exclusively to the humanitarian debris from ethnopolitical wars of the 1990s, tragedies that require more comprehensive solutions than merely emergency relief. The continuing proliferation of war and weapons, of weak economies and political volatility, has accompanied the waning of East-West tensions, which removed many constraints against secession and against the manipulation of ethnic differences for political purposes. A witch's brew is now seething in the international system's cauldron. The idea that humanitarian, political, and security dimensions must be addressed simultaneously is a major new challenge in the chaos of such countries as Liberia and Somalia where state authority has collapsed and the fabric of society frayed to the breaking point.

Moreover, civilians increasingly have become the main targets. In such recent complex emergencies as the situations in Rwanda and Bosnia, the subjugation or annihilation of the opposing civilian population and "ethnic cleansing" of territory have become common war aims. Although many dispute the exact percentages, soldiers formerly were the main fatalities whereas civilians now are.[17] However perverse when viewed from the outside, local parties are committed to killing civilians. As Barry Posen has noted, "in these situations each faction's noncombatants may be the targets of the other's combatants."[18]

Has the proliferation of civil wars and the prevalence of civilian deaths altered the ways that humanitarian actors approach crises? Lawyers are quick to point out that the language of Article 2(7) of the UN Charter remains intact and nonintervention in domestic affairs the norm. But humanitarian imperatives have led governmental, intergovernmental, and nongovernmental organizations to redefine the words when possible "to intervene in matters which are essentially within the domestic jurisdiction of any state." The concept of domestic jurisdiction has changed in substance, if not in law. Sometimes there is no sovereign (the case of failed or collapsed states like Somalia),[19] and sometimes sovereignty is overridden in the name of higher norms (the case of the Kurds in northern Iraq).[20] Observers continue to debate the extent to which the present world disorder is new or old.[21] But the two dominant norms of world politics during the Cold War—namely, that borders were sacrosanct and that secession was unthinkable—no longer generate the almost universal enthusiasm and acceptance that they once did. The automatic and almost reverential respect for nonintervention in the internal affairs of states has made way for a more subtle interpretation according to which, on occasion, the rights of individuals take precedence over the rights of repressive governments and the sovereign states that they represent.[22]

UNITAF soldier shares light moment with Somalis. Credit: UNITAF/159831, Somalia

Heightened Demand for UN Military and Humanitarian Operations

The second characteristic circumscribing international responses to humanitarian tragedies of the 1990s relates to the growth in demand for UN soldiers, which, among other things, spawned a veritable cottage analytical industry about peacekeeping.[23] Secretary-General Boutros-Ghali wrote in January 1995: "This increased volume of activity would have strained the Organization even if the nature of the activity had remained unchanged."[24] And as already mentioned, the nature of military operations and especially of humanitarian action also has changed dramatically.

After stable levels of about 10,000 troops and budgets of a few hundred million dollars in the early post–Cold War period, UN numbers jumped rapidly. After a ten-year hiatus (1978–1988) in deploying new operations, five post–Cold War operations were launched in 1988 alone. Twice as many operations were approved in the following decade as during the previous four decades. The call to the United Nations accelerated as a result of the successful pursuit of the Gulf War. Although the interstate war started this, it was the humanitarian intervention in northern Iraq that really altered the landscape for military-civilian interactions. In the mid-1990s, 70,000 to 80,000 blue-helmeted soldiers were authorized by the UN's annualized "military" (peacekeeping) budget that peaked at some $4 billion in 1995. The United States headed the list of deadbeats as accumulated total arrears in the same year hovered around $3.5 billion and remain so—that is, both the UN debt and the military budget in the heyday of intervention approached three times the regular United Nations budget.[25]

The roller-coaster ride continued. Both the numbers of soldiers and the budget plunged dramatically, by two-thirds. In 1997, for the first time since the decade began, the peacekeeping budget fell below the regular budget. This drop suggested financial and professional problems and "strategic overstretch" by the UN of the type that Paul Kennedy attributes to empires but that seems also to apply to overly ambitious IGOs.[26]

The military part of the United Nations encountered substantial problems of indigestion in fielding operations, as did the civilian part of the world organization. The creation of the Department of Humanitarian Affairs in 1992 was an explicit recognition of the crying need to orchestrate civilian inputs; and the interface between military and humanitarian elements became an obsession in such theaters as the Persian Gulf, the Balkans, Somalia, Rwanda, and Haiti.

The establishment of the DHA responded to the palpable frustrations of major Western donors with the inability of multiple UN agencies and associated NGOs to coordinate effectively their activities in the Gulf. The UN Disaster Relief Office had preceded the DHA but had focused essentially on natural disasters, and it was incorporated into the new body. But the DHA's real purpose was to improve international responses to the massive suffering resulting from the growing number of man-made disasters of the 1990s.

As humanitarian emergencies became more politicized, more militarized, and more intrastate than their predecessors, coordination was increasingly viewed as essential not only to orchestrate complex institutional inputs, but also to situate them in relationship to political and military factors and actors. Long-standing complaints about the lack of cohesion in the UN's civilian humanitarian inputs were exacerbated by the resort to outside military forces under UN command or auspices. Although their number has declined, the issue of military-civilian interactions remains and undoubtedly will remain crucial in the years to come.

"Coordination" is a hobbyhorse of governments and parliaments. Its absence frequently figures in internal reports and resolutions about the bevy of organizations flocking to the scene of tragedies. Within the international public policy lexicon, no expression is more used, or misunderstood. Everyone is for it, although no one wishes to be coordinated if it implies any loss of autonomy.

Antonio Donini makes useful distinctions among three broad categories of coordination within the United Nations:

- Coordination by command—coordination in which strong leadership is accompanied by some sort of authority, whether carrot or stick.
- Coordination by consensus—coordination in which leadership is essentially a function of the capacity to orchestrate a coherent response and to mobilize the key actors around common objectives and priorities. Consensus in this instance is normally achieved without any direct assertion of authority by the coordinator.
- Coordination by default—coordination that, in the absence of a formal coordination entity, involves only the most rudimentary exchange of information and division of labor among the actors.[27]

These distinctions should be viewed not as airtight categories but, rather, as points on a spectrum. Given the sacrosanct autonomy of organizational components within the UN system, coordination by command clearly is unrealistic, however desirable, particularly in the context of coercive military operations. The experience of the DHA under the best of circumstances—for instance, during the first six months after the Rwandan genocide—could undoubtedly be described as coordination by consensus. Under the worst of circumstances—for instance, in the chaos of Liberia—coordination was largely absent, and what did exist could be labeled as coordination by default.

In the absence of meaningful central authority—or "coordination lite" rued by proponents of centralization—some critics and practitioners argue that all UN coordination mechanisms constitute a hindrance rather than a help. Extreme proponents of laissez-faire humanitarian action argue that a coherent strategy is unwise because it works against the magic of the marketplace in which individual agencies pursue independence strategies and arrive at a sound division of labor. A subtler view is that creative chaos is better than botched efforts at coherence, which is all that is possible within the UN system. The process is better self-regulated than poorly coordinated because one less, rather than one more, layer of bureaucracy is preferable. As no one is really in charge and no one can be sure what will work, so the argument goes, why not make the best of it rather than merely adding a ceremonial layer?

An obvious path to improved international responses leads to a better division of labor among the various political and military parts of the UN family and its most important operational humanitarian partners—essentially, the UNHCR, the WFP, and UNICEF. In December

1991, on the heels of the clumsy efforts in the Gulf, General Assembly Resolution 46/182 called for an emergency relief coordinator, in essence to harmonize the diplomacy and especially the implementation of UN humanitarian efforts. In April 1992, then newly elected Secretary-General Boutros-Ghali gave an important boost to the concept by allocating an undersecretary-general post to the new Department of Humanitarian Affairs.[28] Jan Eliasson, the able Swedish ambassador in New York who had helped to negotiate the end to the Iran-Iraq War in 1987 and to shepherd the controversial Resolution 46/182[29] through the General Assembly, became the first occupant.

As a national from an important donor state at the head of a department established in response to donor dissatisfactions, Eliasson logically pursued four tasks seen as crucial by governments that were financing so much of the growing bill for international responses to complex emergencies: gather and manage information; define, prioritize, and consolidate requirements for donors; negotiate interagency frameworks for action and orchestrate field activities; and provide leadership.[30] However, he sorely lacked the necessary management experience to run a major UN department in a complicated area of responsibility. If someone had been found who met the basic requirements for the post, as called for by Brian Urquhart and Erskine Childers,[31] the DHA might have been a different story. For example, the Office of Emergency Operations in Africa (OEOA) had been a success story in the 1980s, largely because the managerial knowledge and political savvy of Bradford Morse and Maurice Strong were powerful enough to break or bend UN institutional rules and practices, just as Sir Robert Jackson had done in the Bangladesh emergency in 1971. Beginning with Mrs. Sadako Ogata's leadership in 1991, the UNHCR has become recognized by donor governments as an accomplished rule breaker akin to the earlier but transient predecessors, Morse and Strong's OEOA and Jackson's Bangladesh operation.

Behind the mask of public eloquence was basic management ineptitude. Not to put too fine a point on it, the DHA had insufficient qualified staff, resources, and authority to accomplish these tasks. Under Eliasson, as well as his successors—Peter Hansen, a respected Danish development economist with lengthy UN experience, and Yasushi Akashi, who had held a number of senior UN posts in New York and in peace operations in Cambodia and the former Yugoslavia—the DHA made little practical difference during its five years of existence. Nor was it successful in internal lobbying on humanitarian issues with the secretary-general and his cabinet and with the Security Council. The so-called reform of 1997 changed little except for acronyms.[32] In January 1998, the "shell game" continued with the creation of the Office for the Coordination of Humanitarian Affairs, although finally this department was headed by a person with both hands-on field and headquarters experience, as well as political savvy, Sergio Vieira de Mello.[33]

UN Subcontracting for Security and Services

Overextension, in both the civilian and the humanitarian arenas, was the consensus diagnosis of the world organization's ills on its fiftieth anniversary in 1995, as well as a prognosis for the near future. The third feature of this description about the context for humanitarian intervention in the post–Cold War arena in some way arises from the first two—namely, subcontracting for military services to both regional organizations or major states, on the one hand, and for humanitarian delivery services to international NGOs, on the other.[34] This feature in many ways builds upon trends toward privatization that had begun before the flurry of new operations after the Cold War.

The pursuit of the Gulf War and the creation of safe havens for Kurds were clear and successful illustrations of military subcontracting, as were NATO's IFOR and SFOR in the former Yugoslavia. A more controversial and less successful example was Somalia. A surge of three Security Council decisions between late June and late July 1994 indicated the relevance of military intervention by major powers in regions of their traditional interests: a Russian scheme to deploy its troops in Georgia to end the three-year-old civil war; the French intervention in Rwanda to help stave off genocidal conflict; and the U.S. plan to spearhead a military invasion to reverse the military coup in Haiti. The decision in Budapest in December 1994 by the Conference (now Organization) on Security and Cooperation in Europe (OSCE) to authorize 3,000 troops from the Commonwealth of Independent States and other OSCE member states after a definitive agreement in Nagorno-Karabakh was another illustration (as yet not realized), as were efforts throughout the 1990s by Nigeria and other countries of the Economic Community of West African States in Liberia.

Military and civilian analysts alike agree that the results from these arrangements have been anything except uniformly positive, as will become apparent. Although there has been a growth in private armies, mercenaries hardly appear the ideal solution for humanitarian intervention.[35] Yet, the evident gap between the UN's capacities and increasing demands for help could be filled by regional powers, or even hegemons, operating under the scrutiny of a wider community of states that would try to hold the interveners more accountable for their actions undertaken with the blessing of a larger community of states.[36]

This is not collective security of the Charter variety.[37] In fact, the

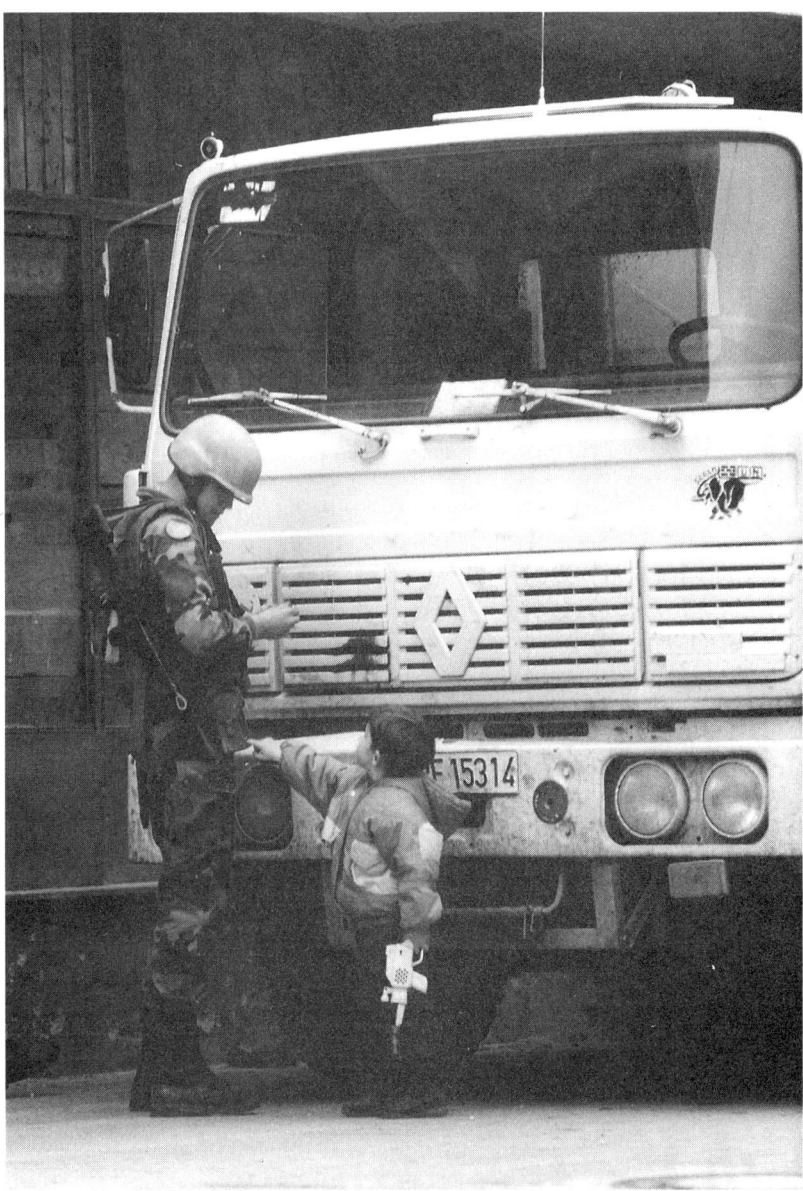

A boy holding a toy gun speaks to a French UNPROFOR (United Nations Protection Forces) soldier standing by a truck in Dobrinja, a heavily damaged "front line" suburb in the besieged capital city of Sarajevo.
Credit: UNICEF/94-0873/Roger Lemoyne

Security Council is experimenting with a type of great power control over decisionmaking and enforcement, whose mitigation and eventual disappearance were behind the UN's founding. Nonetheless, the experiment is increasingly pertinent in light of the inherent difficulties of multilateral mobilization and management of military force.[38] This development may disappoint die-hard UN enthusiasts. Although the relative weakness of developing countries creates additional problems that complicate everything from standardization to payments to hidden agendas, there is no alternative to making better use of regional organizations, without naïveté and with accountability. As former UN Undersecretary-General Marrack Goulding wrote: "It is likely to become the standard approach when the Security Council decides that enforcement action is required."[39] Major powers inevitably flex their muscles in the pursuit of their interests, but they do not inevitably subject themselves to international law and monitoring. However limited, influencing the behavior of would-be subcontractors is a feasible step toward enhanced international peace and security. Limited checks and balances are preferable to unregulated unilateralism.

A second element of the subcontracting phenomenon relates to the growing contribution of international NGOs to mitigate suffering from wars.[40] One of the more striking developments in contemporary international politics has been the burgeoning of nongovernmental organizations.[41] Over the last two decades, human rights advocates, gender activists, developmentalists, and groups of indigenous peoples have become more vocal and operational in contexts that were once thought to be the exclusive preserve of governments.[42] They have injected new and often unexpected voices into international discourse. As globalization proceeds and erodes the control of the state, analysts and policymakers alike seek alternatives to help solve problems. In this context, NGOs emerge as critical actors—private in form but public in purpose.

Their sheer growth has been nothing short of remarkable. Estimates for the number of international NGOs (operating in more than three countries) hover around 20,000, a figure that represents a doubling in the last half decade[43] and an explosion over the last half century—there were only 700 in 1939.[44] National NGOs have grown faster still. Although in the mid-1990s, the UNDP estimated their number to be around 50,000, this figure represented only those authorized to receive support from outside donors.[45] The actual figure is much higher if more specialized researchers are to be believed: 16,000 registered in Bangladesh; 21,000 in the Philippines; 100,000 Christian-based ones in Brazil; and 27,000 in Chile.[46] Grassroots organizations are said to number in the millions.[47] The phenomenon is not limited to the Third World. For example, in France in 1960, approximately 11,000 associations were formed; by 1987, the number had increased to 54,000. In the United Kingdom, some 4,000 new charities were established yearly during the 1980s, reflecting both the importance of the phenomenon and tax incentives.[48]

There is no necessary correlation between growth in NGO numbers and their importance to the activities of IGOs in world politics. Indeed, there has been a rather uncritical acceptance of NGOs by proponents. As Andrew Natsios has remarked, "the international community has grasped the NGO alternative with promiscuous enthusiasm."[49] However, the numbers capture accurately the growing salience of IGO-NGO interactions. Even if their influence is less than either allies or adversaries believe,[50] their existence in such numbers has undermined the contention of states about any monopoly over authority. In fact, IGOs and donor governments have played major roles in the evolution of nongovernmental organizations. Through financial, moral, and institutional support, the UN has contributed to strengthening NGOs, particularly since the 1970s. In return, NGOs have assisted numerous intergovernmental agencies, especially by helping to build local constituencies for UN programs and, more importantly, by acting as implementors of projects. The availability of development aid is generally seen as a major contributing factor to NGO growth in Africa and Asia. Although the phenomenon is not as pronounced as for bilateral donors and other NGOs,[51] UN agencies occasionally have created nongovernmental organizations; but it may be that the UN's main contribution has been in legitimating many local NGOs and in mainstreaming their inputs and ideas.

The combination of rising demands and limited capacities has led IGOs to devolve responsibilities toward other institutions. In particular, UN subcontracting for services to NGOs has assumed remarkable proportions recently—just as it has for military subcontracting.

Delivery of services is the mainstay of most of their budgets and the basis for enthusiastic support from a wide range of donors. As part of a privatization of both development and relief, bilateral and intergovernmental organizations are relying upon NGOs more and more. The last twenty years have witnessed exponential growth, so much so that now the total share of development aid transferred through NGOs outweighs that disbursed by the UN system, excluding the Washington-based financial institutions (that is, the World Bank and the International Monetary Fund). Traditionally, many NGOs have run development programs, but increasingly, emergency relief is becoming, in total financial terms, their most important activity.[52] In 1995, NGOs disbursed at least 13 percent of total public development aid—some $10–12 billion and probably much more since neither emergency food aid nor military help figures accurately in statistics; an ever-growing share (approaching half) was for emergency relief. With a sixfold increase in emergency spending over the last decade, the European Union's switch away from funding for emergencies channeled through governments toward NGOs has been even more remarkable—for governments, from over 95 percent in 1976 to only 6 percent in 1990, and for NGOs, from 0 to 37 percent.[53]

The use of outside military forces has facilitated the sixfold increase in emergency spending over the last decade. Prior to the military's increased expansion into war zones for humanitarian purposes, the International Committee of the Red Cross had a virtual monopoly over emergency delivery in them. The United Nations was constrained by the politics of the Cold War, which essentially meant a restrictive interpretation of its mandate to recognized governments and victims located within the territories under direct governmental control. NGOs usually refrained from helping those in contested areas, at least until the mid-1980s, when individual NGOs began to mount limited cross-border operations.[54]

The widespread use of military forces has encouraged NGOs to leap into the fray; it is possible now for almost any private institution, no matter how insignificant its staff or budget, to mount a program in a war zone. It has also become possible for governments to hire private security groups like Executive Outcomes for protection in countries like Sierra Leone. Moreover, NGO humanitarian relief has become a big business, although how much of the rise in expenditures is due to inefficiencies and increasing administrative costs is not clear. Having literally hundreds of subcontractors delivering similar goods and services in a disjointed and competitive marketplace during the tumult of wars means that part of the dramatic growth must be driven by NGOs themselves.[55] This market phenomenon has led to severe criticism.[56]

This, then, is the substantially altered post–Cold War context: growing numbers of civil wars, a heightened demand for UN military and civilian services, and a growing reliance by the world organization on military and NGO subcontractors. Having explored earlier the roots of today's military-civilian interaction, it is time to turn to a framework to compare costs and benefits of intervention in contemporary humanitarian crises.

2

Framework for Estimating Military Costs and Civilian Benefits from Intervention

Having introduced the key actors on the international humanitarian stage and examined both the historical antecedents of military-civilian interactions and recent trends underlying responses to today's complex emergencies, it is fitting to sketch a framework to guide the subsequent scrutiny of five prominent cases of intervention in the 1990s. As the reader will soon discover, the methodological challenges are anything except simple. The objective is to develop a common schema, even if a template is impossible. Notwithstanding difficulties, data generated by other analysts of northern Iraq (1991–1996), Somalia (1992–1995), Bosnia (1992–1995), Rwanda (1994–1995), and Haiti (1991–1996) are useful and are consolidated in the following five chapters. These data are sufficient, when plugged in to the framework developed in this chapter, in order to make useful, even if less than definitive, judgments about military costs and civilian benefits. This short chapter provides the essential guidelines for readers to keep in mind through the case studies that follow.

Assessing the Bottom Line

Table 2.1 contains the elements of a framework to examine the military costs for donor countries and the benefits for civilians in a targeted

Table 2.1 Estimating Military Costs (for Troop-Contributing Countries) and Civilian Benefits (for Targeted Country) from Intervention

Military costs of intervention for troop-contributing countries	$ Costs	Casualties/Fatalities	Political Impact
	A	B	C

Civilian benefits of intervention for targeted countries	Displacement	Suffering	State of the State
• Humanitarian challenge before intervention	D	E	F
• Civilian benefits after intervention	D′	E′	F′

country resulting from coercive intervention by external military forces. The purpose of this volume is to understand the interactions between outside soldiers and outside civilian humanitarians. The specific task is to compare available data about the nature of outside military involvement and costs for intervening countries, on the one hand, with the magnitude of a humanitarian tragedy in a targeted country and of the postintervention improvements for civilian victims within it, on the other hand. The framework in the following figure is used to the extent possible in subsequent chapters to analyze northern Iraq, Somalia, Bosnia, Rwanda, and Haiti.

In an effort to paint as accurate a picture as possible for each case, the starting point is to establish military costs for intervening countries. To the extent possible, these should be broken down into three components:

- Box A: There should be three indicators of costs: two military and one civilian. The dollar values of the military presence for security purposes should be those officially reported by troop contributors, as well as any well-regarded estimates that are different (usually multiples higher). When possible, the value of the military's providing physical security should be distinguished from its direct humanitarian assistance, and net figures (or incremental costs) should be given to indicate the "true" cost over and above what would have been expended by troop-contributing countries to support troops at home bases. UN budgetary figures should be reported, although these understate the financial costs for industrialized troop contributors and do not take into account the concern surfacing about the loss of purely war-fighting skills resulting from humanitarian intervention.[1] There should be an indication of the changing volume and value of civilian humanitarian aid, the assumption being that such assistance is facilitated by the military's presence. While crude, figures should take into account the total population of an affected area because everyone within it, not simply persons officially at risk, benefit or are penalized by the military's presence.

- Box B: Accidental and battle casualties, and especially fatalities, should be reported. The size, scope, and duration of an operation should be reflected in order to interpret the figures. But an absolute number is probably most relevant because of the relatively low tolerance for deaths in troop-contributing countries unless truly vital national interests are judged to be at stake.
- Box C: There should be an appreciation of conventional wisdom regarding the overall weight of political and parliamentary reactions to a particular intervention. These could be considered a kind of "net political benefit" that influences the subsequent willingness of a country's population, elites, or particular political administration to continue supporting an intervention and future multilateral military operations spurred by humanitarian motives.

The nature of the humanitarian challenge for civilians on the eve of the military intervention in a targeted country should, to the extent possible, be reflected for three criteria. These same criteria should be examined for the period after the outside humanitarian intervention, as a broad-brush-stroke way to measure key possible benefits for civilians:[2]

- Box D: In spite of the well-known controversies about accuracy, involuntary migration is probably the best reflection of the magnitude of a complex humanitarian emergency and should be captured by UNHCR figures about refugees and internally displaced persons. In most cases, the latter category of "internal refugees" (or IDPs) should be accompanied by indications of war victims who have not moved but are living in "refugee-like situations" or as "besieged populations." The UNHCR increasingly refers to "people of concern" to encompass these groups. A rapid improvement (Box D')—measured, for instance, by an increase in voluntary repatriation by refugees or a return by IDPs—in a relatively brief interval after an outside intervention would in many cases provide an important gauge of enhanced security, protection, and some confidence in the future. From a victim's standpoint, repatriation may not always constitute an improvement if the area of return is more insecure than the former area of displacement (for example, repatriations from the Congo to Rwanda or from Abkhazia to Georgia). Moreover, an initial return may be followed by renewed violence and redisplacement (for example, at various times in Tajikistan and Liberia). Although "forced" or "premature" repatriation and tightened asylum policies have become a reality of the 1990s, returns nonetheless usually suggest an improvement, however tenuous, in security.

- Box E: Suffering should be measured by significant changes in hunger, disease, and human rights abuse. The first measurement reflects those whose lives are at risk from a lack of calories, a statistic available from many agencies. Through World Health Organization (WHO) or UNICEF statistics, the second measurement should indicate the status of women and children, the most vulnerable members of a society who are also the most numerous among those involuntarily displaced. Finally, although in theory correlation with intervention should be possible, human rights abuses are probably the most contested and unreliable of statistics within and across cases. And even essential measurements can change from case to case (for example, rape is much more of a factor, however contested the figures, in some conflicts than in others). Nonetheless, a reflection of human rights is essential to capture accurately the nature of suffering in war zones. Again, improvements in these three criteria (Box E') after an intervention would suggest payoffs from intervention in a targeted country, just as a deterioration signaled the onset of the crisis. Here as above, however, the problem of counterfactuals raises its ugly head. To the extent that the intervention contributes inadvertently to the scope and duration of a crisis, the costs associated with these unintended consequences should also be weighed against the gains of, say, lives saved or human rights protected. To put it another way, the relationship between the crisis and the response can be perversely dialectical. The crisis presents human rights problems (for instance, ethnic cleansing that civilian agencies and military forces attempt to address), but the intervention in turn can create new problems (for example, after the creation of safe areas in the for-

mer Yugoslavia). Such interactions cannot be quantified, but they should be kept in mind.
- Box F: There should be a reflection of widespread judgments regarding the ability of governmental authorities in the country in crisis to control territory, exercise administrative authority over its inhabitants, and provide security for them. How much these traditional attributes of sovereignty are present or absent should provide an indication, however subjective, of the extent to which there is a crisis in, or even a collapse of, state sovereignty. Although indicators about a healthy civil society (for example, numbers of opposition groups or media outlets) would be useful indicators for certain countries, the improvement in local governmental authority (Box F') would be more readily visible and also suggest possible benefits from intervention beyond the capacities of outside military forces, and perhaps of others as well.[3] At the same time, more and more observers suggest the importance of moving beyond what Charles King has aptly dubbed "narcissistic" intervention in which the long-term effects of outside involvement are less relevant than they should be.[4]

Methodological Issues

The dramatic acceleration in the number and variety of UN military missions has been widely noted—the Security Council approved over twice as many operations in the last decade as in the previous four ten-year periods combined. The proliferation of analyses about multilateral military operations has been driven by humanitarian impulses; over a quarter of the recent peace operations literature relates to such tragedies.[5] Aware of the usual problems in comparing incomparable cases and the significant geopolitical changes since the collapse of the bipolar system, it is nonetheless crucial to try to draw general policy lessons across disparate cases of the post–Cold War era. However, there are methodological considerations that influence this first attempt to establish costs and benefits of multilateral military operations and humanitarian action in war zones, which hinder letting the data speak for themselves. Three methodological concerns are worth spelling out in some detail.

First, both the armed forces and humanitarian agencies are not any more forthcoming about data, nor do they employ more comparable accounting methods than in the Sudan, where I participated in a 1990 review that highlighted statistical problems, among others.[6] Reliable statistics about the actual costs of delivery (of goods and alternative modes) are sketchy and usually not comparable among sources. Hence, digging for data and compiling them are not the only problems for social scientists. There is still no standard methodology for reporting, even among the members of the Development Assistance Committee of the Organization for Economic Cooperation and Development (OECD).

Exact costs are virtually impossible to establish for a variety of reasons. The U.S. military is often the primary intervening military actor, but its accounting techniques have numerous problems.[7] It is necessary to differentiate between "total costs" and "incremental costs," which is the cost over and above the normal operating expenditures for the resources used during the intervention. Incremental costs are usually incurred "to transport troops, equipment, and supplies and to sustain the military forces in the field."[8] In most cases the incremental costs are given, which makes it difficult to assess the exact cost of what a similar intervention would cost for other agencies or organizations. Moreover, Washington's behavior is typical. And many NGOs do not present accurate data about the exact cost of their programs.

Second, the emphasis on costs and benefits necessarily entails ambiguities. The first is that it biases analyses in favor of delivery over protection, even though both are mutually reinforcing components of hu-

Bosnia-Herzegovina/Sarajevo airport/Logistics Hercules transporting relief items. Credit: UNHCR/S.Foa/07.1992

manitarian action. Effective military intervention in war zones relieves life-threatening suffering by providing emergency assistance and by protecting fundamental human rights. As mentioned earlier, however, it is difficult to measure the latter except by their absence or presence, whereas relief can be quantified more readily. It is also virtually impossible to gauge with any precision how much better or worse the human rights situation would have been in the absence of soldiers, although the perspective of counterfactual analysis is an important one.[9] Moreover, the same hypothetical measurement problem arises when attempting to gauge the costs associated with the purported contributions of humanitarian intervention to prolonging or exacerbating a crisis. Presumably, these indirect costs should be deducted from any benefit. Clearly, more sophisticated methodological approaches are necessary, or one is left with pulling troops in order to test hypotheses.

More attention customarily is paid to delivery than protection, which may favor accounting more accurately for short-term benefits than for longer-term shortcomings. Nonetheless, there can be only limited relief and no hope for solutions without security. Hence, a noticeable improvement in voluntary repatriation would be a significant concrete reflection of the amount of confidence of a threatened population in the value of an intervention, and ultimately in the prospects for improvements in human rights even if Western standards of such protection were not met.

In this regard, it is fair to criticize the military's unwillingness to undertake tasks that it could have agreed to do but did not, or to criticize political authorities who refused to agree to appropriate mandates (for example, for demining territory, disarming belligerents, or arresting war criminals). However, it is unfair to condemn the military for not doing what is not its business to do and what it would never agree to do (for example, reconciliation or addressing the roots of a conflict). It is unreasonable to judge the military in acute emergencies by standards—for example, empowering local communities, avoiding dependence, fostering reconciliation—against which both development and civilian humanitarian agencies measure up poorly.[10] This line of criticism would appear ridiculous in relationship to military help in the face of natural disasters because such assistance failed to address the "roots" of hurricanes or earthquakes. Although more could be done to alter administrative shortcomings, who would argue that it is useless to respond when floods menace Bangladesh or earthquakes strike Afghanistan because the origins of the annual torrential rains or of periodic seismic problems have not been addressed? Somehow such arguments receive more credibility in war zones.

Outside military intervention can improve access and help move relief goods and contribute to an environment in which human rights abuses become less frequent. It can provide time for belligerents to come to their senses and for outside mediators and negotiators to launch activities. But the presence of outside military forces in and of itself cannot be expected to end war. Without a coherent political strategy the decision to use military forces should be seen at most as a necessary and worthwhile temporary respite, not a solution.

As the details of the next five chapters show, there is a fundamental ambiguity in trying to qualify any of the five cases as a "success" or a "failure" in terms of their external and internal impacts. For instance, perceptions in troop-contributing countries about a particular humanitarian intervention are critical for future actions. This external impact would be measured by determining the willingness of states to mount other diplomatic and military efforts and for publics and parliaments to support subsequent humanitarian undertakings. Here, as elsewhere, the calculus of benefits and costs is difficult to treat on a discrete case-by-case basis because of spillover from one intervention to the next. Actions taken in one case may have implications or demonstration effects for others—for instance, the retreat of the USS *Harlan County* from Haiti in 1993 or possible emulation by Hutu forces in murdering Belgian peacekeepers in April 1994 in Rwanda. Such negative consequences emanating from the deaths of U.S. Rangers in Somalia should be considered costs in the initial case; and positive consequences (for example, Operation Provide Comfort) should also be treated as additional benefits. Such spillover cannot be quantified in any meaningful way, but it should be flagged at the outset and reflected subjectively in calculations.

In historical perspective, we would probably have the clearest contrast in the United States between the action in northern Iraq that led to bullish presidential discourse from both Republican and Democratic administrations, on the one hand, and the pessimism and reluctance to take a military lead after the debacle in Somalia, on the other. Yet, military actions still have continued afterward in a variety of situations. Probably the main source of ambiguity in looking to the future results from the following question: How can analysts attempt to measure impacts within affected areas without attaching specific monetary values to human life? Philosophical and moral challenges confront those who assign values to such numbers.

There are inescapable value judgments and differing time frames and objectives used by various actors and analysts along with the hidden agendas that are the essence of world politics and international negotiations. Have military efforts in northern Iraq been a success because 1.5 million Kurds were saved in 1991 and remain alive, or have they been a failure because there was no political solution and Saddam Hussein was ensconced in Baghdad and flaunting international decisions? Were military operations in Somalia successful because death rates dropped in 1993, or were they a long-term failure because billions of dollars were spent to stop the clock temporarily? Were military efforts in Bosnia successful because they saved lives and avoided a wider conflict in Europe, or a failure because the international community has not stood up to aggression, war crimes, and the forced movement of peoples and chose a type of intervention that may have perpetuated the conflict? Were military and police operations to restore President Jean-Bertrand Aristide in Haiti a success because a precedent against a seizure of power by a junta was set and peaceful elections for his successor held, or a failure because fundamentally skewed economic structures remain in place to exploit the vast majority of the population? Were military efforts in Rwanda a success because the carnage was stopped and lives saved, or a failure because the genocide took place and violence spread to new theaters?

Third, some methodological criticism could result from the selection of cases, and so it is important to justify those that appear in this book. The five examples here are not the only historical cases of military op-

Medical personnel from the multinational forces carry an Iraqi refugee into a camp near Safwan. Credit: UN PHOTO 158302/J. Isaac

erations and humanitarian action after the Cold War. This discussion excludes a host of traditional peacekeeping operations in countries with major humanitarian problems (for example, Cambodia, Mozambique, and Angola). It also excludes Liberia and Georgia, where information is very sketchy and where the UN Security Council began to focus attention long after the beginning of outside coercive intervention, thereby making international accountability even less significant here than for the five chosen cases.[11] Nor does the analysis consider outside military forces responding to such natural disasters as volcanic eruptions in the Philippines or monsoons in Bangladesh because they would take us too far from the terrain of war zones.

The five cases were selected because of their political prominence in the mid-1990s for policy analysts and decisionmakers and because sufficient time has elapsed since the completion of the military assignments to permit data to be gathered. These defining events undoubtedly affected calculations in the ministries of defense of the major powers; for example, these five operations provided the basis for conclusions about American foreign policy on the eve of the last presidential elections drawn by the 1996 Independent Task Force at the Council on Foreign Relations chaired by George Soros.[12] Moreover, and essential for the sample here, all were subject to scrutiny by the UN Security Council before the outside military forces intervened and had Chapter VII authorization for coercion.

Whether or not sufficient force was used, the enforcement provision is an essential methodological concern because both the logistics and the security functions of the military were available for warlike situations and not just the humanitarian work often accomplished by traditional UN peacekeepers in their noncoercive roles.[13] The only Chapter VII case missing from the sample is Albania, a relatively insignificant emergency (some 200 deaths and 12,000 refugees in 1996 when Italy began to head an eight-country coalition of willing European states and 6,000 soldiers).[14] This intervention responded to a crisis that was insignificant in relationship to the other five.

These cases illustrate military-civilian humanitarianism without the pretense of neutrality—the existence of a coercive mandate makes quite clear what is perhaps hazier in non–Chapter VII cases. The ICRC, for instance, has championed the view that saving lives and reducing suffering do not advance anyone's political agenda. This view is increasingly under attack in the academic and policy literatures as naïve and wrong.[15] The crises of the post–Cold War era are inspiring a growing literature about the politics of rescue,[16] including the work of Richard Betts, who poignantly pointed to "the delusion of impartial intervention."[17] All decisions about aid have distributional effects with political ramifications, as former U.S. Secretary of State for African Affairs Chester A. Crocker reminded us in commenting upon the November 1996 crisis in what was then Zaire: "Intervention (just like nonintervention) is an inherently political action with inescapable political consequences."[18]

Even without military forces, humanitarian efforts are profoundly political. If done properly, civilian humanitarian efforts, and certainly ones backed by the use of coercion, should alter the balance of power in favor of victims. If they are not carefully designed, they can exacerbate conflicts.[19] Avoiding involvement can be considered "intervention" because those humanitarians who fail to engage themselves on behalf of the oppressed are effectively helping the oppressors. Championed at first by Médecins sans Frontières and other members of the Doctors without Borders movement, the need to be clear about solidarity with victims has been gaining ground in the debate vis-à-vis the more traditional view about the potential for neutrality and impartiality espoused by the ICRC and others. The need for a new type of pragmatic moralism of utilitarian humanitarian ethics adapted to the demands of the troubling contemporary era is a subject that provides the conclusion for this volume.

There are varying circumstances and purposes for the use of force and myriad differences in UN involvement among the five case studies, and even within various phases of the same case.[20] Although in every case U.S. participation was crucial, multilateral military intervention will, and should, be used more frequently in the future, rather than the more unilateral forms of the past. The working assumption here is in line with Stanley Hoffmann's contention that a significant change in the 1990s is that "the emphasis has shifted from unilateral interventions."[21] The political and financial advantages of a blue-colored seal of approval emerge from the cases.

Notwithstanding these difficulties, and as hinted at the outset of this chapter there are sufficient case studies (northern Iraq, Somalia, Bosnia, Rwanda, and Haiti) with data generated by other analysts in order to generalize about military costs and civilian benefits. This information provides the groundwork for broad conclusions in the final chapter about expanding or contracting military-civilian interactions to respond better in future "complex humanitarian emergencies." It would be useful to define this term for this volume: war-induced and sudden catastrophes involving substantial increases in involuntary displacements and in suffering (especially as measured by famine, disease, and human rights abuse) of noncombatants accompanied by a crisis, and oftentimes a collapse, of state authority.

In short, the next chapters dissect the most dramatic humanitarian crises of the 1990s for which the UN Security Council authorized Chapter VII coercion and thereby dared to override the sovereignty of political authorities in targeted countries. These cases of interactions between soldiers and civilians illustrate both the logistics and the security capacities of the armed forces acting in a post–Cold War world in which multilateral humanitarian intervention is preferable to more unilateral interventions of the past.

3

Northern Iraq, 1991–1996: A Difficult Act to Follow?

In the immediate aftermath of the Gulf War and the first Chapter VII enforcement since Korea, international public opinion was sensitized and could not then ignore some 1.5 to 2 million Kurds whose desperate plight constituted a huge humanitarian challenge that appeared virtually overnight. The Gulf War itself had revitalized the notion of collective security, and the international response to the Kurds ushered in a period in which the term "humanitarian intervention" became popular. Indeed, it led to a short-lived euphoria that states would be held accountable for their antihumanitarian actions. Hard-and-fast distinctions between domestic jurisdiction and international responsibilities were set aside with the passage of Security Council Resolutions 687, dictating the terms of the cease-fire, and 688, insisting that "Iraq allow immediate access by international humanitarian organizations to all those in need of assistance." This was the first in a series of elastic interpretations of "threats to international peace and security," a UN Charter provision that Stanley Hoffmann compared during a conference presentation to "an all-purpose parachute."¹

The extent, strength, and rapidity of the Allied Coalition's Operation Provide Comfort (OPC) were impressive from April to July 1991. Over 12,000 American and Allied troops (the main other contributors were France, the United Kingdom, and the Netherlands, but another dozen countries were eventually involved) were deployed on the basis of an authorization from the Security Council. They delivered more than 25

43

Map 3.1 Iraq

Iraq has a population of 22,219,289 (1997), and its capital is Baghdad. It is located in western Asia, with a narrow outlet to the Persian (Arabian) Gulf. It is bordered by Turkey (N), Iran (E), Saudi Arabia and Kuwait (S), and Syria and Jordan (W). Its total land area is 168,754 square miles (slightly larger than California), with 36 miles of coastline and only 12 percent arable land. Main exports are crude oil and refined products and dates.

million pounds of food, water, medical supplies, clothing, and shelter. Soldiers escorted Kurdish refugees from their mountain hideouts back to the safe havens in northern Iraq.

The attention of the international humanitarian system was drawn to the plight of the Kurds in March 1991 when a failed revolt after the Gulf War triggered the flight of almost two million Kurdish refugees to the Turkish and Iranian borders. Operation Provide Comfort has been widely heralded as one of the primary success stories of post–

Cold War humanitarian intervention. For a time, it created optimism about future interventions, certainly in the United States, and a renaissance in the United Nations.

This chapter examines the effectiveness of responses on the Turkish border from May to July of 1991 and thereafter. However, in order to contextualize this intense period of intervention in the early 1990s and since that time, the chapter also examines the history and demography of the Kurds, the Gulf crisis and the larger UN response, and the post-intervention situation. Operation Provide Comfort was complex, and the analysis details the humanitarian crisis in the north and south, the role of the media, UN resolutions, the military and civilian responses, the costs, and finally, the results of the response.

Background and Roots of the Conflict

Considerable debate exists about the exact size of the Kurdish population, partially due to the lack of adequate demographic data, as well as continual migration.[1] Numbering between 20 to 27 million, the Kurds are the fourth largest ethnic population in the Middle East. The majority inhabit southern Turkey (10–14 million), northern Iraq (3.5–4.8 million), northwestern Iraq (6–6.7 million), and Syria (800,000–1 million). There also exists a significant Kurdish population in both Lebanon and the republics of the former Russian Transcaucasian Federation (Armenia, Azerbaijan, and Georgia).

Many argue persuasively that the Kurds are a nation without a state, although others would argue that the requisite political loyalty and identity is lacking and that Kurds other than in the diaspora rarely exhibit cohesive "national" behavior. An ethnic population with strong tribal ties, they have consistently opposed foreign rule and sought self-determination. The historical relationship between the Kurds and the Iraqi government has been characterized by violent uprisings against the government to secure greater autonomy; massive and violent repression of the Kurdish population; periodic attempts at reconciliation between the Kurds and the government, usually granting a degree of autonomous rule that is retracted; and frequent internal dissension, often violent, among various Kurdish factions.

Some observers argue that Iraqi Kurds have a stronger sense of nationalism than counterparts in Turkey and Iran. This difference is largely explained by the policies of Britain, which controlled Iraq until independence, and later by the influence of Faisal II, Iraqi king from 1939 to 1958, who sought to use Iraqi Kurds as a buffer against Iran and Turkey.[2] Throughout the nineteenth and twentieth centuries, the Kurds have been a pawn in games of state competition—by Britain, Turkey, Iran, the United States, and Iraq.

Created by colonial powers only in 1921, Iraq is dominated by its Sunni Moslem population. The existence of the Kurds and a large Shiite population in the south have weakened central state authority. The government has opposed Kurdish secession because of the possible precedent for the Shiite population and because a large portion of Iraq's mineral wealth lies within what would become Kurdistan. In Turkey, by contrast, the roots of the Kurdish uprising lie more in the repression of Kurdish culture than in disputes over resources.

Various Kurdish tribes engaged in minor insurrections against the British throughout the 1920s, but the first major explosion occurred in the 1960s. Since then, there have been cycles of revolt and partial reconciliation with the *peshmergas,* the Kurdish militias, who consistently have used guerrilla tactics against Iraqi conventional forces. By the early 1960s, the Kurdish Democratic Party (KDP), led by Mustafa Barzani, controlled most of northern Iraq, which moved the Iraqi government to agree to a cease-fire in 1964. Kurds were granted partial governance of their districts, and the Kurdish language was recognized. However, disagreements in 1968 between the two major leaders, the KDP's Barzani and Jalal Talabani, who would later found the Patriotic Union of Kurdistan (PUK) in 1976, reignited conflict.

Kurdish insurrections led to the rise and fall of governments, as well as to numerous coups, including the Ba'ath Party's ascension to power in 1968 with Saddam Hussein as vice president. The ascendancy of the Ba'ath Party led to the manifesto of 11 March 1970, "which has been continually referred to over the years as a background for a settlement by both sides, and was declared the basis of the negotiations that took place after the uprising in 1991."[3] This manifesto made both Kurdish and Arabic the official languages of northern Iraq, included Kurds in high public and military positions, granted autonomous rule of heavily populated Kurdish areas, facilitated the repatriation of Kurdish refugees, and granted the Kurds the same rights as other Iraqis. However, a reversal took place with renewed hostilities in 1974, which in turn led to another peace plan in 1975. Later that year, the Kurdish movement was dealt a severe double blow by Barzani's defeat and a settlement signed in Algiers, which ended the long-standing hostilities between Iran and Iraq and eliminated Iranian military aid for the Kurds.

The fall of the Shah of Iran and the rise of the revolutionary Khomeini regime reignited hostilities, which culminated with the invasion of Iran by Iraq in 1980. Throughout this war, the PUK and the KDP received Iranian military aid to facilitate their guerrilla campaign against regular Iraqi forces. The results of the Iran-Iraq War were disastrous, and the resulting economic crisis was a factor in the 1990 decision to invade Kuwait.[4] It is widely believed that one million soldiers were killed on each side during the Iran-Iraq War before the UN brokered an agreement in 1987.

A decisive factor in the massive flight of refugees in 1991 was the searing memory of official repression from 1985 to 1988. The peak was from February until September of 1988, known as the "Anfal campaign" ("booty" in Arabic). With the end of the Iran-Iraq War, resources were liberated for government repression in the north. During this period, between 50,000 to 200,000 Kurds were massacred by Iraqi government forces; 3,000 to 4,000 villages were destroyed; 100,000 Kurds fled to Turkey; and over 800,000 were forcibly moved from their homes.[5] Thus, "only about 1,000 of the 4,000 Kurdish villages which had existed before were still standing and more than one-third of the area of Iraqi Kurdistan was completely depopulated."[6] Government forces used chemical weapons against the Kurdish population in Halabjah.

Prior to the Gulf War,[7] although there had not been a major incursion by Iraqi forces into Kuwait since 1973, Kuwaiti sovereignty over oil had consistently been a source of contention. After Iraqi forces invaded Kuwait on the morning of 2 August 1990, a flurry of UN Security Council resolutions resulted: 660, which called for an unconditional withdrawal; 661, which authorized Chapter VII economic sanctions for the third time in UN history; and 662, which declared the invasion illegal. The United States and other Allied nations invoked Article 51 of the UN Charter to deploy Operation Desert Shield in response to a call for collective defense. In addition to Kuwait's autonomy, the rationale was to protect Saudi Arabia from the possibility of invasion. Coalition forces were called to enforce the sanctions on Iraq by sea, through Resolution 665, and then by air, through Resolution 670.

The August invasion created the first of a series of humanitarian crises related to the Gulf War, this one related to Iraq's original invasion of Kuwait; 850,000 third-country nationals and 300,000 Palestinians from both Iraq and Kuwait fled, primarily to Jordan. After a delay of several weeks, UN agencies managed to repatriate third-country nationals. There were no fatalities in spite of difficult camp conditions. By late March, three out of five camps in Jordan were preparing to close.[8]

Security Council Resolution 678 authorized the use of "all necessary means" against the Iraqi forces if they did not withdraw from Kuwait by 15 January 1991 in order to restore "international peace and security." This was the first time that the UN had explicitly mandated the use of force against an aggressor state since 1950 in Korea. Coalition forces eventually numbered some 680,000 troops, of whom 410,000 were American.

The failure to withdraw Iraqi forces led to the start of a six-week air campaign. Coalition air forces systematically destroyed government and military buildings, air defense installations, ground forces weapons depots, and electrical supply stations. Their campaign destroyed much of the Iraqi civil infrastructure, including the capacity to produce electricity, which in turn incapacitated water and sewage treatment. On 24 February, the Allies commenced a 100-hour ground campaign that liberated Kuwait and further decimated Iraqi forces. Following defeat, the government of Iraq agreed to abide by Resolutions 660 and 662 and signed a cease-fire on 3 March.

Resolution 687 focused on the postwar situation in Iraq and Kuwait and also established the UN Iraq-Kuwait Observer Mission (UNIKOM). It required the disposal and cessation of all Iraqi weapons of mass destruction and nuclear weapons programs, which would be enforced by sanctions, and it created an Inter-Agency Humanitarian Appeal for Iraq.

Following an assessment mission, Martti Ahtisaari, the then UN undersecretary-general for administration and management and now the president of Finland, put forward his assessment that Iraq had been "relegated to a pre-industrial age."[9] Although this was later seen as hyperbole, the cost of reconstruction was nonetheless estimated to be some $100–200 billion. The gross domestic product (GDP) decreased from a prewar $66 billion to $245 million in 1991.[10] Disputed estimates on those killed directly from the conflict range from 56,000 to 120,000 soldiers and 3,000 to 3,500 civilians.[11] Although the extent has been much debated, the health of half a million Iraqis was threatened due to the extended antitank shells mode of depleted uranium fired by A-10 aircraft.[12] Additional suffering resulted from the destruction of infrastructure, and the humanitarian impact of economic sanctions was dramatic.[13]

The Onset of the Humanitarian Crisis

After the Allied victory on 27 February, a power vacuum facilitated uprisings by former soldiers—the Shiites in the south and the Kurds in the north. Southern Iraq was the first insurrection, where the Shiites took the lead and captured the port of Basra and subsequently the major cities in southern Iraq.[14] On 4 March, the Kurdish uprising began in Rania and later spread to virtually all major cities in the region.

Among the factors leading to the Kurdish uprising was the call by then U.S. President George Bush for all minority groups and citizens to revolt and depose the authoritarian regime of Saddam Hussein. The initial success of the uprisings was facilitated by massive desertions from the Iraqi army, which was 80 percent Shiite and also had included some Kurdish militia members.[15] While the situation in the south was largely unorganized, Kurdish factions had formed a loose coalition and were preparing to confront the regime. A report from Middle East Watch describes the process:

> On the day that a city rebelled, masses of unarmed or lightly armed civilians and small contingents of rebels converged in the streets. Shouting anti-regime slogans, they descended on government buildings, especially offices of the security forces. These were then attacked, usually with considerable bloodshed on both sides. Government forces fought back, but then were either killed or captured, or allowed to flee. Once in control, the rebels flung open the regime's prisons and interrogation centers, and seized small caches of weapons.[16]

The Allies argued initially that the ground war had rendered Iraqi forces largely inoperative, but coalition leaders later admitted that they had halted the war before this result was achieved. Evidence now shows that Hussein had anticipated revolts and placed various forces on reserve, rather than dedicating them to the Kuwaiti front. The prospects for a successful insurrection by the rebels—who lacked international support and were equipped primarily with small arms to confront a well-equipped, though partially destroyed, conventional force—were dismal. Furthermore, the cease-fire of 3 March prevented the use of fixed-wing aircraft but not attack helicopters, which have historically been a favored tool for civilian repression. The Bush administration has been harshly criticized for failing to intervene. But it did not seek to get caught in a civil conflict, nor did it intend to depose Saddam Hussein forcefully. There was no better alternative, and furthermore, Iraq would still be a necessary counterweight to the other pariah, Iran. Within two weeks, Iraqi forces had regained control of the majority of northern cities, and the revolt had effectively been quelled.

The result was disastrous and predictable: vicious repression. Basra was the site of intense street fighting. While the rebels were guilty of "slaughtering suspected government officials, Ba'ath Party members and secret police," the response by the Iraqi forces was brutal and included indiscriminate attacks on civilian homes and targets, mass executions, the use of children as human shields, and extreme torture.[17] The southern cities of An Najaf and Karbala witnessed similar events, including indiscriminate helicopter and artillery attacks, rape, and the executions of women, children, and rebels.

In northern Iraq, the rebels massacred Ba'athist supporters and employed torture and mass executions. In the cities of Kirkūk, Tuz Khurmatu, and Sulaimaniya, Iraqi helicopters then conducted missile attacks and dropped napalm. Prior to the rebel victory in Kirkūk, there also had been reports of the collection and deportation of Kurdish men to concentration camps. Aside from human rights abuses, government troops also looted and destroyed homes. The attacks on the civilians did not cease when citizens became refugees.[18]

The number of deaths attributed to the uprising and subsequent repression is controversial, but estimates range from 20,000 to 100,000 dead.[19] At least 30,000 civilians were killed in southern and northern Iraq, and this figure is used here.

This brutality and the fear of even larger-scale repression similar to that of the Anfal campaign led to a mass exodus of Kurdish refugees to the Turkish-Iraqi and Iranian-Iraqi borders beginning on 28 March. Refugees who fled to the Turkish border are estimated at 400,000–500,000, while 1 million and later 1.5 million refugees massed at the Iranian border.[20] Almost 2 million out of the 3.5–4.8 million Kurds fled their homes (40–57 percent), a particularly striking statistic in light of the harsh winter weather and the rapidity of the displacement.

Large refugee flows due to government repression, either by Iraqi or Turkish forces, are not uncommon in Kurdistan; for example, 80,000 had fled into Turkey during the most recent previous massive flight in 1988. However, rather than admitting the refugees as they had done then, Turkey prevented them from crossing the border. Human rights abuses by Turkish border guards and the life-threatening winter conditions of the border-mountain region led to an increasing death rate—between 400 and 1,000 per day—largely due to hypothermia, exposure, exhaustion, and bacteria-ridden drinking water, which led to pneumonia, diarrhea, and cholera.[21] The most thorough data gathering was done by INTERTECT. At the peak of the crisis, 22 percent of the refugees were malnourished (4 percent severely), and 70 percent of all hospital cases had diarrhea.[22] An estimated 4,500–6,700 Kurds died during the initial crisis. Some idea of the seriousness of this phase can be gauged from an early measurement effort: "infant mortality rates (IMR) over the first month of the crisis [were] approximately 18–29 times the IMR in Iraq in the late 1980s."[23] This chapter accepts the lower estimate, which was the most that could be verified following repatriation. However, this estimate does not account for those refugees who fled to the Iranian border, who at the peak were triple the number on the Turkish border.

In addition, the humanitarian crises in the north were complicated by the estimated 10 million land mines that had been planted by the government after 1975, predominantly during the Iran-Iraq War.[24] These mines significantly impeded efforts to repatriate refugees then, and they continue to pose a serious threat to residents.

According to Lawrence Freedman and David Boren, the situation on the Iranian border was even more critical than on the Turkish one. Iran already had 600,000 Kurdish refugees and 2.2 million Afghans (who had fled during the Soviet occupation).[25] The government permitted the Kurds to take refuge in Iran but was unable to provide enough resources to process them rapidly. Freedman and Boren report lines of refugees some 50 to 80 kilometers long. Significantly more data exist on the situation in Turkey, largely because of the scale of the international humanitarian operation. Aid to Iran—which absorbed the largest numbers of refugees and in a manner that should have earned it great praise—was inhibited especially by Washington's desire to treat the Islamic Republic as a pariah. Nonetheless, mortality rates on the Iranian border have been estimated to be similar, although some dispute this likelihood. Within Iran, assistance was furnished by the government in collaboration with the UNHCR. In the province of Bakhtarān, where 400,000 of the refugees were located, evidence suggests a better situation. A survey conducted in May reveals a better situation than on the Turkish border. A less inclement climate may explain the differences.[26]

In southern Iraq, the refugee crisis was less severe because the flat and open geography permitted Iraqi air and tank attacks, and hence civilians hesitated to flee. Even the inhospitable mountains and severe climate was better shelter for the Kurds than their home villages. An estimated 70,000 refugees fled into southern Iran, which further increased the burden for a country already facing a crisis to the north and already home to one of the world's largest refugee populations. Another 30,000 Shiites took refuge with Allied forces in Kuwait and Saudi Arabia. In response to the refugee crisis, the United States created a camp in Saudi Arabia for 30,000 to 50,000 refugees. "By 6 May, 12,300 Iraqi refugees had been transferred from southern Iraq to the Saudi refugee camp."[27]

Although the refugee crisis was not as great as the one in the north, the human rights situation may have been worse. An estimated 500,000 to 850,000 Shiites were encircled by Iraqi forces in the southern marshlands, where they were constantly attacked by artillery fire. UN relief efforts were hindered and prevented by the Iraqi government, which refused to approve any such mission and stopped convoys. Estimates are some 15,000 to 30,000 for deaths on the road in Turkey, in the south, and on the Iranian border.[28]

Humanitarian Intervention, April–July 1991

A large continent of reporters had been following Desert Storm, and many stayed to report the subsequent uprisings, which quickly reached the viewing public.[29] The public outcry about the plight of the Kurdish refugees is considered one of the main forces behind the eventual U.S. intervention, although less of a factor in Britain, where fear of backbench criticism motivated Prime Minister John Major to engage British forces. Furthermore, the lack of a media presence in southern Iraq and on the Iranian border partially explained the lack of international interest. Following the Allied withdrawal, media access decreased, as did interest in the Kurds' plight.

Military Responses

In order to prevent further repression and human rights abuses by Iraqi forces, Security Council Resolution 688 of 5 April 1991 condemned the "repression of the Iraqi civilian population" as a "threat to international peace and security"; "demanded that Iraq . . . immediately end the repression" and "allow immediate access by international humanitarian organizations"; authorized the secretary-general to use humanitarian organs of the United Nations to address the crisis; and appealed to "all Member States and to all humanitarian organizations to contribute to these humanitarian relief efforts."

The resolution did not specifically invoke Chapter VII of the UN Charter, authorize the "use of all necessary means," or mandate OPC and the "no-fly zones" in northern and southern Iraq. However, the resolution's language permitted the Allies to justify the intervention by citing the call for assistance from member states and the insistence that Iraq permit access, by deeming them necessary to prevent the further repression of the Kurds and to create a secure situation, and by noting that these actions had been originally authorized by Resolution 678.

The Security Council's language did not explicitly sanction the intervention, but the intent was clear. According to Jane Stromseth, Resolution 688 and the subsequent intervention demonstrate that the Security Council "was willing to act in response to internal repression when it resulted in substantial transborder refugee flow," was willing to approach "a crisis as a humanitarian problem, sidestepping more contentious political questions of self-determination," and was reluctant "to explicitly authorize the use of military force to stop the state from repressing its own citizens."³⁰

Of the five cases examined in this book, the military response to this crisis was the most expeditious. Only seven days after the refugee flight began, the United States authorized Operation Express Care. With over fifty aircraft provided by the United States, Britain, Italy, Germany, and France, the coalition air-dropped 32,000 pounds of supplies to the refugees on the first day of operations.³¹ Displaying the kind of logistical and transportation capacity available only to the military, by the end of the first week, "1,727,200 pounds of food, water, clothing, tents and blankets were dropped to the refugees."³²

The airdrops should be assessed from a relief, as well as a political and tactical, perspective. Airdrops are costly; and there were numerous reports of shipments falling into minefields and hitting people. Also, many of the items parachuted to the refugees broke upon impact and were unusable, especially the water supplies.³³ One reason that the U.S. military was able to undertake such a rapid and massive relief effort was that both the transport equipment and the supplies were already in the area. Washington had anticipated a longer war (1,000 hours of bombing and only 100 hours of ground warfare) and had plenty of surplus and operational airfields. There was even some speculation that it was just as inexpensive to drop the supplies on the Kurds as to take them back to another depot.

Despite the perhaps limited practical value of airdrops, they provided dramatic opportunities for media coverage and were a public relations success. From a political and tactical standpoint, they demonstrated Allied resolve; and the airdrops required protection and justified the use of air cover to protect cargo planes, which then forced the withdrawal of Iraqi air cover within the theater. Eventually, the airdrops paved the way for the ground intervention. Pictures of C-130 cargo planes parachuting relief supplies were a powerful symbol, particularly because in this case refugees were largely inaccessible by other means. However, modest road transport was used prior to and during the airdrop by other organizations. Within a week, the increased use of helicopters began, which facilitated the orderly distribution of food rather than the chaos and other problems that had characterized the airdrops.³⁴

Despite the provision of emergency aid, the huge numbers of refugees meant that the situation in the camps remained precarious. Following a trip by U.S. Secretary of State James Baker, Washington authorized the deployment of Special Forces (SF) to the camps to organize the field relief effort. The Turkish government announced on 13 April that it would begin to move some of the Kurds to more accessible and sanitary camps within Turkey. The Special Forces' expertise in low-intensity conflict proved to be vital as few NGOs and UN humanitarian agencies were in the area. The SF also served as intermediaries between the Turks and the Kurds, "addressing basic health concerns," coordinating with local leaders, and determining humanitarian needs.[35]

As is its practice, the Office of Foreign Disaster Assistance (OFDA) authorized the deployment of a Disaster Assistance Response Team (DART) to the scene. However, the humanitarian situation continued to deteriorate. Turkey cited its inability to cope with the massive crisis and publicly invited the Allies to intervene at the border and in northern Iraq.

On 16 April, President Bush—in coordination with his counterparts in France, Britain, and Turkey—authorized the creation of a Kurdish safe haven in northern Iraq through Operation Provide Comfort. This announcement was accompanied by a warning to the Iraqi government not to intervene with the creation of the safe haven. The peak of OPC occurred in mid-May, with the United States committing 12,000 troops and another 10,000 troops from Austria, Belgium, Canada, France, Germany, Italy, Luxembourg, the Netherlands, Portugal, Spain, and the United Kingdom. Some 5,000 American, 2,000 British, and 1,000 French troops were actually on Iraqi soil, by which time the operation had flown 4,000 sorties to deliver 25 million pounds of supplies.[36] The initial objectives of the operation were to move the Kurds down from the mountains where it was difficult to provide aid and to lay the foundation for a UN/NGO presence to replace the multinational military forces. But the tactical and operational objectives expanded: to stop the suffering and dying; to move the Kurds out of the mountain camps; and to return the Kurds to their original villages.[37]

The Joint Task Force (JTF) was comprised of the Alpha group, which focused on alleviating the suffering in the mountain camps (objective 1) and the Bravo group, which prepared the Zakho transit camp and facilitated the repatriation of the refugees (objectives 2 and 3). In order to coordinate the actions of the two components within eight camps, two forward humanitarian relief centers were created in Silopi and Diyarbakir, Turkey. Silopi was the center for all road and rotary-wing transport, and Diyarbakir for all fixed-wing transport, as well as a de facto coordination center for the military, UN agencies, and NGOs. The open atmosphere and organization of meetings created by the military leadership in this case served to "facilitate the humanitarian expertise of the NGOs with the logistics and infrastructure of the military."[38]

The decision to move the refugees out of the mountain camps and then back to their homes was opposed by NGOs and the UNHCR be-

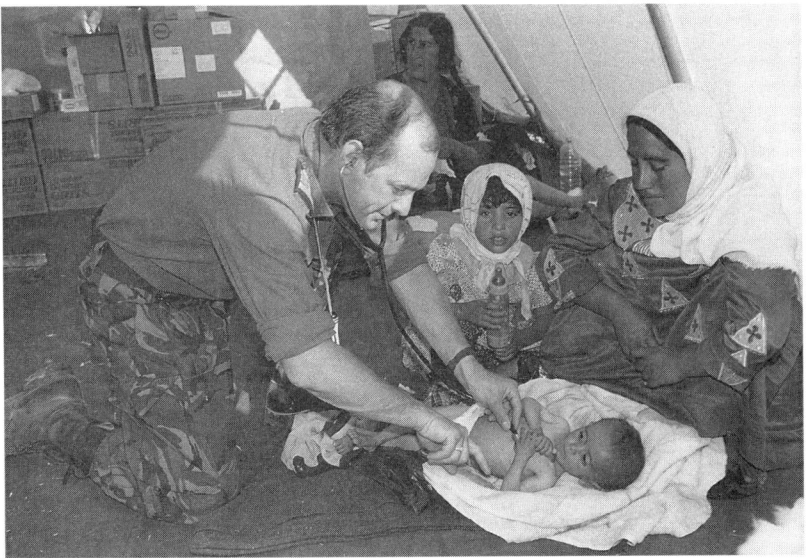

British army medical officer. Credit: UNHCR 21006/05.1991

cause the refugees were supposedly not psychologically prepared for another move. In addition, various policymakers and military leaders in Washington opposed the repatriation and accompanying assistance because of the fear of "mission creep." However, several factors pushed for repatriation. First, the refugees were restless and complained about the quality of food. This type of threatening hostility has been documented to a greater extent in Africa and labeled "relief-induced antagonism," which is the aggressive behavior exhibited by a formerly malnourished population following the alleviation of famine-like conditions.[39] Second, it was logistically infeasible to maintain the refugee population in the mountain camps because they were subject to periodic flooding, and the climate was unhealthy. Moreover, the military and relief workers were anxious to prevent the refugees from becoming dependent on food aid. If the refugees returned, they could become involved in reconstruction efforts and resume normal agricultural activities.

The security needs of the Kurdish refugee population were preeminent. They had fled from areas rather than confront death, torture, or imprisonment. Therefore, repatriation (the operation's objective, along with a military withdrawal) could only occur once the actual and perceived threats to Kurdish safety were addressed. The solution was the creation of a security zone in northern Iraq patrolled by Allied aircraft, which in turn formed the basis to enforce the no-fly zone in June, which interdicted Iraqi flights above the thirty-sixth parallel. In August 1992, another no-fly zone was created in southern Iraq, below the thirty-second parallel, in order to protect the Shiites.

However, even with the protection from Iraqi air attacks, the Kurds were reluctant to move. Frederick Cuny, contracted by the OFDA, developed a five-point strategy to address this problem. First, the transit camps would be created close to the city of Zakho, so that municipal infrastructure could be extended and so that at least refugees from Zakho could return home. Second, in order for the Kurds to determine the security of the Zakho camps, the assistance of Kurdish men was requested for camp construction. The men would determine for themselves the safety of the camps, and many almost immediately returned with their families. Leaders were also brought to the camps, increasing their prestige and allowing the military to determine further their needs. Third, there were around 300 Iraqi police present in Zakho and other urban areas. The military forced them to wear tags, and many were followed and targeted by snipers. With their anonymity eliminated and with constant harassment the order of the day, the Iraqi police almost immediately withdrew completely. Fourth, 300,000 of the Kurdish refugees were originally from Dahūk. By incorporating this city into the safe haven, more refugees would return to their original homes, which would prevent the necessity of a winterized camp in Zakho. The fifth and final step was to adopt a transition plan for the shift of assistance activities to the UNHCR.

On 7 June, the UNHCR assumed responsibility for food distribution and other relief efforts. This was followed by a gradual reduction of Allied forces, with the complete withdrawal by 15 July, aside from small coordination teams in Zakho. In seventy-five days, the U.S. Air Force flew 1,100 sorties and transported 40,000 tons of cargo and 14,421 passengers.[40] Afterward, Allied ground forces were "scaled down from more than 20,000 during the creation of the safe haven to virtually zero."[41]

After the responsibility for providing humanitarian aid was gradually turned over to UN agencies and NGOs, security remained a central factor circumscribing refugee decisions, including Kurdish autonomy. Rather than a UN force, there was a low-key security presence through UN guards clad in blue baseball caps and armed with pistols beginning in May. Known as the UN Guards Contingent in Iraq (UNGCI), these officials and later civilian personnel were able to function because they were backed by a NATO security guarantee. After the withdrawal of Western forces from Iraqi Kurdistan, an eight-nation Rapid Deployment Force of some 2,500 troops remained in southeastern Turkey, along with NATO bombers to deter future Iraqi actions against the beleaguered Kurds. Air sorties were not merely threatened, but they were used to ensure Iraqi compliance. As one group of observers close to the American effort accurately summarized: "The military was clearly most effective in the early stages than in the intermediate- and long-term activities. By coincidence, the NGOs tended to be less effective in the earlier stages and more effective in the later period."[42]

The Civilian Response

In OPC, the military and NGOs were thrown together on a large scale for the first time outside of a national disaster. The NGO Coordination Committee for Northern Iraq (NCCNI) became a center for information sharing, job distribution, needs assessment, and coordination. The existence of the NCCNI also eased relations with the military, which could more easily deal with a single unit rather than with a wide range of independent organizations. A wide variety of NGOs were involved, but the IFRC was especially prevalent in Iran, where it administered some thirty camps for hundreds of thousands of refugees and provided 80 tons of food daily.

A variety of UN agencies (including the UNHCR, the WFP, the UNDP, the International Maritime Organization, WHO, and UNICEF) attempted to alleviate the multiple humanitarian crises caused by the invasion, economic sanctions, the conflict itself, and the massive flight of refugees. In January 1991, the secretary-general requested that the UNHCR be the lead agency. In retrospect, there were a number of problems affecting negatively the UN's ability to coordinate activities in the theater: overlapping responsibilities; differences between the field and headquarters; the lack of formal hierarchy; the slowness to respond at the initial onset of a crisis; and the nonexistence of contingency planning, which should have occurred considering the warnings given by the Turkish/Iranian governments predicting an impending refugee crisis.[43] These problems were hardly new, but their magnitude alongside the military's expeditiousness eventually led to the call within the General Assembly for more centralized coordination. As mentioned earlier, after a lengthy debate in the General Assembly in the autumn, the Department of Humanitarian Affairs began operations the following April.

Two days after Bush's announcement, on 18 April, SRSG Prince Sadruddin Aga Kahn negotiated the Memorandum of Understanding with the government of Iraq that permitted UN humanitarian agencies to operate throughout the country, created a route for the provision of humanitarian aid, and allowed the establishment of the UNGCI. In spite of the original military intervention, this agreement made it possible for the UN to point to "consent" (however grudgingly given) and claim that Charter Article 2(7) was once again respected.

Coordination problems reflected more than the UN's internal inadequacies, however. Iran, Iraq, Turkey, and Jordan placed restrictions on agency access, communication, and monitoring. By the time the UNHCR finally became fully operational, the military and NGOs had already established a solid working relationship. An INTERTECT report harshly criticizes the UNHCR for engaging in a variety of activities that hampered the return of the refugees to their homes— including, for instance, insisting on elaborate interviews to ensure that families were returning voluntarily. On 7 June, the Allies relinquished control of the humanitarian operation to the UNHCR, which along with other UN agencies (especially the WFP, WHO, UNICEF) focused on repatriation in the safe havens. WHO carried out a health assessment. UNICEF provided 275 emergency kits, "each of which could aid 10,000 people for three months. More than 10,000 tons of medical supplies were given out."[44] The UNHCR provided a variety of relief packages containing survival items, such as soap, tents, and blankets.

However, the majority of the Kurds were not on the Turkish, but rather on the Iranian, border. That the refugees on the Turkish border were the primary focus of the intervention is hard to understand in purely humanitarian terms because the situation on the Iranian border was undoubtedly as serious. In April 1991, the refugees there were receiving only 10 percent of their assessed needs.[45]

Several explanations emerge. First, the Turkish government initially refused to admit the Kurdish refugees, while Iran did not. Second, Turkey, as a member of NATO, had a working relationship with the Allies, while Iran was a pariah, especially in Washington. This tense relationship significantly complicated assistance to refugees not only because there was no Allied presence, but also because Tehran wanted the UN to supply the Iranian government directly so that it could then distribute supplies to needy populations. Third, Turkey directly requested Allied assistance earlier than Iran. Freedman and Boren note that Iran did not request a UN military presence but accepted 2,000 German paratroopers and engineers.[46] Although the Allied intervention did not directly target the situation in the facilities, the creation of transit camps and the security created by their presence in the region facilitated indirectly a solution to the crisis on the Iranian border.

Military Costs

Most analyses of international responses to the Kurdish plight reveal the costs and contributions for the relief efforts in the north. In addition to overlooking outside efforts, analysts also miss calculations about relief provided by the Iranian government. By 14 April, for instance, Iran had already allocated $57 million, which was "far in excess of the contributions of any other country."[47] Although the crisis in Iran was two to three times that in Turkey, international assistance to Turkey was substantially higher. Indeed, the value of outside contributions was almost inversely proportionate to the number of refugees. By 17 May 1991, "Iran received $128.9 million in international assistance spent on the Kurdish-Iranian assistance compared to $248 million spent on the Turkish/Iraqi border. The $248 million spent in Turkey combines the UNDRO accounting of $57 million with the $140.1 million in US Department of Defense contributions and $31.6 million in Food for Peace assistance, both of which were distributed as part of Operation Provide Comfort."[48] An official in Iran remarked, "We got the refugees . . . but Turkey got all the funds."[49] One of the first contributions was by the European Community on 8 April, when it pledged $185 million to the Kurdish relief effort.[50] Altogether, the EC would spend some $600 million assisting the Kurds in 1991.

The combined UN humanitarian appeal for vulnerable populations in postwar Iraq was approximately $578.2 million, with $400 million for refugees.[51] Between April 1990 and June 1992, contributions to the UN humanitarian programs in Turkey, Iraq, Jordan, and Iran have been estimated at $1.008 billion, with an additional $885.4 million contributed through non-UN channels.[52] From early April to late May, the U.S. Department of Defense (DOD) spent an estimated $140 million on humanitarian aid. For the entire operation, OPC cost an estimated $800 million. During this period, virtually no military fatalities were incurred. But without the military's formidable efforts to ensure physical security, nothing like this quantity of either military or civilian aid would have been possible. As already mentioned, the success of the effort launched a period of enthusiasm, almost verging on euphoria, for the use of outside military forces in the service of humane values.

Humanitarian Effects

The impressive benefits from Operation Provide Comfort can best be seen in the repatriation rates and the decline in mortality following the Allied intervention in northern Iraq. A decrease in mortality rates is probably the best available method for determining whether an outside intervention has helped alleviate civilian suffering. Emergency mortality rates indicate how much mortality has multiplied as a result of a complex emergency. The normal mortality rate is .65 per 10,000 per day for Iraq, but an INTERTECT report indicated a rate of four to over ten times greater at the outset of the crisis.⁵³ A situation normally is considered an emergency when a rate reaches 1.5 times above the norm.⁵⁴ By the end of April and the beginning of May, the mortality rate had decreased dramatically to between 1.5 and 2, a decrease from 400–1,000 to some 50 deaths per day but still an emergency.⁵⁵ The rates continued to decrease throughout May; and by the time of repatriation, rates had dropped below prewar levels. The speed of the response also lessened the time spent above the emergency rate, which was only eleven days.⁵⁶

[margin note: ↓ infant mortality]

Repatriation does not necessarily refer to a return of all refugees to their original homes; it refers, rather, to their return to the region from where they came. There are still large numbers of the population who are internally displaced within the de facto autonomous zone. The government had destroyed many Kurdish homes, and the Allied-patrolled zone only included a quarter of Iraqi Kurdistan. Nonetheless, OPC's efforts to move the Kurdish population from the uninhabitable mountain region back to population centers and villages were unprecedented in terms of rate and method. Within three weeks of the operation, there were significant returns, and within seven weeks, a complete repatriation had occurred.⁵⁷ By mid-May, there remained approximately 180,000 refugees in Turkey, after 250,000 had migrated to the safe havens and transit camps.⁵⁸ "By the end of August, however, all but 124,300 of them had returned, "most of them utilizing the systems of humanitarian relief centres . . . , mobile stations, and blue routes designed and implemented by the United Nations, and encouraged by the 'moral witness' and stability provided by the United Nations [sic] guards."⁵⁹

Furthermore, within five weeks, the nutritional status of the population had returned to prewar levels, and within eight, the number of diarrhea cases also had returned to normal. As mentioned earlier, the levels of 22 percent malnourishment (4 percent severely) and 70 percent diarrhea remained for two weeks.⁶⁰ In spite of the largely successful operation, suffering had not disappeared. Freedman and Boren point out that "as late as the middle of July there remained around 1.5 million refugees near the Iranian border who were living in makeshift shelters and suffering from sickness, dehydration and malnutrition."⁶¹

The Postcrisis Situation and Continued Responses, August 1991–1996

Longer-term stability is not included in calculations about the benefits of short-term interventions, but longer-term perspectives are relevant in attempting to situate whether, ultimately, costs are commensurate with some movement toward sustainable stability and security. In July 1991, the last American troops pulled out of northern Iraq, but northern Iraq remains unstable at best.

Unlike other situations examined in this book, however, substantial Allied military forces have remained in the area. Hence, the analysis here includes a consideration of the longer-term military presence on the ground beginning in August 1991. There were negotiations among the KDP, the PUK, and the government of Iraq during the Allied operation; but the withdrawal of Western soldiers weakened the Kurdish bargaining position. Immediately following the Allied withdrawal, hostilities resumed between Kurdish and Iraqi forces, resulting in an estimated 500 casualties. The negotiations officially ended on 23 August 1991. In that month, an estimated 40,000 to 100,000 additional Kurds abandoned their homes.[62] However, these events and further Allied gestures that displayed their unwillingness to tolerate blatant Iraqi aggression prompted a cease-fire between the two on 8 October.

From October 1991 to January 1992, the government forces and the Kurdish faction continued mutual attacks, with the government once again bombing Erbil and Sulaimaniya. This was complicated by Turkish attacks against northern Iraq, which included the use of napalm. The result of the renewed hostilities led to the flight of 200,000 to 300,000 refugees from safe havens.[63] Since then other policies directed against the Kurds have included the creation of a 100,000-strong Iraqi force on the border of the Kurdish autonomous zone; the continued "Arabization"[64] of Iraqi-controlled northern cities and towns; the torture of Kurds in Kirkūk; and the declaration of the Kurdish government as illegal.[65]

The humanitarian situation was exacerbated by the economic blockade imposed on the Kurdish autonomous region in October 1991 by Baghdad. This was coupled with the already existing economic sanctions placed upon Iraq as a whole under Resolution 661, which have still not been totally lifted due to the failure of Iraq to comply with the weapons inspection requirements of Resolution 687, although an oil-for-food compromise was agreed in May 1996 but afterward jeopardized by Iraqi machinations. These sanctions have severely affected the trade, government services, agriculture inputs, education, health, water, and sanitation sectors within Iraq and within Kurdish-controlled Iraq as well.

As part of its further strategy to disrupt the economy of Iraqi Kurdistan, Baghdad eliminated the Iraqi 25-dinar note from circulation. As this note was the preferred denomination for trade in Kurdistan, its elimination resulted in the loss of almost $20 million worth of Kurdish savings. The two primary sources of income for the Kurds in northern Iraq are agricultural and government services. Payments for government services were stopped by the government blockade. Kurdish farmers have been unable to restore production completely. They have been consistently hampered by "poverty, mines and the lack of infrastructure," and many are part of "economically depressed collective towns."[66] In 1993, the "embargo also included electric power cut-offs in specific areas, causing the disruption of water and sanitation systems, and interfering with the delivery of food and fuel."[67]

With the creation of safe havens, the Kurdish factions envisaged, once again, the opportunity to create a unified Iraqi Kurdistan. Elections were held for the government of the autonomous region. However, the vote split the Congress in half, giving both the PUK and the KDP about half of the seats, which prevented consensus on any issue. Renewed fighting between the two factions erupted between May 1994 and April 1995 and resulted in 5,000 Kurdish deaths.[68] An Amnesty International report outlines a variety of local abuses by government authorities, including the execution and torture of political figures, assassinations and massacres of civilians due to their political affiliations, and firing indiscriminately into crowds.[69] Both sides continued to use and be used by both the Turkish and the Iraqi governments in their attempts to gain political or military superiority over the other. Both the PUK and the KDP condemned human rights violations while engaging in them. As one analyst summarized,

> In October 1991, the Kurdish population along the border amounted to around 200,000 individuals. After registration, the majority of repatriates continued to live a scattered existence in either damaged villages or in temporary shelter camps, waiting for information about the negotiations between the Iraqi government and the Kurdish Front forces. This is why the population in some of those areas doubled over the last months of 1991. This situation forced the Kurds to become a permanently displaced group, since their movements across the Iranian border were continuous and reflected changes in their temporary sense of security.[70]

In August and September of 1996, Iraqi ground forces would once again invade northern Iraq. This led to the internal displacement of 20,000 people within northern Iraq and the flight of 39,000 refugees to Iran.[71] Iraqi forces conducted house-to-house searches and arrested some 1,500 people. Fatalities were estimated in the hundreds.[72] The KDP also formed an alliance with Baghdad's regular forces in order to eliminate its political rival, the PUK.[73] Although it was initially defeated, the PUK retreated to the mountains and, in a counteroffensive afterward, regained most of what it had lost. The sewage and water treatment facilities systems, already damaged by Allied air attacks, have been looted or harmed by further fighting. Cholera is on the rise, and some 38 percent of children are categorized as "stunted." [The enforcement of the no-fly zones in northern and southern Iraq by Operation Provide Comfort and Operation Southern Watch can be credited with deterring Iraqi air attacks, although they have not prevented the use of artillery. Allied air operations are ineffective at monitoring and preventing human rights abuses and attacks by the PUK, the KDP, and Iraqi forces. The no-fly zones do not cover all of the areas with significant concentrations of Kurds, including Kirkūk and Sulaimaniya. Allied willingness to use force is dependent on Turkish approval, so that OPC has been renegotiated every six months. The Kurds also are not protected by Turkish incursions against the PUK, which usually result in a number of deaths.74]

Moving from relief to development has encountered serious difficulties. Neither the UNDP nor the FAO has been able to initiate large projects to increase local agricultural output, and the Kurds have become dependent on UN agencies for survival, especially during the bitterly cold months. In the winter of 1992–1993, an estimated 2.25 million people were in need of food and fuel assistance, but only 750,000

UNHCR distributes shelter and roofing materials to returnees and displaced persons in northern Iraq. Credit: UNHCR 21075/11.1991

received it. This was coupled with an additional food assistance program from April to December 1993 that was distributed to 300,000 Kurds.

Since late 1992, the funds made available to the UN humanitarian effort have significantly declined. For example, only 43 percent of the funds for the winter 1993 program were available by December of that year.[75] As part of this program from 1992 to 1995, UNICEF distributed 317.5 million liters of water; in 1994, UNICEF provided safe water to over 2.6 million people by supporting 641 water projects, with emphasis placed on those areas with the least access to safe water.[76]

The criteria and methods used to assess the needs of the population and the distribution of the humanitarian assistance have also been sharply criticized.[77] Furthermore, UN agencies are understaffed and consistently targeted by Iraqi forces. In fact, there are reports that Baghdad has at times offered a bounty for UN or other humanitarian workers.

Although there are few specific data by category of expenditure on Operation Provide Comfort, the DOD spent an estimated $425 million in and around Iraq in 1994 and $579 million in 1995.[78] This included the humanitarian activities in northern Iraq, the enforcement of the no-fly zones under OPC and Operation Southern Watch, and UNIKOM. In 1995, the global numbers did not include Operation Vigilant Warrior, which was a U.S. buildup in response to Iraqi military incursions on the Kuwaiti border, estimated to have cost about $200 million. Based on this data, the average costs to the DOD for 1993 and 1996 were between $400 and $500 million annually for operations in and around Iraq. This does not include humanitarian assistance from USAID.

The Effectiveness of Intervention and Conclusion

From an operational and tactical standpoint, Operation Provide Comfort was a success from April to July 1991. Suffering was dramatically reduced and refugees returned, as summarized in Tables 3.1 and 3.2. One of the most successful aspects was the use of logistics capacity of the U.S. military. The humanitarian airlift in support of OPC was the third largest airlift in U.S. military history—only Berlin and Operation Desert Shield were larger in tonnage.[79] As will later be shown in the cases of Somalia and Rwanda, military is more costly than civilian airlift, as well as road and rail transport. In this case, the U.S. military was simply the only option at the onset of the crisis.

The role of individuals cannot be underestimated. The late Fred Cuny has been credited by many as the mastermind behind practical

65

Table 3.1 Northern Iraq: Military Costs and Civilian Benefits from Intervention, April–July 1991

	$ Costs	Casualties/Fatalities	Political Impact
Military costs of intervention for troop-contributing countries	A UN Total: $1.008B among Turkey, Iran, Iraq, and Jordan. $885.4M through non-UN channels. OPC: $800M. EC: $600M altogether. T-Ib: $248M + $57M + $140.1M + $31.6M = $476.7M. I-Ib: $57M from Iran, $128.9M in international aid by 05/91.	B Negligible.	C U.S. used this as a positive example of successful military intervention. Military and IGOs and NGOs optimistic about working with one another. UN creates DHA due to its failure to successfully coordinate during the crisis.
Civilian benefits of intervention for targeted countries	Displacement	Suffering	State of the State
Humanitarian challenge before intervention	D 03/91: 1.5M I-Ib; 400,000 T-Ib: 70,000 Shiites to southern Iran; 30,000 to Saudi Arabia and Kuwait.	E *Hunger*: 03–04/91: 22% malnourished, 4% severely at T-Ib, probably as severe at I-Ib. *Human rights*: 03/91: 30,000 Kurds killed during insurrection. *Health*: 03–04/91: Mortality rate: 400–1,000 per day at T-Ib and probably at I-Ib; 3,600 cases of diarrhea at T-Ib; total deaths: 4,500 at T-Ib.	F Following Gulf conflict: Economic sanctions maintained against Iraq. Much of civil infrastructure destroyed, including in north. Rebellion in north and south. Harsh repression by GOI in response. Massive flow of refugees to borders. High malnutrition, mortality, and disease rates due to lack of food, water, and shelter. Presence of mines.
Civilian benefits after intervention	D' Within 7 weeks of operation, complete repatriation occurred in T-Ib. However, as late as middle of July, still 1.5M refugees at Turkish border. By August, all of Kurdish refugees, on both T-Ib and I-Ib, except for 124,300, would be repatriated.	E' *Hunger*: 04–06/91: Iran: ICRC administers 29 camps, provides 80 tons of food daily. Hunger was eliminated, with only 2 weeks spent at peak rate. *Human rights*: Human rights abuses by both Turkish and Iraqi forces decrease enormously on T-Ib and I-Ib. In the south, Shias continue to be persecuted by GOI. *Health*: 04–06/91: UNICEF provides 275 emergency kits. By end of May, mortality rates had decreased to below prewar level. Diarrhea rates rapidly decreased with only 2 weeks spent at peak rate.	F' Semiautonomous safe haven created, protected by Allied-enforced no-fly zone. Refugees repatriated, most to original homes. However, the humanitarian situation remained precarious, with continued human rights violations and the continued flow of refugees both internally and to Turkey and Iran.

Abbreviations: **B:** Billion **GOI:** Government of Iraq **I-Ib:** Iraq-Iran border **M:** Million **T-Ib:** Turkey-Iraq border

Table 3.2 Northern Iraq: Military Costs and Civilian Benefits from Continued Intervention, August 1991–1996

	$ Costs	Casualties/Fatalities	Political Impact
Military costs of continued intervention for troop-contributing countries	A UN Appeal/Received: 01–06/92: $143.2M/89.1M 07/92–04/93: $201.7M/134.7M 05/93–04/94: $467.1M/95.2M 05/94–04/95: $288.5M/61.2M 05/95–04/96: $138.8M/39.4M Funds from non-UN: 05/93–04/94: $77.9M 05/94–04/95: $53.4M 05/95–04/96: $34.3M OPC provided $24.3M worth of humanitarian assistance through relief and recovery center.	B Negligible.	C Continued decrease of humanitarian funds to the Kurds of northern Iraq. No longer the focal point of attention by international media or policymakers.

	Displacement	Suffering	State of the State
Civilian benefits of intervention for targeted countries Humanitarian challenge of the continued intervention	D 08/91: Fighting between PUK/KDP: 40,000 to 100,000 dead. 10/91–01/92: Fighting between Turkish forces and PKK, and among GOI/PUK/KDP: 200,000 to 300,000 refugees. 08–09/96: Attack by GOI: 20,000 internally displaced and 39,000 to Iran.	E *Hunger*: Continued food shortages; 22% of children are wasted and 37.75% stunted. Winter 1992–1993: 2.25M in need of food/fuel assistance. *Human rights*: 08/91: 500 casualties; 05/94–04/95: 5,000 deaths due to renewed fighting by KDP/PUK, massive abuses by PUK/KDP, 08–09/96: 1,500 arrested. *Health*: Due to sanctions and embargoes, outbreak of children's diseases, shortage of drugs. Cholera is on the rise.	F Population continues to be threatened by fighting among KDP/PUK/Turkish forces/GOI forces. Continued human rights abuses on all sides. Economic embargo has destroyed economy of the area, leading to a 400% price increase between 1991–1993, which continues to rise. Infrastructure has not been repaired. Lack of potable water and electricity.
Civilian benefits of continued intervention	D' Lack of internal relocation, lack of data.	E' *Hunger*: Winter 1992–1993: 750,000 receive food/fuel assistance from UN; 04-12/93, food distribution to 300,000. *Human rights*: 500 UNGCI until June 1992. 300 afterward. UNGCI of questionable value. No-fly zone above 36th parallel and below 32nd parallel have stopped air attacks but not artillery or ground attacks. Cannot monitor human rights. *Health*: 1994: UNICEF provided safe water to 2.6M. 1992–1995: UNICEF distributed 317.5M liters of fuel.	F' Little change from above.

solutions. In contrast, Chris Seiple argues that five more widespread factors contributed to the success. First, despite the fact that the American military was in charge of the coalition, the OFDA's DART was managing the situation and establishing strategy. Second, the military commander on the ground recognized and used DART expertise. Third, the Special Forces initially sent into the Turkish mountains were critical in stabilizing the situation (including the establishment of an initial rapport with NGOs). Fourth, the Army Civil Affairs officers responsible for NGO interaction/coordination, particularly in Zakho, were exceptional professionals. Fifth, NGOs also had superb people leading their efforts.[80]

An INTERTECT report estimated that the overall death rate for this type of crisis could have been expected to be around 450,000.[81] Aside from smaller efforts by the WFP and the IFRC, the military was the first major party to intervene. Involvement by NGOs and the bulk of the UN system lagged. The fact that the crude mortality rate did not soar was explained by the forceful and timely military intervention.

Whatever the humanitarian packaging to justify efforts for domestic audiences, this intervention entailed substantial Western interests that facilitated the commitment of substantial military and civilian resources. Some of these interests made the response less effective and humanitarian; for instance, support for the Kurds could not be overly supportive because of Turkey's concerns, and aid to Iran was inhibited by the desire to isolate the Islamic Republic. This inevitably leads to questions concerning the future status of this operation, as Western interests continue to be redefined and the Allies continue to squabble (at the time of this writing in early 1998) over the proper course of action in response to Baghdad's refusal to comply with weapons inspections. It also leads to queries about operations with far fewer geopolitical interests.

There has been a decreased Allied humanitarian ground presence, and projects have been shifted to UN agencies and NGOs, particularly since the oil-for-food program was agreed in May 1996 and increased substantially in February 1998. With Saddam Hussein periodically testing international resolve—as he did in September 1996 and again in mid-1997 by renewed attacks on Iran, by almost continually trying the terms of diplomacy about sanctions, and by cat-and-mouse games regarding access by arms inspectors—the future is uncertain. Moreover, Iraqi Kurdish parties continue to be divided and are seemingly unable to form a coalition; the cycle of intra-Kurdish violence and political maneuvering is disheartening but historically unsurprising.

In short, the historical significance of the military intervention in northern Iraq will continue to be debated. Although some would question the somewhat artificial focus on the north while ignoring other equally pressing humanitarian problems, this analysis has focused on military-civilian interactions rather than on a host of other problems, including the politics of sanctions and war and their humanitarian costs. The costs were substantial—although they pale in comparison to the $60 billion Gulf War—but so too were the civilian benefits. Because both national interests and credibility for major Western powers were perceived to be on the line, there was the political will to commit military resources to ensure both security and delivery. This is perhaps the clearest case to date of what even such a thoughtful skeptic as Sadako Ogata calls "a rare case of successful humanitarian intervention."[82] It is also true that OPC has limited utility as a model. As Barry Posen notes, "the conditions for a successful safe zone are rarely as propitious as they were in northern Iraq. The Gulf War coalition had already badly damaged Iraqi military forces."[83]

Yet, the longer-term benefits of the intervention remain fundamentally ambiguous. The political situation is uncertain (for the Saddam Hussein regime and for Kurdistan), but the security commitment, at least from Washington, was present in 1991 and remains in 1998, despite dissension among the Permanent Five (especially Russia and France) and provocations from Baghdad. Military fatalities have been insignificant. Although the passage of time has weakened Allied cohesion, the United States nonetheless responded forcefully with cruise missiles and a widened exclusion zone in September 1996 after Baghdad's military support of the KDP against the PUK. The United States also warned both Iran and Iraq when hostilities heated up in mid-1997, moved the USS *Enterprise* into the Gulf, and remained firm in spite of Iraq's efforts to inhibit movement by U.S. nationals working on arms inspections.

Baghdad's machinations continued early in 1998, as this book goes to press, and Kofi Annan returned with a deal from Baghdad, allowing inspectors to be accompanied by diplomats to sensitive sites. The American and British buildups in the Gulf also indicated that peace is unlikely to break out in the near future. The bill for Washington's protection and assistance since 1993 has been steep. Lives have been saved, but northern Iraq is unviable without a continued Western military presence. Moreover, rehabilitation and reconstruction, let alone reconciliation, have yet to begin.

4

Somalia, 1992–1995: The Death of Pollyannaish Humanitarianism?

While the implosion of the former Yugoslavia drew most of the attention at the United Nations, fighting raged in Somalia. Although the Security Council passed several resolutions and two major conferences were held in 1992, no meaningful action occurred, in part because of the inability to focus on more than a single crisis and in part because of divisions within the Organization of African Unity (OAU). In fact, UN agencies had fled the country, and only a handful of NGOs remained. Within a month after his electoral loss, lame-duck President George Bush altered the situation dramatically as he pushed for humanitarian intervention. Buoyed by the initial success and a second dramatic precedent after northern Iraq, those favoring humanitarian intervention were suddenly on a roll. Unfortunately, in less than a year, the tide had suddenly changed with the deaths of Pakistani troops and then U.S. Marines.

In examining military-civilian interactions in this arena, three separate military operations should be distinguished with respect to this troubled part of the horn of Africa. The first UN Operation in Somalia (UNOSOM I) began in September 1992 with the arrival of 500 Pakistani soldiers, who were unable to deploy effectively. Another 2,500 soldiers never arrived because their actual presence was contingent upon the consent of the warring parties. The U.S. Unified Task Force (UNITAF), which the Pentagon termed "Operation Restore Hope" (ORH), took over in December 1992 on the basis of Security Council Resolution 794. The 37,000 soldiers (26,000 of whom were from the United States and

Chapter 4

Map 4.1   Somalia

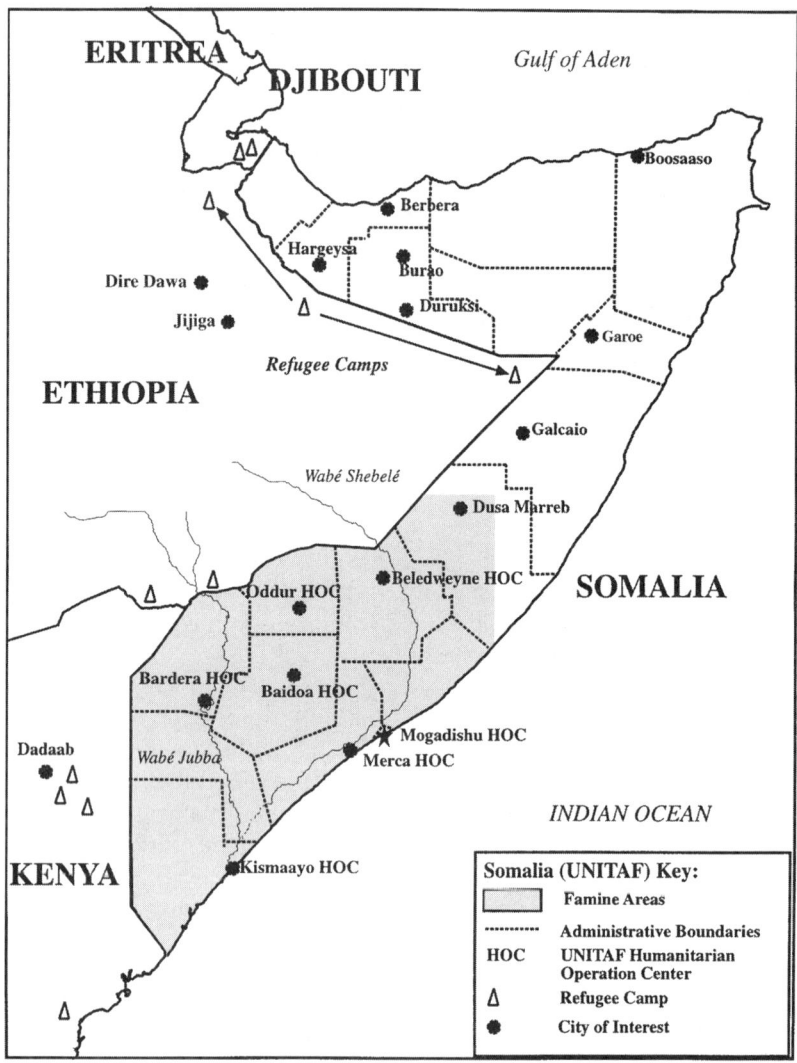

Somalia has a population of 6,590,325 (1997 est.), and its capital is Mogadishu. It is located on the eastern coast of Africa, bordered by Djibouti (NW), the Gulf of Aden (N), the Indian Ocean (E), Kenya (SW), and Ethiopia (W). Its total land area is 246,201 square miles (slightly smaller than Texas), with 1,880 miles of coastline and only 2 percent arable land. Main exports are bananas, live animals, fish, and hides.

the remainder from twenty-three other countries) remained until April 1993 with a unanimous council mandate to use force to ensure the delivery of humanitarian relief.

The second phase by the United Nations, UNOSOM II, took over and lasted until March 1995. Security Council Resolution 814 spelled out the mandate for enforcement action under the direct command and control of the UN secretary-general, which was more ambitious than UNITAF's—not only to ensure access, but also to improve overall security by using whatever force was necessary to disarm Somali warlords. UNOSOM II's maximum strength reached 16,000 soldiers (although 20,000 had been authorized) and logistical troops from thirty-three countries (of whom 1,200 were U.S. soldiers in the Quick Reaction Force and 3,000 logistics personnel).

Before analyzing these phases in some depth, this chapter begins with a brief summary of the background to the trauma of the early 1990s. After the discussion of the three phases, the conclusion describes the costs and benefits of this controversial outside intervention into Somalia's civil war. Although "Lebanonization" had formerly been a favored epithet, it was replaced by "Somaliazation" because fourteen rather than four parties fought over what entered the vocabulary of social science as the model "failed state."[1]

Background and Roots of the Conflict

Somalia frequently has been described as the textbook example of a "collapsed" or "failed" state.[2] Throughout the period of intervention, those involved in "restoring hope"—from the military and civilian sides—no doubt understood too little about, and thus failed to take into account, the sources of state dissolution and the respective roles of the Somali clan system, colonialism, and Cold War geopolitics in the horn of Africa.

Prior to British and Italian colonialism, there was no common Somali identity or centralized control over the territory of what became Somalia. As in the Kurdish case, experts disagree on the existence of a "nation." Although more homogenous than other countries in Africa—with a common ethnicity, language, culture, and religion (Islam)—Somalia's geographical area was occupied by nomadic pastoral groups, organized predominantly by paternal kinship. Nomadism prevented the rise of a centralized political and economical authority and notions of hierarchical society. Conflict was common among lineages, especially in competition for the land and resources necessary for survival. But there were conflict resolution mechanisms within the lineages, known as the *xeer*, which prevented the escalation of conflicts by inhibiting the excessive economic stratification of society. The spread of Islam modified conflict management by adding a mild form of the Shari'ah Islamic Law. Acts of vengeance were diminished through the concept of the *dia*, or the payment of "blood money" compensation to the victim by the violator.

While the basis of organization was direct lineage, groups also were structured by subclans and then clan families, each predominantly associated with sometimes overlapping geographical areas. The six overarching major clan families are the Darod, Digil, Dir, Hawiye, Issaq, and Rahanwein. As mentioned before, each clan family is composed of subclans and then further divided into lineages. Traditionally, lineages continually created and shifted alliances among other groups and subclans.

European powers had been involved in the horn of Africa since the mid-nineteenth century; but the first protectorate was not established until 1896, known as British Somaliland in the north. Soon after, most of southern Somalia was colonized and became Italian Somaliland. There was no overarching perception among the Somali nomads concerning the geographical breadth of the ethnic population, but the distribution of these areas further divided the Somalis among the northern frontier of Kenya, the Ogaden and Haud regions of Ethiopia, and areas of Djibouti.

The new geographical names that accompanied colonialism had negligible effects on Somali society, but other factors eroded more substantially the traditional bases of stability of nomadic cultures. Possibly the largest was the introduction of consumer goods onto the local market, with accompanying monetization and other changes in the economy, and a fundamental shift away from an egalitarian culture resulted, along with a urban migration. A centralized colonial authority was created that was comprised partially of local civil servants trained in European administration. The social structure was further modified with the creation of plantations for the production of bananas and other fruits, providing employment and therefore ending the nomadic lifestyle for many. These three factors radically affected traditional structures. Gone was the antihierarchical focus of the *xeer* since some segments now had access to wealth, education, and power. At the same time, a central state apparatus was maintained with an overarching colonial authority.

Following a ten-year, UN-mandated Italian trusteeship in the 1950s, Somalia became independent in June 1960. However, independence posed new problems. Whereas a local elite capable of running the affairs of state appeared, could the traditional Somali perception shift from the lineage and the clan to the centralized authority of the state? With new elements of power and wealth, traditional methods were adapted to new forms of competition. Migration into the cities expanded relations beyond lineage to clan and subclan levels, and politics became a method of "gaining access to the levers and the resources of the state."[3]

During the immediate postcolonial period, there was growing evidence of a Somali identity of sorts, which mainly evaporated after the Somali defeat by Ethiopia in the Ogaden War. The initial source of internal instability was also the cause of the 1977 Ogaden War, namely, the substantial Ogadeni population in Ethiopia. These people played an important role in the development of a pan-Somali identity. In fact, peace initiatives in 1967 actually contributed to undermining the authority of the parliamentary government. Split along tribal lines for the 1969 election, 62 parties presented 1,002 candidates for only 123 seats.[4] The president was assassinated, thus setting the stage for an army coup that placed Mohamed Siad Barre in power.

Rhetorically, Barre's policy of "scientific socialism" aimed to eliminate "clanism," but the end result of his twenty-two-year rule was strengthening clan-based politics. He forbade the use of clan names; however, his primary method of obtaining and maintaining power was to draw support from his own clan and those linked by lineage and to pit other clans against one another. Virginia Lung has described this policy as a form of "clan clientelism," in which arms, money, and land were distributed to clans in order to maintain his power.[5] Furthermore, Barre harshly repressed other clans through the use of his Soviet-trained secret police, the National Security Service.

Cold War geopolitical competition between Washington and Moscow provided the resources—development and military aid—that Barre manipulated. Scientific socialism had, at first, made the regime a major recipient of Soviet aid. This assistance proved especially useful during the 1974–1975 drought, when pastoral society was decimated after the loss of some five million animals.[6] In addition to a $55 million loan to strengthen the Somali army, the Soviet Union also supplied tanks, aircraft, and ammunition and trained many of the pilots and officers.[7]

With Ethiopia in the midst of its own turmoil that added to the demise of Emperor Halie Selassie, Barre reinvigorated the drive for the unification of all Somali-speaking areas. At first, he only supported the Western Somali Liberation Front within Ethiopia, but, in 1977, he ordered the invasion of the Ogaden region. In a regional square dance, Ethiopia, a former Western client, received aid from the Soviets and Somalia became a Western client. However, U.S. assistance did not play a major role until 1980, months after the Somali invasion had been repelled by the Soviet-Cuban-Ethiopian force in 1978. As part of the eventual friendship agreement, the United States received a strategic base in Berbera for its regional Quick Deployment Force, while Somalia received substantial development aid but relatively little military assistance.

Military, economic, and food aid perpetuated a political system that was not self-sustaining, nor did it fulfill the basic requirements of a sovereign government.[8] Indeed, Somalia was propped up by outside actors: 57 percent of Somalia's gross national product (GNP) in 1987, 100 percent of its development budget, and 50 percent of its annual budget came from international assistance.[9] The national administration, which was the largest employer in Somalia, was composed mainly of Barre supporters engaged in projects to gain access to state resources. Corruption and other informal or illegal activities became the primary method of augmenting income because actual state wages were insufficient to survive.[10]

Food was the key international aid item, obtained, among other things, through the misrepresentation of Ethiopian refugees in northern Somalia. Government statistics exceeded 1.4 million, while the actual number was closer to 400,000 refugees. The excess food aid was diverted to Barre's supporters or sold.[11] The multiplication of food aid was combined with a decrease in domestic production capability so that between 1980 and 1984, some 84 percent of food consumption came from external sources.[12] Food prospects continued to worsen in the late 1980s.

The massive influx of military equipment, especially small arms, was one of the major factors contributing to the insecurity that became prevalent in the late 1980s. Aside from the Soviet Union, Somalia received military assistance from most Arab countries, China, France, Great Britain, South Africa, and West Germany. Washington did not support heavily the Somali military until 1979, when aid multiplied dramatically. Military assistance from 1954 to 1987 totaled some $380 million.[13] Italy was the largest Western donor, training soldiers and providing a total of $124 million worth of equipment by 1980.[14]

The stunning defeat of Somalia during the Ogaden War sowed the first seeds of discontent within Somalia against the Barre regime, culminating with a failed coup attempt in 1974 and the resulting formation of the Somali Salvation Democratic Front (SSDF), a Majerteen-based faction. Barre's clan favoritism became further entrenched and focused predominantly on those groups with whom he had direct familial relations—Ogaden, Marehan, and Dulbohante.[15]

The late 1980s saw the steady decline in Barre's power. The combination of food crises, economic collapse, and the end of Cold War competition in the horn, along with the resulting decline in foreign aid, began to erode Barre's base. Furthermore, the traditional pretext to mobilize nationalist sentiments, Ethiopia, was removed when Mengistu Haile Mariam and Barre agreed to recognize their borders and to stop supporting insurgent groups operating within the other's country.

Recognizing that its primary support had been removed as a result of the agreement, the Somali National Movement (SNM) began an armed revolt in the north that resulted in the occupation of Burao and Hargeysa. Barre's son-in-law, General Mohamed Siad "Morgan," was sent to retake the areas. Morgan's brutal tactics included the complete destruction of Hargeysa, attacks on defenseless refugees, and indiscriminate bombing of civilians. Faced with either extermination or supporting the opposition, there was an increase in civilian support for all opposition factions. Some 400,000–450,000 people from northern Somalia fled to Hartisheik in eastern Ethiopia, and another 600,000 were internally displaced.[16] In total, between 15,000 and 60,000 people were believed to have been killed.[17]

Many weapons used by the government had been supplied by a U.S. special grant of $1.4 million that followed the SNM attack.[18] During the accompanying civil war, Somali defense spending increased from $25 million to $70 million.[19] With opposition rising in the U.S. Congress as a result of human rights abuses, Washington cut foreign assistance, thus ending Somalia's reign as the largest recipient in the horn of Africa. However, the government continued to receive military aid from Italy until 1990 and from Libya until Barre's fall in January 1991.

The rise of clan-based national movements and their success in challenging Barre's rule led to the multiplication of clan-based factions. Spurred by the fear that one group's assumption of power would be detrimental to another's own position, clan-based opposition led to the extreme fragmentation of Somali society. Barre's policy elicited a backlash. By 1990, his only power base was within the Marehan, with the Ogaden and Dulbohante removing support and later forming their own factions.

In June 1990, a group of faction leaders known as the "Manifesto Group" gathered in Mogadishu. Typical of early and subsequent interactions among these various parties, the only area of agreement was the violent overthrow of Barre. Prior to this declaration, the United Somali Congress (USC) had been founded in 1989 in Italy.

The Crisis

The last bastion of Barre's power, Mogadishu, exploded in November when he attempted to attack the Hawiye clan, which primarily composed the USC. By this time, most of the factions had transformed themselves from political parties to military factions, supplied with many of the arms captured from defeated government forces. The fall of Barre in January 1991 was accompanied by an estimated 4,000 deaths.

Mohammed Farah Aideed, a former Barre supporter who had rotated between government service and jail, was directly responsible for Barre's defeat and expected to become president. While he was pursuing Barre in the south, however, Ali Mahdi was elected interim president. Over the next few months, conflict slowly escalated among factions. Attempts at conflict resolution and reconciliation, an example of which was a conference sponsored by the president of Djibouti in May and July 1991, broke down into interclan disputes over property rights and blood debts.[20]

In September, a conflict began between Aideed and Ali Mahdi that effectively split Mogadishu into two heavily armed camps. More than a dozen military-based factions were fighting for power, and this is when "Somalization" replaced "Lebanonization" as the political scientist's most appalling shorthand description. With Barre's departure from Mogadishu in January 1991, the situation became even more chaotic. The shared goal of ending the Barre regime had been realized, which then permitted the clans to focus their violence on one another.

The various national reconciliation conferences included fourteen major factions known by a variety of names and acronyms, including the aforementioned SNM, SSDF, and Ali Mahdi's USC; Aideed's Somali National Alliance (SNA); the Somali Democratic Alliance; the Somali National Union; the Somali National Democratic Union; the Southern Somali National Movement; the United Somali Front; the United Somali Party; the Somali African Muki Organization; the Somali Democratic Movement; the Somali National Democratic Movement; and the split Somali Patriotic Movement between Omar Jess and General Morgan's Somali National Front.

Interfaction relations were characterized by ever-shifting alliances among groups in attempts to consolidate or weaken power. Within a faction, the ability of any warlord to control the actions of his roving militias, composed of soldiers known as *mooryan*, was extremely limited when it was not nonexistent. Knowing no life other than war and violence, the *mooryan* had joined factions to gain access to food and other items. Furthermore, many were under the influence of the narcotic *qat*. The chances of any power-sharing agreement or meaningful cease-fire among the factions was implausible.

Between November 1991 and March 1992, an estimated 30,000 to 50,000 people died, of whom 14,000 were in the Mogadishu area. In the end, 60 percent of government infrastructure was destroyed; the fragile health care system was almost completely decimated; and 70 percent of all livestock perished.

Data on displacement vary because of the permeable borders of the surrounding countries and the ease of transborder movements; a high number of existing refugees, both Somali and other nationals; and the anarchic nature of local society. An estimated 900,000 refugees fled to surrounding countries, 400,000 of whom went to Kenya.[21] In total, about 1.5 million Somalis, or about 29 percent of the prewar population, became either refugees or IDPs.[22]

Within the traditional nomadic lifestyle, coping mechanisms developed to deal with such frequent natural occurrences as drought. However, the drought and the cumulative effect of civil war combined to destroy such local coping capacities. According to a report from the Centers for Disease Control (CDC) and the Refugee Policy Group (RPG):

> [F]ighting destroyed the harvest; militia took household assets necessary for planting and sowing; bandits effectively closed off transport of foods to markets and eliminated any positive incentive for farmers to produce; and, since building household food stores might incite further looting attacks, this fear discouraged farmers from growing anything even for their own households.[23]

The same report argues that there were three distinct waves of famine. Drought greatly exacerbated starvation and helped to create an acute crisis. The first lasted from April until late 1991 in Lower Shabelle, Lower Juba, Mogadishu, and Kismaayo, when fighting between Barre and the factions caused rural to urban displacement and the movement of refugees from Mogadishu to northern Kenya.

Barre's retreat to southern Somalia and the accompanying "scorched-earth" tactics precipitated the second wave of famine beginning in late 1991, which peaked between April and June 1992. The region most affected during this period was the Bay region, with the center of suffering in Baidoa, with over 70,000 displaced persons. The famine in this area caused the threatened population to flee to camps in Beledweyne, Bardera, and Mogadishu.

With much of the population in the famine-prone areas suffering from malnourishment and with the approach of the winter, there were imminent increases in mortality rates and suffering from infectious diseases. The third wave of increased mortality took place from July to mid-October 1992, with malaria, measles, and diarrhea causing a swift rise in deaths.[24] For example, data from displaced persons in Baidoa and all residents in Afgoi show that the average daily crude mortality rate was 16.8 per 10,000 in Baidoa and 4.7 per 10,000 in Afgoi. The role of disease can be extrapolated from the fact that 81 percent of deaths in Baidoa and 53 percent in Afgoi were due to measles and diarrhea.[25] Another study, which cumulatively examined mortality after the third peak, documented that mortality was 7.3 to 23.4 per 10,000 per day and 16.4 to 81.0 per 10,000 per day for children under five.[26] These rates were fifteen to fifty times higher than what is normally seen in developing countries at similar levels of development. For children under five years of age, 32.5 to 56 percent suffered from diarrhea, and levels of wasting ranged from 6 to 80 percent of the population. The under-five mortality had actually been increasing since 1987 as a result of the ongoing conflict and the rising food crisis.[27]

Displacement is prima facie evidence of vulnerability, and half of those who perished were internally displaced because they were "about three times more likely to die than nondisplaced residents." Furthermore, from data gathered in Afgoi and Baidoa, where 74 percent of under-five children died in camps, it can be deduced that displaced under-five children suffered an especially high mortality.[28]

The RPG estimates that 90,000 Somalis died in the conflict between 1985 and 1994; 50,000 died as a result of the fight to depose Barre between 1985 and 1991; some 15,000–40,000 died during the period of interclan conflict (1991–1992); and 10,000 died during the conflict between the various international interventions (UNITAF and UNOSOM II) and Aideed (1993–1995). Prior to UNITAF, the generally accepted number of famine deaths in Somalia was between 300,000 and 350,000—some 30,000 people per month. At the same time, 4.5 million required assistance and 1.5 million risked starvation. While not completely discounting the scale of the famine, the RPG report estimates that 202,000–238,000 people died during the famine. Furthermore, while 4 million out of the 5.12 million Somalis lived in famine-affected regions, 330,000 were at risk of starvation during 1992 and 1993.[29]

Military and Civilian Responses

With insecurity increasing in 1991 and 1992, most government, NGO, and UN humanitarian organizations evacuated staff and suspended programs. The WFP and UNICEF withdrew to their regional offices in Nairobi, Kenya, in March 1991. For example, in the midst of the famine, the WFP delivered only 28 percent of all estimated food requirements, or 19,000 of 68,000 tons.[30] However, a handful of organizations remained and attempted to counteract overwhelming human suffering.

World Vision, CARE, Save the Children–UK, and the MSF remained in extremely volatile conditions. In mid-1992, during the third wave and partially in response to the increase in media coverage, the number of NGOs dramatically increased temporarily, eventually numbering around fifty.

A constant factor was the International Committee of the Red Cross, which maintained operations throughout the violence and war. Operations in Somalia at the time had become the largest in ICRC history since World War II (later surpassed by the former Yugoslavia). During the war over control of Mogadishu, the ICRC and the MFS provided medical assistance to trauma victims, checking 5,000 civilians and actually treating 2,500.[31] In mid-1991, the ICRC distributed "about 2,000 tons of food per month in Mogadishu, about a third of what was needed in the city."[32] In early 1992—during the second crisis—the ICRC provided 54,000 tons of food aid.[33] Operating in the south, the ICRC and the then-extant Somali Red Crescent soup kitchens were active. "By November 1992, 980 of these kitchens were feeding 1.17 million people a day."[34]

The distribution of humanitarian assistance affected the political and economic situation of the recipient area. By preparing and then distributing the meals directly, the ICRC reduced somewhat the need for thievery. Furthermore, theft also decreased through the use of staple food items, such as sorghum, which were not as much in demand.

UNITAF soldiers ride in back of an auto on a Somali street. Credit: UNITAF 159820

However, assistance diminished incentives for local farmers to grow food—a long-standing downside to result from foreign aid. Eventually, the ICRC decreased the use of food kitchens to lessen such dependency. Moreover, since the soup kitchens drew people to feeding areas and the kitchens were in Aideed-controlled territory, Aideed's forces were augmented by civilians seeking a way out of the crisis.[35]

On the humanitarian scene, financial support for civilian airlifts was the first involvement by the United States, Germany, the EC, Belgium, England, Italy, and France. In this manner, the United States supplied 12,210 metric tons of food in 1991 and 79,883 metric tons in 1992.[36] The first U.S. direct response was Operation Provide Relief (OPR), an airlift used as a quick response to the humanitarian crisis that began during the third phase of the famine in August 1992. The goal of the operation was to transport food to local airstrips within Somalia, where humanitarian organizations then distributed it. The military supported logistically the humanitarian effort, rather than acting as the primary contributor and leader. However, the airlift did not actually increase the tonnage of food but replaced the WFP/ICRC airlift with a U.S. military one. Like the early operations in northern Iraq and later missions in Bosnia and Rwanda, the airlift was used to "jump-start" the relief effort without placing ground troops within a potentially hostile situation, from which it would be hard to withdraw.

Military airlifts are expensive, but the additional costs were almost irrelevant in this case in that the military made the decision and bore the costs. As the purpose of the mission was humanitarian, the OFDA dispatched DART to help coordinate. The supplies to be airlifted and the regions affected were determined not by the military, but by UN humanitarian organizations and NGOs. "Between August and November [1992,] with a staff of 600–800 people, Operation Provide Relief conducted 2,486 flights, carrying 28,000 metric tons of relief supplies, equal to 112 million meals."[37] Responding to the increase in mortality due to measles, malaria, and diarrhea between July and mid-October 1992, UNICEF inaugurated a measles vaccination campaign, which by January had inoculated 140,000 people in nine regions. A five-month national campaign followed, which provided vaccines for an additional 500,000 people in sixteen regions.[38]

Although airlifts and food distribution programs were successful in flooding the market and decreasing overall prices, food did not always reach those most in need. Although at the time many observers argued that 80 percent of food was being looted, the range was between 15 and 80 percent depending upon which agency was reporting.[39] Nonetheless, these early efforts saved lives. The activities of the ICRC and other NGOs in early 1992 averted 50,000 deaths and an additional

40,000 between September and December 1992.[40] Earlier military action in response to the famine, on the scale of UNITAF, might have saved 70 percent of those who died, or 154,000 lives.[41]

UNOSOM I

Resolution 733 passed on 23 January 1992, which included an arms embargo authorized under Chapter VII, the Security Council's first substantial action in regard to the Somali crisis. An attempt at a political settlement occurred when James O. C. Jonah, then UN undersecretary-general for special political affairs, was sent to negotiate a cease-fire between Aideed and Ali Mahdi in January 1991.[42] Signed on 3 March 1992, the provisions were never implemented. Authorized by Security Council Resolution 751 on 25 April 1992, the purpose of UNOSOM I was to create and maintain cease-fire agreements between the factions and to provide humanitarian assistance. Through this agreement, fifty military observers, unarmed and dressed as civilians, were deployed to monitor the "Green Line," splitting the Ali Mahdi- and Aideed-controlled areas but not preventing chaos within the zones. The deployment of peacekeepers was to be accompanied by a ninety-day plan to provide direct food and nonfood assistance to 1.5 million Somalis and an additional 3.5 million with seeds and basic health care. This was to have been followed by a 100-day action plan that incorporated UNHCR, FAO, WFP, UNDP, and UNICEF activities and for which $67.3 million of the total $82.7 million appeal was committed. However, increased insecurity prevented moving beyond relief.

The first contingent of 500 troops was not deployed until October 1992, since Mohammed Sahnoun, who had replaced Jonah, had to negotiate for their arrival with the warlords.[43] Limited to operating in Mogadishu, during the first few weeks they did not even leave their headquarters.[44] The predominant focus of the deployment was to create a zone of peace around Mogadishu's airport and port. This concept was eventually extended to four security zones in Berbera, Boosaaso, Kismaayo, and Mogadishu. By this time, the number of troops authorized by Security Council Resolutions 749 and 775 had been increased to 3,500—and later to 4,219—although neither Sahnoun nor the warlords had been consulted concerning the expansion. Originally mandated to observe the cease-fire and to protect UN personnel, the airport, and the port, the expanded operation included deployments in Boosaaso, and the southwest.[45] Frustrated by the failure of member states to act and critical of the lack of initiative within the UN Secretariat, Sahnoun resigned in late October 1992 and was replaced by Ismat Kittani.

The diplomatic efforts by SRSG Sahnoun were active. Negotiating efforts subsequently declined during UNITAF and were virtually nonexistent during UNOSOM II. Recognizing the exclusive and hence detrimental focus on Mogadishu and the lack of legitimacy of the warlords, Sahnoun advocated a policy of "regionalization" in an attempt to construct civil society by empowering traditional bases of authority, such as clan elders, intellectuals, religious leaders, and the emerging professional class.

Negotiations and relations between Mogadishu's two main warlords were tenuous. Aideed's forces were more powerful and numerous than Ali Mahdi's; Aideed thus believed that without outside international intervention his forces would win. By associating the UN's efforts with Secretary-General Boutros Boutros-Ghali, who had been the deputy foreign minister in neighboring Egypt, he insinuated that there were UN political ambitions in Somalia. In contrast, Ali Mahdi was more enthusiastic about UN involvement. Tense relations were not helped by alleged use of UN military airlifts to supply Ali Mahdi with weapons and currency. In late October, Aideed expelled the UN humanitarian coordinator and refused to guarantee the security of Pakistan troops. Attacks against the UN force steadily increased.

Jarat Chopra argues that the application of traditional Chapter VI peacekeeping doctrine to the situation in Somalia was inherently flawed.[46] The purpose of such a consent-based operation is to separate warring states after they have reached an agreement. Somalia was in the midst of internal war between faction-based warlords who lacked domestic legitimacy and respect for civilians. The application of a Chapter VI mandate to this crisis legitimated the warring factions as leaders; their consent was requested by the UN prior to the mission and before any further deployments. They and their armed forces thrived—economically, politically, and militarily—on anarchy. Although the faction leaders could not initially be excluded from the political reconciliation process, their role may decrease in the future.

UNITAF

In what has become a prime example of the supposed "CNN [Cable News Network] effect," the role of real-time television footage of famine victims and rampaging looters in focusing the attention of U.S. policymakers on providing military assistance has been the subject of controversy.[47] At the same time, actions by humanitarian agencies within Somalia were pivotal in aggressively drawing media attention and visits by U.S. congressional representatives to the area, which also spurred action. The public overwhelmingly supported President

Bush's initiative. The underlying reasons for U.S. intervention certainly went much deeper than a "humanitarian impulse" and included alleviating international pressure for U.S. ground involvement in Bosnia, providing examples of the future roles of the military in order to deter budget cuts, and easing relationships with the Arab world following the Gulf War. Furthermore, the consensus in the Bush cabinet was that the mission was "doable," considering the desert terrain and situation.[48]

On 25 November, George Bush, who had only weeks earlier been defeated in the 1992 election, proposed to the secretary-general that Washington would lead an interventionary force. Boutros-Ghali presented five possible variations for intervention to the Security Council: the complete deployment of the 4,219 troops of UNOSOM I; total withdrawal; and three variations on the use of force, including the U.S.-led initiative, which was in fact the only real option on the table. On 3 December, Security Council Resolution 794 created UNITAF and authorized it "to use all necessary means to establish a secure environment for humanitarian relief operations in Somalia as soon as possible" under Chapter VII of the UN Charter. According to the United States, the operation's main functions were "to secure the main ports of Mogadishu and Kisma[a]yo; to openly supply routes and secure other towns and other major feeding areas; and to prepare the way for UNOSOM II to take over."[49] The resolution authorized some 28,000 American troops, but in the end 26,000 were deployed to the region, accompanied by an additional 10,000 troops from more than twenty other nations.[50]

The weak UN command and control structure was obvious, as was Washington's long-standing commitment to avoiding such modalities. The U.S.-led contingent was primarily composed of the First Marine Expeditionary Force (MEF), a high-intensity, quick-acting combat force that had been used during Operation Provide Comfort.[51] Focused primarily on short-term deployments, the use of the MEF suggested a certain reluctance at the outset to long-term commitments. Noticeably missing from the intervention—unlike Operation Provide Comfort, Support Hope, Restore Democracy, and the IFOR—was the inclusion of a battalion from Army Civil Affairs, which in the aforementioned operations played a vital role in reconstruction, domestic liaison, and humanitarian support. The U.S. contingent also did not include a military police (MP) unit, which would have been useful in order to train and equip a police force because there was none after the chaos of the preceding period.

On 9 December, the first amphibious units arrived in Mogadishu with no opposition and a generally welcoming citizenry, along with live press coverage. The factions were not consulted on the deployment of UNITAF; however, subsequently they both offered a largely symbolic agreement. Furthermore, Aideed attributed his acceptance to a belief that Washington did not share the UN's colonial ambitions. Fear of UNITAF motivated many of the infamous "technicals"—trucks with mounted heavy machine guns that both roamed the city causing chaos and were hired by humanitarian agencies for protection—and other militias initially to move out of the city. Although this benefited Mogadishu, suffering in the countryside increased.[52]

After securing the port and airports, troops then began to deploy the other eight Humanitarian Relief Sectors (HRSs); Kismaayo, Merca, Oddur, Beledweyne, Bardera, Gialalassi, Baledogle, and Baidoa. The operation covered only 40 percent of Somalia (in the southern and central famine belt) and about 60 percent of the population. Furthermore, the emphasis on Mogadishu—where one-third of all UNITAF troops were stationed—increased the legitimacy of Ali Mahdi and Aideed.

Unlike Operation Provide Comfort, in which the military was the first international actor to respond in Iraq, UNITAF was deployed to Somalia in the midst of a well-established NGO presence that had been present, albeit in reduced form, continuously throughout the duration of the crisis.[53] A Humanitarian Operation Center (HOC) had already been used by UN organizations and NGOs. Also unlike OPC, in which the Civil-Military Operations Center (CMOC) served as a vital coordination point for addressing humanitarian needs, the CMOCs in Somalia were not central for the military and were instead referred to as "Civil-Military Liaison Centers," the title of which indicated a different relationship. Consultations and partnership were replaced here by more of a one-way military briefing for NGOs.

Operating as a coalition rather than a unified force, national contingents operated regionally, and their behavior and discipline varied. Familiar with the area due to previous operations in nearby Djibouti, the 2,100 troops from the French Foreign Legion displayed the value of using small, highly mobile, specialized forces in the Somali countryside.[54] Recognizing the implications of deploying in main cities, the forces integrated quickly with villagers and engaged in community rehabilitation activities. With a similar philosophy, the Italian forces also maintained close community relations in those areas where they were based.

The UNITAF forces in Kismaayo, predominantly Belgian but joined by some U.S. troops, were the first to become engulfed by violence with factions, which served as a dire harbinger. General Morgan and Omar Jess, who was allied with Aideed's SNA, had been fighting for control of the area. UNITAF had recognized Jess as legitimate and, as a result, repulsed an early attack by Morgan against Jess's weapons cantonment area. However, when Morgan attacked again, UNITAF did nothing, and the SNA in Mogadishu protested that UNITAF was biased.

From a humanitarian standpoint, about a month and a half after the initial deployment, 40,000 tons of relief supplies had been delivered—about 25,000 tons of food aid delivered by road and 8,000 tons of long-term rehabilitation items such as seeds and tools.

UNOSOM I was characterized by relatively few resources but by an aggressive focus on a domestic political solution; but UNITAF and to a lesser extent UNOSOM II were mirror images with tremendous military and humanitarian resources but no political component.[55] Many observers argue that UNITAF spent its energy treating the symptoms and not the actual causes of the illness or disease. Moreover, Chris Seiple even argues that there was no overarching humanitarian strategy. Emphasizing the provision of food to end starvation, Washington's strategy did not adequately enough reflect even day-to-day tactical realities on the ground.

UNITAF was accompanied by echoes of Vietnam.[56] The impact of the "body-bag syndrome" on the unwillingness of political authorities in troop-contributing countries to intervene should not be underestimated. Interactions with civilian populations are vital for humanitarian efforts, but the underlying philosophy of UNITAF was that the indigenous population was acted "upon" rather than "with." The intense security precautions of the U.S. forces drove an ever-growing wedge between the people and UNITAF, and dire repercussions would ensue during UNOSOM II. The separation also affected American perceptions and stereotypes of Somalis by maintaining the image of drugged-out, gun-toting militias.[57]

The lack of an overall strategy, the operational defects of the mission, and domestic political considerations all can be seen in the controversy of disarmament faced by UNITAF forces. From the beginning of the December 1992 intervention, U.S. leadership had clearly opposed any concerted attempt at disarming the multitude of gunmen roving Mogadishu's streets. A rift reappeared between Secretary-General Boutros-Ghali and President Bush over the necessity of disarmament. According to UNITAF's mandate, the primary objective to be realized before a U.S. withdrawal was the creation and maintenance of a secure environment. The official American reluctance contrasted with the view of most experts and practitioners who saw disarmament as essential, not peripheral, to the realization of the objective. Although it did not carry out house-to-house searches, UNITAF did seize various small weapons caches. Altogether, UNITAF collected 1,270,000 rounds of light ammunition, 2,255 small arms, and 636 heavy arms.

The practical difficulties of disarming a country like Somalia should not be minimized. Throughout the Cold War, Somalia had received massive shipments of small arms and other weapons. A report by the UN Institute for Disarmament Research (UNIDIR) estimates a total of 500,000 such weapons in Mogadishu alone.[58] Moreover, exceptionally porous borders facilitated arms shipments from Ethiopia and Eritrea. There is even some evidence that weapons were being sent from Serbia. Even if disarmament had been more successful in the short term, the presence of so many weapons suggested that only a change in the political situation could have created long-term stability. Confiscating and destroying weapons is one thing, but eliminating their role in society through political reconciliation and economic development is quite another. In Somalia, however, neither task was accomplished.

Despite the vociferous objection by U.S. policymakers of activities involving "reconstruction," "rehabilitation," or the dreaded "nation building," UNITAF's involvement in such projects was inevitable. Although MP units were not included in the MEF, 3,500 police were trained to monitor food distribution points.[59] Furthermore, UNITAF soldiers built bridges and repaired sanitation areas and roads, oftentimes after-hours and in their spare time.

U.S. Central Command had initially planned to withdraw by the end of January—a totally unrealistic estimate, at the time and in retrospect—so that the mission would not have to be assumed by the new Clinton administration. UNITAF did not totally withdraw, but by the end of February, troop strength was down to 16,000. However, 5,000 additional troops were provided by various international contingents. The rush to exit Somalia by UNITAF proved disastrous for the handover to UNOSOM II. There was virtually no joint planning between the UN and UNITAF. Moreover, the transition was not phased out because there were lapses between the withdrawal of U.S. troops and the deployment of their replacements. This contrasts, for example, with the lengthy and smooth handover by Operation Restore Democracy to the UN Mission in Haiti that is discussed later in this volume.

A variety of U.S. policymakers credited UNITAF with saving over one million Somali lives.[60] In contrast, an RPG and CDC report indicates that the famine had already peaked prior to the intervention and that, therefore, the operation itself perhaps did not save as many lives as originally thought. The dominant cause of mortality was communicable diseases, which became more potent to poorly nourished victims.

The UNITAF intervention occurred when fewer than 10,000 people were dying per month, essentially because most of the weakest victims had already succumbed. "Many of the deaths (during this period) were likely to have occurred with or without UNITAF's intercession," and "the combined UNITAF and relief efforts interventions might be said to have speeded up the conclusion of the famine curve by one full month," thereby saving 10,000 to 25,000 Somalis.[61] UNITAF's contributions created an atmosphere in which interference with relief convoys was no longer tolerated, farmers could return to their lands, and displaced populations no longer "congregate[d] in disease-prone feeding centers."[62] The ultimate breakdown of UNOSOM II, which then placed the surviving population again at risk, also should be placed on UNITAF's balance sheet.

UNOSOM II

The background for the first Chapter VII operation under UN command and control was the Addis Ababa National Reconciliation Conference of 15 March 1993. With fourteen various factions but no elders or intellectuals, the postconference unraveling was predictable. As described above, factions had the least to benefit from the creation of a unified state. Furthermore, each faction represented such a small constituency and region that only the vaguest and most superficial consensus on issues could be reached.

As part of the agreement, a Transitional National Council (TNC), eighteen Regional Councils, and ninety-two District Councils were to be created. Since the factions would have the most representation from the national level, they wished to create the TNC first and then exercise its authority nationally. However, the Somali crisis required making use of traditional structures (authority from the bottom up). Paper agreements were hardly the same thing as implementation.

Several days prior to the reconciliation conference, a UN-sponsored meeting on humanitarian assistance to Somalia involved the ICRC, UN agencies, NGOs, and some Somali representatives. Resulting in the pledge of some $130 million of the total $166.5 million estimated need, the program addressed ten primary areas, including repatriation of 300,000 refugees and one million IDPs, construction of a new police force, support for women, civil reconstruction (water and sanitation), agricultural and livestock development, and education.[63]

As a further example of the surrealistic character of the agreement, the factions agreed to disarm within ninety days. Beyond the factions' obvious unwillingness to disarm, the ability of UNOSOM II to supervise and manage this process was even more questionable. There was no set disarmament program to inherit from UNITAF; and when the transition occurred, only 25 percent of UNOSOM II troops were effectively deployed.

Security Council Resolution 814 authorized UNOSOM II to assume control from UNITAF on 3 May 1993. Chapter VII authorization was necessary because, according to the UN secretary-general, a secure environment had not been created. UNOSOM II was mandated to monitor the cease-fires between the various factions and prevent any violence; to seize all small arms and guard heavy weapons cantonment areas; to protect UN, NGO, and ICRC personnel and equipment; to continue demining; to protect all ports and airports for humanitarian delivery; and to assist in repatriation of refugees and the displaced.[64] There were to be four operation phases: the transition from UNITAF; the complete deployment of UNOSOM throughout all of Somalia; the transition from military to civilian political activities; and the transition and deployment out of Somalia.

UNOSOM II's authorization included 20,000 troops with 8,000 logistics staff and an additional 2,800 civilian staff. This was augmented by the addition of a 1,300-strong troop of the U.S. Quick Reaction Force from the Tenth Mountain Division. As mentioned, only 25 percent of the force had been deployed by May. By February 1994, when the operation was about to wind down, only 400 of the 2,800 civilian staff had been deployed. The nine UNITAF HRSs were combined into five UNOSOM Areas of Responsibility (AORs) in Kismet-Bardera, Bade-Oddur-Baledogle, Mogadishu-Merca, Gialalassi-Buulobarde, and Belet-Uen-North.

With inadequate resources, UNOSOM II was given the task of complete countrywide disarmament and political reconciliation. The operation never extended beyond the second phase, troops were deployed predominantly in Mogadishu, and the political activities were weak in the resolution and virtually nonexistent on the ground.

Weaknesses of UNOSOM II can be seen as symptoms of the lack of balance between military and political components. The primary aspect of the Addis Ababa agreement had been the election of national, regional, and district councils; but UNOSOM II did not include an election contingent. Furthermore, the AORs for the force did not coincide with the traditional administrative divisions of Somalia.[65] If the district and regional councils had been created, the interaction between the two would have been difficult. Yet, during the operation there was no political input whatsoever from civilian staff.

One of the most fundamental weaknesses was command and control. This was the first enforcement operation in which the UN secretary-general was in charge. The attempt to apply a coalition-style structure like UNITAF's to a multinational peacekeeping operation in

A French United Nations soldier stands guard at a street corner in Mogadishu, while children open a shop's gate. Credit: UNICEF/93-BOU0634/Betty Press

which no one contingent was dominant ultimately proved fatal.[66] Headquarters staff had very little authority beyond Mogadishu, and the various contingents determined their own actions mainly by consulting with their home governments rather than with the central UNOSOM command. Many refused to redeploy to areas as "ordered" by UN authorities. The wide variations of the rules of engagement (ROEs) for different contingents was reflected in the overall lack of coordination among them and the infeasibility of UN command and control over Chapter VII operations.

Tensions between Aideed and UNOSOM exploded on 5 June, when twenty-four Pakistani soldiers were killed and fifty were wounded in an ambush that followed a UNOSOM inspection of Aideed's radio station. This event catalyzed the move from a peace operation to war for UN forces on 12 June. Primarily driven by U.S. decisionmakers, Resolution 837 called for the arrest of those responsible for the attack—in other words, Aideed. Between June and October, UNOSOM II engaged in war against Aideed, in a Wild West style that included a reward poster. On 12 June, the U.S. air attack on Aideed's headquarters left the warlord unscathed but bombed a group of elders discussing reconciliation. The death total ranged from 20 (UNOSOM estimate) to 215 (ICRC estimate). As a result, even the minimal political agenda disappeared, and all civilian staff were withdrawn into the compound.

Although Belgian and French forces withdrew, the deployment of U.S. Rangers on 31 August further signified U.S. desires to "hunt" Aideed. Extensive propaganda efforts were made to create a true enemy of Aideed and his supporters. There was no attempt to place him in context—that is, he was a legitimate leader with a long-standing following, to say nothing of the fact that his son was a member of the Marine Corps serving in the theater. The efforts to demonize him and his followers led to disastrous results. On 3 October, Rangers attempting to rescue survivors from a downed helicopter were ambushed. In the end, eighteen died and seventy-eight were wounded. The public outcry prompted plans for a phased U.S. withdrawal over six months. On 25 March, the final U.S. forces withdrew, leaving only fifty Marines to guard the U.S. liaison office. The American public and the Pentagon agreed with Samuel Huntington, who presciently had written a year earlier that "it is morally unjustifiable and politically indefensible that members of the armed forces should be killed to prevent Somalis from killing one another."[67] It is unclear how much Huntington, the American public, or the Pentagon knew how closely they echoed Neville Chamberlain.

The impact of American fatalities in Somalia on U.S. policy toward peacekeeping and the United Nations in general can be seen in Presidential Decision Directive 25 (PDD-25), which was issued in May 1994.[68] Under the order, the United States would not become involved in any peace operation that was not judged doable or within U.S. strategic interests. The long list of seventeen qualifications sharply limits U.S. participation in future armed humanitarian intervention.[69] The notion that troops should not be deployed unless an administration can predict the precise cost, duration, and end results represents "a Somalia corollary to the Vietnam syndrome in American foreign policy," as Gideon Rose has stated. Rose also correctly points out that the notion of exit strategy has nothing to do with military strategy, but mainly with post–Cold War politics, which confuses observers: "The key question is not how we get out, but why we are getting in."[70]

The first application of this new doctrine was Rwanda, in which the United States neither addressed the genocide nor engaged in security, but provided logistical support for a humanitarian response to the refugee crisis. Regarding the impact of the directive on Rwanda, one senior U.S. Department of State (DOS) official remarked in an interview, "It was almost as if the Hutus had read it." This is a subject to which the analysis returns in the Rwandan case.

The announcement of an impending U.S. withdrawal ended any hopes of UNOSOM II success. The primary focus of the operation now became self-protection. By early 1994, over half of the forces were concentrated in Mogadishu.[71] In May 1994, UN forces pulled back to Baidoa, Kismaayo, and North Mogadishu. Finally, in March 1995, 1,800 U.S. Marines were sent to cover the "retreat"[72] of the final UNOSOM contingents. The humanitarian situation was further complicated in early 1994 by a cholera outbreak that once again emphasized the impact of infectious diseases on mortality. The outbreak, which was not contained until midyear, killed more than 1,000 people and affected 27,000.[73]

In the period since UNOSOM II's withdrawal, Belgian, Italian, and Canadian troops have been accused of violence against the civilian population. Also disheartening has been the willingness of some UN legal personnel to cover up human rights abuses, including unlawful detention.[74] The lack of legal recourse for Somalis widened the gap between the indigenous population and outside military forces. In hindsight—and in view of the Canadian and Belgian cover-ups—the interventionary forces operated with a level of impunity whose worst aspects resembled the behavior of militias.

Costs and Benefits

Table 4.1 summarizes the various costs associated with the interventions, although they are somewhat difficult to separate for analytical purposes. The total costs of the three separate military phases are estimated to be about $3 billion, with U.S. government funds constituting the majority ($2.28 billion).[75] Operation Provide Relief cost $20.1 million, for which the United States had agreed to front the entire cost. Whereas UNITAF was initially estimated to cost $750 million, the actual bill was $1 billion, and the incremental costs for U.S. forces $692.2 million. Japan contributed $100 million to a trust fund. These figures do not include the costs incurred by the other participating nations. U.S. operations following UNITAF withdrawal, known as "Operation Continue Hope," required $94.7 million, of which the DOD expects to be reimbursed for $43.7 million from the UN.[76] In addition, the U.S. government provided $311 million to the $322 million in humanitarian aid, predominantly through USAID.[77] Although UNOSOM I was never fully deployed, the operation cost $42.9 million. The total cost for UNOSOM II was $1.64 billion; originally the annual cost beginning in 1993 was going to be $1.55 billion.[78]

The variety of humanitarian interventions in Somalia proved ex-

Table 4.1 Somalia: Military Costs and Civilian Benefits from Intervention, 1992–1995

	$ Costs	Casualties/Fatalities	Political Impact
Military costs of intervention for troop-contributing countries	A DOD: Total $1.5B; 20.1M (OPR); 692.2M (UNITAF/ORH); 461.5M (UNOSOM II). UN: 1.64B for UNOSOM. Net: U.S. government–2.28B. Total: $3B.	B UNOSOM I: 6. UNOSOM II: 244 casualties (with 136 fatalities).	C UNOSOM II is used as the primary example by many U.S. politicians of the flaws of the UN. Impact is felt in U.S. foreign policy in Bosnia, Haiti, and Rwanda.

	Displacement	Suffering	State of the State
Civilian benefits of intervention for targeted countries			
Humanitarian challenge before intervention	D 1992: 1.5M IDPs and refugees. 1993: 1.6M. 1994: Some repatriation; 80,000 flee from Hargeysa.	E *Hunger:* 1992: 4.5M in need of assistance; 1.5M at risk of starvation; 202,000–238,000 died from famine, maybe 300,000; 1993: 2.6M in need; 10,000 died due to famine. 1994: 1.1M in need. 1995: 1.0M in need. *Human rights:* 1992: 15,000–40,000 died due to fighting. 1993: 10,000. Total: 90,000 dead due to fighting. *Health:* Disease is often the cause of death for famine victims. 1993: 5,000–27,000 affected by cholera outbreak.	F Since 1988 when the Issaq clan revolted against Barre in the north, Somalia has been in the midst of civil conflict. Barre was overthrown in 1991. The resulting situation is what some have called "anarchy," with subclans fighting for control of regions of the country. Both factional fighting and banditry. Complete breakdown of civil administration, destruction of infrastructure, and so on.
Civilian benefits after intervention	D' 1993: Decrease in movements. 1994: 57,000 repatriated; IDPs cut by half.	E' *Hunger:* 1992: ICRC/NGOs fed 1M; saved 90,000. 1993: UNITAF saved 10,000–25,000. *Human rights:* 10,000 Somalis wounded/killed by interventions. *Health:* UNICEF immunized 640,000 in 1992–1993.	F' Following UNOSOM II pullout, occasional fighting among factions and widespread banditry. Still no infrastructure. Relative peace in north. Mogadishu is most insecure with little hope for return of state and government as normally understood.

tremely costly in terms of human life—for intervening governments, for the UN, and for Somalis. Eight soldiers lost their lives throughout UNOSOM I.[79] During UNITAF, seventeen soldiers lost their lives: eight were American, four Belgian, two French, one Moroccan, one Canadian, and one from the United Arab Emirates.[80] UNOSOM II was the most costly with 136 personnel killed: 143 military personnel, three international civilian staff, and one local staff person. As mentioned earlier, the political spillover, particularly in Washington, was overwhelmingly negative. Moreover, an estimated 10,000 Somalis were either injured or killed due to the combined interventions: 100 Somali fatalities during UNITAF and 1,500 fatalities and 6,000–8,000 wounded during UNOSOM II.[81]

The disequilibrium between the military and humanitarian components was striking. The net cost to the United States of ORH amounted to about three times Washington's total aid contributions to Somalia since independence and about the entire amount of overseas development to Africa for a year. At the same time, the lowest estimate for humanitarian aid was that it amounted to 0.7 percent of the nonincremental total costs, and even the highest estimate was only 10 percent.[82] Jan Eliasson, the UN undersecretary-general for humanitarian affairs in July 1993, observed that outsiders "were spending ten dollars on military protection for every dollar of humanitarian assistance"; Mohammed Sahnoun lamented that "it cost $2 billion in peacekeeping to deliver $50 million of humanitarian assistance."[83] Even if one takes the higher estimate, the relative weight of humanitarian assistance as part of the total seems disproportionate. As John Sommer appropriately asked, "What level of military intervention can be usefully introduced in situations of need without becoming counter-productive?"[84]

Yet, determining whether military expenditures were justified depends on the perspective of the evaluator. In 1992, some 4.5 million people were in dire need of assistance, and 1.5 million risked starvation. These figures improved substantially as a result of a combination of factors: better access and security combined with market forces, improved weather, and renewed agriculture. Andrew Natsios, who headed the OFDA at the time, argued that food prices were the most critical element and believed that "while the airlift actually substituted for other means of delivery, rather than adding net new food into the country, the psychological effect on traders who had been hoarding stocks on such was to cause them to release the stocks, thus causing the price decline."[85] The harshest critics of Washington's intervention have claimed that the obstacles to food delivery were not as bad as commonly assumed and that famine had actually receded by December.[86] Even if one is persuaded by this argument, however, UNITAF hardly hurt Somalia. It was effective in opening up roads and providing security for humanitarian relief so that those who had not already died could leave camps and plant crops, and those without resources could receive food aid.[87] After substantial discussion in New York, including an unfavorable comparison with the "white man's war in Bosnia" by Secretary-General Boutros-Ghali, at least states were moved to act vigorously.

In terms of the oft-used and readily available indicator of suffering and vulnerability, there was a dramatic improvement in the numbers of displaced persons because the 1.5 million people driven from their homes during the height of the crisis in 1992 had decreased by December 1994 to about 465,000 refugees and 300,000 IDPs.[88] The estimated toll of 400,000 or even 500,000 deaths in the two years preceding December 1992 resulted directly from interclan warfare, internal power struggles, and repression, or indirectly from famine. This high level of vulnerability was halted, and emergency delivery finally took place on a large scale. The lives saved during the UNITAF phase alone may have been worth the effort, according to a summary by the Refugee Policy Group:

- The estimated population of Somalia during 1991–1993 was 5.1 million.
- Of this total population, some four million Somalis lived in famine-afflicted regions in southern Somalia, where they faced extreme food insecurity and heightened risk to infectious disease.
- Of these four million, some 330,000 Somalis were at imminent risk of death during 1992 and 1993.
- Of those at imminent risk, 110,000 lives were sustained (deaths averted), due to health, food, and other interventions that reached over one million Somalis.
- Of the 202,000–238,000 famine-related deaths that did occur in 1992, at least 70 percent (154,000) could have been prevented had proven primary health strategies been implemented earlier and more widely.[89]

Postcrisis Epilogue and Conclusion

In a depressing description of the lack of long-term impact of the various interventions, one observer interviewed by Sommer said:

Fifteen months ago when George Bush dispatched 25,000 U.S. Marines here, Somalia was a country with no government, no electricity, no telephones, only a few schools, and no security on the streets because of widespread banditry. Now, as the United States nears the end of its withdrawal, and after all the death and destruction by antitank missiles, Somalia is still a country with no government, no electricity, a few more schools, a few satellite telephones, but still no security due to widespread banditry in the streets.[90]

Fighting still occurred among the factions, and the ordinary person somehow managed to eke out an existence. Yet, in 1995, about one million Somalis still depended on international food aid.

Some have speculated that the factions weakened considerably following the international withdrawal. The warlords could no longer exploit various representatives of the international community for money and food. The UN withdrawal may have resulted in more benefits than a continued deployment under the untenable political conditions of 1995. Dying much as he lived, on 2 August 1996, Aideed was killed by a stray bullet. Mogadishu had continued to be an area of contention between Aideed's SNA and Ali Mahdi's USC. However, following Aideed's death, prospects for peace appeared hopeful by Somali standards, as both sides declared and mainly respected a cease-fire. Meanwhile, in the north, an area spared both the famine and the subsequent interventions, an independent Republic of Somaliland operates relatively peacefully, although it has not been recognized by the UN.

In short, this is among the more unsatisfactory cases of military intervention under analysis in this volume. When the last UN soldiers pulled out in March 1995, the ultimate result of military help and humanitarian delivery was unclear. It was a "non-event," wrote Gérard Prunier, and "life went on pretty much the same way as it had gone on during the late UNOSOM 2 period."[91] Three years and some $3–4 billion had left the warring parties better armed, rested, and posed to resume civil war. Full-scale violence has not erupted, and the country remains without anything resembling a central government or state services. Yet, lives were saved, and subsistence agriculture and pastoral life have been renewed.

Humanitarian intervention may be necessary, but it also clearly is insufficient. Sommer concludes: "Indeed, the central irony of recent Somali history is that a humanitarian manifestation (mass starvation) of an underlying political problem elicited a military response. This response, while helping to meet short-term humanitarian needs, further complicated the fundamental political problem—with potentially antihumanitarian consequences."[92]

Gains from humanitarian intervention in the short term cannot hide the stark reality that a commitment to longer-term nation building is also a requirement. As Barry Posen notes, "advocates of these humanitarian operations should understand that success will require the commitment of substantial resources, perhaps for quite a long time."[93] Whether or not it is inadvisable to intervene to save lives, even if there is no stomach for nation building, however, is a morally uncomfortable hypothesis to recommend testing.

5

Bosnia, 1992–1995: Convoluted Charity?

If the success of the intervention in northern Iraq and the initial effort in Somalia had led to optimism about military-civilian interactions, the wavering international response to the implosion of the former Yugoslavia led to pessimism and even despair long before the deaths of eighteen U.S. Marines in Mogadishu. Two approaches were unsuccessfully married. The first emphasized diplomacy with humanitarian assistance to alleviate suffering in Bosnia; and the second stressed the need for coercion as the only way to stop the violence and gross human rights abuse in the former republic. A traditional peacekeeping operation was transformed into a coercive military effort, but without the means to be effective and with considerable damage to the reputations of both military forces and civilian humanitarians, not to mention the suffering of victims.

The soldiers of the UN Protection Force (UNPROFOR) in the former Yugoslavia were an essential part of the landscape circumscribing humanitarian action, beginning with Security Council Resolution 749 in February 1992 until after the Dayton Accord and NATO's IFOR were agreed in December 1995. The discussion here does not deal with UN blue helmets playing a preventive role in Macedonia or those who were charged to act as a buffer between Croats and Serbs in the Krajina and western Slavonia in the so-called UN Protected Areas (UNPAs). The UN's military component in the Krajina and Slavonia clearly had substantial and negative humanitarian impacts because its inability to

Map 5.1   Former Yugoslavia

Bosnia has a population of 2,656,240 (1996), and its capital is Sarajevo. It is part of the Republic of Bosnia and Herzegovina, located in southeastern Europe and bordered by Croatia (N, W), Yugoslavia (S, E, SE), and the Adriatic Sea (SW). Its total land area is 19,776 square miles (slightly larger than Tennessee), with 13 miles of coastline and 20 percent arable land.

achieve objectives (collecting weapons and facilitating the return of refugees) ultimately led to an offensive in western Slavonia in May 1995 and especially to the thirty-six-hour Operation Storm beginning late in August 1995. This latter and largely Croatian offensive resulted in the displacement of approximately 200,000 civilians and soldiers, the largest refugee flow in Europe since the Soviet crushing of the Hungarian revolt in 1956.

The focus here is on the UNPROFOR soldiers in Bosnia because the 2.7 million needy victims in Bosnia-Herzegovina were the main motivation for the largely Western military response under UN and later NATO auspices.[1] The suffering that accompanied displacement and war has been thoroughly documented. Statistics include a doubling of infant mortality rates and perhaps 200,000 deaths and 20,000 rapes. According to two observers, "Human rights abuses have followed the tide of the military conflict and have included the detention of civilian populations, mass killings, torture of both civilians and captured military personnel, mass systematic rape, forced eviction from homes and villages, shelling of urban centres and obstruction of humanitarian relief."[2]

The emphasis on Bosnia is apt because UNPROFOR there was a Chapter VII operation—although the protection of humanitarian personnel was the first and predominant objective, more important than the welfare of civilians in the so-called safe areas.[3] At the moment of the Dayton agreement, their numbers had grown to some 22,000 soldiers (of a total of some 37,000 from over thirty countries), and these were reinforced by an additional 12,500-strong NATO Rapid Reaction Force, as well as substantial air cover. UNPROFOR's total costs to the United Nations in 1994 and in 1995 were about $1.5 billion each year, of which something like 70 percent can be explained by the humanitarian-motivated efforts in Bosnia. NATO's costs in support of the UN effort were substantial, but they are not available, although they should be.

Bosnia-Herzegovina is predominantly associated with the conflict and humanitarian suffering in the former Yugoslavia, but the international community was first drawn to the region by the crisis in Croatia and Slovenia. The situation in Kosovo has been largely ignored compared to the others, although the potential for a humanitarian emergency has always been obvious and verged on igniting a new crisis in the Balkans in the spring of 1998. The assorted activities of the UN and other organizations—military, humanitarian, or political—and their changing functions cut across the areas and periods analyzed. The ongoing severity of human suffering in spite of the various forms of intervention adds to the complexity of the argument. These factors make this case the longest discussion in the book.

In order to understand the decay of a state once considered a multicultural model, this chapter begins with a brief historical survey of the former Yugoslavia, focusing on the political, constitutional, military, and economic structures of Josip Broz Tito's regime. Included within this analysis is the role that these structures played in the post-Tito years and their evolution in the midst of fragmentation. This is followed by a brief outline of the beginnings of the short Slovenian conflict and the Serbo-Croatian conflict before the text continues with the gruesome details of four years of diplomatic dithering in Bosnia, along with painful military-civilian interactions. In order to reflect different situations on a single map and in spite of the apparent historical inaccuracy, Map 5.1 situates cities, events, and UN sites from 1991 to 1995 on the territory of the former Republic of Bosnia-Herzegovina, with political divisions reflecting the Dayton agreement of November 1995.

Background and Roots of the Conflicts

The area now occupied by the former Yugoslavia lay at the crossroads of two great empires prior to World War I, the Hapsburg (Austro-Hungarian) and the Ottoman.[4] In the early twelfth century, the Hungarian Empire began to exert influence within the region—first in Croatia, and then in Slovenia and Vojvodina by 1490. In 1389, Ottoman interests in the region became apparent when, following the invasion of Macedonia, Ottoman forces deposed the Serbian nobility. Within a century, the Ottoman Empire partially controlled Montenegro and completely dominated Serbia, Bosnia, and Herzegovina. However, at the turn of the nineteenth century, both Montenegro and Serbia obtained varying degrees of autonomy. The result of the conflict between these two empires was the disposal of the Serbian population throughout the region, especially in the Croatian Krajina and Vojvodina.

The first decade of the 1900s saw the end of Ottoman influence from the region after the Balkan Wars. The region's powers—Greece, Bulgaria, Italy, Serbia, and the Hapsburg Empire—continued to fight over territory. The volatility of the region was illustrated when the assassination of Hapsburg Archduke Francis Ferdinand by a Bosnian acting for a Serbian nationalist group led to the declaration of war by the Austro-Hungarian Empire against Serbia and quickly to the outbreak of World War I.

Following the defeat of the Central Powers, a unitary state was created between the southern Slavs and the Serbs. Under the "Vidovdan" Constitution, the heir to the Serbian monarchy became the head of Yugoslavia. Under Serb domination, a Croat separatist movement emerged, resulting in autonomy for Croats in 1939. Two years later, Yugoslavia faced disintegration when, as a result of a treaty between the leadership and the Axis powers, a Serbian coup d'état facilitated the Axis invasion.

The war years were dominated by the presence of three movements: the Ustashe, a predominantly Croatian group closely allied with the

Nazi occupiers; the Chetniks, a Serbian royalist group; and Tito's Partisans, a multiethnic Communist force mobilized against the Nazi invaders. The Ustashe committed a variety of atrocities against the Serbs in Croatia during the war, including running Nazi-style concentration camps, while the Chetniks also abused non-Serbian civilians. After a successful guerrilla campaign, the Partisans began to liberate areas of Yugoslavia; and following the end of the war, the Federal Republic of Yugoslavia was created with Tito as prime minister. He was declared president for life in 1974, and his leadership was a center of stability and unity within the federation until his death in 1980.

Tito's accomplishments were prominent in four areas: the constitution, military structure, the economy, and policy toward ethnic groups. Although Tito was a strongly ideological Communist, relations between Belgrade and Moscow were tense throughout his rule. In 1948, Yugoslavia was expelled from the Cominform, although it remained a member of the Warsaw Pact. Yugoslavia was a founder of the Non-Aligned Movement and eventually became an observer in the OECD in Paris. This position between East and West provided Yugoslavia with a certain freedom for maneuver.

The original constitution created six republics (Serbia, Montenegro, Bosnia-Herzegovina, Macedonia, Slovenia, and Croatia) and two autonomous regions (Vojvodina and Kosovo). It permitted only one party. Throughout his years in power, Tito adjusted the constitution, but the most dramatic changes occurred in 1974, when reforms incorporated the rights of national minorities into the federal structure, calling special attention to the rights of Muslims.

Initially, Yugoslavia followed the Soviet economic model, resulting in a variety of largely unsuccessful experiments with collectivization and industrialization. By the 1960s, the government looked to create "market socialism." The system was more decentralized than the Soviet model, with individual factories having significant control over targets and production. But Yugoslavs received social services from the state, and only a minority of the population earned a living outside of state-controlled enterprises.

The structure of the Yugoslavian military and defense forces is vital to understanding the warring sides and their military tactics in the 1990s. Shaped by the internal resistance against Nazi occupation, Yugoslav military strategy reflected both conventional and guerrilla tactics. More importantly, it reflected Yugoslavia's unusual position in the world, neither pro-Soviet nor pro-Western. It was a country at the strategic crossroads of the two contending blocs, perhaps one of the very few that actually merited the "nonaligned" label. In order to be dependent on neither side for its military supplies and equipment, Yugoslavia purchased weapons from both Eastern and Western blocs and had its own burgeoning military industry capable of producing 70 percent of its military needs. The military consisted of two parts: the Yugoslav National Army (JNA) and the Territorial Defence Forces (TDF). The JNA comprised 220,000 troops in 1980 but decreased to 150,000 by the actual collapse of Yugoslavia.[5]

The JNA could hardly counter a Soviet or NATO invasion, but the second military structure, the TDF, was composed of highly mobile, community-based units. The purpose of this "people's army" was to engage invading forces in a protracted guerrilla conflict, which would serve to slowly gnaw at the military strength and political will of the invading force. The remnants of this decentralized structure surfaced later in Bosnia-Herzegovina; small paramilitary groups, at best loosely associated with a broader hierarchical command structure, complicated outside attempts to secure cease-fires or even modest discipline.

The roots, and the subsequent definition, of the conflict in the former Yugoslavia have been debated by academics, practitioners, and politicians. A variety of theories pointed to the decline of Communist power—the Tito regime and the Soviet Union—which led to the resurgence of long-standing ethnic hatred; other interpretations emphasized that the conflict reflected grandiose Serbian, and later Croatian, nationalist dreams. To some extent, each of these is partially accurate; but they reflect the symptoms rather than the underlying disease.

According to Susan Woodward, the three primary elements of stability were the former Yugoslavia's unusual position in the international community during the Cold War; the constitutional structure of the federation; and the security, both economic and political, provided to the people by the state. All of these came under considerable pressure in the late 1970s and evaporated by the late 1980s.

Much can be inferred about Serbian policy by examining the demographic structure of the Yugoslav Federation. Of a population of 23.5 million people in 1991, 36.2 percent were Serbian, 19.7 percent Croat, 10 percent Muslim, and 9 percent Albanian, with Slovenes, Macedonians, Montenegrins, and others making up the difference.[6] While the Serbs were the largest ethnic group, they were also geographically the most diffused. As of 1991, 65.8 percent of the residents of Serbia were Serbs; however, if Kosovo were not included, the percentage would jump to 87.3 percent. Serbs also composed 57.2 percent of the autonomous province of Vojvodina and 12 percent of Croatia. Furthermore, 23 percent of all Serbs resided in other republics. The demographic structure of the two autonomous zones also reflected their stability. Both directly bordered the Serbian republic during the federal period; both have been incorporated in the new Federal Republic of Yugoslavia

(FRY). However, the presence of a Serbian majority in Vojvodina saved it from most conflict, while Kosovo—which is 90 percent Albanian—remains on the brink. This dispersal has led to a victim mentality and a sense of being underrepresented among Serbs, when in fact they were overrepresented in governmental institutions and in the economy relative to their numbers within Yugoslavia as a whole.[7]

Economic stability came under increasing threat during the debt crisis of the late 1970s. Due to its dependence upon Western manufactured goods, Belgrade did not really have the option of defaulting on loans and distancing itself from the Western economic system—a tactic pursued by Third World debtor countries. The high interest that followed the debt crisis proved destructive to the Yugoslavian economy, even though debt actually decreased between 1983 and 1989. Inflation increased steadily and, by 1989, had reached an annual rate of 2,500 percent.[8]

Economic liberalization and stabilization were instituted under the Markovic plan, which included issuing a new currency and decreasing state control. While it was accompanied by a temporary decrease, the inflation rate once again began to soar in 1990. Furthermore, the collapse of communism and the Persian Gulf War eliminated many importers of Yugoslavian exports. The result was increased dependence on local resources and even a reversion to a subsistence economy for many citizens. The growing dissolution of the state economy was accompanied by an increase in banditry, organized crime, and black market activity. Possibly the region hit hardest by the economic decline was Serbia, thereby providing fertile ground for the manipulation of ethnic hatred and scapegoating for the population's increasing poverty.

Tito had initiated a variety of reforms prior to his death in order to protect the cohesion and stability of Yugoslavia. In order to deter a power struggle from occurring among the various republics, a collective state presidency was created, which was composed of all eight federal units (the six republics plus the two autonomous regions). The revised constitution sought to balance political centralization with pluralism and the rights of individual republics with ethnic majorities. After Tito's death in 1981, the League of Communists of Yugoslavia was split between pro-state Serbia and pro-confederation Slovenia and Croatia. Belgrade's power weakened considerably. Coupled with the fallout from the global economic crisis, each republic began to look inward and to rely increasingly on its own largely ethnic leadership.

Serbia was the first to defy the constitution by limiting the rights of its two autonomous provinces. The central theme for Yugoslavia's wars was the rise of ethnic nationalism and its subsequent domination of politics. Accompanied by the growing economic crisis, Serbian President Slobodan Milosevic gradually utilized ethnic nationalism to consolidate his power in Belgrade. Serving as both a catalyst and a response, Croatian and Slovenian leaders pushed for independence. The widespread violence that began in 1991 thus reflected the combination of a constitutional crisis that exponentially weakened the central authority, the steady collapse of the economic system undergoing the transition from a command to a market economy, the end of the Cold War, and the willingness of regional leaders to play the "nationalist card."

Conflicts, Crises, and Responses in Slovenia and Croatia

Slovenia and Croatia declared independence on 25 June 1991. In both cases, the declarations had been preceded by constitutional amendments that asserted each republic's sovereignty and right to secede, followed by a referendum held within the country concerning secession.[9] Almost immediately following the Slovenian declaration, the JNA attacked Slovenia and began a ten-day war, which was a skirmish in comparison with the later conflicts in Croatia and Bosnia. Slovenia's population was the most ethnically homogenous of the former federation, with the 1991 census reporting 87.6 percent of residents as ethnically Slovene and only 2.4 percent as Serbian. Slovenian independence posed little threat to such a small Serb minority—indeed, there was no historical Serbian claim on Slovenian territory—and the logistics of long-distance supply were formidable. Consequently, Belgrade and the JNA retreated. The relatively quick war had neither Serb paramilitary units nor the widespread atrocities that would pervade in clashes in other parts of the former Yugoslavia.

The onset of conflict drew the attention of Europe and regional institutions. The European Community emerged as a dominant—though at times reluctant—player. Ironically, its desire to present a common European foreign policy complicated policymaking. Fearing that dissolution would create a precedent and facilitate the breakup of the former Soviet Union, the United States and its allies in the EC originally supported the Serbian position toward the maintenance of a federal Yugoslavian state. However, Germany emphasized self-determination, which therefore supported the Croat and Slovene moves for independence or at least cofederation. A troika of foreign ministers of three member states (Italy, the Netherlands, and Luxembourg) was sent to communicate the EC's "common" foreign policy. The first result was a brief cease-fire, which was conceived to become permanent following the return of the troika accompanied by the threat of EC-imposed sanctions. The EC plan resulting from the internal compromise incorporated the immediate withdrawal of the army, the induction of Milorevic into the federal state presidency, and the delay of independence for three months.

The Conference on Security and Cooperation in Europe (CSCE) played an important role during the early phase of the crisis by creating the Conflict Prevention Centre and the Crisis Support Office. The result was CSCE support for EC peace efforts followed by the decision to send an observer mission to Slovenia, place an arms embargo on all of the former Yugoslavia, and cease all international assistance to the fragmenting state.

The fighting that resulted from the subsequent Croatian declaration of independence would not be as easy to extinguish. As mentioned, there was a significant Serbian minority within the former republic of Croatia, as well as a prior history of internal repression dating from World War II. Multiparty elections and the subsequent rise to power of Croatian nationalists in the form of the Croatian Democratic Union in May 1990 increased the Croatian Serbs' fear that they would become victims of an independent Croatia, as they had been of the Ustashe during the Nazi period. For their part, Croatian Serbs held a referendum in late August and early September 1990, which resulted in a declaration of the Serb Autonomous Region of Krajina in October and a later declaration of secession and desire to join with Serbia in March. Interethnic violence steadily increased.

Following the declaration of independence, the war in Bosnia began in earnest. The cease-fire in Slovenia allowed the JNA to focus instead on Croatia and particularly the Krajina, where the existence of a concentrated and significant Serb minority was of vital interest to Belgrade and the Serb-controlled JNA. Furthermore, while the newly formed Croatian Military Forces was assisted by the National Guard and police units, the Serbian forces were comprised not only of the local paramilitary militia, the Territorial Defense Forces, but also supported by the JNA, the police, and paramilitary groups from the Republic of Serbia.[10] The combined Serb forces gained control over one-third of Croatia in July and August.

By the end of 1991, some 6,000 to 10,000 people, predominantly civilians, had been killed and another 10,000 wounded. Croats were displaced by Serb forces in the Krajina, while Croat forces displaced Serbs in other communities. By mid-August, an estimated 90,000 people had become refugees due to the fighting in eastern Croatia. In total, over

250,000 Serbs and 100,000 Croats were displaced by the initial round of fighting. William Durch and James Schear point out the importance of the stress placed upon the communities by this displacement, as ethnic radicals fled to more moderate areas and created a substantial voice for revenge.

Attempts at resolving the crisis and ending the conflict were futile, and a series of cease-fires was violated. Between the Croatian declaration of independence and late 1991, half a million refugees required assistance.[11] By late October 1991, the secretary-general had asked the UNHCR to respond to the situation.

During the initial phases of the crisis and prior to the conflict in Bosnia, the UN's activities in the former Yugoslavia were consensual. On 9 November 1991, at the request of the six republics, the Security Council authorized the deployment of UNPROFOR in the areas occupied by the Serb factions, based upon a cease-fire negotiated by the SRSG, former U.S. Secretary of State Cyrus Vance. As a direct result, on 25 December 1991, Security Council Resolution 743 created UNPAs in order to facilitate demobilization, disarmament, and conflict resolution, as well as to provide humanitarian relief. While UN involvement was demonstrated on paper by these agreements and resolutions, UNPROFOR was not physically present until March 1992.

UNPROFOR soldiers in Stari Vitez, Yugoslavia. Credit: UN PHOTO 186716/J. Isaac

Conflict, Crises, and Responses in Bosnia-Herzegovina

The international response to the humanitarian crisis in Bosnia-Herzegovina—especially to the massive violation of fundamental human rights—was feeble in comparison with the other cases in this volume and in light of the severity and magnitude of suffering that continued in spite of outside military involvement. Unlike the other four cases in which outside forces were mandated under Chapter VII of the Charter, UN peacekeepers were authorized only to protect humanitarian personnel. Furthermore, while in the other cases the actions authorized by the Security Council materialized, UNPROFOR acted like a peacekeeping instead of a war-fighting force, a failure that led one to label the effort "collective spinelessness."[12] The reasons were myriad, including the West's collective worries about Russian nationalism and attempts to support Boris Yeltsin, which led to an unwillingness to target Serbia, Moscow's traditional ally. Also, there were uncertainties about how to deal with a reunified Germany's role in the region and, more specifically, Bonn's traditional ally, Croatia; the lack of focus of the Clinton administration on foreign policy; and the unease with Muslims, however "unfundamentalist," and their problems in the heart of Europe.

All of these actors meant that the international responses were characterized by a wide variety of actions, at times conflicting. Following a brief introduction to the crisis, this section analyzes the initial deployment of UNPROFOR and the Sarajevo airlift. There follows an analysis of UNPROFOR's protection of humanitarian assistance and the early role of NATO. The dilemmas posed by ethnic cleansing and the international response to such human suffering are incorporated in the last part. The events beginning with the creation of "safe havens" and ending with the Dayton Accords conclude the description, which is followed by an analysis of the costs of international action throughout the entire period.

In this war there were three local contending factions rather than two, as in Yugoslavia's other conflicts. Although the total Muslim population was relatively small in the former Yugoslavia as a whole, it was concentrated, constituting the largest ethnic group in Bosnia-Herzegovina, which is also where most Muslims lived. The only other republic with a substantial Muslim minority was Montenegro, with 14.6 percent. In Bosnia and Herzegovina in 1991, 43.7 percent of the population was Muslim, 17.3 percent Croat, and 31.4 percent Serb.

The declaration of sovereignty by the Bosnian government on 15 October, which stressed the inviolability of its borders, resulted in a declaration of autonomy and unity by Serbs in the occupied Krajina and in Bosnia. Moreover, the government called for the creation of an Assembly of the Serb Nation of Bosnia-Herzegovina and a referendum for a common Serbia. As expected, the referendum stressed support for the maintenance of a federal Yugoslavia. The Serbian regions of Bosnia-Herzegovina did not possess as clear a majority of Serbs, whereas the Serb areas in Croatia's Krajina did. An autonomous region would either have to incorporate peacefully the other minorities or expel forcibly or conquer them.[13] The latter strategy prevailed, and conflict spread to Bosnia-Herzegovina, escalating in early April 1992, with JNA forces supporting Bosnia Serb paramilitary groups. The initial onslaught of Serbian forces overwhelmed the poorly equipped Muslim-Croat forces and quickly resulted in Serbian control of some 70 percent of Bosnia. This percentage remained fixed by the end of the summer and for the next three years, as the Serbs could not exercise effective control over more.[14]

The Sarajevo Airlift

UN involvement in Bosnia-Herzegovina began on 25 October 1991, when UN Secretary-General Javier Pérez de Cuéllar requested that the UNHCR assist IDPs and refugees. However, the UNHCR's mandate evolved from providing relief and protection to the displaced to being designated the "lead agency" for the UN response by Boutros-Ghali in May 1992.[15] At the end of 1991, the total number of refugees was estimated to be 100,000, only a small fraction of the major displacement that would soon occur.[16] Five months later, at the end of May 1992, the number of displaced already had increased to 300,000.

UNPROFOR was extended to Bosnia-Herzegovina on 5 June 1992, through Security Council Resolution 758, which authorized the protection of the Sarajevo airport for the arrival of the UNHCR's humanitarian airlifts. Two successive Security Council resolutions (761 and 764) increased the UNPROFOR presence in Sarajevo. The resolutions also included provisions for the withdrawal of the Serbian antiaircraft and heavy weapons batteries from around the airport.

While the UNPROFOR mission in Croatia had originally been stationed in Sarajevo, the headquarters moved to Zagreb following the outbreak of hostilities in Bosnia. On 10 June, the first deployment of UNPROFOR, in the form of fifty military observers, arrived at the Sarajevo airport. These forces were augmented by the addition of a battalion composed of a thousand infantry personnel, ten military observers, forty civilian police, and technical and support staff.[17] The purpose was not to protect the population from armed attack, but to feed and clothe them.

The airlift quickly became central to U.S. involvement in Bosnia. On the one hand, when road convoys were blocked or slowed by the increase of hostilities, air transport provided secure passage to hard-to-reach areas—especially when the no-fly zone was declared and enforced by NATO—as well as allowing a range of rapid reactions to changing circumstances. On the other hand, air transport was far more costly than that by road or rail, and possibly wasteful. In this case, the airlift was predominantly contributed by NATO and was not billed to the United Nations. At the same time, Fred Cuny speculated that the overall political impact of the airlift focused attention on Sarajevo and diverted it from Serb atrocities in other areas of Bosnia.[18]

The humanitarian impact of the airlift for the people of Bosnia cannot be denied. For three years, the airlift—in which twenty nations were involved—supplied essential items: "From 3 July 1992 to 31 January 1993, the humanitarian airlift . . . brought in 2,476 aircraft carrying 27,460 tons of food, medicines and other relief goods."[19] By mid-1993, for example, "a total of 56,707 metric tons of relief supplies reached the Bosnian capital, about 37,000 by truck and the rest by airlift." In 1994, 55,000 metric tons were delivered by the airlift, double that provided over land.[20] Between July 1992 and April 1995, the airlift delivered 175,000 tons of food and other items to the city.[21] The closure of the airport in April 1995 created a food crisis, which was not resolved until the airport reopened in September of that year as a repercussion of Bosnian-Croatian offensives and NATO assertiveness.

Protecting Humanitarian Assistance

On 13 August 1992, Security Council Resolution 771 authorized the use of "all measures necessary"—through Chapter VII of the Charter—to "facilitate in coordination with the United Nations, the delivery of humanitarian assistance to Sarajevo and wherever needed in other parts of Bosnia." On 14 September, UNPROFOR's mandate was broadened in Resolution 776 to protect UNHCR convoys, which had often come under violent attack by belligerents. The number of battalions increased from three to seven, and three support units were established. By the beginning of 1993, UNPROFOR was composed primarily of NATO troops under a UN flag and numbered only 8,723 troops.[22] The stark discrepancy between the firm actions authorized by resolutions and the feeble reality of state support for effective implementation on the ground was becoming clear. Enforcement would have required, according to some estimates from NATO specialists in Brussels, at least 100,000 troops; in Washington, the Joint Chiefs of Staff estimated that between 60,000 and 120,000 troops would be required to secure humanitarian aid and an additional 400,000 to create and

Relief supplies arrive in Sarajevo.
Credit: UNHCR/P. Kessler—August 1992, Photo 22081

enforce peace.[23] Even making allowances and discounting the "Powell doctrine" of overwhelming force, clearly the UN presence was woefully inadequate.

Beyond its dimensions, the interpretation of the mandate itself was feeble and inconsistent. The operational test for a Chapter VII mission lies with the rules of engagement for troops; however, UNPROFOR troops had those of traditional peacekeepers—that is, only for self-defense and not for civilian protection. Even if more aggressive ROEs had been authorized, UN soldiers on the front lines were underequipped—in terms of both hardware and political support at home.

The geographic distribution of UNPROFOR left much to be desired. The Serbs' halting a French troop convoy in November 1992 symbolized the lack of field strength. A decision was made that UNPROFOR should be stationed only in those areas controlled by Muslims and Croats, although UN military observers did operate in Serb areas and a Russian contingent was deployed there in early 1994. Small paramilitary groups from all factions continued to plague UN attempts at providing humanitarian relief. Beginning in early 1992, convoys and other humanitarian efforts were hindered by the actions of small militias establishing roadblocks and periodically attacking convoys and humanitarian workers. Cease-fires negotiated with the authorities often were disregarded by these undisciplined groups, which would either impose additional demands or refuse access. Before they were given uniforms and accorded legitimacy by others, many of these young men had been spending most of their days in cafés.

At the same time and in a more positive light, UNPROFOR provided intelligence briefings on the human rights situation, and the force often escorted humanitarian convoys in insecure areas. Later, UNPROFOR also engaged in such engineering work as road and bridge reconstruction.

Early NATO Action

The earliest UN coercive actions were an arms embargo on the former Yugoslavia and broad sanctions against Serbia banning all nonhumanitarian items. In this case, the Security Council's decisions were backed by effective enforcement action. At first, NATO and the Western European Union provided naval enforcement for the resolution, through Operation Maritime Guard and Operation Sharp Fence. On 22 November, these missions were combined into Operation Sharp Guard. Resolution 787 authorized additional enforcement by permitting the boarding and inspection of all naval vessels to ensure compliance with the embargo.

The sanctions and the arms embargo proved to be a special handicap for the poorly armed and landlocked Bosnian-Muslim government. The Serb and even the Croat forces appropriated far more military equipment than the Bosnian Muslims from the JNA, and they were also able to procure more illegally because of their more favorable geographical locations. Therefore, not only did the Muslims find themselves outnumbered, but also drastically and increasingly underequipped. In many ways, the sanctions and embargo constituted an outside intervention, or at least interference, in favor of Serbia.

The international arms embargo also did not prevent the internal transfer of weapons within the former Yugoslavia. Support to Bosnian Croats and Bosnian Serbs came from the Croatian Army (HVO) and the JNA, respectively. UNPROFOR's mandate was extended through Resolution 787 to include the deployment of observers to Bosnia-Herzegovina's borders, who were authorized to confiscate or turn back all banned goods and personnel but who were unable to do so.[24]

The main impacts of the Security Council's decision to authorize economic sanctions were increased civilian suffering and complications for relief.[25] The majority of the refugees in Serbia and Montenegro were Bosnian and Croatian Serbs who had fled armed conflicts. Rather than residing in refugee centers, 96.9 percent, or 572,000 refugees, lived initially with host families.[26] The remaining 3 percent lived in a few collective centers established by the Yugoslavian Red Cross. Since the refugees lived with families who were dependent upon the Serbian economy, the refugees' standard of living and the abilities of outside aid agencies to help were penalized by sanctions. The result was a weakened economy that was obliged to support an ever larger and poorer population. In this case, sanctions symbolized action and had an impact, although the exact contribution to the eventual settlement at Dayton is far from clear.

Since FRY (that is, Serbia and Montenegro) inherited about 85 percent of the JNA's equipment, the Serb forces in Bosnia also benefited from airpower, to which Croatia and the Croat Bosnian armies had limited access and to which the Bosnian forces had none. Attempts at limiting the scale of the fighting resulted in the declaration of a no-fly zone over Bosnian airspace by Security Council Resolution 781 on 9 October 1992. The resolution exempted UN and other humanitarian flights. At first, the resolution was not enforced but simply "patrolled" by NATO-supplied AWACS aircraft and by seventy-five personnel on the ground who inspected airfields. Between November and March, there were some 465 reported violations. Following the bombing of two villages, the need for more than observation was emphasized by Resolution 816, which led to the authorization of NATO to "enforce" the zone. The on-and-off threat of NATO retaliation, in the form of air strikes, was the primary coercive method. The Netherlands, the United States, France, Turkey, and the United Kingdom had all volunteered. Intermittent air strikes served as an enforcement tool whose potential was lessened because of the need to prevent placing NATO ground troops where they risked becoming targets. The tactic succeeded in bringing the parties closer to the bargaining table. However, the lack of agreement between Washington (with no forces on the ground) and London and Paris (whose casualties were the most substantial among the contributors) meant that NATO's seriousness was doubted, in retrospect a quite accurate assessment. And the threat became less effective. In three years of operation, between October 1992 and December 1995, over 7,552 violations were reported, which certainly points to a very limited notion of a threat.[27]

The unwillingness to react militarily with any seriousness in the former Yugoslavia until August 1995 provides a case study of what not to do in a humanitarian crisis. In the words of Rosalyn Higgins, subsequently elected to the International Court of Justice, "We have chosen to respond to major unlawful violence not by stopping that violence, but by trying to provide relief to the suffering. But our choice of policy allows the suffering to continue."[28] This inaction left many of the inhabitants of the region mistrustful of the United Nations and lent a new and disgraceful connotation to "peacekeeping." Bound by the traditional rules of engagement (fire only in self-defense and only after being fired upon), UN troops never fought a single battle with any of the factions in Bosnia who routinely disrupted relief convoys. The ROEs led to appeasing local forces rather than to enforcing mandates. Among the most unsafe locations in the Balkans, indeed the world, were the so-called safe areas that are discussed later in this chapter. Partisans of gallows humor suggested that there was a missing letter ("S" for "Self") in the acronym for the international military presence, which should have been the UN Self-Protection Force.

UN peacekeepers in Croatia were unable to implement their mandate because they received no cooperation from the Croats or Krajina Serbs. In Bosnia, the situation was even more problematic. The UN force there was present under Chapter VII, but it lacked the capability to apply coercive force across a wide front. Under such conditions, observed Major Richard Barrons, chief of staff of British forces, at their headquarters in Split, "Day One success can turn into Day Two failure, unless you are prepared to conduct full-scale conventional war in support of humanitarian objectives." Even those UN soldiers who might have been prepared to challenge Serbian troops would require "a completely different package of forces."[29] Unable to create the conditions for its own success, UNPROFOR was not militarily credible. Shortly before resigning in January 1994 from a soldier's nightmare as UN commander in Bosnia-Herzegovina, Lieutenant General Francis Briquemont lamented the disparity between rhetoric and reality: "There is a fantastic gap between the resolutions of the Security Council, the will to execute those resolutions, and the means available to commanders in the field."[30]

The world organization's fiftieth anniversary in October 1995 should have been the occasion to recall that the United Nations was supposed to be distinguished from its defunct predecessor, the League of Nations. The provisions for economic and military sanctions in the UN Charter had been designed to back up international decisions to counteract aggression and to halt atrocities in just such situations as the one in Bosnia. Yet, with additional gallows humor, many in Zagreb and Sarajevo referred repeatedly to the UN soldiers as "eunuchs at the orgy." What exactly did the eunuchs do?

Ethnic cleansing and the quandary of protection. Beginning in March–July 1992, images of pallid faces peering through the barbed wire of concentration camps reappeared in Europe. Serbian atrocities, especially against Muslims, led the way so that Croats jumped into the fray and eventually Muslims as well.³¹ While all sides engaged in a variety of atrocities upon other ethnic groups, the Muslim population was the most substantial victim of such acts. Although Serbs protested that international efforts were not evenhanded, the breakdown in victims can be somewhat accurately surmised from the ethnic breakdown of the first seventy-six individuals indicted by the International War Crimes Tribunal in The Hague: about 70 percent Serb, 25 percent Croat, and 5 percent Muslim.³² The degree of responsibility for these atrocities by the Serbian leadership, both military and political, has ranged from direct planning and participation to silent complicity. "Ethnic cleansing" entered the popular lexicon, a euphemism to describe removing representatives of the "wrong" ethnic group from an area to gain numerical, political, and military control by employing whatever tools are most effective—incentives, forced movement, threats, rape, or death.

One of the first well-documented examples of ethnic cleansing and of the failure of UNPROFOR and the UNHCR to protect civilians was the attack of Srebrenica by the Bosnian Serbs in July 1992.³³ The size of involuntary displacement—over two million persons alone in Bosnia—made ethnic cleansing one of the primary aims of the wars.

One of the more disturbing aspects of the conflict in Bosnia was the use of rape as a weapon of war and nationalist policy. According to the chair of the Commission of Experts on International Humanitarian Law, the "vast percentage of sex based crimes, rapes in particular, were committed by Serb and Bosnian Serb forces." Three methods were used by the Serbs against the Muslim population: paramilitary groups would publicly rape women, leave, and the following JNA troops would offer the population transport to the safe areas in order to cleanse an area; women would be confined to concentration camps and raped, so that their future psychological stability would be destroyed; women were sent to concentration camps where they would be tortured.³⁴ If a woman conceived a child in the camps, she would be forced to carry it.

Coping with ethnic cleansing created painful choices for humanitarian agencies: to try to protect the population in situ within the threatened enclaves, thereby possibly exposing them to additional human rights abuses or even death if the approach was unsuccessful; or to help move them and thereby abet ethnic cleansing.³⁵ At first, the dominant strategy for the UN was that of "preventive protection," through which people who had not left their homes were aided and defended in order to prevent them from becoming IDPs or refugees. However, such a strategy requires both the will to protect and the resources to back it up, including a large civilian staff with significant geographic distribution, financial resources, and military might.

Protection efforts were at best modest. For example, "at the end of 1993, UNHCR had about 25 officers with protection responsibilities in the former Yugoslavia."[36] The UN Centre for Human Rights also sent monitors, but their numbers and resources were extremely limited. The Special Raporteur of the Commission on Human Rights reported on the status of abuse through field reports and interviews in order to increase international awareness. In spite of some heightened visibility for human rights issues, the lack of follow-up led Tadeus Mazowiecki to resign publicly and with great indignation.

Despite the painful lack of human resources devoted to legal protection, the UNHCR should nonetheless be credited with saving "thousands of people who were trapped, whether by negotiating cease-fires, assisting and protecting them where they were, or evacuating them."[37] The physical presence of international actors—soldiers as well as civilians—no doubt decreased violations in areas where they deployed. Most abuses occurred in those areas with no international presence, which was 70 percent of Bosnia since UNPROFOR was not deployed in the Serb-controlled regions. When human rights monitors became targets, their visibility and movements were more limited. In addition, reporting on abuses often resulted in increased hostility toward victims, followed by accusations of partiality against international staff and sometimes the cessation of aid. Balancing the tensions between successful emergency delivery and protection within the UNHCR is always difficult, but in this case the problem was particularly acute.

After the creation of the Commission of Experts on International Humanitarian Law in late 1992 by Resolution 780, the International War Crimes Tribunal in the former Yugoslavia was established the following May. Underfunded and understaffed, the first persons were actually tried in 1996. Notwithstanding the different views about the utility of prosecution and a few exceptional arrests,[38] the lack of vigorous pursuit of indicted war criminals by NATO's IFOR and SFOR after Dayton became a source of embarrassment for those who claimed to occupy the moral high ground.

Suffering and relief. The shortcomings of UNPROFOR and the UNHCR in the human rights arena were understandable in light of the magnitude of requirements for emergency assistance. By ignoring the causes of Yugoslavia's wars and permitting the violent expression of largely manipulated ethnic grievances, however, the humanitarian symptoms grew steadily and often exceeded the response capacity of the international system, especially between late 1992 and early 1993. By late 1992, there were over two million displaced persons within Bosnia-Herzegovina. The approaching winter required additional help, and

UNPROFOR battalions delivered "some 34,600 tons of relief supplies . . . to an estimated 800,000 beneficiaries in 110 locations."[39]

Assistance was mostly in the form of food aid, with the UNHCR as the primary contractor. UNICEF and the WFP were initially absent from the arena because the former Yugoslavia had been historically a net donor rather than a recipient of international assistance. The WFP and UNICEF became operational in late 1992, and the World Health Organization in summer 1993. The WFP was responsible for food distribution and provided 320,000 metric tons of food valued at $225.6 million between November 1992 and July 1993.[40] UNICEF provided food assistance to a total of 1.5 million women and children by 1993, including the 70,000 children enrolled in its feeding program in Sarajevo.

Serb attacks on the Muslim enclaves isolated the residents within them or created additional displacement toward them. For example, the population of Srebrenica expanded from 7,000 to 30,000 in 1993. A pattern emerged. After a Serb attack, the population of one area would flee to a more secure enclave. The rapid increase of population would place stress on housing, health care, and food; after the enclave had been weakened, the Serbs would then attack it and begin the cycle again.

In 1993, the magnitude of displacement and overall humanitarian needs was staggering. In the first six months of 1993, the total number of people requiring international aid throughout the former Yugoslavia escalated to 4,269,000, which included 847,000 refugees, 1,634,000 displaced persons, and 1,788,000 additional war-affected persons. In Bosnia, the total number of those displaced had increased to 2,280,000, or over half of the prewar population of four million. In fact, the UNHCR was reluctant to publicize the numbers, fearing at the outset that they might possibly cause donor reluctance. Estimates at the time were as high as 230,000 people killed or missing and 60,000 seriously wounded.[41]

Humanitarian agencies at first were unable to respond adequately. Between January and September 1993, only 52.4 percent of food requirements were met for the needy in Zepa, 42.9 percent for those in Srebrenica, and 26.4 percent for those in Goražde.[42] However, due to NATO airdrops, Zepa received an additional 1,000 tons, Srebrenica 2,000, and Goražde 3,000. Due to continued insecurity, the UN was able to meet only 57 percent of estimated food requirements for 1993. This was not a financial problem—in fact, adequate funds were available[43]—but one of political will. The UNHCR, as lead agency, and the other international and nongovernmental organizations were operating in the midst of insecurity. Belligerents used food as a weapon against civilians and consistently broke cease-fires. Fighting continued to block or slow humanitarian convoys, particularly with the outbreak of fighting in central Bosnia in 1993, which cut the convoy routes, while ethnic cleansing continued virtually unabated.[44]

Moreover, food did not necessarily reach those most in need. Humanitarian agencies often were obliged to provide aid to those less in need as part of a Faustian pact to gain access to threatened populations elsewhere and to demonstrate evenhandedness. For instance, the UNHCR was accused by the Serbs of not supporting adequately refugee populations within Serbia, but it was also condemned by non-Serbs for providing too much assistance to Bosnian Serbs. Of Sarajevo's 380,000 targeted population, 24 percent were in the Serb-controlled area whose residents were less needy and whose ethnic brethren were targeting the rest of the city. In February 1993, during the Serb attack on Cerska and Konjevic Poel, the United States attempted to bring relief to the population through airdrops. The United States was later joined by Germany and France, and by November, 9,000 tons of food and medical supplies has been delivered.[45] The question of who should distribute humanitarian assistance was not solved by using the Bosnian government to facilitate distribution because much of the aid ended up on the black market. As a result, the residents of Sarajevo were receiving less than 100 grams of food a day.[46]

UN efforts were complemented by nongovernmental ones. The ICRC's operations accounted for almost half of its annual budget of some $1 billion and ranged from visiting prisoners to sanitation, food assistance, and family reunification. Between January and September 1993 alone, the ICRC distributed "32,000 tons of relief supplies to about 600,000 persons each month, supplied 215 medical facilities with medicines and surgical supplies, and exchanged two million family messages."[47] Emphasizing neutrality and impartiality—as well as its traumatic experience in Somalia—the ICRC decided to contract independently for transportation and to distance itself from the UNHCR and UNPROFOR's so-called physical protection under Chapter VII. Within this period, the number of NGOs in the former Yugoslavia doubled (from 65 to 126), of which 91 were international and 35 local.[48] Many governments, especially that of the United States through its OFDA and the European Union through its ECHO, distributed government funds for humanitarian assistance. Twenty-two international NGOs became implementing partners of the UNHCR, as subcontracting became the major delivery mechanism for both governmental and intergovernmental funds.[49] Serbia received the least international aid—only twelve NGOs were involved in 1993—which added to the belief in Serb-majority areas that the members of the so-called international community were anti-Serb.

Safe Havens and the Weapons Exclusion Zones

Negotiations between the various belligerents resulted in the Vance-Owen plan in March 1993, which was named after the special representatives of the UN and the EU, respectively.[50] The plan divided Bosnia-Herzegovina into ten territories, with each ethnic group receiving three apiece and Sarajevo becoming multiethnic. However, the plan was rejected by the Serbs, who physically controlled over two-thirds of the territory and believed that more could be gained by engaging in extended war.

After the departure of Cyrus Vance, Thorvald Stoltenberg became the SRSG and, with Lord Owen, negotiated the Owen-Stoltenberg plan in June 1993. Rather than attempting to maintain a unified Bosnia-Herzegovina, the plan divided Bosnia into three ethnic states linked together by a confederated assembly. Instead of reflecting the percentage of each ethnic group, this plan distributed geographic areas to reflect more accurately the territorial gains actually made by the Serbs and Croats during the wars. Sarajevo and the surrounding regions were to be administered by the UN. This plan was rejected by the Bosnian-Muslim government.

Shortly thereafter, the Muslim-Croat marriage of convenience dissolved with the emergence of vicious armed conflict in eastern and central Bosnia. The onset of fighting between these temporary allies further undermined the ability of the assortment of humanitarian organizations to provide assistance. Only one-half of requisite relief was received in western Bosnia during the first six months of 1993. In spite of the arms embargo, the Bosnian Muslims made surprising gains by repairing arms production facilities, procuring arms from various Islamic nations in contravention of the embargo, and purchasing some through Croatian and Serbian sources. The Bosnian Croat forces—known as the Croat Defence Council—were aided by the HVO, with the deployment of an estimated 3,000–5,000 troops on Bosnian soil where Croats dominated, mainly in those areas contiguous with Croatia proper.

On 16 April 1993, a new approach was initiated by the UN in an attempt to provide assistance when the Security Council authorized the creation of a safe area in Srebrenica under Chapter VII. This measure resulted from the public outcry elicited by the dramatic televised gesture of the UN commander in Bosnia, French General Philippe Morillon, to remain in the city until it was declared "safe."

A month later, the declaration of safe areas was expanded to Sarajevo, Goražde, Zepa, Tuzla, and Bihać by Resolution 824. The extension of the mandate did not include a comparable increase in troop size or equipment for UNPROFOR. UN Secretary-General Boutros-Ghali estimated that 34,000 additional troops would be necessary to fulfill the mandate. However, even his "light" option was not met because only 2,000 troops of an authorized 7,600 were deployed immediately, resulting in the resignation of the UNPROFOR force commander. The total deployment of only 20 percent of the original estimated troop strength would eventually require over half a year. Although total strength had increased from seven to twelve battalions, with eight support battalions now in place, the result was a situation in which the "safe areas were not safe, protection was extended to food but not people, and the vicious customs of war in the Balkans were condemned without consequence to the perpetrator."[51]

After a much-publicized mortar attack on a Sarajevo market—for which the responsibility was logically assigned to the Serbs but without adequate investigation—NATO threatened to bombard Serb positions surrounding Sarajevo unless all heavy weapons were withdrawn from the 12-mile Sarajevo "weapons exclusion zone" by midnight on 21 February 1994 and handed over to the UN. Accompanied by the downing of four Serbian aircraft, this was the first case of successful NATO brinkmanship that reversed two years of saber rattling. Before this, during January 1994, the toll of the artillery bombardment averaged six deaths per day. In total, the two-year siege of Sarajevo had killed 10,000 citizens and wounded 60,000.[52] The Serb forces complied within two days, and though the Serbs had not completely withdrawn all weapons, the air strikes were not carried out and the siege was ended.

At the same time, on 23 February and after substantial arm-twisting by Washington, the Bosnian government and the Bosnian Croat sides agreed to a cease-fire and to renew their marriage-of-convenience vows. This partnership was followed by a framework agreement that established the Bosnian-Croat Federation on 10 May, which would eventually facilitate the autumn 1995 offensive and ultimately the Dayton Accords, however shaky a foundation for the longer run. But just as NATO, the United Nations, and the Clinton administration began to hope that these modest military actions would end the siege of Sarajevo and facilitate a diplomatic solution, the Serbs began new ethnic cleansing activities in Prijedor and Banja Luka and also attacked the safe area in Goražde. The effort resembled a medieval siege in which the attacking forces deliberately targeted civilians directly through shelling and indirectly through resource strangulation tactics.

Two American F-16s carried out another NATO "first" on 10–11 April, bombing Serbian ground positions outside of Goražde. Although the stated purpose of these strikes was to protect the handful of UN observers and relief workers in Goražde, the real target was the Serbs. The attacks enraged the Bosnian Serbs, who responded by killing a British soldier, shooting down a British Harrier aircraft, detaining 200 UN personnel, and taking over Goražde. The Serbs called NATO's bluff, for neither the first nor the last time. NATO member states collectively seemed to have forgotten that successful coercion requires a demonstrated capability to defeat an enemy and not merely to sting. A pattern was developing in which the Western alliance threatened but did not respond straightforwardly to Serbian aggression because they feared all-out war between the 100,000-strong Serbian forces and the significantly outnumbered UN forces.

A 22 April NATO ultimatum demanded the imposition of a 20-kilometer weapons exclusion zone and a 3-kilometer Serb withdrawal from safe areas. In Tuzla, the Serbs complied after a fashion by withdrawing their weapons, but Bosnian Serb troops remained within the zone, dressed as civilians or policemen, and thereby complicated relief efforts. NATO had also empowered the UN commander in Bosnia to set up exclusion zones around three other safe areas (Zepa, Srebrenica, and Bihać) in the event of attack or the infiltration of heavy artillery. Admiral Leighton W. Smith Jr., the U.S. commander of NATO's air cover for UN operations in Bosnia, subsequently proposed using force to menace the Serbs who were shelling Tuzla, but UNPROFOR's French force commander, General Betrand de Lapresle, refused. With the advent of the weapons exclusion zones, UNPROFOR deployment peaked with 22,500 troops, 300 military observers, 250 international civilian staff, and 500 local staff.

The profound ambiguity of the term "safe area" became apparent. The purpose was to protect civilians within them from violence, although the military weakness of UNPROFOR made this term such a misnomer that denizens of safe areas suffered more from insecurity than many civilians living elsewhere. The Bosnian government took advantage of safe areas to base military and paramilitary forces within them, which added to the Serb's impression that the UN had sided with the Bosnian government. In August, Sarajevo was increasingly violated, resulting in two additional NATO air strikes.

In the winter of 1993, humanitarian organizations were confronted with many of the same problems faced a year earlier. The number of those in need had risen to 2.7 million people, and the UNHCR and UNPROFOR initiated Operation Lifeline in order to secure humanitarian delivery routes. By early 1994, only 20 percent of all planned relief was reaching its destination, and reportedly as much as 50 percent of all food assistance was being diverted to soldiers.[53] By late 1994, the distribution of humanitarian assistance had become more effective. In total, "about 356,000 metric tons of food, or about 85 percent of their estimated food requirements, were delivered to Bosnians." However, by no means was distribution equal throughout Bosnia, either geographically or temporally: Bihać received only 33 percent of aid for 180,000–205,000 people, with none delivered during the siege in November; Goražde, Zepa, and Srebrenica, which had either already been attacked or would be, received 65 percent of aid for 104,000 people. Overall, 77 percent of the convoys reached their destinations, but where they were most needed they were the least effective. In addition, 59 percent of all convoys to safe areas were successful, with 44 percent in Bihać and 62 percent in the eastern enclaves.[54]

In July 1994, the "contact group"—which had been formed earlier in that year and was made up of representatives of the United States, France, Germany, Britain, and Russia—offered the warring parties in Bosnia a take-it-or-leave-it partition of the country into more or less equal halves. It was thought that a combination of carrots (easing economic sanctions against Belgrade) and sticks (the threat of NATO military action and the lifting of the arms embargo against the Bosnian Muslims) would prompt all Serbs—of Bosnia, Croatia, and Serbia—to accept 49 percent of Bosnian territory instead of the 70 percent that they controlled. The Vance-Owen plan had been judged a year earlier as morally and politically bankrupt, although it had proposed even less territory as a reward for Serbian aggression. The Bosnian government accepted the contact group's plan unconditionally, but the Bosnian Serbs attached so many conditions that their acceptance amounted to a rejection. In a referendum the following month, 96 percent of the Bosnian Serbs who voted flatly rejected the plan.

Again, verbal rebukes rather than action emanated from the contact group. In spite of the humanitarian consequences and doubtful impact of sanctions (indeed, they seemed to stimulate a rally-around-the-flag nationalism), there was a call for more. Despite two symbolic attacks in August and September—against an antitank gun and an abandoned tank—it soon became clear that there was insufficient political will to employ meaningful airpower against the Serbs or to arm the Muslims, which was increasingly favored by Washington.

In a curious twist of logic mixed with wishful thinking, the contact group instead took up a Russian proposal to ease sanctions against Belgrade. The Serbian government agreed to permit the deployment along the Yugoslav-Bosnian border of 135 civilian observers under the supervision of retired Swedish General Bo Pellnas to monitor its compliance with its announced decision to stop supplying the Bosnian Serbs with war material. In exchange, the contact group decided in late September to reward Serbian President Milosevic with a temporary (100-day) easing of certain sanctions related to commercial travel and participation in international sporting and cultural events. At the same time, the contact group, in its wisdom, refused the promised lifting of the arms embargo that would have allowed the Bosnian Muslims to arm themselves more adequately.

Although ethnic cleansing had ebbed between February and June 1994 in northern Bosnia, it reappeared in July in Bosanska Krajiana and Bijeljina, with reports of rape, expulsion, murder, extortion, and slave labor by Serb forces.[55] In fact, there had been an agreement between the Bosnian Serbs and the Bosnian government to cease hostilities and to release all prisoners of war. As a result of both the Serbs' ethnic cleansing and the Bosnian government's successful offensive in Ozren and Travnik, the agreement lasted barely two months. The agreement improved the situation in Mostar and increased UN mediation efforts in the Brcko, Tuzla, and Orasje areas.[56]

In early November, after an unexpected string of victories in the Bihać pocket by the Bosnian army, nationalist Serbs counterattacked with artillery, tanks, and aerial bombing. Since 1992, Bihać had been the sight of an internal struggle between Muslim secessionists and the ultimately successful Bosnian-Croat Federation. The use of airpower based on the Udbina airfield inside the Serbian-controlled Krajina, an area of Croatia patrolled by UN troops, included the dropping of napalm and cluster bombs. These blatant violations of the no-fly zone and the UNPA embarrassed the United Nations. Furthermore, Serbian soldiers routinely received weapons and fuel from Serbia in violation of Belgrade's agreement with the contact group.

In response, the Security Council authorized NATO to attack Serbian ground targets as well as Serbian aircraft over Bosnian airspace. The sixth NATO attack—by thirty-nine U.S., British, French, and Dutch aircraft—damaged the Udbina runway and the airfield's antiaircraft defenses but left Serbian aircraft untouched. Such a result was unthinkable unless orders had been given to avoid damaging aircraft. Shortly thereafter, some fifty NATO aircraft attacked three Serbian missile sites—two in Bosnia and one in the Krajina—after attacks on two British planes on routine patrol. Air strikes remained largely symbolic and only marginally punitive.

Some observers incorrectly heralded these gestures as a possible sign of a new commitment on the part of the West to use force. The United Nations, afraid that continued action would provoke retaliation against its troops and international aid workers, asked that the bombing be

UN APCs at British Battalion in Stari Vitez. Credit: UN Photo 186738/J. Isaac

stopped. UN inspectors on the Bosnian border did not object, as fuel and, no doubt, weapons shipments from Serbia passed through Serb-held parts of Bosnia en route to the Krajina. The remains of a pilot whose jet fighter crashed near Bihać were identified as those of a member of the Yugoslav (Serbian) air force, which clearly demonstrated that Belgrade continued to support the rebel Serbian forces. Moreover, the abrupt appearance of surface-to-air missiles in both the Krajina and Serbian-occupied Bosnia—also linked to Belgrade—now posed a threat to NATO aircraft and permitted Serbs to advance and recoup lost territory.[57]

In order to prevent further attacks, the Serbs again seized humanitarian personnel—including over 400 UNPROFOR soldiers. UN forces demonstrated that they were unable to protect themselves, let alone Muslim civilians. Washington's criticism seemed a cheap shot in light of the total absence of ground troops. Notwithstanding valor on the ground, Paris and London ironically refused to utter the word "hostage," because to have done so would have indicated the threat to their own nationals, which in turn would have led to public outrage and a demand for action.

The United Nations and troop-contributing governments downplayed the fact that the detained troops were Serbian pawns. British General Sir Michael Rose was in charge of UN forces in Bosnia and euphemistically called them "life insurance" against bombing raids.

The fate of UNPROFOR and of some four million people dependent on the United Nations for their daily survival hung in the balance as governments endeavored to save face. Boutros-Ghali discussed openly a UN withdrawal, and 2,000 U.S. Marines were deployed in the Adriatic in case they were needed for an evacuation. Although there had been no commitment of ground troops to stopping the war, President Clinton announced that the United States would commit up to 25,000 soldiers to a force two or three times that size in order to evacuate the 24,000 UN troops from Bosnia.

By December 1994, Serbian attacks on the safe areas of northern Bosnia resulted in the expulsion of 10,000 non-Serbs in three months.[58] Areas controlled by the Bosnian Serbs were ethnically cleansed—most notably, Banja Luka, Prijedor, and Bijeljina. Washington soon joined Paris and London in appeasement. Flights of NATO warplanes over Bosnia were halted so that the Serbs would free the UN hostages and accept reformulated peace terms. In mid-December 1994, former U.S. President Jimmy Carter arrived in Bosnia to mediate—which, in fact, resulted in solidified Serbian gains in exchange for a renewable four-month cease-fire and a cessation-of-hostilities agreement that might permit UNPROFOR to interpose itself eventually between the hostile parties. The agreement held as winter set in, and the belligerents began yet another series of negotiations. As the cease-fire (by some accounts, the thirtieth to have been negotiated in the preceding three years) went into effect on New Year's Day, Bosnian President Alija Izetbegovic spoke to his compatriots over the radio: "We will negotiate where we can and make war where we have to. If the enemy does not show readiness for reasonable political solutions within the next four months, the cease-fire will not be extended."[59]

By the end of 1994, the total number of refugees, war victims, and IDPs stabilized at 2.74 million, almost 50 percent of the prewar population of Bosnia. The contested but widespread estimate of those killed—mostly civilians—was 250,000.[60] By early 1995, disappearances were believed to number 26,000; and 50,000 people were victims of torture. Over 150 mass graves were reported, each containing as few as five and as many as 3,000 bodies.[61] Because of embarrassment and difficulties in access (that is, the social stigma attached to victims and the unwillingness of women to admit that they were victimized), estimates of the number of females raped vary between 20,000 to 50,000.[62] Less well-documented health, disease, and psychological effects should be added to these statistics, as they will continue to take their toll.

In December, Croatian President Franjo Tudjman announced that he would not allow UNPROFOR to remain in the Krajina when its mandate expired at the end of March 1995. Although the threat was not new, it appeared serious because evidence was growing that the Serbs would never relinquish the quarter of Croatia that they occupied so long as UN soldiers shielded them. The West resisted, understanding that withdrawal of these troops could open up the possibility of a renewed Serbo-Croatian war.

In mid-March, Tudjman withdrew his demand. His emphasis on the dangers in a permanently divided Croatia resulted in the reduction of UN troops (from about 14,000 to 8,750). Those remaining were to be redeployed to monitor the international borders with Serbia instead of only the cease-fire lines in the Krajina, and UNPROFOR's name was changed to the UN Confidence Restoration Operation (UNCRO). The objectives were to show that the Serb-occupied Krajina was still part of Croatia, to impede arms shipments from Serbia to Serb rebels, and to permit the UN soldiers to continue holding the lid on the Bosnian cauldron. In effect, the UN's actual downsizing and withdrawal would await a Croatian military offensive a few months later. The UN headquarters in Zagreb became the command and control center for UNCRO, along with the other two missions: UNPROFOR in Bosnia, which remained named as such, and the UN Preventive Deployment Force in Macedonia.

Meanwhile, hostilities continued in Bihać, and war preparations continued in Tuzla and Travnik by government forces. Following a continual unraveling of the cease-fire in early spring, the United Nations finally called in NATO bombers for two successive days in late May 1995. Prodded by the Clinton administration, UN commander Lieutenant General Rupert Smith agreed to target the Serbian arms depot in Pale, the Bosnian Serb capital. In what could be described as "Bihać revisited," the Serbs responded as they had earlier after milder air strikes. They held over 300 UN soldiers hostage—chaining several to such potential targets as bridges in order to serve as human shields—recovered heavy arms from the UN-controlled collection sites, and fired the deadliest shell of the war into the supposedly safe area of Tuzla.

Extrapolating from past reactions, including backing down in the face of comparable Serbian tactics in Bihać, Serbian leaders were skeptical that NATO would press its assault. They were correct. UN blue helmets were eventually released; but this was not in the "unconditional" manner originally demanded by the United Nations. Rather, their release appeared a quid pro quo for the UN's agreement to abide strictly by the principles of traditional peacekeeping—diplomatic shorthand for no more NATO air strikes, the demand made by Bosnian Serb General Ratko Mladic and President Radovan Karadzic, who were soon to be officially indicted as war criminals.

On paper, the military reaction appeared more muscular; moreover, in June, NATO defense ministers, joined on the occasion by those from Sweden and Finland, established two separate Rapid Reaction Forces. Security Council Resolution 998 approved the addition of 12,500 heavily armed soldiers for Bosnia—an increase of over 50 percent—from the British Twenty-fourth Airmobile Brigade in central Bosnia and the joint English, French, and Dutch one in Croatia. In August 1995, for the first time, the United Nations had artillery, light tanks, and battlefield-support helicopters. More importantly, there would be no "dual key," meaning that the NATO firepower would no longer be subject to a veto by the civilian head of the UN operation, then SRSG Yasushi Akashi. In addition to other problems, the approval of the new force also provided an ideal occasion for the Republicans in Congress to continue the larger battle to scale back U.S. contributions to the United Nations.

Although humanitarian motives figured prominently in justifications for the UN mission, concern about the safety of peacekeepers had always been the primary reason for the recalcitrance to respond vigorously. As noted earlier, many Bosnians had commented with derision that the word "Self" should have been inserted before "Protection" in UNPROFOR's title. As if to prove the point, before leaving his command in Bosnia, General Rose had coined the expression "Mogadishu line" to indicate that strict impartiality by UN soldiers was a necessity to avoid their becoming participants in the war, as had been the case in Somalia. It was argued that consolidating positions, rather than remaining scattered in locations around Bosnia, was necessary in order to use force more effectively at a later time. Yet, this argument has a hollow ring in light of three previous years of feebleness. Beefing up military capacities for self-protection made clear yet again that UN soldiers were more concerned with protecting themselves than with implementing any humanitarian mission. The latter necessarily would have involved crossing General Rose's boundary to the other side of the line on behalf of victims.

The situation in 1995 continued to deteriorate, and humanitarian delivery suffered accordingly. For example, "in June, UNHCR was able to deliver only 20 per cent of targeted supplies to the six safe areas and only 8 per cent to Sarajevo."[63] In July, the Serbs overran safe areas in eastern Bosnia. The symbolism was ironic. As Dutch peacekeepers retreated and widespread massacres of Muslims took place, the first safe area to be eliminated was Srebrenica. It was here that the vacuous policy of safe areas had actually originated in March–April 1993, when Lieutenant General Morillon had made his televised personal stand. This prevented the town from being overrun then by rampaging Bosnian Serbs and resulted in the Security Council's designation of Srebrenica and five other locales as "safe areas." On this occasion, however, the Serbs proved unstoppable, and there was no willing media star to take Morillon's place on the stage.

As pointed out earlier, Srebrenica had actually served as a magnet for many of those displaced by the process of Serb ethnic cleansing, resulting in a dramatic growth in population. In addition to worsening the overall humanitarian situation, there was now a larger concentration of victims to be cleansed. UNPROFOR checkpoints fell into Serbian hands on 9 July, and all civilians were given forty-eight hours to leave the city. With the Serb invasion imminent, one of the more horrific events of the war followed—what became known as the "Death March" of 15,000 civilians who did not trust the Serb evacuation and fled on their own. During the flight, the column was repeatedly shelled and fired upon by Serb forces. Altogether, 40,000 people fled the fallen safe area, of whom 25,000 were "escorted" to Potocari by the Serbs.[64] Serb forces collected military-age men with the result that 6,000 were executed. After taking Srebrenica, the Serb forces then focused upon Potocari, resulting in the transfer—coordinated by the ICRC—of 23,000 refugees to Tuzla. Information from refugee interviews attests to mass executions and torture. Following the fall of Srebrenica, the Bosnian Serbs next directed their attack against Zepa, which fell on 25 July, due to the inability of Ukrainian peacekeepers to resist Serbian advances. Goradze was the next obvious target because the Serbs sought, as they had since 1992, an uninterrupted and "cleansed" swath of territory in eastern Bosnia bordering on Serbia itself.

After the fall of Srebrenica and Zepa, NATO announced a decision to use airpower to deter further attacks. The latest in a series of lines drawn in continually shifting sands was around Goražde. However, the most important result was that the NATO announcement catalyzed Croatia. With Serbian forces preoccupied, the Tudjman government mobilized soldiers to recover the Krajina and eventually other areas in western Bosnia.

In spite of the arms embargo, Croatia's long coastline and cooperation by Hungary had permitted Zagreb to procure heavy weapons for its 100,000-man army and 180,000 reserves. The HVO had also been receiving technical assistance and training from a number of sources, including a Virginia-based company formed by retired American officers called Military Professional Resources, Inc.[65]

In only a few days, the Croatian army overran Knin, the capital of the self-styled, breakaway republic, and recovered most of the Krajina that had been occupied for four years. The West talked, but Croatia acted. NATO's bluster had seemingly tied down the Bosnian Serbs. Karadzic and Mladic had just been indicted by the International War

Crimes Tribunal and were busy infighting over civilian and military prerogatives. In any case, they did not come to the aid of their Croatian Serbian counterparts who were quickly routed. Ironically, the most concentrated refugee flow of the war—and as noted earlier, the largest in Europe since the Hungarian uprising in 1956—resulted from a successful Croatian military campaign. The estimated 125,000–150,000 refugees and 50,000 soldiers this time were all of Serbian origin. They fled into Serbia itself and toward Serbian-dominated Bosnia, especially Banja Luka. UN blue helmets accelerated their withdrawal; the 14,000 troops had only been reduced to 13,000 in spite of the March agreement to number 8,750 en route to 2,500 by November. The so-called UNPAs were "protected," by Croatian rather than United Nations soldiers.

The result was a 5 October countrywide cease-fire among all parties. Bosnian-Croat forces had also defeated the forces of the rebel Fikret Abdic from Bihać, resulting in the displacement of 25,000 of his followers to Croatia. Bosnian-Croat forces committed documented human rights abuses both during and after the offensive.[66] Furthermore, the exodus of 50,000 Bosnian Serbs to Banja Luka led to additional cases of ethnic cleansing in retaliation against the few remaining Muslims and Croats in that largely Serbian outpost.

In late August 1995, Serbian shells had killed thirty-eight people in the same Sarajevo market where twice as many deaths had catalyzed the first NATO air strikes in February 1994. The West's response involved both artillery from the Rapid Reaction Force and NATO warplanes. The explanation for the largest military action since the founding of the Western alliance in 1949 was twofold: Serbs were on the defensive and their leadership in disarray after the Croatian trouncing in the Krajina; and UN soldiers had withdrawn completely from the exposed areas in eastern Bosnia, thereby removing blue-helmeted targets potentially endangered by Western air attacks. The two-week operation included 3,400 sorties against Serb targets, focusing primarily on Bosnian Serb air defenses, communications, command and control, and ammunition depots.[67]

Prior to the air strikes, Washington significantly altered its political approach by assigning U.S. Assistant Secretary of State Richard Holbrooke to focus on the situation. Initial Serb intransigence to negotiations was overcome partially by the NATO air operation and the military prowess of the Muslim-Croat Federation. Additional threats were used: further air strikes, lifting the arms embargo for the Bosnian government, and possible provision of troops from Muslim countries. As such, the parties got close enough to the bargaining table to agree on four basic principles: the creation and maintenance of a sovereign Bos-

Bosnian Muslims wait at a checkpoint manned by Croatian and Bosnian police officers and monitored by United Nations soldiers.
Credit: UN PHOTO 186709/J. Isaac

nian state within the republic's original borders; the creation of two semiautonomous areas—the federation and Republika Srpska—within this state; a territorial division of 51/49 percent; and the right of the two regions to interact independently and enter into agreements with bordering countries.

In November 1995, the multiple sides—the Federal Republic of Yugoslavia, the Republic of Croatia, the Republic of Bosnia and Herzegovina, the Federation of Bosnia and Herzegovina, and the Republika Srpska—met in Dayton, Ohio, to discuss what would become a peace agreement. The agreement went beyond the division of the territories and size of various corridors, and it contained provisions for the creation of a new federal constitution, compliance with the International War Crimes Tribunal, full access by human rights monitors, free and fair democratic elections, the repatriation of refugees and displaced persons, joint arms control, and the deployment of a NATO Implementation Force.

The surreal nature of avoiding the realities of partition subsequently would become clearer. From the perspective of military-civilian interactions, however, there was an immediate irony. After the official signing of the peace agreement in Paris in 14 December, some 60,000 soldiers from IFOR assumed military control on 20 December 1995 and were replaced a year later by a smaller SFOR.[68] But there was no doubt about the military seriousness and wherewithal of these troops. As UN official Shashi Tharoor commented wryly in an oral presentation, "UN peacekeepers were present when there was no peace to keep, and NATO warfighters arrived when there was no war to fight."

The Balance Sheet and Conclusion

Table 5.1 summarizes essential data regarding the costs and benefits of military intervention in Bosnia from 1992 to 1995. Stated starkly, the task of fostering a secure environment was a dismal failure. In spite of over 167 fatalities (most in Bosnia, although UN figures do not provide this breakdown) and almost 1,500 casualties among the UN's soldiers, "force protection" rather than security for Bosnians was the order of the day. France and Britain sustained about half of the fatalities in the Balkans prior to IFOR, which contributed to the diplomatic venom between a rhetorically passive Europe with troops on the ground and a verbally aggressive United States without soldiers in the war zone.

Whatever one's views about European and American motivations, clearly some of the least safe territories in the Balkans were under UN protection in six safe areas. Ethnic cleansing and other war crimes continued virtually unabated until November 1995. The unwillingness by the West to put military teeth in what *The Economist* caricatured as "the confetti of paper resolutions" led more and more caustic observers to adopt the description of UN soldiers as "eunuchs at the orgy." Would starvation and human rights abuse have been worse without the UN's weak military? Such counterfactual speculation is not without its attractions, but testing would require considerable moral fortitude. Moreover, without the ability to quantify the perverse dialectical relationship between outside help and prolongation of the conflict, this analysis leads in the direction of more muscular intervention.

UNPROFOR is a depressing illustration (although UNOSOM II could be similarly considered) of collective failure in spite of substantial expenditures and even greater investments in rhetoric. Without putting too fine a point on it, the United Nations is incapable of exercising command and control over combat military operations for humanitarian or any other purposes. Although world politics have changed, UN capacity has not kept pace. The ability to plan, support, and command peacekeeping, let alone peace-enforcement, missions is scarcely greater now than during the Cold War. And this situation will not change in the foreseeable future because states will not empower the United Nations with the wherewithal to contradict Michael Mandelbaum's judgment that "the U.N. itself can no more conduct military

Table 5.1 Bosnia and Herzegovina: Military Costs and Civilian Benefits from Intervention, 1992–1995

	$ Costs	Casualties/Fatalities	Political Impact
Military costs of intervention for troop-contributing countries	A UNPROFOR: 02/92–09/95: $2.82B of which USDOD provided $786M. USDOD: $784M airlift and ODF. UN humanitarian: $1.355B. USAID: $348.1M. Total: $4.5B. IFOR: 1996–1997: $2.5B for U.S. only.	B 1992–1994: 90 peacekeepers killed and 900 wounded. By 03/95: 167 killed.	C Sarajevo airlift; no-fly zone; sanctions and embargo enforcement; air strikes; UN protection of humanitarian convoys. Led to crisis in UN system, EC/EU, and NATO and doubts about Western leadership in the post-Cold War world.

	Displacement	Suffering	State of the State
Civilian benefits of intervention for targeted countries Humanitarian challenge before intervention	D C: 1991: 250,000 Serbs; 100,000 Croats. BH: 1991: 100,000 refugees; mid-1992: 300,000 IDPs; late 1992: 2M IDPs; early 1993: 2.28M IDPs; end 1994: war victims + IDPs + refugees = 2.7M; 07–08/94: 125,000–250,000 Serb refugees to Serbia; 10/94: 25,000 refugees from Bihac to Croatia, 50,000 Serb refugees to Serbia. S: 96.9% of 572,000 refugees in Serbia live with families.	E *Hunger:* C: 1991: 0.5M refugees require assistance. FY: early 1993: 4.259M in need. BH: Winter 1993–1994: 2.7M in need. *Human rights:* C: 1991: 6,000–10,000 killed; 10,000 wounded. BH: From 1992: ethnic cleansing, expulsion, torture, rape; early 1993: 230,000 killed or missing; 60,000 seriously wounded; 1992–1994: siege of Sarajevo killed 10,000 and wounded 60,000. Total: 250,000 killed, 35,000 wounded, 26,000 disappearances, 50,000 torture victims, 20,000–50,000 rape victims.	F State structures ill-suited to the dynamics of integration across ethnic lines and the complications of national self-determination taken to logical extremes.
Civilian benefits after intervention	D' *Displacement/Repatriation:* Even after IFOR, very little improvement. End of 1995: 1.3M IDPs; 1.4M war-affected people: 800,000 refugees.	E' *Hunger:* SA: 07/92–01/93: 2,476 sorties carrying 27,460 tons of relief; 1994: 55,000 tons; 07/92–04/95: 175,000 tons; winter 1992–1993: UNPROFOR delivered 34,600 tons of relief to 800,000 beneficiaries, WFP 320,000 tons of food, UNICEF assisted 1.5M; early 1993: between 26–50% of food needs met in enclaves, only 53% altogether in 1993. ICRC: 32,000 tons to 600,000 persons each month; early 1994: 20% relief reaching destination. 50% diverted to soldiers; late 1994: 85% of needs met; mid-1995: UNHCR delivered 20% of need to safe areas and 8% to Sarajevo. *Human rights:* Periodic limited protection in certain areas. In the end, UNPROFOR did not prevent the massive atrocities. *Health:* Early 1993: ICRC: operated 215 medical facilities.	F' The emergence of more ethnically homogeneous territory makes "nation-state" governance accurate for the near future.

Abbreviations: **BH:** Bosnia/Herzegovina   **C:** Croatia   **FY:** Former Yugoslavia   **S:** Serbia   **SA:** Sarajevo Airlift

operations on a large scale on its own than a trade association of hospitals can conduct heart surgery."[69] This realization had become conventional wisdom within the UN Secretariat by the end of Boutros-Ghali's term and has continued into Annan's. The implications for military-civilian interactions are clear: Serious military force will not be under UN direction while civilian efforts almost certainly will.

The direct costs of UNPROFOR alone between its inception in February 1992 and September 1995—scarcely two months before the transition to IFOR—have been estimated at $2.82 billion. Of UNPROFOR's total costs, $786 million was contributed by the United States, which funded almost 32 percent of the operation according to the formula that has been reduced by Congress to 25 percent and is now under discussion at the United Nations itself.[70] In total, including the fund supplied to UNPROFOR, the DOD spent more than any other U.S. government agency on Bosnia, with total expenditures amounting to $1.05 billion.

Beginning in July 1993, UN and international resources dramatically increased. Afterward, member states authorized roughly $1 billion per year to finance UNPROFOR's operating costs. From July 1993 to March 1994, UNPROFOR cost 387 million. Between April and September 1994, costs increased to $535 million. The peak of the operation, in terms of cost, occurred between October 1994 and March 1995, when the bill for six months was $658.7 million; the costs from April until September 1995 were $614.7 million.

Data concerning UN humanitarian activities can be found in the reports from individual agencies and, later, from the interagency consolidated appeals. From December 1991 to October 1993, the UN released seven consecutive appeals, which for the period totaled $1.675 billion and covered 4.259 million people.[71] Between May and September 1992, the total amount requested increased from $174 million to $561 million. The largest increase occurred between December 1992 and March 1993, when the total request jumped from $642 million to $1.335 billion. In per capita terms, allocations increased from $7 per month in 1992 to $16 per month in Bosnia and $21 per month in Croatia. By the end of 1993, the UNHCR's operations had grown from a staff of 19 to 700 in 29 offices, accompanied by a budget of $295 million, which later would reach some $500 million. It was not without reason that Mrs. Sadako Ogata sometimes described herself as the "desk officer for the former Yugoslavia" because half of the UNHCR's total budget was devoted to the hapless Balkans.[72] Expenditures remained at about these levels through 1995.[73]

Aside from the U.S. assessment of UNPROFOR costs, the DOD also reported a total of $784 million in incremental costs from 1992 to 1995.

These costs were predominantly in support of airdrops, the airlift to Sarajevo, and support and participation in Operation Deny Flight (ODF). USAID spent $348.1 million on food, humanitarian assistance, and support for other humanitarian organizations operating in Bosnia. Total U.S. expenditures in the former Yugoslavia between 1992 and 1995 were $2.186 billion, with 1994 representing the peak of $959 million.

This was a costly operation not only in financial terms, but in terms of international personnel as well. Between 1992 and 1994, 90 peacekeepers were killed (almost all from hostile military activity), and 900 were wounded.[74] By March 1995, the number of UN fatalities had increased to 167 (3 military observers, 159 military personnel, 1 civilian police, 2 international civilian staff, and 2 local staff).[75] Although the figures include the fatalities in FRY and Macedonia, virtually all of the UN fatalities occurred in Bosnia-Herzegovina. War was the problem, not a lack of access to food. Humanitarian aid was an alibi for weak diplomatic and military efforts. Fred Cuny, in an inimitable one-liner, summarized the proverbial bottom line: "People did not die from starvation but from bullets." He told me on another occasion, "If the UN had been around in 1939, we would all be speaking German."[76] The UN to which Cuny was of course referring was the arena for state decisionmaking. Major powers simply failed to back multilateral responses to sustain their decisions.

The Dayton agreement amounted to a defacto partition of Bosnia to form three more homogeneous ethnic zones.[77] As there were no effective safeguards for those refugees or displaced peoples returning to their homes, the only choice for those returning from Europe or elsewhere in the former Yugoslavia was to go back to a village or city where their ethnic group was dominant. In spite of calls for freedom of movement, some 50,000 fewer Bosnians live in areas controlled by another group than prior to Dayton. Ironically, the elections and other elements of the peace process have been used to consolidate ethnically homogeneous swaths of territory. Ivo Daalder has noted that the international presence has ironically allowed "powerful hard-line elements on all sides to exploit Dayton's implementation, which they view as little more than the continuation of their conflict by other means."[78]

In early 1996, the United States had provided 27,000 troops for IFOR, of which the majority were deployed directly in Bosnia. The incremental cost of U.S. participation is believed to have been $2.5 billion for operations in 1996 and 1997.[79] One year after Dayton and despite IFOR's and then SFOR's presence, from the 4 million who had been on international assistance during the war, some 1.3 million people still remained displaced with an additional 1.4 million categorized as "war-affected" persons. And only a tiny number (about 30,000) of those who had "returned" had in fact returned to their original communities where they had been in the minority. An additional 800,000 were residing either in other republics of the former Yugoslavia—184,000 in Croatia, 250,000 in the Federal Republic of Yugoslavia (Serbia), 24,000 in Slovenia, and 7,000 in Macedonia—or in other European countries, especially Germany.[80]

This case is the most striking one under review in which civilian benefits are least impressive in relationship to the investment in military means. The humanitarian impulse has been prevalent in the post–Cold War world, but the dramatic increase in the number of interventions since 1991 has been tempered with sobriety after the debacle in Bosnia—and in Somalia and Rwanda, as the preceding and following chapters indicate.

Humanitarianism as a visceral expression of concern for the victims of armed conflict and political disorder has traditionally been spearheaded by nonstate actors. That states themselves have given such official prominence to humanitarianism in their policy architectures and as a justification for military expenditures is evidence of the extent to which this orientation has become a prominent feature of both contemporary transnational civil society and interstate relations.[81]

There is, however, a dramatic downside to what might otherwise be considered a positive moral development at the international level, which is receiving increasing attention in the philosophical and policy literature.[82] Rushing to rescue victims may, depending on the circumstances, be a palliative or even a counterproductive measure. The international responses to Yugoslavia's wars indicate that the "politics of rescue" are a poor excuse for policy.[83] They build erroneously on the metaphor of saving a drowning stranger by ignoring the politics and distorting the context of humanitarian efforts. In the Yugoslavian context, they do not confront the clash between the need for peacebuilding and partition.[84]

Political strategies to create an enduring sociopolitical order sometimes require reining in or refining the absolute impulse to save lives and alleviate the suffering of noncombatants with all available humanitarian means.[85] In the prescient prose of Alain Destexhe—the former secretary-general of the International Office of Doctors without Borders and now president of the International Crisis Group and member of the Belgian Senate:

> All over the world, there is unprecedented enthusiasm for humanitarian work. It is far from certain that this is always in the victims' best interests. . . . In dealing with countries in ongoing wars of a local nature, humanitar-

ian aid has acquired a near-monopoly of morality and international action. It is this monopoly that we seek to denounce. Humanitarian action is noble when coupled with political action and justice. Without them, it is doomed to failure and especially in the emergencies covered by the media, becomes little more than a play thing of international politics, a conscience-solving gimmick.[86]

When confronted with the crisis caused by Yugoslavia's dissolution, the West used the United Nations to pursue a course of shameless diplomatic compromise mixed with inadequate military responses and well-intentioned but counterproductive humanitarianism. Combined with the negotiating charade by Belgrade and Pale, UN action substituted for more creative Western diplomatic pressure, more vigorous military action, or arming the Bosnian Muslims to defend themselves.

Until the Croatian military offensive of August 1995 catalyzed a Western response, the sum of international efforts in the former Yugoslavia had constituted an intervention—but one that worked in favor of Bosnian and Croatian Serbs and their patrons in Belgrade. The idea of limited and neutral intervention is, as Richard Betts has pointed out, a "delusion," and "the West's attempt at limited but impartial involvement abetted slow-motion savagery."[87]

The moral of international military responses in the former Yugoslavia is that halfhearted or symbolic action is worse than no action at all. There is a real military-civilian puzzle: Before this crisis, a standard criticism of lackadaisical military responses was that humanitarian crises did not affect NATO countries directly; and yet, when a crisis occurred in Europe, the response was highly ineffective. This is not to minimize the serious difficulties of intervening in ethnonational conflicts generally or of working around the perennial obstacles to UN action. Nor is it to deny the value of traditional peacekeepers in contexts where consent is present. In the former Yugoslavia, however, earlier and more robust NATO military intervention should have taken place, or the warring parties should have been left to settle their disputes among themselves. Instead, appeasement produced the worst possible outcome: large expenditures, unspeakable suffering, and diminished NATO and UN credibility—which Boutros Boutros-Ghali called "mission impossible"[88] and Holbrooke deemed "the greatest collective failure of the West since the 1930's."[89]

6

Rwanda, 1994–1995: Better Late than Never?

In three years to the day, the mood toward humanitarian intervention had changed 180 degrees. In April 1991, the outside military effort in northern Iraq seemed to indicate that even the overnight appearance of some two million refugees was not an impossible task to be countered by military-civilian interactions. Then, in April 1994, the world stood by and watched a televised genocide in Rwanda.

Military forces were integral to the international response to the suffering that emanated from the 1994 genocide in Rwanda. The UN Assistance Mission in Rwanda (UNAMIR) had been present in Kigali for about eight months when the bloodbath began on 6 April 1994. The Security Council reduced these UN military forces a few days later after the murder and mutilation of ten Belgian soldiers—almost half the outside military fatalities for the entire period under review. The decision to increase troop strength took place after at least 500,000 people were murdered and 4 million others (about 50 percent of the country's population) involuntarily displaced—about half were officially refugees and half IDPs. There were two stand-alone military initiatives: a two-month French security effort, Opération Turquoise, from June to August, to stabilize the southwestern part of the country on the basis of Chapter VII through Security Council Resolution 929; and the massive two-month U.S. logistics effort, Operation Support Hope (OSH), from July to August, in order to provide relief to the Goma region in Zaire. There were also a number of national contingents that deployed to this region in support of the assistance efforts by the UNHCR.

Map 6.1 Rwanda

Rwanda has a population of 7,737,537 (1997), and its capital is Kigali. It is a landlocked country in central Africa bordered by Uganda (N), Tanzania (E), Burundi (S), and Zaire (W). Its total land area is 10,170 square miles, about the size of Maryland, with 29 percent arable land. Main exports are coffee, tea, tin, cassiterite, and wolframite.

A discussion of the roots of the 1994 crisis sets the stage for an analysis of this profoundly disturbing example of military-civilian interactions. Military force was too little and too late, while military logistics were useful but expensive. Yet, the late intervention is pregnant with lessons for future complex emergencies.

Background and Roots of the Conflict

The genocide in 1994 was not the first example of state-sponsored ethnic violence in Rwanda, or in neighboring Burundi; but the scale was unprecedented within the African Great Lakes region, as was the attention it received from the international media.[1] One result was a search into the historical and anthropological background for the roots of these gruesome events. The attributed reasons range from the legacy of colonialism to environmental stress to simply ancient ethnic hatred. Peter Uvin argues persuasively for a series of factors:

> extreme pauperization and reduction of life chances for a majority of the poor, especially from 1985 onwards; the Front Patriotique Rwandais invasion and the civil war that followed; and uninformed and uneducated peasant mass treated in an authoritarian and condescending manner; a history of impunity, human rights violations, corruption, and abuse of power; a deep-felt frustration and cynicism by many poor people; rapidly growing regional ethnic and social inequality; political strategies employed by small elite groups in search of protection against the pressures of discontent and democratization; the existence of past and current acts of violence; and a history of institutionalized, state-sponsored racism.[2]

Debate rages about the anthropological reality of Hutu-Tutsi-Twa ethnic divisions, but their numbers are agreed: On the eve of the genocide, of a population of 7.6 million, 85 percent were Hutu, 14 percent Tutsi, and 1 percent Twa. Notwithstanding the varying views among social scientists, the Rwandan population believes that ethnic differences exist—and at several junctures, they have justified horrific activities on the basis of this shared belief. These divisions thus are social and political realities. Indeed, constructivists would argue that the bases for international relations in general are just as fictitious, but the reality of "imagined communities" of states has clearly concrete consequences, both positive and negative.[3]

Much of traditional Rwandan history has been invented by European priests and scholars. In particular, the astute manipulation of precolonial ethnic and social constructions within Rwanda originates from the ethnic favoritism toward the Tutsi exhibited first by German and subsequently by Belgian colonizers. There is no documentation of any significant armed conflicts between Hutus and Tutsis of the same magnitude as that of the postcolonial period. Earlier violence mainly reflected attempts by the king (*mwami*) to exert influence over areas removed from his effective control, or what Gérard Prunier labels the "periphery."[4] Decades of European colonialism reinforced the social bases of differences in the society to such an extent that a persuasive case can be made for its transformation.

In 1899, Germany colonized Rwanda and Burundi and created German East Africa, which it occupied until 1918. After Germany's defeat in World War I, the League of Nations surrendered the colony as part of the settlement to Belgium, which also controlled neighboring Congo. As a result of the so-called science of ethnic classification, the characteristically tall and thin Tutsi were considered superior to the shorter and heavier Hutu. This served as the basis for Belgian favoritism between 1918 and 1959, until shortly before independence when the balance dramatically shifted to the Hutu majority.

While Rwanda-Burundi was no longer a Belgian territory after World War II, it was placed under Belgian-administered UN trusteeship until 1961, when a referendum ended the monarchy and established a republic.

The transition from a monarchy to an elected form of ethnically based governance began with massive ethnically based violence in Rwanda, where over 20,000 Tutsis were massacred in 1963 and thousands were displaced. After his initial election, President Grégoire Kayibanda structured elections in 1969 that resulted in the overwhelming victory of his party. In a move to consolidate his power base, Kayibanda purged Rwandan political society of any dissident voices who had opposed him or his party during elections. While there had been multiparty politics during the elections, over the following twelve years of his rule, Kayibanda's would become the only legal political party.

In the early 1970s, Kayibanda saw his power gradually weakening because of regional competition between the north and the south for political positions and favors in one of the poorest and most densely populated countries on earth. To maintain his authoritarian grip, the president resorted to anti-Tutsi propaganda, which was an effective device with 85 percent of the population.[5] In the face of growing poverty and population, most civil institutions and businesses were purged of their Tutsi employees. The continued rise in ethnic violence in rural areas prompted a bloodless military coup by Major General Juvénal Habyarimana—whose power base was in the north—on 5 July 1973. Whatever the value of arguments about ethnic differences, they were effective tools of political struggle for control of resources and power in 1963, 1966, and 1973. The early years of the Habyarimana regime minimized the blatant manipulation of anti-Tutsi sentiments and politics, but "institutional discrimination" eliminated Tutsis from virtually every arena except the private sector.[6]

Beginning with the Hutu revolt in 1959 and continuing through successive outbursts of ethnically based massacres, a Rwandan Tutsi expatriate community established itself in Uganda and eventually numbered some 200,000 people. They played a vital role in supporting the young Yoweri Museveni during his successful ascension to power. The Tutsi-Ugandan Alliance for National Unity became a force for change in a Uganda that had long ago ceased being the "jewel" of British East Africa.

In order to further consolidate power, by 1974 Habyarimana's *Mouvement Révolutionnaire National pour le Développement* (MRND) dominated the political scene. The early result of the centralized political organization was a rapid increase in living standards for most Rwandans, who experienced a rise of per capita income and further improvements in health, hygiene, and education largely fueled by outside financing.[7] In the 1980s, Rwanda became one of the most aided countries in the world: 11.4 percent of its GNP originated from development aid in 1986 and 22 percent in 1991.[8]

The Rwandan economy steadily weakened during the 1980s. Depending on the year, 60 to 80 percent of the government's revenues resulted from taxing coffee, virtually the only export. In 1983, the price of coffee plummeted and, along with massive devaluation, dramatically worsened Rwanda's debt. Furthermore, the return of refugees from Uganda in 1982 and from Burundi in 1988 added to the pressure on local resources and land. Growing internal tensions sounded the death knell for the Rwandan economy as GDP declined by 30 percent and production by 33 percent between 1990 and 1993.[9]

The plight of poor Rwandans worsened even more dramatically. Development projects mainly benefited the elite, who also accumulated scarce land that was then rented to the poor. Income inequality grew two and one-half times from 1982 to 1994,[10] and about half of the population was spending 75 percent of its income merely on food. With one of the highest population densities in the world (285 people per square kilometer) and with only 10 percent of the population living within cities, Rwanda is in a "demographic trap."[11] The stress of the 7.6 million people on the land led to dramatic deforestation and soil erosion. The impact of "structural violence on children is seen in the under-five child mortality rate of 20 percent, the fact that 50 percent of children under five are stunted, and that 30 percent are suffering from moderate to severe malnutrition."[12] Estimates for the population growth rate ranged between 2.9 and 3.4 percent, implying a doubling of the population at least every twenty-four years.[13]

After years in exile and with the active support of the Ugandan government, the Rwandan Patriotic Front (RPF) invaded Rwanda in October 1990 and penetrated to within 20 miles of the capital, Kigali, before being forced to retreat. This guerrilla campaign served as one of the causes of the 1994 genocide because it provided the occasion for the constant manipulation of fear among Hutus by the media and governmental extremists.[14] Most of the Tutsis in the RPF were second-generation descendants of the original refugees who had fled to Uganda to escape earlier ethnic violence and had never lived on Rwandan soil. Skilled in the methods of guerrilla warfare, they also had gained access to Ugandan weapons and were backed by governmental troops in exchange for their earlier loyalty to Museveni; at the time, the RPF was composed of 6,000 Tutsi soldiers and 3,000 Ugandan regulars. Regional rivalry led Museveni to support the minority Tutsi government in Burundi and the minority Tutsi guerrilla opposition in Rwanda. In addition to his gratitude for Tutsi help during his own struggle for power, Museveni was also angered at the Rwandan government's active support for rebels within Uganda attempting to overthrow his regime.

After the initial RPF success, France and Zaire sent military aid and troops to assist the Habyarimana government. Belgium also sent troops, although they were primarily used to protect their own nationals. Under increased international pressure and RPF demands for democratization, President Habyarimana enacted a series of power-sharing agreements in 1990. The reforms incorporated moderates and some coalition parties into his government, while simultaneously solidifying his own power. These reforms also strengthened extremist Hutu groups, the most serious being the *Coalition pour la défence de la république* (CDR) and eventually the *akazu*, which included the president's wife and a small elite of extremists from the army.

By 1992, the MRND and the CDR had each formed its own armed militia. The MRND's was known as the *interahamwe* and the CDR's as *impuzamugambi*. Their combined strength was estimated at 30,000 to 50,000 soldiers. Beginning in late 1992 and increasing steadily in 1993 and early 1994, political elements of the government expanded training and arming the Presidential Guard, various militias, and elements of the military in preparation for what was to become the genocide. Rwandan government military expenditures grew rapidly in preparation for the 1994 bloodbath; between 1990 and 1991, they increased 40 percent, and another 20 percent in 1993.[15] Armaments were supplied mainly by France, which had become the mainstay for supply and training throughout the Habyarimana era. In fact, the government continued to receive arms and distribute them to civilian militias continually, even after the Arusha Accords in 1993.

The RPF invasion provided Hutu extremist groups with ample evidence that their worst fears had been justified. The primary tool for broadcasting their message of hatred for Tutsis was the Radio-Télévision Libre des Mille Collines ("The Independent Radio-Television of the 1,000 hills"). The entire Tutsi ethnic group became the "enemy," in spite of substantial intermarriage and other social and official mixing in previous decades. On several occasions between 1990 and 1993—October 1990, January–February 1991, March 1992, and December

1992–February 1993—at least 2,000 civilians were victims of politically motivated killings.[16]

The Organization of African Unity was the first outside organization to try mediation in the deteriorating situation. The attempt to send an observer group had failed mainly because only Uganda, Tanzania, Burundi, and Zaire—all with close ties to one of the two parties— volunteered to send observers. However, after negotiating a cease-fire between the two parties in July 1992, the OAU placed a fifty-man Neutral Military Observer Group. In the end, forty observers were deployed.

In order to halt the ongoing dissemination of additional military supplies to the RPF coming from the Ugandan military forces, the Security Council authorized the UN Observer Mission in Uganda-Rwanda (UNOMUR) on 22 June 1993. This operation arose from the two-year regional negotiation that had resulted in the 1993 Arusha Accords. The pact, which was initialed in the nearby northern Tanzanian town for which it is named, incorporated what would prove to be unworkable national reconciliation and power-sharing measures, including provisions for the repatriation of the Tutsi refugee population; incorporation of the Tutsi minority into the government power structure, through ministerial and legislative positions; and the integration of the RPF into the regular army.

After Arusha, the Security Council created the UN Assistance Mission in Rwanda (UNAMIR). This operation subsumed UNOMUR's mandate and went further. As part of a four-step deployment, the mission was supposed to engage in a series of activities, including facilitating and observing the cease-fire through demobilization and integration; establishing a weapons secure zone in Kigali; demining; repatriating refugees; coordinating humanitarian assistance; and monitoring overall security, the police, and the peace process.[17] In the first phase of the operation, UNAMIR—numbering 1,217 troops— continued to monitor the cease-fire, provided some security, and took steps to integrate the RPF into the national army. The integration process quickly stagnated. For example, between January and February 1994, UNAMIR ominously intercepted four planes loaded with armaments in Kigali.[18] By the time of the genocide, 2,548 peacekeepers were on the ground, the total number authorized by the original mandate.

The Arusha Accords were considered by many observers and diplomats to be a workable model for reconciliation, but the willingness of the government to abide by the provisions and the actual applicability of the timetable for implementation were questionable from the outset.

With the proliferation and growth of extremist groups and armed militias, the ability of Habyarimana to assert control was decreasing.

The Onset of the Crisis

The 1994 tragedy in Rwanda had two parts. The first was the systematic genocide carried out by Hutu extremist groups and the government against Tutsis as well as moderate Hutus. The second was the ultimately successful invasion by the RPF forces initiated immediately after the massacres had begun.

In an attempt to rescue the Arusha Accords, Habyarimana met with the representatives of the RPF and President Cyprien Ntaryamira of Brunudi in Dar es Salaam, the Tanzanian capital. While returning, their plane was shot down on 6 April, in what many believe to have been an act of sabotage. Immediately following the crash, Hutu extremist groups—composed primarily of the Presidential Guard, elements of the Rwandan Armed Forces (FAR), the *interhamwe*, and the *impuzamugambi*, as well as ordinary citizens—began to massacre Hutu opposition leaders. Although these groups alleged that the RPF and southern Hutu groups had targeted the plane, available evidence suggests that the Presidential Guard was the plausible culprit because it was perhaps most threatened by any sort of reconciliation. Roadblocks were established, and armed gangs with predetermined lists of victims systematically worked their way through Kigali. Even traditional centers of refuge, such as hospitals and churches, became the sites of massacres. Within a week, over 20,000 victims had been slaughtered as the killings spread to the east and the southwest.[19] Also among those who died in the initial rampage were ten Belgian peacekeepers guarding the prime minister, Agathe Uwilingiyimara. The blue helmets, employing an unwise extrapolation of traditional peacekeeping principles, had laid down their arms and were slaughtered along with the prime minister.

By the end of April, an estimated 200,000 people had been massacred. After six weeks, the estimate had increased to 500,000 civilians. After Habyarimana's death, extremist Hutu groups quickly established an interim government. Composed of several parties, their shared purpose was simple: Tutsi extermination. Initially, this interim government was tacitly recognized by SRSG Jacques-Roger Booh-Booh. However, by late May, the interim government had fled Kigali after the RPF's successful invasion.

First in Tanzania and later in Goma, the largest and fastest refugee flows in the region's sad history took place. Some two million Rwan-

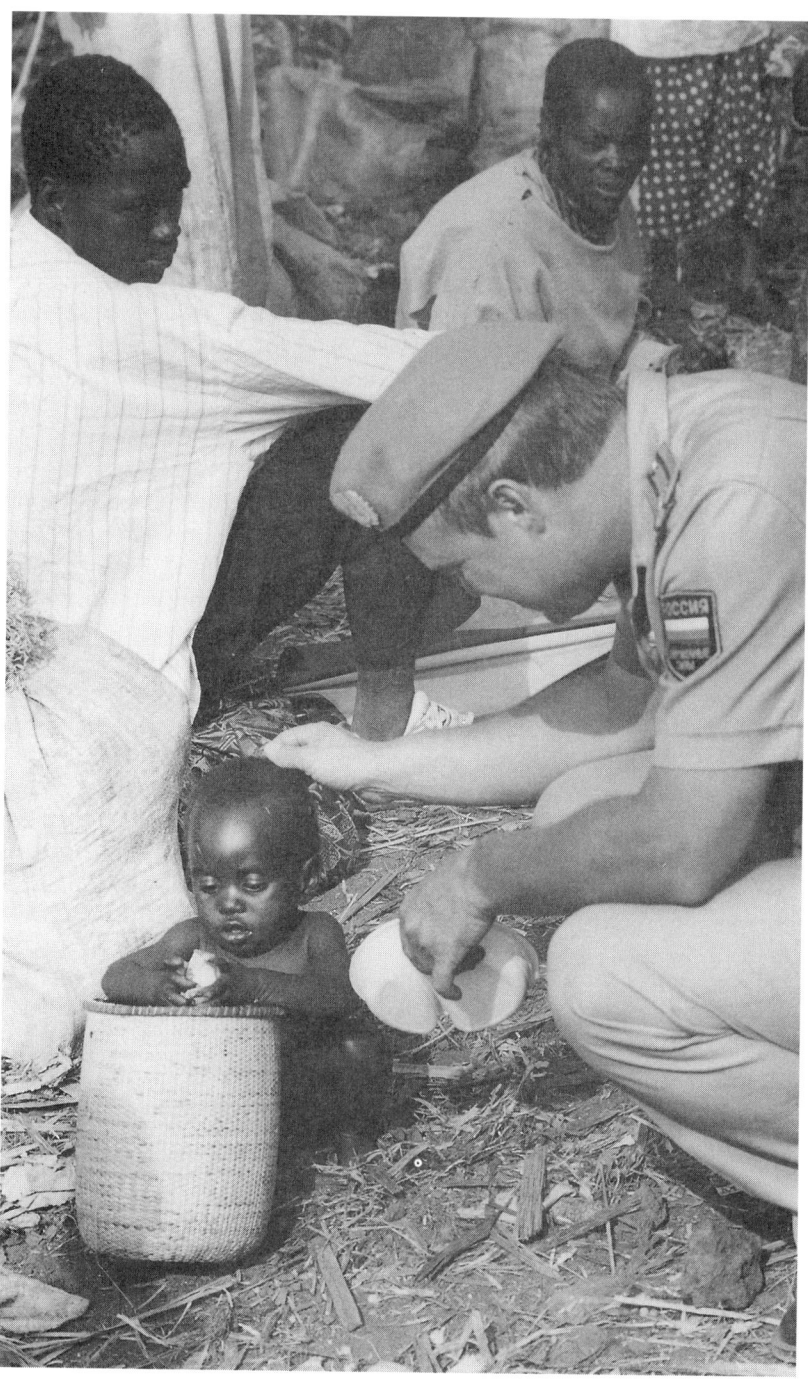

A United Nations soldier from Russia plays with a baby in a camp at Ruhengeri. Credit: UN PHOTO 186790/J. Isaac

dans, both Hutu and Tutsi, fled in the wake of the original genocide and the RPF offensive. Some 50,000 displaced Rwandans had settled in the central region, and 200,000 predominantly Tutsi fled to the northern RPF-controlled areas. Of the 200,000 Burundian (mainly Hutu) refugees in the south, only 80,000 remained. Fearing for their lives, they returned to Burundi. On 29 April, after additional RPF advances in the north, some 250,000 Hutus fled to Ngara, Tanzania, in a span of twenty-four hours, thereby becoming the world's largest refugee camp and one that had materialized virtually overnight. Furthermore, an additional 8,500 refugees were in Zaire; between 5,500 and 10,000 were in Uganda; and between 16,000 and 47,000 were in Burundi.[20] In Burundi during May, the crude mortality rate was between 0 and 8 per 10,000 per day; however, by July, it had declined to 0 to 2 per 10,000 per day.[21] As in northern Iraq and later in Goma, the primary cause of death was diarrhea.

The massacres were complemented by vast sexual violence. Some 15,700 cases of rape were reported, but the actual figure may have been 250,000 to 500,000.[22] Like genocide, rape was systematic. Furthermore, due to the high prevalence of HIV/acquired immunodeficiency syndrome (AIDS) and the subsequent transmission to many rape victims, the process of genocide undoubtedly will continue.

Additional data concern the role of children during the conflict. As in other recent wars, children have been victims as well as perpetrators of violence;[23] but the vast majority were victims—over 300,000.[24] Between 88 and 96 percent of all children witnessed massacres, 87 percent lost a parent, 82 percent were threatened with weapons, and 66 percent witnessed the death of a parent or other family member.[25] In the end, 70 percent of all refugees were children, including some 100,000 unaccompanied minors.

Military and Civilian Responses

As the genocide raged, physical threats to outside humanitarian personnel also increased. Most UN organizations and international NGOs withdrew from Kigali and then Rwanda to the safety of Nairobi. The ICRC and Médecins sans Frontières–France were exceptional among the group in that they continued to operate in spite of the impossible situation. In the midst of lethal chaos, the two organizations joined forces with the remaining UNAMIR troops. Local staff were even more vulnerable than their expatriate counterparts, and many were targeted and massacred by the Hutu militias.

The refugee camps in Tanzania were populated primarily by Hutu refugees, and they illustrated one of the thorniest dilemmas within refugee camps elsewhere in the region, particularly in eastern Zaire where the UNHCR eventually recruited Zairean soldiers as a kind of local protection force.[26] Of the 250,000 refugees, some 30,000 were among those who had planned, initiated, or actively participated in the genocide. There were no outside peacekeepers or other military forces to attempt to separate the refugees from the perpetrators of genocide. In fact, the latter quickly established political dominance over the other refugees. War criminals in many cases assumed responsibility for distributing food and other supplies, hence international assistance was diverted to militias and, more clearly than in other cases, fueled the continuing instability.[27] As Mrs. Ogata lamented in a speech at the Holocaust Museum in Washington, D.C., in 1997, "No country offered to get help. My staff had to continue feeding criminals as the price for feeding hundreds of thousands of innocent women and children."[28]

How to respond when humanitarian aid is manipulated proved an acute dilemma for those on the ground. Was it better to feed the criminals and the needy, or feed no one? In mid-1994, such sentiments were set aside. By early 1995, however, the situation and sentiments had changed. Feeling increasingly unwilling to become accomplices to the possibility of continued atrocities, several agencies chose to withdraw—led by the International Rescue Committee and the MSF, whose staffs had originally been in the vanguard of the relief effort. Others were compelled by humanitarian imperatives or their intergovernmental mandates and remained within the camps.

UNAMIR, April–July 1994

The original UNAMIR mandate was to facilitate the cease-fire and political integration of the warring factions. With the onset of genocide and the renewed RPF offensive, the original purpose of UNAMIR was superfluous. Typically, the rules of engagement for peacekeepers permit the use of force only in self-defense. Canadian General Romeo Dallaire, commander of the UNAMIR force, requested an expansion of the ROEs to incorporate the protection of civilians. He also requested, unsuccessfully, doubling the force. The mandate was not modified until 29 April—four weeks after the genocide had begun. And immediately following the onset of the bloodbath, the Security Council actually reduced the number of peacekeepers when the Belgian contingent withdrew following the massacre and dismemberment of ten soldiers. Feeding upon the earlier reaction in the United States after the deaths of eighteen Marines in Somalia, targeting the Belgian contingent was a deliberate and successful tactic to create the conditions for a UN withdrawal. Targeting soldiers from the former colonial power whose citizenry had little stomach for the ugliness of ethnic violence in the African Great Lakes region proved an accurate calculation of Belgian sentiments.

In the midst of utter chaos in Rwanda, the UN Security Council had three options: alter the UNAMIR mission from peacekeeping to enforcement and significantly increase the military resources provided; decrease the mandate and troop numbers; or implement the complete withdrawal of UNAMIR. In order to avoid being embroiled in a seemingly chaotic atmosphere while appearing also not to completely abandon the local population, the Security Council passed Resolution 912 of 21 April. One UNHCR official privately called it "a shameful black day in UN history." Kenneth Roth, the executive director of Human Rights Watch, described the resolution at the time as "a thin veil over another massacre."[29] The authorization for the peacekeeping force decreased from 2,500 to 270. UNAMIR's lowest level was 500 troops, predominately from Bangladesh, because slow procedures meant that they were still in the country when cutbacks and the retreat were reversed.

The UN secretary-general called for a reversal of the decision and for the expansion of UNAMIR. Within a week, debate concerning the structure of possible intervention was between the UN Secretariat's recommendation to create internal safe areas and Washington's to support safe areas across the borders of neighboring countries. While the UN proposal required more troops, the U.S. proposal encouraged displacement.

In spite of rumblings about an all-African force, nothing materialized for lack of political will and transport.[30] The final compromise was the expansion to a 5,500-strong force with a somewhat expanded mandate. Although not referring to Chapter VII, Resolution 918 authorized the protection of civilians and humanitarian relief operations. In this case, the primary push for the expansion was from developing countries, especially in Africa, and middle powers that wished to "shame the council into action."[31] The resolution made no reference to "genocide." The State Department and the White House, as well as counterparts elsewhere, realized that such language would require stronger military intervention based on the international agreement to act under the terms of the 1951 Convention on Genocide. As part of the resolution, an arms embargo was enacted, although most of the massacres had already been committed with such available and low-tech weapons as machetes.

The mandate's expansion did not alter realities on the ground. By 18 June, UNAMIR had only 354 troops and 124 military observers provided by African nations.³² Furthermore, these troops were equipped with only light arms and had no logistical support of their own or from the West. Authorized levels were not reached until October 1994, half a year after the beginning of the crisis.

In spite of its limited resources, UNAMIR was able to contribute to humanitarian action in Kigali, albeit on a limited scale. The force created havens for potential victims and negotiated cease-fires and access for aid groups. An outstanding example was the protection of 10,000 civilians in Kigali's Amahoro stadium and at the King Faisal Hospital.³³ UNAMIR also protected some aid convoys and supported aid organizations.

Daily patrols by UNAMIR sought to deter human rights abuses. They escorted convoys and transported 5,000–6,000 civilians to safe locations,³⁴ but on various occasions UNAMIR personnel allowed violations to occur before their eyes. UNAMIR also served in a logistics role prior to the massive UNHCR and unilateral humanitarian efforts. The airlift, managed by peacekeepers, transported repatriated humanitarian personnel and supplies. UNAMIR can be credited with saving 25,000 lives.³⁵

These facts lead naturally to ask whether earlier and more forceful action by the Security Council would have led to better protection for at-risk populations. The presence of UN peacekeepers—no matter how feeble—served to deter at least some human rights abuses. If, with a force of only 354 soldiers, UNAMIR was capable of protecting 25,000 Rwandans from imminent massacre, then how many lives could have been saved by a more sizable and robust deployment?

The great powers were silent, presumably because of their reluctance to become entangled in a chaotic internal conflict and their perceived nonvital national interests in the region. Washington was the primary obstacle, as it continuously blocked attempts to respond. The basis for this stance was a desire not to pay for an operation that the Untied States believed would inevitably fail, as well as the new U.S. policy under PDD-25, which argued against intervention in areas and countries outside of U.S. strategic interest.³⁶ Ironically, or perhaps logically in light of the Somalia experience and the public reaction to it within the United States, this approval of the 180-degree reversal away from the Clinton administration's earlier policy of "assertive multilateralism" was approved at the beginning of May, halfway through the genocide. The costs in Rwanda should at least partially be reflected in the balance sheet for Somalia.

Opération Turquoise

Citing the lack of troops actually in the theater of conflict, France declared that it would deploy troops in Rwanda in late June, with or without UN support. The role of French intervention in Rwanda through Opération Turquoise admittedly was different from the other military efforts under discussion in that the "troops of a UN-mandated humanitarian force had, less than a year previously, been occasional but direct participants in the conflict."[37]

The Security Council endorsed the Chapter VII Opération Turquoise on 22 June 1994. The green light for the operation in the southwest was a kind of quid pro quo for council approval shortly thereafter of Russian intervention in Georgia and the U.S. invasion of Haiti.[38] The operation was authorized to "use all necessary means" in order to "identify and protect threatened civilian populations on Rwandan soil and to assist the injured." Therefore, the mandate to end the violence was approved fifteen weeks and an estimated half million deaths after the killing had commenced. By 20 June, the number of refugees had increased to 514,000 and the number of IDPs to 1.4 million.[39] As mentioned earlier, judgments about success or failure vary. With one-quarter of the population either dead or displaced, the approval of Opération Turquoise could be seen as a failure by the community of states to make a prompt decision. At the same time, from the point of view of forestalling future additional deaths, displacement, and disease, it could be seen as a partial success.

The decision by France to intervene unilaterally was controversial. French ulterior motives were suggested, including the desire to reclaim technologically superior weaponry provided to FAR prior to the genocide; French historical support for the Hutu government; and French neoimperialism in Africa, both economic and linguistic (the so-called Fashoda complex stemming from a nineteenth-century incident and the desire to staunch the expansion of English in francophone countries).

A variety of French compromises dampened opposition to the initiative. First, the operation had a two-month duration (to withdraw by 22 August). Second, the operation became multinational with the integration of troops provided by six African countries (Senegal, Chad, Congo, Guinea-Bissau, Mauritania, and Niger), known as the French-speaking African Battalion (FRAFBATT). Following the withdrawal of French forces, FRAFBATT was integrated into UNAMIR II. Third, the neutrality and purely humanitarian nature of the operation was strongly stressed. These compromises did not completely dissipate the RPF's hostility to the presence of French soldiers.

They were deployed in two separate areas: Goma, Zaire, was the logical and support center for the operation; and southwestern Rwanda was the operation area. Immediately following Security Council approval, some 2,500 troops and 700 vehicles were deployed to the area within a week.[40] The force was initially comprised of French special operations forces and legionnaires, although it would later incorporate logistical, medical, and humanitarian personnel as well. Despite this logistical effort, insecurity initially worsened. On 4 July, a humanitarian safe area was established in the south, Zone Humanitaire Sure (ZHS). One of the primary reasons was to prevent both genocidal retribution by the RPF against Hutus and a refugee tidal wave like the earlier one to Goma.

Threats to the ZHS came from the invading RPF, who were wary of the French operation and of the civilians whom they protected; and from the genocidal Hutu paramilitary groups, who had fled the RPF and were considered a source of instability and violence. A 250-strong Rwandan gendarmerie was created of Hutus who dissociated themselves from the various militias and were willing to cooperate with the new government. Opération Turquoise also protected humanitarian convoys traveling into the zone. The operation created a secure and stable enough environment so that humanitarian organizations were able to operate.

Within the first days of operation, some 8,000 Tutsis and later an additional 1,324 were rescued.[41] Within the southwest, the French-led force protected an estimated 11,500 to 14,000 civilians, remaining Tutsis, and other at-risk groups.[42] Other Tutsis and opposition groups had already been massacred because genocide had first spread to the south. Beyond the security activities that comprised its primary purpose, Opération Turquoise also undertook relief support and modest direct relief. The large number of IDPs in the southwest quickly stretched capacities of the international safety net to the breaking point. An estimated 20,000 displaced persons perished within these camps as a direct result of the unhealthy conditions.

The most noticeable contributions were in health and sanitation. The operation encompassed a standing medical unit, the Elément Médical Militaire d'Intervention Rapide (EMMIR), and a mobile emergency response team, Bioforce. With a staff of 49 personnel, EMMIR treated 300 civilians per day. Bioforce was especially vital, operating locally and cooperating with NGOs. From 22 June to 30 September, the operation "carried out 1,100 surgical operations, 17,000 medical consultations, 11,000 days of hospitalization, 90,000 ambulatory treatments, 24,000 vaccinations, and 24 births."[43] The engineering capacity of military forces proved helpful, with soldiers restoring electricity and rebuilding roads and bridges.

French forces also used Bukavu, Zaire, as an operational center, but the decision to use Goma as a logistical and command center had other impacts. One of the primary reasons that so many Hutu refugees had fled to Goma in the first place was the promise of security from supporters of the former Hutu regime. This result ensued because, as the center for the logistical effort, the capacity of the airport was substantially increased and the outside military presence fostered stability. Originally able to accommodate only a few medium-size flights per day, capacity was rapidly expanded to twenty-five large flights per day. French forces also directly participated in relief distribution and assistance. As in other operations, soldiers often used their time off to help with distribution and reconstruction.

Throughout the civil war and the genocide, RPF military gains led to the departure of Hutu refugees. On 4 July, the RPF gained complete control of Kigali. However, by this time only 50,000 of its 300,000 citizens remained, and 25,000 more would soon be displaced.[44] The invasion of the northern town of Ruhengeri on 13 July triggered the flight of 500,000 to 800,000 refugees to Goma on 14–15 July.[45] There is considerable debate concerning the actual number who fled to Goma, with some estimates exceeding one million; but the earlier record for the rapid rise of a staggeringly large camp in Tanzania was broken. This analysis accepts the middle range used above and provides mortality data within it. It was estimated that "between 15,000 and 30,000 Hutus had crossed the border per hour into Zaire."[46] With Goma quickly overwhelmed by the masses and people dying on the streets, the refugees migrated further north to the camps of Mugunga, Kibumba, Katale, and Munigi.

The lack of clean water and adequate sanitation facilitated the rapid spread of disease among refugees. This was of course coupled by dehydration and exhaustion. "By July 17, it was estimated that one refugee was dying per minute due to cholera, dehydration, and exposure."[47] The crude mortality rate (CMR) at the peak of the crisis, from 14 to 31 July, was between 28.1 and 44.9 per 10,000 per day, whereas the preconflict CMR was 0.6 per 10,000 per day. Those most vulnerable were unaccompanied children and infants, for whom the CMR was 20 to 100 and 100 to 800 per 10,000 per day, respectively.[48] In total, there were an estimated 10,000 unaccompanied refugee children.[49]

An estimated 50,000 people died in Goma, some 6 to 10 percent of the refugee population. Some 85 to 90 percent of all deaths were associated with diarrhea, cholera, and dysentery. The appearance of what seemed like a medieval epidemic may have been the story that sparked dramatic media coverage.[50] Furthermore, 90 percent of all deaths occurred outside of clinics.[51] The case fatality rate for diarrheal disease during the initial part of the crisis was 22 percent. Almost all refugees had cholera, although only 10 percent showed symptoms. Those children under five who did not perish from these combinations of disease

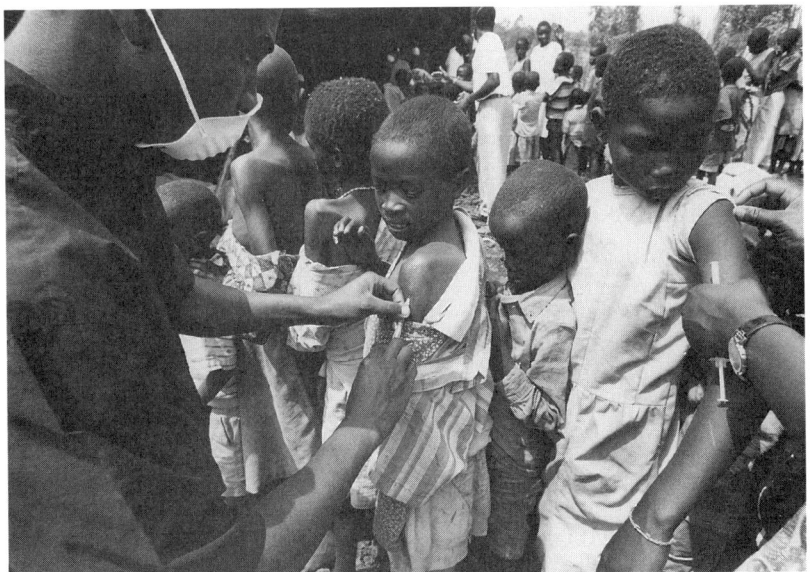

Two girls receive needle vaccinations from health workers, while other children wait in line at the Ndosho camp for unaccompanied children in the town of Goma. Credit: UNICEF/94-0277/Betty Press

suffered from acute protein-energy malnutrition, which ranged between 5 and 8 percent. In addition, of those who fled, 47 percent did not bring any type of shelter.[52]

As mentioned, the crisis peaked in late July, before the true effects of the various unilateral interventions in response to the Goma influx were effective. These responses did not begin to have an impact on the health of refugees until the third week of the crisis. Many argue that if earlier and more aggressive action had taken place, the case/fatality ratio would have declined precipitously.[53] Even in comparison with the flow of refugees and the international responses in Bosnia, Somalia, and northern Iraq, this was a most dramatic crisis. In light of the country's size, it could be categorized as the worst of the lot.

By 24 July, over 2.1 million Rwandans had become refugees, with an additional 1.2 million IDPs in the French zone and 1.2 million elsewhere.[54] Including the minimal estimate of 500,000 dead, approximately two-thirds of the precrisis population was either dead or displaced.

Prior to the deployment of additional unilateral support missions, Opération Turquoise participated in a variety of attempts to ease suffering. Aside from the work of Bioforce and EMMIR, one of the most beneficial services was to bury cholera victims in Goma. Heavy equipment and mechanical excavators were required to penetrate the volcanic soil; the military operation had used this equipment on the airport so that it was not available to NGOs and UN agencies.

The most immediate UN humanitarian response in Goma was by the WFP, which had been involved in providing humanitarian relief in the southwest, Bukavu, and Ngara. Within forty-eight hours, the first WFP airlift arrived carrying 40 tons of food, which was followed by a road convoy arriving on 21–22 July, carrying a combined 900 tons.[55] Furthermore, the airlift by Church World Action–Rwanda had arrived on 16 July carrying 14 tons of food aid and relief personnel.

The rapidity of forced population movements to Goma and the equally rapid onset of a humanitarian crisis with a lethal epidemic seemingly eliminated the earlier Western opposition to intervention. Taking advantage of the presence of a large number of correspondents on the continent for the elections in South Africa, intense and dramatic media coverage led to other external military efforts.[56]

Mel McNulty argues that Opération Turquoise discredited both France's role in Africa and the validity of foreign military intervention in general.[57] However, the evidence of "failure" presented consists of French withdrawal, condemnation by the OAU, and continued violence in the African Great Lakes area. It is relevant to indicate that the withdrawal was part of the resolution, the condemnation by the OAU was prior to the intervention, and regional stability can hardly be a legitimate criterion for a two-month intervention. It is more worthwhile to quantify the humanitarian benefit of a military intervention.

Operation Support Hope

The largest of the military-humanitarian support efforts was the U.S. Operation Support Hope. Involving 3,000 troops drawn from regular military forces and reservists, its purposes were to carry out water purification and distribution in Goma; to improve airfield services in Goma and Kigali; and to organize airhead and cargo distribution from the airport in Entebbe, Uganda.[58] Any reference to peacekeeping or enforcement was avoided in favor of President Clinton's "disaster response." On the ground, both within the military command structure and during interactions with other agencies, the American role as supporter and facilitator rather than as leader, was stressed, as had been the case in Somalia and northern Iraq and would be the case in Haiti. From an organizational standpoint, OSH contained a new element of U.S. military disaster response. Instead of deploying entire divisions, the military provided smaller logistic contingents. As in the other four cases in this book, the U.S. Army Civil Affairs units were useful.

The operation was coordinated by the European Command in Germany and composed of two task forces: Joint Task Force Bravo in Kigali and Joint Task Force Alpha in Goma. The operation was run in Kigali, Entebbe, and Goma by the Civil-Military Operations Command. In the other four cases, the CMOC was used to coordinate the activities of the military with those of NGOs and UN agencies; in Rwanda, the CMOC played a subordinate role to the UN. The central UN authority was the UN Rwanda Emergency Office (UNREO), with the DHA taking the lead in Goma. The military had relatively few direct interactions with NGOs; instead, the UN grouped requests and put them forward to OSH, which then responded.

Prior to the deployment, the military had briefly used airdrops. The damage caused by missing target areas led to abandoning the technique more quickly than in northern Iraq and Bosnia. In Goma, OSH tackled head-on the primary cause of mortality, namely, the lack of clean water. At first, the military approached the problem through the use of reverse osmosis water purification units. However, this system produced low quantities of high-quality water, whereas what was required was high quantities of potable water. The military shifted to the provision of tankers that would produce 3,000 liters per hour by quickly chlorinating the water during travel to the destination. By 12 August, enough water was being produced per day to fulfill the survival requirement of 5 liters a day—although 15 liters per day is considered preferable. By 27 August, the amount produced per day exceeded available storage facilities. The combined actions of all forces increased water production from 0 to 4 million liters per day.

The military's secondary function in Goma was to enlarge airport capability. As mentioned, Opération Turquoise had already increased the capacity, but the addition of night runway lighting and air traffic controllers allowed twenty-four-hour use. Furthermore, the deployment of in-flight refueling tankers to the area prevented the possibility of overwhelming the airport for certain routine operations. Some NGOs reported that cargo was being unloaded within a quarter of an hour, a formidable performance according to those veterans interviewed. In Kigali the primary goal of OSH was to rebuild the airport, which reopened on 8 August. Additional assistance was also provided in the southwest, where aerial reconnaissance provided information to humanitarian organizations concerning refugee flows and also served to reinforce perception of security among civilians.

The U.S. airlift flew 903 sorties, carrying 46 percent of all aid to the region, while the UN airlift provided the remaining 54 percent, or

1,150 sorties.⁵⁹ The strategic, or intertheater, distribution center was Entebbe, where the flights would then be directed to other areas by the Combined Logistic Center, which was donated to the United Nations prior to American withdrawal.

Praise for airlift and logistics measures is often tempered somewhat by complaints from NGOs, whose staffs are reluctant to call for free military airlifts because they have learned from experience that cargo is not always delivered at the required time or to the right destination. The cost of civil transport is believed to be 40 percent lower than military transport. Other modes, predominantly road and rail, are six to eight times cheaper. Furthermore, the capacity of road versus air transport also needs to be considered. A C-130 cargo plane has a payload of 13 metric tons, while many trucks have payloads of 40 metric tons.⁶⁰ Confronted with the necessity of delivering 0.5 kilograms of food per day to 800,000 refugees, an exclusive reliance upon air transport would quickly have proved financially ruinous.

The magnitude of Washington's response in Rwanda was noteworthy; but its delayed, limited, and short-term nature led some to credit OSH only begrudgingly with "expediting a process that would have happened anyway."⁶¹ However, the purpose was to respond rapidly to humanitarian needs and withdraw once the crisis was manageable by the UNHCR and the other civilian organizations. For example, OSH withdrew from Goma on 28 August, when the mortality rate was still 500 per day. The force completely withdrew from the theater on 28 September.

Aside from criticism about timing, the reluctance to provide direct security has greater validity. The U.S. force was credited with creating enough security so that humanitarian organizations could move effectively into the region. The very presence of American soldiers, rather than any specific war-fighting activities, was the reason. The overriding concern for "zero body bags" behind PDD-25 also impeded the development of the kind of military-NGO relationships that had been beneficial in northern Iraq and even Somalia. Other criticism has focused on the delays caused by the overwhelming security provided for OSH convoys. One NGO noted wryly that when the OSH forces departed, the number of convoys actually increased by two to three per day.⁶²

Additional Unilateral Support

In addition to the French and American operations, eight countries provided direct military resources; the size and the nature of the unilateral operations differed considerably, but they are part of an unusual mosaic of military-civilian interactions. As part of a long legacy of participation in peacekeeping operations, Canadian troops as part of UNAMIR numbered 400 at the onset of the genocide. Those soldiers played a vital role in early April, when a Canadian-organized airlift transported expatriates and Belgian troops out of Rwanda and supplies for UNAMIR into the country. This was the only transport during the early period of the crisis, during which many other organizations were withdrawing.

Under the service packages agreement, Canada undertook two operations: Operation Passage for medical reasons and Operation Scotch for air transport. Operation Passage comprised 200 personnel, largely medical personnel but also including security, support, and engineering staff. Operating near Goma between 25 July and 21 October, some 22,000 patients were checked and treated. Based in Nairobi, Operation Scotch delivered 2,600 metric tons of supplies to Kigali, Goma, and Bujumbura and an additional 6,000 people to and from Kigali.[63]

Soldiers from the Netherlands had been involved in Rwanda since UNOMUR. Under UNAMIR, the Dutch contingent trained and equipped the Zambian contingent. Operating between 4 August and 4 September, the 104-strong Dutch force provided 100 vehicles—split between heavy trucks and light transport—10 mobile kitchens, and electric generators. The military allied with Médecins sans Frontières–Holland and the Dutch NGO Memisa, thereby providing relief to 400,000 refugees in two camps near Goma. Furthermore, Dutch grants to the UNHCR funded meningitis vaccines for 150,000 civilians and supplied other medical and health supplies. The Dutch operation is an apt example of the potential for a "low-profile and gap-filling" method of military humanitarian assistance.[64]

Germany, Australia, and New Zealand provided air transport services. The single-plane New Zealand operation carried 1,750 tons of supplies and 250 passengers in August. Based in Nairobi and Johannesburg, the German operation flew 175 sorties carrying 2,500 tons in total, which included a 300-bed field hospital and 17 water purification plants. Australia also supplied water purification and transport equipment.

Israel and Japan focused primarily on fulfilling medical needs. Named "Operation Interns for Hope," the Israeli Defence Forces mission provided both air transport and medical assistance from 25 July to 31 August. The 100-bed hospital, staffed by 80 medical and support staff, treated 3,000 refugees. Beginning in October, when other countries had already withdrawn, the 260-strong Japanese contingent also contributed sanitation and water purification assistance in Goma. Almost one-half of the troops were specialists.

One of the more unusual contributions came from Ireland. Rather than directly intervening, soldiers and civilians were seconded to the UNHCR and two Irish NGOs. Government personnel predominantly included specialists in the fields of engineering, medicine, logistics, security, communications, and administration. There was an unusual blurring of the cultural divide that typically separates the military and civilian sides of such operations, with documented instances of considerable flexibility between what sometimes have been impenetrable cultures. For example, one of the NGOs (Concern) made use of active-duty soldiers who were out of uniform—or rather, dressed in the NGO "uniform" of a T-shirt with its logo—on the front lines.[65]

Eleven countries also provided assets in response to the UNHCR request for service packages. In many ways, the actions of the Western military forces more closely resembled a UN humanitarian agency or an international humanitarian NGO than strictly military operations. They undertook little that reflected their war-fighting capabilities, although the magnitude and speed of logistics reflected the kinds of capacities that are financed by governments mainly to be in a position to wage war effectively. In response to the Goma crisis, the UNHCR specifically requested that member states provide service packages in a number of fields: airport services, logistics base services, road services and road security, site preparation, provision of domestic fuel, sanitation facilities, water management, and airhead management.[66] The military influx into Goma was also accompanied by the influx of NGOs.

A substantial criticism related to the development of such "service packages" by the UNCHR, which permitted ten donors (and especially the militaries of France, the United States, the Netherlands, Israel, and Ireland) to choose what to provide rather than to provide what humanitarian agencies determined was required. According to Larry Minear and Philippe Guillot:

> Because governments exercised the opportunities to pick and choose among elements of the United Nations to support in this particular crisis, it became arguably more difficult for the world body to attract the full range of assistance needed. Weighing peace-keeping functions in volatile settings against humanitarian support roles, governments in all likelihood committed fewer troops to the tougher security assignments, opting instead for the lower-risk, higher-visibility, and undiluted command and control arrangements the service packages afforded.[67]

UNAMIR II, September 1994–July 1995

One of the more positive contributions of UNAMIR occurred on 22 August. In conjunction with UNREO and the new government of

Rwanda, the UN military successfully assumed control of the southwest following the French withdrawal. Only 50,000 to 70,000 of the 1.4 million IDPs in the zone fled to Bukavu, although speculation earlier had led many to predict several multiples of this figure.

The multifaceted international response had stemmed the crisis within various refugee camps, but no medium- or longer-term solution was even under discussion. In September, UNREO estimated that there were "2,129,200 Rwandans in neighboring countries with: 1,332,200 in Zaire, 510,000 in Tanzania, 277,000 in Burundi, and 10,000 in Uganda. With some 2 million refugees and about 1.8 million internally displaced persons, almost half of all Rwandans were uprooted by the events of 1994."[68]

In an attempt to reconstruct the judicial system, punish those responsible for the genocide, and end the culture of impunity within Rwanda, the International Criminal Tribunal was created by Security Council Resolution 955 on 8 November 1994. Over 32,000 Rwandans have been arrested and are being held under appalling conditions; few have yet to be tried. Prison conditions that violate international standards have led to further deaths and a host of complaints from human rights organizations.[69]

On 30 November 1994, UNAMIR's mandate was expanded by Resolution 965 to include the protection of UN and other humanitarian personnel. But the overall security situation deteriorated throughout 1995. The former members of the extremist government and its military were playing an increasing role within the camps. They obliged refugees, through either the threat or actual use of force, to remain, and they often controlled the distribution of goods and services within the camps. Indeed, the camps had become a staging ground for renewed civil war.

From January 1995 to April 1996, UNAMIR was phased out. On 9 June 1995, UNAMIR's mandate was reduced, which led to a decrease in troops to 2,330 by 9 September and to 1,800 by 9 October.[70] On 8 March 1996, UNAMIR's mandate expired. The new RPF government argued that the inability in 1994 to stop genocide was indicative of a larger international incapacity to do anything serious about the camps, especially in eastern Zaire. Moreover, the government asserted with some evidence and great conviction that the UN's military presence actually had permitted additional time for the Hutu regime in exile to rearm and prepare to resume the war.

The Costs and Benefits in Review and Conclusion

Table 6.1 summarizes key costs and benefits from the preceding discussion, but the breakdown by period is also of interest. From its inception

Table 6.1 Rwanda: Military Costs and Civilian Benefits from Intervention, 1994–1995

		$ Costs	Casualties/Fatalities		Political Impact
Military costs of intervention for troop-contributing countries		A Total incremental cost: $650M. UNAMIR: $198M. Total humanitarian assistance: $1.3B. Total: $2B.	B 18 fatalities.		C Unilateral commitment of troops is less likely to occur due to cost and domestic political reluctance. However, more of a call for military's logistical utilities rather than security humanitarian organizations.
		Displacement	Suffering		State of the State
Civilian benefits of intervention for targeted countries	Humanitarian challenge before intervention	D 1994: 2M refugees; 1.8M IDPs.	E *Hunger:* N/A. *Human rights:* 1994: 500,000–1M killed due to genocide; 1995: 2,000–8,000 in Kibeho massacre; 250,000–500,000 rape victims. *Health:* 1994: 46,000–63,000 IDPs died due to dysentery; 30,000 due to cholera.		F Following the death of the president, systematic purges of Tutsis and moderate Hutus. Destruction of civil infrastructure and government. "Failed state" on Somalia model.
	Civilian benefits after intervention	D' 200,000 refugees and 147,000 IDPs repatriated.	E' *Hunger:* N/A. *Human rights:* UNAMIR protected 25,000 civilians; Opération Turquoise, 14,000. *Health:* N/A.		F' Displaced populations continue to be a political and economic problem. Still dependent on foreign assistance. Political reconciliation is proceeding slowly at best. Another humanitarian crisis in late 1996.

until September 1994, when it was combined with UNAMIR, UNO-MUR cost merely $2.354 million. Between its authorization on 5 October 1993 and the beginning of genocide in early April, UNAMIR cost $35.3 million; the total cost for operation from the beginning of the crisis in April 1994 to June 1995 was $261.3 million; and the total cost from June to 31 December was $96.68 million.[71] The U.S. share for all UNAMIR activities between 1992 and 1995 was $109.5 million.[72]

The French government has not provided verifiable information concerning Opération Turquoise, but early estimates showed $240 million for sixty days. Before June, the operation had been originally estimated to cost $1 billion, although the figure was later reduced. The actual costs are undoubtedly in between, but most observers judge the actual to have exceeded the estimated $240 million by two or threefold.

According to U.S. Department of Defense estimates, the incremental cost for OSH was $107 million, with an additional $36.4 million in 1995. The disjointed DOD budgetary data lead some observers to speculate that the actual costs may be two to eight times greater than the original estimate.[73] The UN has reimbursed the DOD for $10.6 million at the cost of Operation Support Hope.

Other U.S. authorizations supported humanitarian agencies in the field. In the case of the OFDA, a DART team was also deployed to the region. Altogether, USAID spent $199.1 million between 1992 and 1995, almost half of which was spent in 1994. Costs for U.S. assessments for peacekeeping operations are drawn from the State Department budget, which also authorized some $120 million for support of activities beyond the peacekeeping assessment. The United States spent $573.7 million on peace operations and humanitarian activities in Rwanda between 1992 and 1995.

The total Canadian contribution to the crisis in Rwanda was about $75 million (or $103 million in Canadian dollars [C]), of which C$23 million (C$10 million incremental) was for Operation Passage and C$19 million (C$1 million incremental) for Operation Scotch. Canada spent C$66 million for UNOMUR and UNAMIR (C$27 million incremental). The Japanese military intervention cost $59 million. Although available data for Dutch contributions amount to only $2.25 million, the actual value of the services was considerably more. The military operation from New Zealand cost $1.4 million, with an additional $2 million in governmental humanitarian assistance and $7 million from domestic NGOs. Australian relief was diverse, with $35 million Australian dollars (A) for the UNHCR service package and A$30 million from domestic NGOs. Israel's medical contingent cost $7 million, and there is no public information on Germany's or Ireland's cost.[74] Though the reported incremental cost for the various unilateral missions from June to October was $650 million, the actual figure may have been two to three times higher.[75]

Overall humanitarian assistance, both military and civilian allocations, amounted to a staggering $2 billion in 1994 alone.[76] The majority (60 percent) was devoted to refugees, with the remainder for IDPs. Even more dramatic was the fact that 20 percent of all international emergency assistance in 1994 went to Rwanda, a sum that represented about 3 percent of all official international aid that year.[77]

In terms of expatriate human cost, between October 1993 and March 1996, twenty-six UNAMIR personnel lost their lives—three military observers, twenty-two soldiers and other personnel, and one civilian police.[78] The largest number occurred during the raid upon the Belgian UNAMIR troops, when ten were butchered.

With the lack of international efforts to prevent or respond to the genocide, the fragility of the Rwandan state, and the flux in refugee camps, benefits from the various military and civilian sources can be viewed only as short-term relief. Whether lives saved will be threatened in the future is, as in other cases, a pertinent line of inquiry. UNAMIR's weakness—both its mandate and the physical resources allotted by member states—was obvious. Yet, even actions of the limited force of 500 were noteworthy in protecting some 25,000 civilians from extermination. Due to the initiatives by a variety of NGOs, UN agencies, and military forces, the mortality rate in Goma "dropped sharply from an estimated 6,500 per day on 27 July to less than 500 per day on 6 August."[79] The unilateral military operations, especially OSH, did not occur until after the peak mortality had been reached.

With the overthrow of the Hutu-led interim government by the RPF, the scale of human rights violations decreased but did not disappear; and the conditions in prisons were particularly egregious. The momentum of interethnic violence continued on a reduced scale—predominantly as a government tactic to consolidate political power and eliminate dissent. In order for psychological reconciliation to begin, there must at least be some recognition of responsibility for the genocide. However, the current status of the hearings of the International Criminal Tribunal in Arusha—as of this writing, not a single person has been convicted and adequate documentation to satisfy international standards is nonexistent—does not bode well. Without investments in both data gathering and prosecution, the tribunal is stillborn.

Although the substantial lifesaving efforts in 1994 and 1995 are hardly negligible, it is noteworthy that the really substantial repatriation of two million refugees began in late 1996, not as a result of UN-sanctioned intervention, but when Tutsi guerrillas attacked the infamous Hutu camps in what was then eastern Zaire. Aided by neighboring countries (especially Uganda and the new RPF government in Rwanda) and by the overall weakness of Mobutu Sese Seko's crumbling regime, Laurent Kabila's forces liberated the refugees and chased war criminals. This military campaign, and the subsequent takeover of what was renamed the Congo, was not without abuse and violence. However, the solution to the problems resulting from the exodus of Hutus in 1994 was closer than relying upon largely rhetorical international effort, including the aborted Canadian-led proposal for a multilateral force that had been on the Security Council's docket since autumn 1996.

Fostering a secure environment, the military's clear comparative advantage for which there is no substitute, was dwarfed by its logistics efforts in Rwanda in the eye of the genocidal storm. The military's cautious standard operating procedures, accompanied by widespread concerns among governments about a possible quagmire, paralyzed international military responses for two months while as many as 10 percent of all Rwandan's were murdered and what has been estimated as at least 250,000 women were raped[80]—clearly the most tragic human rights abuses documented in the cases under study. It can be argued, however, that Opération Turquoise probably prevented another refugee crisis of the record-setting magnitude of the one in Goma, when almost one million refugees appeared virtually overnight accompanied by a cholera epidemic and widespread dysentery that killed what is variously estimated to be between 50,000 and 80,000 people.

The military thus was more successful in doing what civilians normally do better, namely, providing direct assistance to some four million people in need. The various forces delivered massive quantities of food (some 270 metric tons in 1994 alone), clothing, medicine, shelter, and water. As a report of the Joint Evaluation of Emergency Assistance to Rwanda concluded:

> Widespread starvation did not occur. For the refugees and many of the IDPs the food and supply system, dominated by [the] WFP and to a lesser extent the ICRC, was vital to their survival and performed well. Given the magnitude and the scale of the population movements and the distance of the beneficiary populations from coastal ports, this was a substantial achievement.[81]

Outside armed forces thus made essential contributions by using their logistical and organizational resources, but only *after* the genocide had occurred. The most obvious and prevalent criticism was that political authorities did not authorize the military to use its comparative advantage to halt the carnage.

A French soldier protecting a camp in Gikongoro.
Credit: UN PHOTO 187769/J. Isaac

Two other concluding observations are pertinent here. First, it is not without irony that rapid military action in April proved totally unfeasible, but the costs of the genocide, massive displacement, and a ruined economy (including decades of wasted development assistance and outside investment) were borne almost immediately afterward by the same governments that had refused to respond militarily a few weeks earlier. In the estimations of the Joint Evaluation:

> April–December 1994 relief operation cost about $1.4 billion with 85 percent coming from governments and official sources, and 15 percent from private sources. Of the government funds, 50 percent came from the US/EU, and 50 percent was channeled through the UN (85 percent of this money went to UNHCR and WFP which further channeled the money to NGOs. The ICRC was responsible for 17 percent of all flows.[82]

Second, total costs and benefits are especially thorny in light of such considerations as opportunity costs and diminishing availabilities of public funds for development. UNAMIR's expenditures averaged about $15 million per month, with military fatalities of twenty-six. The figure for the French two-month effort is officially about $250 million, and the American incremental costs for the same period "totaled at least $650 million, although they may have exceeded that amount by a factor of two or three."[83]

The vast bulk was channeled to maintaining refugees in asylum countries rather than their repatriation or assistance to the new government. The multidonor Joint Evaluation by some fifty-three experts questioned the allocation of resources in the following way: "Thus in those instances where military aircraft operated over the same routes as functioning road transport routes, such as between Entebbe and Goma, the use of military aircraft to carry cargoes that could have traveled by road was between 20 and 40 times more expensive."[85]

Rwanda illustrates, probably better than any of the other cases discussed herein, that media coverage may elicit humanitarian responses even if it is insufficient to provoke timely and robust military ones. When gruesome enough images appear in the media, cost savings become less of a preoccupation than in the daily bill-of-fare of parliamentary cost cutting. There is evidence that many wealthier societies, particularly those of the West, are viscerally and ethically unable to ignore massive tragedies, even though the initial reaction may be to do nothing. There are fewer risks for politicians from humanitarian assistance, however costly and inefficient, than from early preventive action by military forces with possible casualties or the potential for protracted involvement in a civil war.

In the spring of 1998, Bill Clinton was the first American president to visit Africa in two decades. After arriving in Kigali some four years after the tragedy described in this chapter, the president stated:

> The international community, together with nations in Africa, must bear its share of responsibility for this tragedy, as well. We did not act quickly enough after the killing began. We should not have allowed the refugee camps to become safe haven for the killers. We did not immediately call these crimes by their rightful name: genocide.[86]

The irony in these remarks is noteworthy because Washington specifically had opposed action in Rwanda in the first place, fearing that the risks outweighed the potential rewards. The decision then was codified in PDD-25, which limited American participation in peace operations. The president subsequently even told the General Assembly that the United Nations had to learn "when to say no." It would be wishful thinking to imagine that the president and the infamous "international community" had learned the lesson and now were prepared "to say yes."

7

Haiti, 1991–1996: Why Wait So Long?

Haiti has struggled against domestic despots and outside interference since winning independence from France in 1804. Particularly throughout the twentieth century, it has suffered alternatively from U.S. military and economic interventions and neglect, a fact that ironically is replicated in microcosm in the case of military-civilian interactions in this chapter.

During the period of crisis under review, from 1991 to 1996, and especially after 1993, Haiti had all the attributes—in particular, massive migration and human rights abuse, as well as a devastated economy—of countries that have suffered from violent armed conflicts. It was also the target of international coercive actions, such as economic and military sanctions under Chapter VII of the UN Charter that resemble those in the other war-torn countries analyzed in this volume. Moreover, the basis for outside intervention in this case was the restoration of a democratically elected government; this precedent has crucial implications because of its potentially widespread relevance for international responses elsewhere.

Although Haiti did not really endure a civil war in the 1990s, there is still much to be learned from recent experience concerning civilian-military interactions. The historical background to the crises in this decade provides an appropriate way to examine what turns out to be another case in which the benefits to civilians substantially outweigh the costs of the outside military intervention.

Map 7.1 Haiti

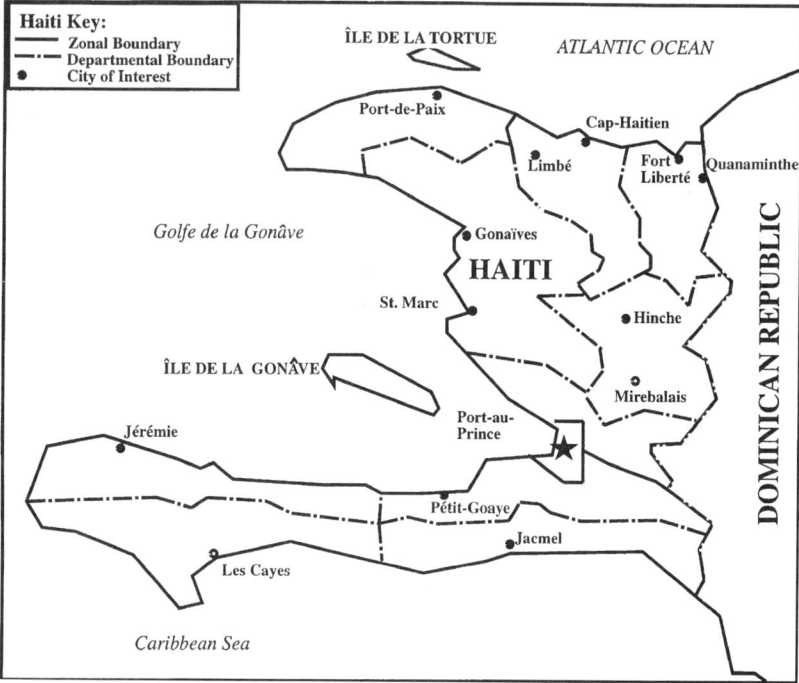

Haiti has a population of 6,611,407 (1997), and its capital is Port-au-Prince. It is located in the western part of the island of Hispaniola in the northern Caribbean Sea; the Dominican Republic occupies the eastern part of the island. Haiti's total land area is 10,714 square miles (slightly larger than Maryland), with 1,100 miles of coastline and 20 percent arable land. Main exports are light manufactures, coffee, and other agriculture.

Background and the Roots of the Conflict

As is shown later, the two-year economic sanctions and embargoes imposed on Haiti led to the further erosion of human rights and the overall quality of life for the vast majority of the Haitian populace. However, even before the September 1991 coup against the elected government of Jean-Bertrand Aristide that provides the point of departure for the case here, Haiti's economy had stagnated for almost two centuries.[1] How did what was once considered France's richest colony become one of the poorest countries in the world and the poorest in the Americas? According to one observer, three factors account for Haiti's underdevelopment: "the interaction between the growth of the population and soil erosion; the lack of technological progress in agriculture (which is where the vast majority of the population earn their living); and the predatory nature of the governments which have ruled the country for more than one and a half centuries."[2] This chapter emphasizes the third factor while taking into account the other two.

An old Haitian adage states, "Constitutions are paper, bayonets are steel,"[3] an apt and succinct summary of the political atmosphere in Haiti since 1804. Haitian history is characterized by short presidencies, failed reform, corruption, violent conflict, and the eventual deposition either by force or by the voluntary exile of the past leader. There have been forty-one leaders since independence and not a single democratic transition until 1996.

Whether internally by the use of coups or internationally by invasion, political change normally has occurred through the use of military force—as it did again in 1994, through the U.S.-led military intervention to restore the first democratically elected government. Force has also been used to create what has been called a "phantom-predator" state, in which the few control the majority of resources while the many eke out a harsh daily existence largely as subsistence farmers. The state provided virtually no services, other than repression and taxation. The purpose of the military—which in other countries normally defends its citizens from outside aggression—was designed in this Caribbean island only to repress internal opposition.

In 1804, following a twelve-year slave rebellion against the French authorities led by Toussaint-Louverture, Haiti became the second colony in the Western Hemisphere to gain its independence. While the grassroots upheaval was greeted initially with optimism by the country's inhabitants, the economic and political isolation—especially by the United States and other colonial powers—quickly emphasized to Haitians the consequences of rebellion. The fear was that the slave rebellion would proliferate and affect similar slave-based economies in the Caribbean and the American South. Indeed, Haiti was not recognized by the United States until 1862, after the Emancipation Proclamation. French recognition came at an even steeper price in 1825, 125 million francs to be exact, which served as an indemnity for the colony's loss.[4]

Yet, the departure of the French slave owners did not eliminate the legacy of colonialism and hierarchial rule. Instead, it was replaced by a new form of internal repression. The first few decades of independence saw the emergence of the two factions that have alternatively cooperated and competed, often violently, until the present day: the military and the economic elite.

The invasion by the United States in 1915 was justified to counter largely German and European military, political, and economic ambitions in Haiti.[5] Although the occupation contributed to the modernization of Haiti with the construction of roads, health services, sanitation, and additional infrastructure, other results were more ambiguous. Forced labor was used to increase the wealth of the occupiers and the elite. Furthermore, not only did infrastructure extend the reach of the state, but the repressive arm itself was strengthened when Washington built a well-organized, disciplined, trained, and equipped military, known as the Garde d'Haiti, the name of which was subsequently changed to the Forces Armées d'Haiti (FAdH).

Following almost two decades of occupation by the United States, the local military began to play in 1934 a more active role in Haitian politics. However, until 1947, the United States still exercised a kind of authority by ensuring that a president of its own liking was in power. François "Papa Doc" Duvalier, a former black nationalist leader, assumed power in 1957 through an election in which he received the majority of votes under questionable circumstances. Though it temporarily ended the cycle of what seemed endless coups, his fourteen-year presidency was characterized by repression of dissent, personal consolidation of power, and purges of the military and the economic elite. In 1964, the legislature declared him president for life. After his death in 1971, the title passed to his son, Jean Claude, "Baby Doc."

During the Duvalier regime, the state's primary organizational structure was the military. For administrative and enforcement purposes, the country was divided into nine departments, each of which was further subdivided into districts and subdistricts.[6] These were then separated into 565 sections, with leaders of each exercising complete control over the lives of the population in his (never her) section. According to Robert Maguire, "they have been the police and have served as judge, jury, executioner, and extortioner in their realm. In other words, section chiefs exercised the power to arrest, fine, sentence, imprison, tax, torture, and otherwise arbitrarily control those within their jurisdiction."[7] To counterbalance the power of the military and to further terrorize the population, a paramilitary group was established known as the *"tontons macoutes."* The predatory power of the state was also furthered by yet another source of violence, the so-called *attachés*, who were associated with both the *tontons macoutes* and the section chiefs.

Washington supported both Duvaliers as part of Cold War Caribbean policy to prevent the spread of communism and to politically and economically isolate Cuba. Baby Doc received further assistance during the Carter administration by pledging to achieve better governance and human rights standards. In the 1980s, U.S. foreign assistance declined from $43.5 million in 1983 to $34 million in 1985, and still further to $26 million the following year, as human rights abuse continued.[8] The provision of economic and development aid had entrenched privileged elites.

Slowly, however, the number of grassroots and self-help organizations increased and was coupled with the emergence of a small middle class, whose interests often clashed with the traditional Haitian elite. Eventually, the combination of the decline in foreign aid, the loss of support from the business elite, and mass demonstrations resulted in a coup that ended with Baby Doc's flight on a U.S. Air Force jet to southern France, where he still resides.

The end of the reign by the Duvaliers in 1986 unleashed fear and mass migration of Haitians, some illegally and others legally. Members of the Haitian elite fled repression by Duvalier by going to Paris, Montreal, and New York. However, illegal migration by poor Haitians proved to be more politically sensitive in the United States. The flight of 13,500 Haitians between January and October 1980 prompted the joint 1981 U.S. Haitian Interdiction Agreement. This agreement allowed the U.S. Coast Guard to intercept and repatriate all illegal Haitian refugees and the United States to screen all refugees to ensure that they had not migrated for political purposes. These actions were reinforced by the 1980 U.S. Refugee Act that reiterates distinctions between economic and political refugees. Haitian refugees were normally characterized as economic refugees, while displacement from neighboring Cuba was considered political. This agreement led to the interception and return of 22,716 illegal Haitians from 1981 to 1991.[9] Between them, the "Boeing people" and the "boat people" created a Haitian diaspora numbering about one million.

Following the military coup against Baby Doc, the ranking military officer, General Henri Namphy, assumed control of the government through a civilian-military junta, the National Council of Government. The new constitution was approved in 1987 but not put into effect until 1990. It included provisions for the election of a bicameral Parliament, mayors, administrators, and a president. The president, with the Parliament's consent, had the power to appoint the prime minister, cabinet ministers, and the Supreme Court.[10] The human rights situation in post-Duvalier Haiti hardly improved, as pointed out by the Inter-American Commission on Human Rights. Attempts to create political and social change in 1987 were thwarted by political violence, including the massacre of 200 peasants at Jean-Rabel by government forces.[11] Following a further series of military coups, Ertha Pascal-Trouillot was sworn in as provisional president until the political elections of 1990.

Haiti's economic situation remained basically unchanged. Before the

1991 coup, GDP per capita had been declining by 2 percent per year.[12] Tremendous income disparities had also formed a consistent pattern in Haiti. For example, by the early 1980s, 1 percent of Haiti's population controlled 55 percent of its GNP. A 1984 study estimated that 75 percent of the population lived in absolute poverty, which may have been an underestimation. Furthermore, the limited economic progress made during the Duvalier regime quickly deteriorated following their ouster. From 1986 to July 1995, 28,000 jobs were lost in the assembly sector.[13] The life expectancy in 1990 was fifty-four years; 9.4 percent of children died in their first year; only 41.7 percent of the population had ready access to drinking water; only 47 percent were literate; 7 percent of children aged between three and fifty-nine months and 10.7 percent between twelve and twenty-three months were at risk of death due to malnutrition. These are the poorest overall statistics in the Western Hemisphere.[14]

The country also has had rapid population growth, rural to urban migration, and deforestation (97 percent of the country). Massive soil erosion has resulted, which reduced dramatically the farmland production on which the bulk (at least 70 percent) of the population depend for their existence. Underemployment and declining standards of living in rural ares have led to migration to urban areas in search of employment in the manufacturing sector. Slums, the most important of which is Cité Soleil in Port-au-Prince, serve as centers of social instability and violence.

The daily struggle has been deepened by the AIDS pandemic.[15] According to a detailed 1989 survey, 14,000 Haitians already were HIV positive, but only 20 percent of HIV cases were reported even then. Since the early 1980s, the dreaded disease has evolved from primarily afflicting men to afflicting a growing number of women—40 percent of all AIDS cases—and children. This issue is doubly complicated by the sexual histories of Haitian women. A recent survey revealed that out of a control group of about 1,000 individuals, almost half (45 percent) had first sexual experiences that were nonconsensual.

The 1991 Elections and the Onset of the Crisis

In 1991, the first democratic elections occurred in Haiti. Both the Organization of American States (OAS) and the United Nations declared them to be generally "free and fair." UN involvement was supported by General Assembly Resolution 45/2 of 10 October 1990, which had created the UN Observer Group for the Verification of Elections in Haiti.

Haiti, 1991–1996

Haitians take to the streets of Port-au-Prince to celebrate the election of Father Aristide. Credit: UN PHOTO 177258/Milton Grant

Jean-Bertrand Aristide, a populist priest who had been dismissed from the Silesian order in 1988 for his vocal political engagement and opposition to the government, won 67 percent of the vote. Over three million Haitians had registered their support for the platform of "transparency, participation, and justice." Although Aristide had been given a clear mandate for political change, the main victors in legislative elections ironically were supporters of the economic and military elite.

Washington's traditional support for reform by moderate political groups rather than more radical grassroots organizations continued after Aristide's election. Some parts of the U.S. government, most notably the DOD and the Central Intelligence agency (CIA), provided both monetary and political support for opposition parties and "democracy by elites." They later were the base for the coup in 1991, which was not the first attempt to push Aristide from power. Almost immediately following his election, Roger Lafontant, the former minister of the interior and a Duvalierist, attempted to hold interim President Pascal-Trouillot hostage. However, the people of Haiti quickly demonstrated and, with the surprising support of the military, halted the attempted coup.

Aristide's policies and presidency between February and September 1991 have been the subject of considerable analysis. International lending institutions quickly provided the Aristide regime with $511 million in grants and loans, but he was immediately condemned for "cronyism" and placing associates in positions of authority. His decision to retire senior military officers and to discuss civilian control of the army and the police led to predictable opposition from the well-entrenched elite who also felt threatened by his explicit and implicit references to income redistribution. Other policy proposals included moves to end corruption, elimination of the section chiefs, and attempts to punish political and military leaders who had been involved in past human rights abuses. There were excesses by his populist followers, including some much-publicized and brutal retaliations against the former forces of order (or disorder in the case of the *tontons macoutes*). The forced repatriation of Haitian refugees from the Dominican Republic in July 1991 also intensified economic pressures.

On 29 September 1991, military forces led by General Raoul Cédras, commander and chief of the FAdH, overthrew Aristide in a violent coup. Aristide fled initially to Venezuela and eventually to Washington. The crisis resulted in human rights abuses by the regime,[16] the flight of refugees and displaced persons, substantial humanitarian dislocation created by economic sanctions, and later the forceful repatriation of the refugees by the Bush and Clinton administrations.[17]

Data about human rights violations by what became known as the "de facto regime" are difficult to gauge because of irregular geographic coverage by human rights monitors, the use of small paramilitary groups, and the isolation and subsequent lack of information about rural areas. The most accurate information covers those periods when the OAS and other human rights monitors were present, and their coverage was far better in urban than in rural areas.

Although Haiti's history has consistently been marked by repression of opposition parties and of the poor, the human rights violations following the coup were unprecedented. The de facto government quickly moved to eliminate Aristide's supporters, the Lavallassiens. The first day after the coup, ten radio stations were destroyed. Scores of Aristide's supporters were reportedly killed immediately following the coup, with the total number killed estimated to be 300 to 500.[18] Methods included brutal beatings, torture, disappearances, execution without trial, corruption, extortion, gang rape, assassination, mutilation, and the destruction of property.

International Responses Prior to Military Intervention

The Initial UN/OAS Response

The Organization of American States condemned the coup on the day it took place.[19] On 3 October, the "Organization's Ministers for Foreign Affairs . . . adopted a resolution demanding his [Aristide's] immediate replacement, and recommending the economic, financial, and diplomatic isolation of the military regime, and the cessation of all non-humanitarian aid."[20] An additional resolution passed on 8 October included a variety of other provisions stressing the illegitimacy of the de facto regime and created a civilian mission to work toward the reestablishment of democracy and to facilitate Aristide's return to power. The basis for these resolutions was the Santiago Commitment to Democracy and the Renewal of the Inter-American System and a resolution on representative democracy, both signed in 1991. These agreements, in a significant departure for a region that has traditionally been extremely hostile to outside interference of any type, especially when spearheaded by Washington, called for appropriate action by the OAS in the event that the democratic process was interrupted in a "sudden or irregular manner."

UN Security Council actions were neither as rapid nor as vigorous, largely due to the widespread unease among many developing countries that such action would set a precedent concerning intervention in the name of democracy and human rights. Although the Security Council failed initially to take collective action aside from a statement by the president condemning the coup, the UN General Assembly passed a resolution on 11 October that supported the return of Aristide and called for Security Council support of OAS actions.[21]

In February 1992, the OAS, Aristide, and members of the Haitian Senate and Chamber of Deputies met to negotiate and sign the Protocol of Washington, the goal of which was Aristide's return. The de facto government decried the protocol as unconstitutional. Another OAS resolution followed on 17 May that sought to monitor the embargo and attempted to punish those naval vessels that broke it by denying them future access to other port facilities in the region. The embargo would prove to be porous[22] because the OAS lacks enforcement mechanisms to ensure compliance and is prevented from doing so by the UN Charter.[23] Furthermore, in November, the U.S. legislature passed an exemption to the embargo for U.S.-owned manufacturing companies in Haiti.

Also in November, UN Secretary-General Boutros Boutros-Ghali appointed Dante Caputo as his special envoy. President Aristide requested, and subsequently the UN and the OAS agreed to deploy, the International Civilian Mission in Haiti, or the MICIVIH, an acronym based on its French name, the Mission Civile Internationale en Haiti, in order to monitor human rights abuses by the de facto authorities. The UN contributed 200 staff to the mission, including 133 human rights monitors; and the OAS contributed an additional 133 observers.[24] The first human rights report from the mission was released on 3 June 1993. This effort illustrated a growing cooperation between the universal and the regional body.[25]

The presence of an international human rights mission documented violations, but the oppressive practices of the Cédras regime increased throughout 1993. By April 1993, an estimated 3,000 Haitians had been killed since the coup in September 1991.[26] Between June and August 1993, there were more than 300 cases of arbitrary arrest largely due to "the attempts of the victims to exercise their right to freedom of expression: distribution of pamphlets, putting up posters or attempting to organize and participate in pro-Aristide demonstrations."[27]

UN Economic Sanctions

Despite UN and OAS actions, the restoration of democracy was largely at an impasse. The de facto regime had held Senate elections and placed a new president, Emile Jonaissant, in power, but the results were rejected as invalid by the community of states. Following a request by Aristide's government in exile, the Security Council passed Resolution 841 on 16 June, which, under Chapter VII of the UN Charter, imposed an arms and fuel embargo; it also froze all government funds and those of the de facto regime.

Economic sanctions exacerbated local conditions. It is widely acknowledged that sanctions often harm vulnerable groups more than they alter the policy of the target government. In Haiti, the poor were forced to cope with the health and hunger-based effects of the sanctions, while elites maintained, or in many cases improved, their standards of living. Once sanctions come into effect, anything that can be smuggled has a premium price, and the people best equipped to set up smuggling operations—in terms of overseas contacts, access to paramilitary protection, transportation, and border controls—are the very elites whose position the sanctions are trying to undermine. Far from causing harm, then, sanctions provide a lucrative way of making money. Nonetheless, Haitians as well as the exiled Aristide regime supported their imposition as one of the few international efforts that appeared feasible in order to help facilitate the return of the democratically elected government.

The precise impact of sanctions on civilian suffering has been questioned because of the poor statistical base.[28] Cesar Chelala argues that the sanctions "accelerated the critical situation in the country and ... had serious consequences for the already low healthy status and quality of life of the Haitian people."[29] The same report estimates that 60 percent of children below the age of five are malnourished, with 3 percent severely so. The number of under-five children moderately and severely malnourished increased by 100,000 between 1991 and 1994.[30] In 1993, according to a report by a Harvard team—controversial because the baseline data were so poor that the conclusions seemed suspicious—the impact of the sanctions led to an estimated 1,000 excess child deaths per month.[31] Also, as an indirect result of the sanctions, the number of cases of pulmonary tuberculosis, malaria, pneumonia, and typhoid increased. Furthermore, the "incidence of mental illness is believed to have increased because of the climate of social and political instability, violence, and the rise in the use of drugs."[32]

Beyond the human suffering caused by the sanctions, they further crippled the economy. GDP fell 20 percent between 1992 and 1993, and an additional 10.6 percent in 1994.[33] Moreover, the "government's deficit widened, trade fell sharply, the gourde [the country's currency] plummeted, and unemployment climbed to 75 percent."[34]

Between 50,000 to 70,000 jobs were lost in the Haitian formal sector.[35] Especially affecting food and fuel, the prices of goods, known in Haitian Creole as *"lavi ché,"* increased at times by 100 percent during the period of the sanctions.[36]

Haitian Boat People and U.S. Foreign Policy

In response to the violent campaign of the de facto regime against Aristide's supporters and other Haitians, an estimated 300,000 people were internally displaced. This was known as the process of *marronage*, during which those who feared repression continually moved from one area to another, whether from urban to rural or vice versa.[37] According to Chelala, this migration resulted in the further spread of AIDS among the population.[38] An estimated 60,000 to 100,000 refugees fled Haiti by small craft for the shores of Florida and the Dominican Republic between 1991 and 1994.[39]

The policy of the Bush, and subsequently of the Clinton administration, toward these boat people has been condemned by a variety of groups because it violated international human rights and refugee law. Initially, the Bush administration summarily returned refugees without an interview. However, this policy was suspended by a lower court, and the refugees were brought to a holding site, where they were to be screened. Between November 1991 and April 1992, refugees were interdicted by the U.S. Coast Guard and taken to Guantánamo Bay, Cuba, where a Joint Task Force had been established. The population ranged from 3,000 to 12,000 and were 75 percent male. At the camp, 35 percent had malaria, 9 percent tuberculosis, 6 percent measles, 5 percent syphilis, and 7 percent were HIV positive.[40] Over the period of its existence, the JTF provided medical care to some 18,000 of these migrants. Between September and November, some 38,000 refugees were interdicted, with 26,000 returned and 10,500–12,000 refugees granted asylum in the United States.[41] Of those granted asylum, 200 HIV-positive Haitian refugees were forcefully kept in the Guantánamo camps. After being kept at these camps for two years, a court order condemned this practice and allowed the refugees to enter the United States.

In February 1992, the U.S. Supreme Court overruled the lower court and supported forced repatriation. This was followed by President Bush's order on 24 May 1992, which stated that all Haitian refugees would be immediately returned to Haiti without a screening process. Estimates of the total number of Haitians interdicted and returned vary considerably. According to Patrick Costello, between September 1991 and 1993, 53,375 refugees were interdicted and returned.[42] Amnesty International has issued a lower figure, with 31,938 returned in the first nine months following the coup and only 7,832 between May 1992 and 1994.[43] Costello's figure is widely accepted and used here.

The in-country processing procedure was created in Haiti as part of the Bush order to offer political asylum to those with a legitimate fear of oppression. However, this procedure was fraught with problems: Haitians applying for asylum became the target of further attack; and the procedure was slow because of the large number of applicants, estimated at 55,000. In any case, most applicants were rejected. The consequences after such a turndown often were further ill treatment by the de facto regime, including torture and in a few cases execution.

The Civilian Response

Prior to the coup, there were two varieties of action by NGOs: providing emergency relief, which necessarily involved working with the elite; or striving for economic, social, and political change through small-scale development activities. Many critics argue persuasively that such international humanitarian aid had "no impact and no sustainability" on the overall lives of the massive Haitian poor.[44]

Although some humanitarian organizations evacuated personnel after the coup, many UN agencies and NGOs sought to alleviate the humanitarian crisis but were faced with internal and external problems that hampered their ability to ease suffering. The sanctions and embargo on fuel and other necessary items also complicated their efforts; these items were simply not available without violating the embargo or dealing with smugglers. These organizations often were forced to enrich the very people who were the source of suffering in the first place. They did not want to recognize the legitimacy of the de facto government by communicating with officials, but they also required government approval to carry out activities. Ironically, other necessary items, such as housing and warehouse space, could be rented only from the elite who had opposed Aristide and supported the coup.

In March 1993, the UN issued a $62.7 million interagency consolidated appeal for the main UN agencies involved in Haiti: the UNDP, UNICEF, the UNHCR, the Pan American Health Organization (PAHO, an affiliate of WHO), the FAO, and the WFP.[45] However, only $9.6 million materialized, and agencies were obliged to rely on their own funds but were alternately unable to cover the shortfall. By September 1994, these agencies were providing 940,000 Haitians with food and improving water supply and sanitation. In order to eliminate the effects of the fuel sanctions on humanitarian agencies, between January and September 1994, PAHO provided 1.2 million gallons of diesel fuel and 206,000 gallons of gasoline to aid organizations.[46] According to one group of analysts, "the Haitian crisis showed UN humanitarian agencies in their most uncoordinated and least effective light," although some NGOs proved to be effective in providing food and shelter to the internally displaced fleeing oppression.[47] The lack of consensus about helping or isolating Haiti made the task of humanitarians impossible.

Governors Island Agreement

Despite the negative humanitarian and economic impact of the sanctions, they drew the de facto leaders to the bargaining table. The result was the Governors Island Agreement of 3 July 1993, which included provisions for the return of Aristide, the lifting of sanctions, the retirement of Cédras, the presence of 1,000 UN blue helmets to ensure the modernization of the army and the separation of the police from the army, and the nomination of a prime minister. The agreement was harshly criticized by many because coup leaders were given amnesty and permitted to remain in Haiti, where they would be able to threaten democracy. Sanctions were immediately lifted by the Security Council as part of the agreement when Robert Malval, Aristide's appointed prime minister, assumed office in July 1993. Such optimism proved illfounded.

As the deadline for the transfer of power from the Cédras regime was approaching, human rights abuse dramatically increased. This was facilitated by the creation of the Front Révolutionnaire pour l'Advancement et le Progrès en Haïti (FRAPH) in 1993, which was closely associated with the military and the former Duvalier regime and which would later be renamed Front Armée du Peuple Haitien. Not only did FRAPH consist of many former *attachés*, but it also assumed many of their duties. There are also well-substantiated allegations that the CIA had close working contact with FRAPH and used this group to help undermine and discredit Aristide and his supporters.[48] In a dramatic example of FRAPH's impunity and power, on 11 September, Antoine Izmery, a businessman and close associate and supporter of Aristide, was dragged from a church and executed outside by FRAPH members and *attachés*.

A most stunning example of the failure of international commitments was the USS *Harlan County* debacle.[49] The initial deployment of the UN Mission in Haiti (UNMIH) forces, which included 200 U.S. soldiers, was to occur on 11 October. However, an angry mob of armed *attachés* was demonstrating at the dock in Port-au-Prince. In a solitary decision that reflected the ongoing collective trauma in Somalia, U.S. authorities ordered the *Harlan County* to withdraw. Not surprisingly, political violence increased, including the 14 October assassination of Guy Malary, Aristide's justice minister. As a result of attacks and growing instability, the MICIVIH was evacuated on 16 October. With the reputation of the UN once again on the line, between 13 and 16 October 1993, the Security Council not only reimposed sanctions, but also added a naval blockade. Under the OAS and the earlier UN sanctions and embargo, the flow of goods had been hindered but not prevented. By May 1994, the more effective naval blockade consisted of eight U.S. Ships, one Canadian, one Dutch, and one Argentine.[50] Through the naval blockade and the establishment of a Dominican border monitoring mission—known as the "Military Observer Group" and comprised of U.S. and Canadian troops—the sanctions became far more effective, if not airtight.

Humanitarian problems continued for the poor, although the temporary respite from sanctions had allowed the regime to replenish its supplies.[51] In a raid by government forces on 27 December 1993, between 250 to 1,000 houses were burned in Cité Soleil. There is no accurate assessment of casualties, with reports varying from dozens to as many as seventy.[52]

U.S. Policy Reversal

President Clinton harshly criticized the Bush administration's Haitian policy during the 1992 election campaign, but he continued to return all refugees after being inaugurated in January 1993. Repercussions against returned Haitians continued. For example, between January and May 1994, 139 of the 904 Haitian migrants returned were arrested on the dock.[53] This reversal seemed part of a pattern of presidential indecisiveness; other 180-degree changes included the reversals of the announced policies in Bosnia and gays in the military. Aristide increasingly was in a position to condemn U.S. inconsistencies to the media and to other policymakers. Exasperated with the lack of progress, Aristide rescinded the 1981 U.S. Haitian Interdiction Agreement. Largely due to pressure, including the hunger strike of African-American activist Randall Robinson and efforts by the Congressional Black Caucus, Clinton eventually eliminated the prior policy of immediate forced repatriation. He replaced it with a policy that brought the refugees to Jamaica in order to determine whether they were political or economic migrants. Due to the overwhelming response by the refugees, the "safe haven" policy emerged, which involved bringing the refugees to the Guantánamo Bay military base. By early August, 16,000 Haitians had taken refuge at Guantánamo; and 29,417 refugees were interdicted and brought to the base.[54] This exodus further pressured the Clinton administration.

The media portrayal of Aristide, his Lavalas movement, and the de facto regime evolved along with U.S. policy. At first, Aristide was harshly criticized, while the military leaders where viewed more favorably. During this period, the primary focus of the American media was on the plight of the boat people. Until the Governors Island Agreement collapsed, Aristide was depicted as intransigent and Cédras as conciliatory. A dramatic shift in media portrayal occurred in mid-1994, following the USS *Harlan County* incident and the increase in human rights violations reported in part by the MICIVIH. Throughout the crisis, human rights organizations played an important role as the primary pressure groups on U.S. and international policy.[55]

A Solution Approaches

Human rights violations increased at a particularly alarming rate between January and July 1994. There were reports of 296 homicides,

91 cases of enforced disappearance, and 66 rapes between 31 January and 31 May 1994, most in Port-au-Prince.[56] Amnesty International estimates that an additional 54 homicides occurred between early June and July.[57] There were reports of entire villages being massacred. Assassinations, including that of another politically engaged clergyman, Father Jean-Marie Vincent, and disappearances increased. Many corpses were left in the streets to terrorize further the population. Those who were not executed were often subjected to extreme prison conditions and torture, of which a primary example is the prison in Les Cayes and its commander Norelus Mandelus, who personally committed atrocities.[58] During a raid on a shantytown in March 1994, "some 40 women were reportedly raped, including an 8-year-old girl and a 55-year-old woman. In only one instance was the victim raped by fewer than three men."[59] On 22 April 1994, members of the FAdH, FRAPH, and *attachés* killed twenty to fifty civilians in Raboteau.

On 11 July, the MICIVIH was forced to evacuate its posts in Haiti for a second time by the de facto government, after it had temporarily returned six months earlier in late January. During this period, the monitoring group had become increasingly aggressive in its reporting, and its expulsion was sharply condemned by the OAS and the Security Council.

The debate about the utility of military intervention continued. On 31 July 1994, the Security Council passed Resolution 940, which, under the provisions for coercion of Chapter VII of the UN Charter, authorized the creation of the U.S.-led Multinational Force (MNF), or the Pentagon's Operation Restore Democracy. As Haiti was "a threat to international peace and security," the operation was authorized to use "all necessary means to facilitate the departure from Haiti of the military leadership, consistent with the Governors Island Agreement, the prompt return of the legitimately elected President and the restoration of the legitimate authorities . . . and to establish and maintain a secure and stable environment that will permit implementation of the Governors Island Agreement."

China and Brazil abstained from the vote even though the resolution's language stressed the unique situation and response. There were numerous reasons why it took so long to extract a response from the Security Council. But the Chinese and Brazilian abstentions highlight the disagreement among member states about intervention on the basis of democratization and human rights. Humanitarian intervention on behalf of civilians being deprived of access to relief is already controversial enough, on behalf of human rights victims it is more so, and on behalf of a democratically elected government it is even more controversial. Issues of sovereignty and domestic jurisdiction have hardly disappeared, although the nature of political and ethical considerations remains in flux.[60]

The MNF would be followed by the UNMIH, which was a Chapter VI peacekeeping, rather than a Chapter VII enforcement, operation and was mandated to "assist in sustaining the secure and stable environment established during the multinational phase; . . . assist in the professionalization of the Haitian armed forces and the creation of a separate police force; . . . [and] assist the legitimate constitutional authorities of Haiti in establishing an environment conducive to the organization of free and fair legislative elections." The mistake in the Governors Island Agreement was not repeated in Resolution 940 because sanctions would not be lifted until Aristide had reassumed his position as president within the country.

This resolution was followed by two attempts at creating a diplomatic solution to the political crisis. The first attempt prior to the intervention in August was a failure, when the de facto leadership refused to meet with UN emissary Caputo. The second was on 17 September, within hours of the imminent intervention by the MNF force, when President Clinton sent three representatives—former President Jimmy Carter, chairman of the Joint Chiefs Colin Powell, and Senator Sam Nunn—to Haiti in a last-ditch effort to negotiate a peaceful solution. The result was an agreement that granted amnesty to the coup leaders if they left Haiti, lifted economic sanctions when Aristide returned, called for the cooperation of the FAdH with the MNF, and provided for legislative elections. Only Carter and Jonaissant signed the agreement; neither Aristide nor a representative of the UN was part of the process.

Although "consent" of sorts emerged from the last-minute agreement negotiated between the de facto military authorities and the U.S. delegation headed by Jimmy Carter, the willingness to authorize and use force was an essential part of military and diplomatic calculations and tactics with important lessons for the future. The actual use of force proved unnecessary, but deterrence requires credibility and a demonstrated willingness to make good on Chapter VII coercive threats. The MNF's willingness to use overwhelming military force is crucial for the following analysis.

Military Intervention: Costs and Benefits

In an ironic twist, U.S. military forces were returning to Haiti to confront institutions that they had helped to nurture there. According to President Clinton, the purpose of U.S. intervention was to "protect our interests, to stop the brutal atrocities that threaten . . . Haitians, to se-

A Canadian military policeman, part of UNMIH, talking with local youth during his patrol of the streets of Port-au-Prince.
Credit: UN/DPI Photo UNI187337C by Eskinder Debebe

cure our borders and to preserve stability and promote democracy in our hemisphere."[61] Unlike the other four cases in this volume, the primary goal of military intervention in Haiti was neither to deliver nor to secure access for the delivery of humanitarian aid. However, the military's war-fighting capacities, as well as eventually its logistic and engineering ones, were in evidence. As in other cases, the military was deployed to mitigate human suffering.

The pace and evolution of U.S. involvement in Haiti had allowed the American military to begin contingency planning for different intervention scenarios almost a year before the actual deployment. This included planning for a mission that would incorporate military civic action, civil assistance, humanitarian assistance, and psychological operations (PSYOP).[62] Prior to the agreement, the military was planning for an enforcement operation that would be dangerous and involve combat. However, this quickly shifted to a Chapter VII operation that more closely resembled traditional peacekeeping with a more assertive mandate.

On 19 September, some 22,000 troops invaded. This force was comprised of 21,000 U.S. soldiers with an additional 1,250 soldiers from the Caribbean Community and Common Market and twenty-eight other nations. The so-called Powell doctrine of overwhelming force was used to "quickly establish a dominating physical and psychological presence," which would deter any acts of aggression by the armed opposition. The Haitian army did not respond to the invasion due to the Carter agreement. Furthermore, the intervention forces were greeted warmly by the Haitian population.

At first, the MNF was condemned for failing to prevent human rights abuses by what remained of the former repressive apparatus—whether it was by the *attachés*, the *tontons macoutes*, FRAPH, or the FAdH. The importance of this issue was emphasized during two incidents in late September. On 29 September, members of the de facto security forces attacked civilians with grenades. The next day during a pro-Aristide march, members of FRAPH killed five civilians and wounded seventy with U.S. troops watching, as CNN and other media groups recorded the event. There was an initial aversion among the U.S. forces to pursue actively disarmament and routine police work. However, because withdrawal was dependent upon stability, the rules of engagement were clarified, and the following day MNF forces invaded FRAPH headquarters and arrested leaders. In early October, the leader of FRAPH called all members to cooperate with the MNF and supported the reinstatement of Aristide and democracy.

Possibly the most vital elements in obtaining and ensuring stability in Haiti are reforms of the military, police, and judicial systems. At first, U.S. policymakers sought the modernization of the Haitian military, but Aristide pushed for reforms to eliminate it. Between December and February, he decreased the army's numbers from 7,500 to 1,500 and then dismissed all senior officers. In April, with the withdrawal of Allied forces, Aristide would completely dissolve the military.

The intervention was accompanied by a deployment of 600 international police monitors. Furthermore, an Interim Public Security Force (IPSF) was established, consisting of 3,000 former members of the Haitian security forces. In December, an additional 900 refugees from Guantánamo became part of the IPSF following a brief training program. This force would be replaced by graduates from the new police academy, who would comprise the 6,000- to 7,000-strong Haitian National Police. The police force was due to be completely replaced by mid-1996; however, the process had been fraught with delays and funding shortages. The IPSF was faced with a variety of problems, including lack of equipment and training. Prior to its deployment, it was widely believed that former FAdH members had been evaluated to ensure that they had not been involved in egregious human rights violations. However, it was later revealed that only senior officers had been screened.

Here as elsewhere, a major hindrance to the creation of stability was the proliferation of small arms. Following the dissolution of FRAPH and the military, and largely due to the weak structure of the new Haitian security forces, many weapons were stolen and hidden throughout the Haitian countryside by former soldiers, FRAPH members, and *attachés*. There are still an estimated 50,000 illegal arms in the country.

The second internal report on Operation Restore Democracy from 10 October cites the success of the intervention in searching and seizing weapons caches, protecting public safety, and establishing a stable and secure environment. As a sign of the secure environment and as a renewed commitment toward human rights, the MICIVIH returned on 22 October.

As in northern Iraq, U.S. Special Forces would play a vital role during the MNF deployment and, subsequently, during the handover to the UNMIH. In a departure from previous practice, SF units were placed in every department specifically to limit human rights abuses by the section chiefs and paramilitary organizations.

As in other humanitarian operations, U.S. Army Civil Affairs units, composed primarily of reservists, proved effective. They engaged in a variety of public works and civic assistance activities, including road clearing and construction, reforming the judicial and police system, and health and sanitation projects.[63] In one article, a colonel notes that UN and U.S. policymakers actually constrained nation-building activities: "It was difficult for CA [Civil Affairs] operatives to convince US and UN leaders that education should be a high priority. For the most part, the UN's hierarchy views the USCA units only in terms of humanitarian assistance, not as a vital nation assistance force."[64] Soldiers from these units were assigned to various ministries in order to provide advice on governance. The MNF also made use of a Civil-Military Operations Command, used to coordinate the actions of UN agencies, NGOs, and the military.

A new military section, the Military Information Support Team (MIST), was created as a tool for providing information specialists and linguists during the operation.[65] The team provided insight into the social, economic, and political structures and helped identify short- and long-term goals for the operation. Furthermore, MIST engaged in PSYOP, which was necessary considering the tense political atmosphere, the traditional reactions to U.S. imperialism, and the rapid spread of misinformation. These operations consisted of supporting the return of the Haitian Congress, creating *Radio* and *Television Democracy*, and distributing information on humanitarian civic action projects. PSYOP informed the local population on the U.S. presence, minimized criticism, and discouraged hostility.

On 31 March 1995, the 20,000-strong MNF withdrew and was replaced by the 6,000-strong first UN Mission in Haiti, which included 2,500 U.S. troops. As an illustration of planning and smooth handover, at the time of the transition 5,500 of the 6,000 authorized troops already were present in Haiti. The U.S. contingent was composed of the Special Forces units deployed in twenty-five locations, Army Civil Affairs officers in ten areas, and a 550-troop Quick Reaction Force, which served to maintain the appearances and some reality of overwhelming force. The UNMIH was accompanied by 567 civilian police monitors, 250 international civilian staff, and 200 local staff.

Table 7.1 contains the essential costs for this effort. In 1994, total U.S. funds amounted to over $530 million—with $372.1 million from the DOD, $18.1 million from the DOS, $0.5 million in support of the UNMIH, $123.9 million from USAID, and $16.7 million in other funds. In 1995, total U.S. funds amounted to over $900 million—with $568.7 million from the DOD, $78.6 million from the DOS, $51.9 million for the UNMIH, $187.6 million from USAID, and $40.9 million in other funds. Total U.S. assistance from 1992 to 1995 was $1.6167 billion. Of this figure, DOD incremental costs account for $952.9 million, which was used predominantly to fund the MNF, embargo enforcement, and the UNMIH, as well as the processing of refugees at Guantánamo Bay. Some $114.6 million from the State Department was used mainly for assistance to refugees and victims. USAID allocated an estimated $489.1 million to NGOs for food distribution and health assistance. Furthermore, the USAID funds were used, especially in 1994 and 1995, to develop a new judicial and police system for Haiti. The combined $60.1 million in other funds was used by the Departments of Transportation, Commerce, Justice, Health and Human Services, and the Treasury to provide a variety of services related to peace operations and the refugees at Guantánamo Bay.[66]

To provide a point of comparison, in 1992, total U.S. funds amounted to $79.7 million—$9.3 million from the DOD, $2.7 million from the DOS, $66.0 million from USAID, and $1.7 million in other funds. In 1993, total U.S. funds amounted to $130.4 million—$2.8 million from the DOD, $15.2 million from the DOS, $111.6 million from USAID, and $0.8 million in other funds.

As of 31 May 1996, with the next phase of activities about to begin, total expenditures for the UN Support Mission in Haiti had reached $315.79 million. During the MNF intervention, there was one fatality

Table 7.1 Haiti: Military Costs and Civilian Benefits from Intervention, 1991–1996

	$ Costs	Casualties/Fatalities	Political Impact
Military costs of intervention for troop-contributing countries	A 1992: U.S. costs: $79.7M. 1993: U.S. costs: $130.4M. 1994: U.S. costs: $453M, majority for MNF. 1995: U.S. costs: $568.7M, majority for MNF. Total DOD: $953M. UNMIH as of 05/96: $315.79M.	B MNF: 1 U.S. soldier. UNMIH: 4 military, 2 civilian personnel killed.	C Intervention was 3 years after initial crisis to restore democracy. Ease partially removed impression that intervention impossible and risky.

	Displacement	Suffering	State of the State
Civilian benefits of intervention for targeted countries			
Humanitarian challenge before intervention	D 1991: 300,000 IDPs. 1991–1994: 60,000–100,000 refugees/boat people. 09–11/92: 26,000 refugees returned by U.S. 08/91–08/93: 53,375 returned. 1994: 29,417 refugees kept at Guantánamo naval base.	E *Hunger:* Effects of sanctions: 60% children malnourished, 3% severe; 1991–1994: number increased by 100,000; 1993: 1,000 excess child deaths per month. *Human rights:* 09/91: Repression, torture, rape, execution, corruption, disappearance, 300–500 believed killed; 04/93: 3,000 killed since coup; 06–08/93: over 300 cases of arbitrary arrest, U.S. condemned for questionable human rights practices toward refugees; 12/93: 250–1,000 homes burned in Cité Soleil; 01–07/94: increase in human rights violations. *Health:* Increase in TB, malaria, pneumonia, typhoid.	F 1991 coup that replaced Aristide with Cédras regime. Human rights violations by government and suffering caused by sanctions and embargo.
Civilian benefits after intervention	D' Virtually all of 29,417 Haitians interdicted repatriated.	E' *Hunger:* 03/93: UN agencies providing 940,000 Haitians with food; MNF brought substantial assistance and ended sanctions. However, people still live in the midst of poverty. *Human rights:* UN human rights mission reported on violations. MNF decreased violations and restored Aristide to power.	F' MNF restored Aristide to power. Rebuilt some of destroyed infrastructure and began to reconstruct judicial and police system. Trained 3,900 for interim police force. Smooth transition to the UNMIH and first democratic transition in Haitian history. 50,000 armed former militia/FRAPH/*attachés* remain.

when a soldier was shot and killed while engaging in disarmament activities at a roadblock. The UNMIH troops fared worse; by 30 April 1996, four military and two civilian personnel had been killed.

Was it worth it? As noted at the outset of this chapter, human suffering in Haiti reflected the human rights abuses of the de facto regime; the imposition of sanctions by the international community; displacement, both internal and external, of the Haitian population; and the forced repatriation and consequences of the Bush and Clinton administrations' policies toward the boat people. The humanitarian results of the intervention can be summarized positively in three ways.

First, the definitive lifting of international sanctions after Aristide's return on 15 October 1994 and the subsequent flow of goods into Haiti alleviated the worst of the acute humanitarian suffering. However, the living conditions of the poor continue to be precarious, as shown by the high infant mortality rate, low life expectancy, high malnutrition rate, low vaccination rate, and the subsequent prevalence of disease.

Second, the intervention led to a dramatic and almost instantaneous decrease in human rights violations by FAdH forces. Throughout the crisis, human rights violations had ebbed during periods of international presence. During the MNF intervention, the army, which was the primary tool of repression, was disbanded. Schools and shops reopened, and life returned to "normal," although the norm in Haiti is distressingly low.

Third, due to the return of Aristide and stability to Haiti, "most of the 24,917 Haitians interdicted . . . in 1994 . . . opted to repatriate voluntarily."[67] Not only does this emphasize the valid political nature of their original flight, but also the increased enthusiasm with which the intervention and the subsequent return of Aristide was greeted. Some 5,000 refugees still had not returned by late December, but soon 20 percent would repatriate voluntarily and the others against their will.

The Postcrisis Situation and Conclusion

While the unprecedented peaceful democratic transition of government from Aristide to René Préval in February 1996 serves as a point of optimism for the future of Haiti, substantial obstacles remain. The transition from the MNF to the UNMIH has been used as a model for how the transition from coalition to UN peace operations should occur.[68] Planning for the transition from the U.S.-led enforcement to the UN, the peacekeeping mission began eight months prior to the transition with the incorporation of a UNMIH planning staff into MNF only one month after the intervention had begun. Furthermore, there

On the outskirts of Cap-Haïten, local police train new policemen. Canadian Civil Police (right), part of UNMIH, observe the training.
Credit: UN/DPI Photo UNI87350C by Eskinder Debebe

was a mutually approved transition plan, which ensured that the peacekeeping mission was not unprepared and underequipped from the outset. The presence of an American general as the first UNMIH commander and solid relations between him and the SRSG were essential for the smooth and effective change in command and control.

During the first month of the UNMIH, there was no increase in political violence. However, there was continued instability and criminal activity, including the raiding of humanitarian aid warehouses by armed gangs. The efforts to institute judicial, legal, and penal reforms had been only partially successful.

Aristide's five-year term had been interrupted by the coup. As the date for the scheduled democratic elections approached, the question arose as to whether he would attempt to remain in office. In November 1996, due to a variety of factors including U.S. pressure, Aristide confirmed his decision to step down. This was followed by the elections on 17 December. Aristide's appointed successor and member of the Lavalas movement, René Préval, won the election with 89.7 percent of the vote, although only 28 percent of the population turned out for the elections. Enjoying less popularity than his predecessor, Préval's limited public support impeded his ability to move forward with unpopular reforms.

In February 1996, U.S. forces withdrew from the UNMIH. However, a group of 450 soldiers from an engineering unit remained in Haiti; after temporarily withdrawing (in order to satisfy the presidential pledge that all American soldiers would leave), it returned to continue public works and training. Immediately following the MNF intervention, economic growth reflected the rapid influx of international development assistance—a 4.5 percent increase in real GNP. This was accompanied by a 30 percent decline in inflation and the recovery of the value of the Haitian gourde by the end of September.[69]

Since the 1970s, the boat people have symbolized economic and political instability. In the first few months following the MNF intervention, repatriation increased and the flow of refugees decreased and then virtually disappeared for a time. The U.S. Coast Guard interdicted only 867 Haitians in the first ten months of 1995, with none in five of these months. However, on the eve of the elections in November 1996, the Coast Guard interdicted and then summarily repatriated 1,162 refugees. Furthermore, the government signed agreements with the Bahamas and French Guyana for the voluntary return of 800 and 4,000 refugees per month, respectively. A potentially unsettling situation resulted from the 1,000 Haitians who were forcefully repatriated by the Dominican Republic, which had been accused of a variety of human rights abuses.[70]

As the final UN peacekeepers pulled out of Haiti in December 1997, the mood was one of frustration with the lack of nation building, but not with the efforts of outside soldiers. The purpose at the outset was to arrest the untenable humanitarian deterioration and to give Haiti a chance to restore more democratic government. The outside forces removed the criminal de facto regime and helped begin a process that improved prisons and established a more professional and less brutal National Police Force. As a *New York Times* editorial summarized at the time, "Haiti shows why outsiders should not count on rapidly changing a political culture deformed by centuries of dictatorship. . . . Outsiders cannot build a working Haiti. They can, and have, established a more secure and free atmosphere, a necessary prerequisite."[71] Haiti is perhaps the most dramatic example of the unrealistic expectation that humanitarian intervention followed by other short-term inputs can work miracles. The most biting criticism of such efforts is found in the work of David Rieff, who argues that humanitarian intervention is just a sop to the Western conscience, enabling the avoidance of the chronic issues of Third World poverty and governmental mismanagement.[72]

Nonetheless, Haiti's balance sheet favors the use of outside military intervention to the benefit of human values even if the longer-run situation is ambiguous. There were few complications and only six total military fatalities. The perceived success helped resuscitate the image, at least temporarily, of the possible utility of American military intervention in a region that had traditionally resisted outside pressures of any type from the United States. The most severe shortcomings, with implications for future conflict management, resulted from doing too little to improve the police, penal, and judiciary systems, which were part of the mandate. Although some training and equipment were provided, it was insufficient for a country with no experience or professionals in these areas. Moreover, fundamental economic relations remained unchanged. The disparity in the distribution of wealth and power between a tiny elite and the vast majority of the local population makes Haiti one of the world's most inegalitarian societies. This polarization had led to the rise and fall of Aristide, and violence is likely to remain part of the future picture. Ironically, the most important humanitarian impact of the Chapter VII military intervention may well have been the end of the coercive economic sanctions also under Chapter VII that had devastated the local economy and the Haitian poor.

The perception that vital interests of key states were threatened eventually spurred leadership and risk taking. The geography of the crisis brought into prominence not just Washington, but also Ottawa (in the police and UN military operations) and several Caribbean countries. The rapid and painless attainment of security was dramatic, especially because of the precedent to intervene and restore democracy. In spite of the costs, the effective projection of military force and the resulting humanitarian benefits have led some observers, and certainly this author, to question the logic of the UN Charter's calling for nonforcible economic sanctions *before* forcible military coercion.[73] A swifter military intervention undoubtedly would have proved more humanitarian than a "tightening of the screws" through economic sanctions. It would have maintained the major achievement of replacing the de facto regime with the constitutional authorities but avoided the massive immediate suffering and long-term structural dislocations of the economy from sanctions. "Sanctions, as is generally recognized, are a blunt instrument," writes Boutros-Ghali. "They raise the ethical question of whether suffering inflicted on vulnerable groups in the target country is a legitimate means of exerting pressure on political leaders whose behavior is unlikely to be affected by the plight of their subjects."[74]

8

Humanitarian Intervention: Costs, Benefits, Quandaries

Tentativeness has characterized much of the prose in the preceding chapters, perhaps to a greater extent than the reader would have wished. However, the framework, the cases, and the analysis lack the clarity, specificity, and objectivity that statistics are supposed to convey. Definitive depictions and judgments are problematic for each of the five cases; and the goal here is to suggest comparisons across them. At this stage it seems preferable and safer to suggest visually and qualitatively the value-laden judgments emanating from a comparison of suggestive data across the five case studies. In this way, the reader can identify whether and why his or her bottom line differs from my views at this time.

As such, Table 8.1 is only a slightly modified version of what earlier had been billed as a "first crude and subjective attempt"[1] to capture a comparative interpretation of data across cases (columns) and across criteria (rows). After two years of poring over available data and interpretations, the figure still remains a graphic way to capture an ambiguous reality. The legend indicates that the more white the circles, the more successful a particular case was in comparison with others in this sample; and the more dark the circles, the more unsuccessful. The judgments are perhaps not as subtle as some would like—the only three options are all black or all white or an equal mixture—but the figure accurately depicts my considered evaluation of available data. Hence, more successful operations are characterized by a relatively graver humanitarian challenge before an intervention in a particular

Table 8.1 Depicting Military Costs and Benefits across Cases

		Northern Iraq (1991–1996)	Somalia (1992–1995)	Bosnia (1992–1995)	Rwanda (1994–1995)	Haiti (1993–1996)
	1. Military Costs $ Value • Military Security • Military Logistics • Civilian Humanitarian Aid Casualties/Fatalities Political Impact	○ ○ ◐ ○ ○	● ● ◐ ● ●	● ◐ ● ● ●	● ● ◐ ● ◐	○ ○ ○ ○ ◐
○ Least Costly ◐ Costly ● Most Costly						

	2. Civilian Crisis (before Intervention)
	 Displacement
	 Suffering
	  • Hunger
	  • Health
	  • Human Rights
	 State of the State
		◐ ● ● ● ○	◐ ● ● ○ ●	● ◐ ● ● ●	● ● ● ● ●	○ ○ ● ● ◐

○ Least Critical ◐ Critical ● Most Critical						

	3. Civilian Benefits (after Intervention)
	 Displacement
	 Suffering
	  • Hunger
	  • Health
	  • Human Rights
	 State of the State
		○ ○ ◐ ● ●	◐ ○ ○ ● ●	● ◐ ● ● ●	● ◐ ◐ ○ ◐	○ ◐ ● ○ ○

○ Most Beneficial ◐ Beneficial ● Least Beneficial						

targeted country, relatively more substantial improvements in the humanitarian situation after such an intervention, and relatively more bearable military and political costs to the main troop-contributing countries.

Perhaps the most subjective part of weighing and then judging available data stems from the necessity to reflect an adequate appreciation of the challenge on the ground at the time of an intervention. As with Olympic diving, the degree of difficulty should be combined with the degree of execution to determine a fair assessment of the overall utility and success of a particular intervention. Assigning a value to "difficulty" would reflect three judgments: how dangerous and chaotic a particular humanitarian situation; how physically challenging a specific terrain; and how ambitious an operation's mandate. The MNF in Haiti, for example, would undoubtedly receive high marks for execution on the first two but with a relatively low degree of difficulty in comparison with far more dangerous and challenging operations on the ground in the other four cases under review. At the same time, even the partial pursuit in Haiti of the mandate to enhance local police, judiciary, and penal systems was considerably more ambitious than for the other cases, where such efforts received rhetorical rather than operational resources; and this too should be factored into a composite assessment.

Although it is beyond the temporal scope of the present framework, it would not be irrelevant to revisit targeted countries a decade after an intervention to determine whether the outside intrusion had a positive or negative impact on the containment, mitigation, and potential resolution of a conflict that had led to the humanitarian crisis and outside military and civilian responses in the first place. One analyst recently has proposed that longer-term considerations should really be part of any evaluation of a short-term intervention, which otherwise "can thus become narcissistic, with questions about the long-term effects of external involvement pushed to the back of the queue."[2] Methodologically, of course, this type of weighting would be as impossible as its use is politically infeasible.

Conflict resolution is outside the terms of reference for the military per se. However, policy analysts and decisionmakers are obliged to ask whether a humanitarian intervention has prevented, slowed down, or exacerbated subsequent violence. This line of inquiry might lead toward a greater emphasis on either of two tasks. The first would be those like disarmament and demilitarization. The complexity of these tasks is well illustrated in the cases. In the former Yugoslavia, an embargo penalized the Muslims (and Croats), and the situation was only redressed through NATO and surreptitious purchases. At the opposite extreme was Somalia, a country awash in small arms where little effort was made to remove them. In Iraq and Rwanda, the level of small arms was irrelevant—in Iraq because the well-armed government forces had to be confronted by a conventional force, and in Rwanda because the killing was done by low-tech machetes. In Haiti, arms were fewer and their removal and control was a priority.

The second task concerns the choice for the military to remain until some semblance of local order and legitimacy are restored (for example, through improvements in police and the judiciary and through elections). From the cases in this book, a plausible hypothesis is that longer-term benefits for conflict resolution may emerge from the type of intervention that occurred in Haiti where efforts were made to strengthen local institutions essential for the functioning of what had been a phantom state.

The simplistic notion of a time-bound "exit strategy" suggests that a humanitarian intervention is a mechanical task, rather than a strategic effort characterized by uncertainty and changing tactics on the ground. When substantial interests are involved, the notion of an exit strategy is superfluous, as demonstrated by the open-ended commitments in the Persian Gulf (or in Korea after forty years). But without such interests, perhaps it is better not to get started in the first place.

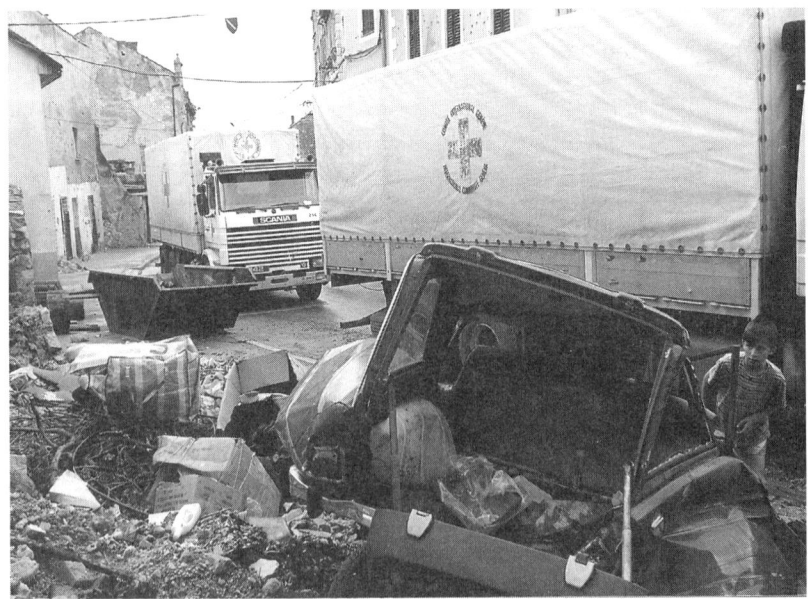

A child in Bosnia surveys the destruction in a war-torn city. Credit: ICRC Photo 93-113/5

"In Somalia, American policymakers should have recognized long before the firefight in Mogadishu that the humanitarian crisis could not be resolved without addressing the country's political anarchy, which would prove too much for a weak U.N. force to handle."[3]

In light of all the previous uncertainties, some would perhaps question the wisdom of an analyst's efforts to draw conclusions. Nonetheless, Iraq and Haiti are at one end of an analytical spectrum with civilian benefits (in terms of lives saved, improved access to alleviate famine and disease, and fewer human rights violations) worth the military costs. Bosnia (prior to the Dayton agreement, which is the focus here) would be at the opposite end as a case illustrating that the high economic and political costs and low effectiveness of military forces are not commensurate with civilian benefits. In between, Rwanda would probably be closer to the successful end of the spectrum (after July 1994, because military expenditures before this time were trivial), and Somalia the failure (particularly in terms of the political backlash against multilateralism in the United States, although not in terms of lives saved). At the same time, a shift in subjective appreciation or emphasis toward or away from particular data or priorities could push Rwanda and Somalia closer to one end of the spectrum or the other. Some analytical comfort resides in the coincidence between the lowest three scores here and Stanley Hoffmann's judgment of the UN's "perceived failures: Somalia (where the record is complex); Rwanda (where indeed the UN did not cover itself with glory); and above all Yugoslavia."[4]

The impact of forceful multilateral military operations on humanitarian action in war zones is neither as harmful as many detractors think nor as helpful as proponents often argue. Establishing a bottom line for either of the two basic humanitarian functions—logistics and security—requires value-laden judgments. The downside to military logistics consists largely of looking at a particular military operation and asking, "What is it worth?" Every case demonstrates that the military is the most costly option—the best data, from Rwanda, indicate that military aircraft are four to eight times as expensive as commercial ones, and the latter mode already is twenty to forty times as expensive as normal road transport, which in turn is more expensive than bulk shipments by rail.[5] As the late Fred Cuny wrote in 1991, the Berlin crisis "seared in public memory" the importance of this mode of transport "no matter that the airlift is the most expensive means of delivering a commodity."[6] In certain situations, military options, and especially their airlift capacity, may be the only ones available. Certainly northern Iraq in the spring of 1991 was such a case. And even the unilateral and multilateral efforts in Goma in mid-1994 demonstrated that an effective humanitarian response can sometimes require the human resources, logistics, and rapid deployment capacities available only to the military.

Moreover, expenditures by defense departments sometimes are genuine add-ons, and then high costs are not directly deducted from allocations for efforts by civilian agencies. Being clear about the sources and alternative uses for public funds is essential. Assuming that a sum approaching the resources disbursed by or attributed to the military within a particular crisis somehow could be handed over to civilian humanitarians, even in the medium to long run, would be simplistic. Yet, such an implicit assumption permeates a host of "what if?" analyses in much of the literature criticizing the ostensibly lavish costs of military humanitarianism.

It is more pertinent to ask questions about the relative costs and approaches of different militaries. For example, according to back-of-the-envelope calculations, the 8,000 U.S. soldiers in NATO's SFOR presence in Bosnia in 1997–1998 cost some $2.5–3 billion of the approximately $7 billion annual total.[7] Accordingly, one should question how much of this bill reflects what other militaries—especially European ones who mix more freely with local populations—regard as an obsession with self-protection and how much as a legitimate concern stemming from the U.S. position as both a preeminent power and a target. Indeed, the hyperprotective and isolationist measures in the former Yugoslavia led to the description of American troops as "Ninja turtles," which was contrasted to the European approach of soft hats and mixing. The low-key approach is not only cheaper, but also arguably more effective. At the same time, it requires skills not taught in boot camps but, rather, in police academies.

It is impossible to determine the extent to which civilian emergency relief, let alone military humanitarianism, is being deducted from resources allocated to development, although this too is often the implication in critical analyses noting the steady side-by-side decreases in overseas development assistance and increases in emergency aid. Such criticism is in many ways beside the point because in today's world "conflict should be taken for granted." As Dutch Minister for Development Cooperation Jan Pronk has also remarked, emergency and development assistance are difficult to distinguish when "ever more countries linger in prolonged states of half peace/half war."[8] Other serious criticisms, although even more difficult to substantiate, are that outside military helping hands ultimately "increase the nonmilitary operations of local armies . . . [and] undermine the process of democratization."[9] or are part of a new paradigm "to manage the symptoms of global polarisation and exclusion."[10]

Evaluating commercial alternatives to replace military logistics depends essentially on their existence and, if none, on the value attached to individual lives—by the militaries that contribute such logistical assistance and by domestic pressure groups who make themselves heard. Civilian humanitarian organizations are learning to live with this reality and are adopting procedures with standby arrangements for staff, equipment, and supplies in order better to engage and collaborate with armed forces when they are committed to a particular humanitarian crisis.

Although neither readily calculable nor necessarily evident from the figures, interviews over the years suggest that a potential disadvantage of resorting too quickly to military logistics is that this option possibly discourages the armed forces from undertaking tougher, security-related tasks—what Michael Pugh, editor of *International Peacekeeping*, poetically has dubbed "mission cringe."[11] In light of the pressures on governments "to do something," there is a seductive appeal in sending the military to furnish emergency goods and logistics rather than security. In fact, the preoccupation with having a clear exit strategy and avoiding mission creep, in Washington and other Western capitals, makes it appear easier and more attractive to provide clean water than to challenge genocide or even to embark on demining.

Rather than new methods and training to permit more effective and less expensive humanitarian delivery by the armed forces, there emerges a central and stark finding from the successes in northern Iraq and Haiti, from the successful elements of the French presence in Rwanda, and even from moments in Somalia and Bosnia. The emphasis should be on the direct provision of security by armed forces in war zones. Adam Roberts concludes his overview of international responses in this decade: "If the practice of the 1990s has proved anything it is that humanitarian assistance cannot realistically be considered in isolation from security. . . . Protection is properly seen not as an occasional add-on to humanitarian relief supplies, but as a key aspect of the international community's response to wars and crises."[12] Guaranteeing access or supporting the work of civilians through armed convoys or air cover is directly related to the military's ability to wage wars—even if such a capacity is only a threat, as it was in Haiti. There is no alternative source of supply for military muscle.

Calculating the costs and benefits of using the military when belligerents deny access is considerably more controversial than evaluating logistics, which is problematic enough. This is especially the case because the West lacks leadership and a willingness to stay the course when fickle electorates tolerate only something close to a zero-casualty foreign policy. The situation is exacerbated, as Michael Walzer points out, by the widespread acceptance of "the indiscriminate use of modern fire power to save soldiers from trouble and risk."[13] As mentioned numerous times, knowing where to deploy in a civil war is not easy, nor is mobilizing the political will to see an intervention through more than a brief period. But there simply is no substitute for the armed forces in order to foster a secure environment. Whether this capacity will be utilized with any frequency in the future is an open question.

The notion of costs may need to be further refined when attempting to pinpoint longer-term impacts on a targeted country resulting from the application of outside military force to stave off an emergency. Both direct and indirect costs in the longer run resemble those of humanitarian aid in that they are fundamentally subjective and incalculable with any degree of precision, however fancy the analytical tools. Yet, it undoubtedly is still instructive to pose thorny questions emanating from a longer-term perspective even if the answers are qualitative rather than quantitative. In the same way that analysts are discovering how outside aid influences the dynamics of wars, and even exacerbates them under certain circumstances, it also is important to contextualize the limitations of multilateral military operations. Will the application of military might enhance the role of violence in determining local leadership? Will the abandonment of the norms of nonintervention lead to further instability and the weakening of the nascent institutions of civil society? Should the military take the lead under such circumstances? Will the use of outside military force postpone reconciliation among local parties and confronting the root causes of conflict? Will any foreign power be willing and able to commit its soldiers for anything except the short term?

Looking Ahead

That intervention is so costly and has such mixed results does not mean that states will agree to move earlier to save resources or lives, although that is the conclusion reached by many fervent advocates of prevention. Even late responses are becoming rarer, a fact brought home poignantly in late 1996 and 1997 with the unraveling of the African Great Lakes region. Several thoughts related to six directions for future research come to mind.

The first concerns establishing the precise financial, bureaucratic, and cultural reasons that a unitary presence in complex emergencies is impossible. The orchestration and management of the various inputs and programs of the UN system—the military, political, humanitarian, and human rights dimensions—is extraordinarily complex, a task that does not become easier when economic and social inputs are infused in a postwar phase. A clear chain of command is required in war zones, where the entire system and the largest international NGOs working as subcontractors could and should constitute a coherent and effective response mechanism. Rather than extant feudal arrangements, a single body is necessary to set priorities, to raise and distribute resources, and to coordinate emergency inputs.

This seemingly obvious—but politically and bureaucratically problematic—consolidation of the UN presence has been recommended by me[14] and a variation by former WFP executive director James Ingram in the form of a revamped International Committee of the Red Cross.[15] Disparate views of course remain among Western governments about the exact shape of such a mechanism. Moreover, their bilateral aid agencies themselves are not necessarily more efficient and sincere—in fact, often the call from governments for "UN coordination" is duplicitous in light of their collective and individual unwillingness to do less national flag-waving in humanitarian tragedies.

Centralization moves in and out of mainstream intergovernmental discussions depending on the existence of a world-class crisis. For instance, former U.S. Secretary of State Warren Christopher's "nonpaper" at the July 1995 session of the UN Economic and Social Council proposed considering "whether and how to consolidate the emergency functions of the UN High Commissioner for Refugees, the World Food Programme, the UN Children's Fund, and the Department of Humanitarian Affairs into a single agency."[16] These views are not a monopoly by Washington. For example, Pronk stated at the 1996 General Assembly: "At the field level, integration and efficiency for the sake of comprehensive conflict prevention could be enhanced if there would be only one UN-representative in a country, representing the entire UN-system, including the specialised agencies."[17]

Christopher's and Pronk's views about consolidation reflected the trauma of Rwanda, just as earlier calls for reform in the General Assembly in 1991 had reflected the fumbling in the Gulf crisis. Albeit still controversial, centralization emerged from the unprecedented multinational, multidonor evaluation of the international response to the Rwandan tragedy;[18] but it evaporated once again from the international agenda because there was no Rwanda-like crisis in 1996, 1997, or as of this writing in 1998. However, the need for a consolidated UN presence in war zones is bound to return when a Burundi, Congo, or Kosovo really explodes instead of merely seething. Some officials quietly are still pushing the issue that would, in fact, build upon a host of earlier proposals by other seasoned practitioners.[19]

In spite of the compelling logic, consolidating the UN's emergency capabilities within a new institution appeared too visionary an option in earlier drafts of the secretary-general's 1997 report *Renewing the United Nations System: A Programme for Reform*.[20] However, it was at least to have appeared as an annex. The implication was that this imaginative option was politically and bureaucratically infeasible but *not* undesirable. Moreover, unlike the transfer of responsibilities to the UNHCR (which was another and more pragmatic option under consideration), the centralized structure would have necessitated constitutional decisions by member states. Yet, as detailed earlier, the reform led to mainly a change of acronyms rather than any meaningful consolidation. An urgent item for the research agenda is to establish the host of constraints that time and time again prevent more meaningful centralization in spite of all the evidence about the potential benefits.

The second avenue for future research concerns investigating judiciously the geopolitics of prevention. A "stitch in time" resonates nicely in multilateral ears. But such a desirable framework usually also provides the least plausible rationale for states' use of UN military operations. Stephen Stedman has compared them to "alchemy" and I to a "pipe dream."[21] Preventive diplomacy is the latest conceptual fashion—according to Michael Lund's honest formulation, "an idea in search of a strategy."[22]

Such preventive actions as fact-finding missions and human rights monitors are not only being discussed, but their use expanded; they have, in fact, been mainstays in UN activities for half a century. Economic and social development have also been central to the world organization's mission, but they have received added emphasis because they too are now also viewed as essential to help prevent armed conflicts. The tone of too many of these discussions—for example, by the Carnegie Commission on Preventing Deadly Conflict,[23] the Aspen Institute, the Volkswagen Stiftung, the Council on Foreign Relations, and the U.S. Institute of Peace—resembles that of a homily: The way to avoid civil wars is to eradicate their political and economic roots through the introduction of wise government and civil society, of rationality, of prosperity with distribution. The results from substantial aid and investment in the former Yugoslavia and Rwanda are hardly encouraging for those like the former UN secretary-general wishing to make a case for "preventive development" as a "necessary complement to preventive diplomacy."[24]

But a new element with the potential to forestall massive displacement and suffering would be both better information and a military capacity to respond. The former, consisting essentially of various aspects of early warning, occurs in peacetime, is feasible, and could be improved, although no truly independent UN intelligence-gathering capacity is politically plausible. But the second and essential preventive capacity for times of crisis is nonexistent. Although it has been heralded by many as a first success, the symbolic deployment of a UN detachment to Macedonia has worked only because the international bluff has not yet been called. It also is an unusual, not to say atypical, case from which generalization is deeply problematic.

To be a successful deterrent, preventive soldiers must be backed by contingency plans and reserve firepower for immediate retaliation against aggressors. Thomas Schelling has provided the classic argument for the incremental application of force combined with a clear, imminent, and real threat to inflict more pain in the event of noncompliance.[25] In the case of UN preventive deployment, this would amount to an advance and genuine authorization for a Chapter VII coercive response in the event that a modest preventive force is challenged. Otherwise there is no other basis for deterrence than hope. Acknowledging, for example, that the combined forces of the Yugoslav National Army and the Bosnian Serbs would have been very hard to intimidate, automatic backup is nonetheless essential. Although fervent proponents of humanitarian action often argue that doing something is better than nothing, UN credibility can ill afford additional and inevitable black eyes that result from giving in to the impulse reflected in former Secretary-General Boutros-Ghali's comment to a journalist about the former Yugoslavia: "If we had not been there, it would have been worse."[26] If there is no response when the UN's bluff is called, the currency of preventive UN military action will be devalued to such an extent that preventive action should not have been attempted in the first place.

States have made modest improvements—for example, a round-the-clock situation room, satellite telephones, and consolidated administrative services. Moreover, the Canadian and Dutch have been joined by twenty-two other countries, "the friends of rapid reaction," and have proposed a mobile military headquarters capable of fielding command teams within hours of a Security Council decision. In addition, Western countries (Austria, Canada, Denmark, the Netherlands, Norway, Poland, and Sweden) have signed an agreement to set up a 4,000-member force for use for a maximum of six months before regular UN peacekeeping troops arrive. Although the existence of such a capability would perhaps be helpful in exercising a restraining effect on combatants, the real problem is the reluctance of states to move quickly and to authorize forces large enough to be effective if national interests are perceived to be low or costs disproportionately high. Underlying this reluctance, among other things, is the fear that extrication will be necessary.

In Bosnia early in 1993, the UN secretary-general asked for some 35,000 soldiers immediately to protect the so-called safe areas, but it took months to get barely 7,000 into the field. The record indicates the basic correctness of the original estimates and request.[27] Perhaps it is time to revisit the notion launched by the first secretary-general, Trygve Lie, for earmarking troops rather than an independent reaction force. In 1997, for example, sixty-five states had declared their readiness to make some 85,000 soldiers available for a standby arrangement system.

The hope is that a growing preoccupation with saving public resources could alter such myopia. However, the political risks from sustaining fatalities or getting bogged down in a quagmire are usually high enough to outweigh any purported economic savings from acting sooner rather than later. Allocating and disbursing billions of dollars of humanitarian aid after violence has erupted is easier for risk-averse politicians and policymakers than moving precipitously to commit armed forces early in a conflict cycle.[28] There are low domestic political costs for humanitarian aid coupled with a minimal loss of credibility in case of failure (that is, the opposite of potential military fiascoes). The usual result is halfhearted and inconsistent policy, as Hoffmann has written: "Caught between reasons to act and fear of the risks, governments tend to initiate halfhearted measures . . . without sufficient political commitment to pursue them seriously . . . result[ing] in internally inconsistent policies whose success is at the mercy of the strongest parties to the conflict."[29]

A third area for future research concerns the impact of the much-contested "CNN effect."[30] What are the causal links between media coverage and policy changes in governments and agencies, particularly decisions to contribute troops and resources? Can the media's effect foster the humanitarian urge to come to the rescue but not to override risks for politicians if national interests are not at stake? As one former senior U.S. military officer has noted, "Few leaders are willing to invest their political capital in risky, controversial international interventions with uncertain outcomes."[31] As one of his junior colleagues wrote, "The lack of political resolve strongly indicates that the humanitarian/NGO community and the military have a common enemy: an inattentive and uninformed civilian leadership (irrespective of the country) and, as a result, a wishy-washy public mandate."[32]

As pundits and professors are fond of indicating, democratically elected governments can rarely imagine action whose time horizon extends beyond the next public opinion poll, and certainly not beyond the next electoral campaign. Dithering in 1996 and 1997 in the African Great Lakes—to Burundi's seething ethnic cauldron and to lawlessness in Zaire (later Congo) and Rwanda—indicated that the terms of international discourse have changed. Yet, the willingness to deploy troops clearly lags substantially behind the rhetoric, whatever the media attention accorded to a particular crisis. The reality of the CNN effect appears considerably less influential than conventional wisdom proclaims, but there is precious little data about cause and effect in terms of coverage and policy changes.

A fourth future research focus concerns time frames. The potential for third-party military forces in complex humanitarian emergencies is necessarily short-term and should not be exaggerated. The Mohonk Criteria for Humanitarian Assistance in Complex Emergencies specify that "military forces should be used only as a last resort."[33] This of course refers to making maximum diplomatic efforts and not being trigger-happy. Yet, for security purposes, the military should be involved as early as possible, before a simmering situation boils over.

In this context and as indicated earlier, it is germane but hardly fair to ask whether military action slows down coming to grips with such longer-term issues as rehabilitation, reconstruction, and conflict management. Roberts, for one, has criticized the incomplete nature of inter-

Food is distributed to Rwandan children who lost their parents in recent massacres. Credit: UN PHOTO 186798/J. Isaac 1059L

vention: "What is deplorable, though, is the pretense that, in the absence of a serious long-term purpose, it suffices to call an action 'humanitarian.'"[34] According to this line of argument, for example, protecting the Kurds since 1991 has saved lives but left them prisoners in their own land—targets of Baghdad and unwelcome in neighboring countries—and divided among themselves.

Nonetheless, "nation building" (for many in the U.S. Congress, "the 'N' word") has hardly been a success anywhere, no matter who is in charge or for what period. The usual criticism of the UN's peacekeeping operation in Cyprus—that there is no incentive after three decades for the belligerents to negotiate or invest in the future—thus also is relevant for military-civilian interactions in the post–Cold War era. The use of traditional Chapter VI UN peacekeepers or Chapter VII humanitarian enforcers ideally should be part of a comprehensive political strategy to resolve conflict—what Jarat Chopra has called "peace-maintenance."[35]

The military is not a substitute for longer-term nation-building efforts or a sensible means to address the oxymoron of a "protracted emergency"; but it can be a helpful ally, a necessary if insufficient step toward improving the chances of stability. Most importantly, as former U.S. Congressman Stephen Solarz has written;

> Political reconciliation and stabilization are always desirable. But confidence that they will be achieved in a given case should not be a prerequisite to stopping genocides or manmade humanitarian catastrophes. . . . [W]hen hundreds of thousands of lives are at imminent risk, the inability of an intervention to preclude any future unrest is a weak counterargument to prompt and decisive action.[36]

The existence of a political vacuum for conflict resolution is not the fault of soldiers, but of the governments that send them. Moreover, criticizing the military for a failure to consult more with local authorities and to address the socioeconomic roots of armed conflict and begin reconciliation is to suggest criteria that will never be met. At bottom and as Pugh has remarked: "It has to be remembered that peace support operations reflect failures in world politics. They attempt to deal with the manifestations of problems rather than problems themselves."[37]

As mentioned earlier, the criticism of failing to alter root causes would appear ludicrous and be dismissed for natural disasters. Negative judgments about the longer-term results of military-civilian interactions in war zones are as relevant or irrelevant as those about the inability of military help to offset the longer-run impacts of natural disasters. The essence of valid criticisms about any outside effort is the extent to which the country is better off as a result. Keeping the future in mind is, however, a useful reminder of the importance of pushing for a political strategy in conjunction with an intervention. The absence of a long-run commitment, though, should not be an excuse for not making maximum use of military resources in both natural and man-made disasters.

There may be an additional irony in the so-called continuum from relief to development.[38] Conventional wisdom calls upon donors and aid organizations to move more quickly toward the kinds of projects and activities that have failed in the past and even to make greater commitments of the kind that are diminishing everywhere.[39] As such, development thinking itself is in crisis.[40] With massive humanitarian needs, emergency help is, sadly, precisely what is most required from outsiders. And in countries in chronic instability, relief will remain a crucial part of outside involvement for decades even if something akin to agreements halt armed conflict.[41] Distinctions between emergency and development assistance in war-torn societies are blurred; but this is quite different from lamenting the growth of emergency assistance in the face of increasing life-threatening suffering resulting from wars or the reappearance of massive famine in a country like North Korea.[42]

The issue of appropriate time frames leads to a host of questions whose answers are anything except obvious. What if the use of military force in complex emergencies resembles development aid, which some observers have argued actually has been not only wasteful but counter-productive, and thus leads to more violence and war? Are there questions about the military similar to one from a study that argues that "the acceleration or the attempt to accelerate economic, social, and political change often intensifies the historic tensions among different groups in society"?[43] What if humanitarian interventions resemble structural adjustment, so that even if they attain their short-term objectives they can contribute to more armed conflict in the longer term? What if, as another study argues, securing lasting peace in ethnic conflicts is often best pursued by placing opposing groups into demographically separate and defensible enclaves?[44] Under these circumstances and in spite of the widespread humanitarian "impulse"—some like the ICRC would say "imperative"—perhaps outsiders should simply wait for battle fatigue, or for the weaker belligerents to be subjugated or eliminated?

Perhaps most unsettling is a fifth area for future research, namely, the repugnant notion of triage.[45] Humanitarian practitioners estimate that ten to twenty times more could be accomplished with the same limited resources by attacking what UNICEF's late executive director

Jim Grant first called poverty's "silent" emergencies, rather than the "loud" emergencies caused by warfare.[46] This theme has been echoed by many, including the last UN secretary-general at the end of his term.[47] Indeed, there is the question here of selecting which emergencies will receive attention and which will be set aside.

Nicholas Stockton, the emergencies director of Oxfam, for instance, has pointed to the "existential reality where 'normal' poverty disposes of many more victims than the number that die in humanitarian emergencies, and where 'development' when conceived of as material progress, is actually moving in reverse for many millions of people."[48] Each day, for example, 35,000–40,000 children worldwide perish from poverty and preventable diseases. What claim should they have on the resources that now go to soldiers and civilians who intervene in civil wars? The perverse situation exists that heavy investments would be required in many local public services to attain the minimal standards obtained in humanitarian emergencies. What is the meaning of "tough love" in this context?

We clearly require more satisfactory answers. But until we have them, should we refrain from humanitarian intervention? If both practitioners and scholars are so unsure about whether military or civilian medicine is going to help or hurt patients in the longer run, is it sensible to forge ahead with alacrity? This line of argument adds still more fuel to the fire ignited by scathing criticisms of emergency relief in Somalia, Bosnia, and Rwanda—namely, that it has contributed, albeit inadvertently and unwittingly, to the continuation of war. It also requires considering the ICRC's contention that outside military intervention justified exclusively in terms of protecting humanitarian assistance is unviable and its interpretation of the Geneva Conventions and Additional Protocols that do "not permit the imposition of humanitarian assistance by the use of force."[49]

A sixth area for possible research concerns trying to test the hypothesis that the altered politics of the post–Cold War era permit better accountability for actions undertaken on behalf of international institutions. Better than other cases in this book, Iraq illustrates the extent to which the UN is no longer peripheral to international peace and security. President Clinton's address on 17 February 1998 to the Joint Chiefs of Staff and other Pentagon officials about Washington's diplomatic gymnastics to confront Baghdad's machinations over arms inspections illustrated how, Jesse Helms notwithstanding, even the sole remaining "superpower" continues under many circumstances to need the world organization.[50] Such situations provide some leverage for enhanced accountability.

The preceding pages have tried to distinguish what many commentators as well as students overlook—namely, the existence of "two United Nations."[51] The first is the arena where governments meet and make decisions, and the second is comprised of the various officials and soldiers who actually implement those decisions. It is meaningless to say that the UN "succeeds" or "fails" without specifying which United Nations. States always play a role in success or failure, and sometimes UN personnel also do, but usually both contribute to good and bad outcomes.

The end of the Cold War is variously dated from Mikhail Gorbachev's ascension to power in March 1985, the collapse of the Berlin Wall in November 1989, or the implosion of the Soviet Union in December 1991. For the United Nations, the dramatic turning point was Iraq's brutal occupation of Kuwait in August 1990. Saddam Hussein threatened the "mother of all battles" but instead became a hapless braggart who crumbled before a unified international coalition. Indeed, the Security Council's original decision to go to war was followed by Resolution 687, which dictated the terms of the cease-fire and which Hussein might now label the "mother of all resolutions." UN deliberations and actions were characterized by unanimity among the great powers and enforcement through collective security, akin to what the original framers of the UN Charter had imagined in 1945.

The euphoria about the UN's role that resulted from the reversal of Iraqi aggression and the subsequent rescue of almost two million Kurds was, of course, short-lived. As stated at several junctures, optimism about multilateral conflict management—captured prematurely by then President George Bush's "new world order"—quickly ceded to far more cautious and sober assessments. Collective spinelessness by both UNs in the face of ethnic cleansing in Bosnia, genocide in Rwanda, and the debacle in Somalia ushered in an era of pessimism and UN bashing as favorite pastimes in Washington's Beltway and elsewhere.

Nonetheless, today's world politics are different from the Cold War variety, which is suggested as this book goes to press by Washington's approach to the conflict with Baghdad. The United Nations—both the arena and the actor—often is in the limelight. States were never the billiard balls used in realist metaphors, but this simplification formerly was more accurate as a somewhat useful abstract to analyze the logic of the international system. States were never as impermeable to norms, transnational influences, and international organizations as the image implied. However, now that sovereignty has eroded in a number of ways and world politics have changed, no simple theoretical construct captures the complexity of contemporary affairs.[52]

The former produces decisions that provide the framework within which American diplomacy and military action often occur. Prior to 1998, the United States had used airpower against Iraq four times since the end of the Gulf War, and few disputed the international legal authority to do so because of Security Council Resolution 687. Seven years of economic sanctions and no-fly zones were important infringements upon Iraqi sovereignty. The crisis that began in November 1997 over access was based on a "material breach" of the cease-fire because Iraq refuses to respect its "unconditional" agreement to elimination by the UN of chemical, biological, and missile capacities and to "immediate on-site inspections." These were international, not American, decisions.

The "other" United Nations, the somewhat independent actor, also has been crucial on the ground in Iraq. For example, more weapons had been destroyed by the UN Special Commission (UNSCOM)—led first by Swedish Ambassador Rolf Ekeus and later by Australian Ambassador Richard Butler—than by six weeks of bombing during the Gulf War. In fact, successful detective work by UN inspectors, whom Bill Clinton called "the eyes and ears of the civilized world," had led to the crisis. As Deputy Prime Minister Tariq Aziz said, "UNSCOM is the adversary." UN relief agencies cared for virtually an entire country of 22 million people. In May 1996, eased sanctions led to a restricted "oil-for-food" program managed through a UN-administered escrow account. The proceeds actually went where they should—one-third to compensate Kuwaiti victims of the 1990 Iraqi invasion and to pay UN administrative expenses including those of weapons inspectors, two-thirds to purchase aid for civilians—rather than to Saddam's coffers. The top official of this other UN, Secretary-General Kofi Annan, arrived in Baghdad at the eleventh hour to strike a deal and avoid air strikes while still securing unconditional access by the inspectors. Whatever the eventual outcome of the situation in Iraq, it is worth asking a number of questions.

If the United States is the most important world power and there were solid international legal grounds to justify military action against Iraq, why was the Clinton administration proceeding so deliberately before acting? Why were Secretary of State Madeleine K. Albright, Secretary of Defense William S. Cohen, and UN Ambassador Bill Richardson globe-trotting to mobilize support for a UN Security Council vote? Why did Washington and London seek another political blessing, thereby risking vetoes from Moscow and Beijing and disgruntlement in Paris? Quite simply because the United Nations provided a tactical political advantage, or in Robert Keohane's words: "Even an unchallenged superpower such as the United States would be unable to achieve its goal through the bilateral exercise of influence; the costs of such massive 'arm-twisting' would be too great."⁵³

The president accurately argued that Saddam Hussein "alone will be to blame for the consequences," but this statement had to be interpreted in light of a significant development in world politics regarding the need in the post–Cold War era for international approval of actions, even by major powers like the United States. This is a new phase for outside military intervention. During the age of empires, imperial masters openly intervened when and where they wished. Then, as a result of decolonization, major powers increasingly opted for less noticeable economic and political arm-twisting in order to foster their interests by proxy, rather than for more obvious military forces. But when they made use of their armed forces, there was no requirement to seek, and no advantage arising from, international approval. Finally in the 1990s, a third phase is becoming apparent with the desire to secure an international imprimatur for military deployments by major powers. Big powers inevitably resort to military intervention to pursue their interests, but now they allow themselves to be subjected to international scrutiny.

Seeking approval from the Security Council for outside intervention represents a crucial change in international relations. The United States (and presumably Britain, Canada, and Australia, which had all indicated their intention to contribute to the American-led military buildup) would undoubtedly have proceeded without a new UN blessing in early 1998. But a blue-tinted stamp of approval from the world organization afforded them a political advantage, and this results in some leverage for the community of states to hold others more accountable for their actions. In this regard, former Secretary-General Boutros Boutros-Ghali argued: "They may herald a new division of labour between the United Nations and regional organizations, under which the regional organization carries the main burden but a small United Nations operation supports it and verifies that it is functioning in a manner consistent with positions adopted by the Security Council."⁵⁴

In this context, "accountability" means the ability to ensure that a mission subcontracted by the international community to a powerful state or a coalition reflects collective interests and norms and not merely the national imperatives and preferences of the subcontractor. There are very limited means to ensure lawful behavior and compliance by states generally, and ensuring accountability is more problematic when a powerful state seeks international approval of an intended or an ongoing military deployment. Nonetheless, an intergovernmental decisionmaking organ (especially the Security Council) is in a position to refuse approval and hence can demand that specific conditions pertaining to the character, size, timing, and goals of an operation be met before the potential subcontractor is given an international blessing. Ensuring accountability consists of three elements: an effective mechanism in the field, meaningful content to restrictions governing the behavior by the subcontractor's soldiers, and costs associated with noncompliance.

In principle, major powers with a long democratic tradition are more likely to be embarrassed by criticisms of their aberrant behavior under a subcontract from an international authority than are authoritarian governments. However, it is worth exploring when precisely the need for international sanctioning of actions by major powers affords the opportunity to require more of them. Skeptics will no doubt argue that this is a slender reed on which to hold while the community of states takes a next step toward the better maintenance of international peace and security; but it appears preferable to gunboat diplomacy. Although major powers inevitably flex their muscles when their geopolitical interests are at stake, they do not inevitably subject themselves to international monitoring and law. Although hardly a panacea, mapping steps toward more accountable subcontracting nonetheless would seem to represent progress toward a more stable order.[55]

In short, the logic of these questions leads us to pursue more fundamental research about the complexities of international responses to sustain humane values in times of war. Whether the sum of the experience in the five cases examined in these pages falls definitively on the plus or minus side of the ledger remains largely an open question. Moreover, adding the terrible toll of Liberia, Sierra Leone, and Chechnya to the ongoing plight of East Africa and another thirty ongoing civil wars shatters any pretense of omniscient humanitarianism. The absence of consistent and hearty diplomacy and military action suggests a possible return to the "bad old days," akin to those of the Cold War, when abusive treatment by political authorities of "their" populations was largely beyond effective international challenge. In Algeria, for instance, the government believes that it falls into the category of not being subject to intervention.

Over time, it may be possible to conduct better comparisons across incomparable cases making use of the theoretical guidance preferred by Alexander George.[56] At the present moment, I am quite aware of the sui generis commentary that can be easily directed at my judgments. To take the example of Haiti and the positive judgment about intervention, it would be difficult to draw general lessons in light of the unusual specificities that contributed to success: the strong interest of the United States as regional power; Haiti's proximity to the main-

A UNMIH peacekeeping soldier from Canada stops to greet a young Haitian boy, as he patrols the streets of Port-au-Prince.
Credit: UN/DPI Photo 87334C by Eskinder Debebe

land and its island geography; the lack of allies for the de facto regime; the acquiescence or support of all the region's countries; agreement among Security Council members about legitimacy; first-time UN co-operation with the OAS and so on.

The validity of judgments is also diluted at present by the methodological problems of counterfactual analysis[57] flagged in Chapter 2 and present throughout the five case studies. In addition to being hard to quantify, many of the costs and benefits should be subjected to a "what if?" line of inquiry. The most important relationship concerns outside intervention and possibly worsening or prolonging armed conflicts, which has been the subject of much of the most strident criticism of well-meaning but sometimes inept humanitarian action of the 1990s. As indicated earlier, any crisis and its resulting international responses are perversely dialectical in that the crisis presents problems to which humanitarians respond. But these responses frequently create new problems (and costs). These unquantifiable interactions were a concern highlighted at the outset and repeated here because one's subjective evaluation of intermingling costs and benefits contributes to the nature of final judgments.

In pursuing a future research agenda, a final cautionary thought comes to mind: Analysts should be wary of dramatic pronouncements that are too closely tied to contemporary events and headlines. Many observers, including myself, are relearning not to make linear extrapolations from the most recent experiences. For instance, in April 1991, the dominant mod in policy and analytical circles after the Gulf War and Operation Provide Comfort was that "we could do anything." And barely three years later, almost to the day in April 1994, the prevailing mood was totally different, namely, that "we could do nothing" to halt genocide in Rwanda.

At present, the climate for military-civilian interactions in humanitarian crises is similar to that of the early and mid-1980s when the exoticism of UN peacekeeping concerned mainly *cognescenti*.[58] This had followed other periods of enthusiasm (after 1956 and again in the mid-1970s following efforts in the Middle East) as well as of despair (in the mid-1960s after the Congo). There are bound to be instances in which traditional peacekeeping, peace enforcement, and everything militarily messy in between will be relevant policy options for humanitarians as we enter the twenty-first century. Politics will prevent consistent responses, but some will occur. The fact that international responses will vary should not imply that observers should support not doing anything anywhere. And when action occurs, civilian-military interactions should reflect the lessons from the past. That, it seems, is the proverbial bottom line.

Humanitarian Quandaries

Can politics and humanitarianism be insulated from each other, or are they inevitably and inextricably enmeshed? It should come as no surprise that I support the latter interpretation. And the intersection of humanitarianism and politics has implications for the principles of neutrality, impartiality, and consent that are dear to the ICRC and many other institutions. A few years ago, I and a colleague claimed "sovereignty is no longer sacrosanct."[59] It would perhaps be fitting to adapt that now because "principles are no longer sacrosanct."

No one would disagree that during the post–Cold War era there have been numerous micro and macro examples of well-intentioned but ultimately counterproductive humanitarian action. Undoubtedly there are numerous bottom lines and interpretations of particular incidents, but virtually every analyst and humanitarian practitioner would agree that at least some of the well-intentioned outside efforts in Bosnia, the African Great Lakes region, and Somalia made matters worse rather than better. The commitment to saving lives and relieving suffering can have the unwanted and unintended consequences of fueling conflict, even of worsening some political crises, and also of eroding the longer-term coping capacities of target societies.

In this case, reflections and not reflexes are required because, in David Rieff's poignant prose, "despite the best intentions of aid workers, and at times because of them, they become logisticians in the war efforts of warlords, fundamentalists, gangsters, and ethnic cleansers."[60] One is not obliged to agree with John Hutchinson's pejorative connotations about the nature of this virtue in his highly critical history of the ICRC[61] in order to state frankly that it is insufficient, as ICRC official Cornelio Sommaruga has argued repeatedly, to praise apolitical humanitarianism as an "act of charity."[62]

Political humanitarianism, designed either to end violence or to transform conflict, is not necessarily a threat. Rather than a danger for humanitarians, such an approach could be viewed as an opportunity. There are risks in that humanitarian aid can be held hostage to politics without any payoff, but then again there are risks associated with any action. Careful empirical research is required to test the hypothesis, but it is plausible that placing humanitarian activities within a conflict resolution framework may ultimately work in favor of humanitarian interests, to bring substantially more benefits to victims than naïve and misplaced humanitarian action.

That we are asking such questions and that certain governments are pursuing strategies of political humanitarianism suggest that the pendulum within the community of humanitarians seems to have swung toward the Doctors without Borders school to intervene on behalf of the victims, to have a political agenda in mind and employ humanitarian action within a political strategy on their behalf. The notion that humanitarian action can and should be autonomous is giving way to the notion than the two types of action—political and humanitarian—cannot be dissociated, or at least that these actions should not be undertaken in isolation but in parallel. Andrew Natsios has noted that "the advocates of neutrality are losing ground in the debate."[63] Political humanitarianism is a legitimate response to the recognition that "humanitarianism is not enough" and cannot replace robust diplomatic and military action.[64]

There is no need to denigrate the heroic and unselfish acts of humanitarians or the value of compassion. Although it would be comforting to state otherwise, evidence contradicts relatively optimistic contentions from observers like Sommaruga and Roberts. Rieff has noted that to disagree that "barbarism is back"[65] is wishful thinking, or a "humanitarian illusion," and that "disillusionment is the beginning of wisdom in the analysis of this terrible reality, this time of piety and iron."[66] A striking fact of contemporary international society is that the numbers of individuals and organizations acting to foster humanitarian norms and facilitate humanitarian action has risen dramatically, as has media attention. The paradox is that barbarism is increasing apace.

To return to an earlier remark, "principles are no longer sacrosanct" but must be contextualized. A truly disturbing realization for humanitarians in the 1990s has been the diminishing relevance of rigid principles when confronting totally unprincipled actors. Although humanitarian action has never been easy, it was formerly more plausible to abide strictly by principles and be effective. Decisions were, for instance, more straightforward. The consistent application of neutrality, impartiality, and consent coincided with visceral reactions to rush to rescue war victims; and this combination almost always produced satisfactory results.

The 1968 Biafran War was considered an anomaly, although it was this event that triggered the founding of the MSF as a "counter" ICRC[67] and foreshadowed the debate that engulfs us today. The post–Cold War era has routinely witnessed a host of similarly disturbing and ambiguous realities in war zones. Context is as important as principles because the latter often clash. Thoughtful reflection thus has come to assume an increasing role relative to visceral reaction.

At the outset of the 1990s, Larry Minear and I spelled out what we called the "Providence Principles."[68] In a practical handbook for field practitioners, the presentation at that time already used "principles" in a somewhat unusual manner. It connoted more flexibility and pragmatism than may have been acceptable to many ethicists and moral philosophers. This approach was not opportunism but, rather, a step toward pragmatism, appropriate humanitarian ethics for a new and troubled period.

Rather than moral absolutes, the Providence Principles took this more utilitarian tack and were presented as norms toward which to strive, but without the illusion that success was guaranteed. Differences among principles exist and will continue to exist—in the interpretation given to them by various individuals and agencies, in the importance of some relative to others, and in the extent to which a given principle or principles will prevail in particular circumstances. Indeed, the validity of this utilitarian approach has been reinforced by subsequent experience and particularly by the analysis of the five case studies in these pages. From sustaining vulnerable groups in the African Great Lakes while feeding thugs and fueling the war, to moving threatened populations in Bosnia while facilitating ethnic cleansing, operational situations in the 1990s have been tortuous for victims as well as for their humanitarian benefactors.

In fact, the discourse of moral philosophy has become prevalent in contemporary analysis. Michael Ignatieff struggles with the "impalpable moral ideal: that the problems of other people, no matter how far away, are of concern to us all." Unfortunately, he continues, "almost everyone who tries to live by this ideal has a bad conscience; no one is quite sure whether our engagement makes things better or worse."[69] Just as Bill Maynes has put forward "ethical realpolitik" as an alternative for American foreign policy,[70] Mark Duffield has called for a "new ethics of working in political crises . . . [where] 'good guys' no longer exist."[71] Joanna Macrae has stated, "The idea that it is easy to distinguish the bad guy from the good woman and child is no longer sustainable."[72] In fact, in reviewing recent literature, a Norwegian group concluded that "growing awareness of the complex consequences of humanitarian assistance has sharpened the division between the 'pure humanitarians' and the 'solidarity humanitarians.' " In short, the ICRC view that principles are sacrosanct increasingly confronts an alternative that "neutrality is a form of moral bankruptcy."[73]

In spite of protestations from those who will cry "oxymoron," situational ethics are required. These can no longer be considered pejoratively in comparison with unassailable principles, what Myron Wiener has dubbed "instrumental humanitarianism."[74] The clear articulation of principles remains important in order to safeguard against the slippery slope of shameless opportunism. But when principles bump into one another, compromise and tough trade-offs are inevitable. Those who deviate from principles should be aware of the costs—and extenuating circumstances in all five cases indicate why such deviations are necessary and desirable. Those with principles who are clear about the costs of deviating from them will be more successful in helping victims than those with none or with inflexible principles.

Frequently, the word "dilemma" is employed by analysts and practitioners alike to describe painful situations in the five cases; but the word "quandary" would be more apt. A dilemma involves two or more alternative courses of action with unintended but unavoidable and *equally* undesirable consequences. If consequences are equally unpalatable, then remaining inactive on the sidelines is a viable and moral option, rather than entering the scrum on a battlefield. But the use of the military brought at least some benefits in all cases analyzed in the preceding pages, and quite substantial ones in northern Iraq and

Haiti. That more harm than good was done makes most empirical sense in the case of UNPROFOR's pathetic presence from 1992 to 1995 in Bosnia. Depending on one's point of departure and evaluation of available data, Rwanda and Somalia are more ambiguous.

Humanitarians find themselves perplexed, or in a quandary, but they are not and should not be immobilized in times of war. The key lies in making a good-faith effort to analyze the advantages and disadvantages of any military or civilian course of action and choosing what oftentimes amounts to the least-worst option. The calculus is agonizing but inescapable for those who engage themselves in war zones.

Far from occupying the high ground, humanitarians with fervent and rigid ideological commitments to principles are often ill at ease or even paralyzed in many of today's humanitarian crises. Because action is necessary to alleviate life-threatening suffering, a more instrumental approach to humanitarian decisionmaking is required. For evaluating the painful trade-offs implied by various policy choices, the situational morality championed by John Dewey emerges as desirable from the preceding analysis of military-civilian interactions. A humanitarianism that is thoughtful and contextual is more appropriate than one with an automatic application of principles for four reasons: There are often conflicting goals; good intentions can have catastrophe consequences; there are alternative ways to achieve ends; and even if none of the choices is ideal, victims still require decisions about outside help. The overall approach could resemble just war doctrine—each situation is so highly contextual that analyses and not formulas are required. The task is thus to be flexible rather than to take preset criteria and apply them blindly.[75]

Many of the decisions in northern Iraq, Somalia, Bosnia, Rwanda, and Haiti—but especially those involving the application of coercive military force—required selecting least-worst options. As the philosopher Thomas Nagle advises: "Given the limitations on human action, it is naive to suppose that there is a solution to every moral problem."[76] Thus action-oriented institutions and staff are required to contextualize their work and not blindly apply preconceived notions of what is right or wrong. Making decisions in war zones could perhaps benefit from the analogy of "clinical ethical review teams," whose members are on call to make painful decisions about life-and-death matters in hospitals.[77] Although certain religious traditions claim that principles should be applied automatically, new technologies present unfamiliar situations in which principles clash and yet decisions are required. Tough love—or what in a domestic context the British prime minister has described as "compassion with a hard edge"—is necessary in today's hospitals and wars. Finding solutions to challenges is emotionally wrenching but intellectually doable and operationally necessary. Humanitarians who cannot stand the heat generated by situational ethics should stay out of the post–Cold War humanitarian kitchen.

Mary Anderson, one of the more thoughtful analysts of development and of humanitarian action, recommends identifying the range and variety of ways in which outside assistance worsens rather than relieves violence. Her own bottom line for humanitarian help is "do no harm," part of a new "Hippocratic Oath of Aid."[78] In reducing rhetoric and lowering expectations, her advice rings particularly true for military-civilian interactions and is becoming part of the conventional logic of practitioners. Oxfam, for example, is calling upon humanitarian agencies to conduct "conflict impact assessments" before undertaking what otherwise might have been a knee-jerk reaction to rescue those suffering.[79] Understanding better the limitations of military coercion and of charity is a wise point of departure for humanitarian crises of the post-post-Cold War era.

Notes

Introduction

1. Raimo Väyrynen, *The Age of Humanitarian Emergencies*, Research for Action No. 25 (Helsinki: World Institute for Development Economics Research, June 1996).

2. For these and other disheartening statistics, see UNHCR, *The State of the World's Refugees, 1997–98: A Humanitarian Agenda* (Oxford: Oxford University Press, 1997); International Federation of Red Cross and Red Crescent Societies, *World Disasters Report, 1997* (Oxford: Oxford University Press, 1997); and DHA *Humanitarian Report, 1997* (New York: United Nations, 1997).

3. For contrasting partisan views, see Warren Christopher, "America's Leadership, America's Opportunity," *Foreign Policy* 98 (Spring 1995): 6–27; Bob Dole, "Shaping America's Global Future," *Foreign Policy* 98 (Spring 1995): 29–43, and Jesse Helms, "Saving the U.N.: A Challenge to the Next Secretary-General," *Foreign Affairs* 75, no. 5 (September–October 1996): 2–7. For a more academic overview, see John Gerard Ruggie, *Winning the Peace: America and World Order in the New Era* (New York: Columbia University Press, 1996). See also Charles William Maynes and Richard S. Williamson, eds., *U.S. Foreign Policy and the United Nations System* (New York: Norton, 1996).

4. Francis Fukuyama, *The End of History and the Last Man* (New York: Free Press, 1992). For a discussion on the phenomenon of fragmentation, see Lori Fisler Damrosch, ed., *Enforcing Restraint: Collective Intervention in Internal Conflicts* (New York: Council on Foreign Relations Press, 1993); Michael E. Brown, ed., *Ethnic Conflict and International Security* (Princeton, N.J.: Princeton University Press, 1993), and *The International Dimensions of Internal Conflict* (Cambridge, Mass.: MIT Press, 1996); Ted Robert Gurr and Barbara Harff, *Ethnic Conflict in World Politics* (Boulder, Colo.: Westview Press, 1994); Gidon Gottlieb, *Nation against State* (New York: Council on Foreign Relations Press, 1993); and "Reconstructing Nations and States," special issue on *Dædalus* 122, no. 3 (Summer 1993). For discussions of the difficulties of negotiating the end to such wars, see I. William Zartman, ed., *Elusive Peace: Negotiating an End to Civil Wars*

(Washington, D.C.: Brookings Institution, 1995); and Fed Osler Hampson, *Nurturing Peace: Why Peace Settlements Succeed or Fail* (Washington, D.C.: U.S. Institute of Peace Press, 1996).

5. See James Rosenau, *Turbulence in World Politics: A Theory of Change and Continuity* (Princeton, N.J.: Princeton University Press, 1990), and *The United Nations in a Turbulent World* (Boulder, Colo.: Lynne Rienner Publishers, 1992).

6. Commission on Global Governance, *Our Global Neighbourhood* (Oxford: Oxford University Press, 1995). For other visions, see also South Centre, *For a Strong and Democratic United Nations: A South Perspective on UN Reform* (Geneva: South Centre, 1996); Independent Working Group on the Future of the United Nations, *The United Nations in Its Second Half-Century* (New York: Ford Foundation, 1995); and Gareth Evans, *Cooperating for Peace: The Global Agenda for the 1990s and Beyond* (St. Leonard's, Australia: Allen & Unwin, 1993). For an evaluation of these proposals, see Michael Barnett, "Bringing in the New World Order: Liberalism, Legitimacy, and the United Nations," *World Politics* 49 (July 1997): 526–551.

7. See Thomas G. Weiss, David P. Forsythe, and Roger A. Coate, *The United Nations and Changing World Politics*, 2nd ed. (Boulder, Colo.: Westview Press, 1997); and Inis L. Claude Jr., "Peace and Security: Prospective Roles for the Two United Nations," *Global Governance* 2, no. 3 (September–December 1996): 289–298.

8. For a discussion of the impact of Somalia, see Tom J. Farer, "Intervention in Unnatural Humanitarian Emergencies: Lessons of the First Phase," *Human Rights Quarterly* 18, no. 1 (February 1996): 1–22; and Thomas G. Weiss, "Overcoming the Somalia Syndrome—'Operation Rekindle Hope'?" *Global Governance* 1, no. 2 (May–August 1995): 171–187.

9. Quoted by Alison Mitchell, "Clinton's About-Face," *New York Times*, 24 September 1996, A8.

10. Both are found in Boutros Boutros-Ghali, *An Agenda for Peace, 1995* (New York: United Nations, 1995).

11. Kofi Annan, *Renewing the United Nations: A Programme for Reform* (New York: United Nations, 1997), document dated 16 July 1997; references are made to paragraph numbers throughout.

12. The term "military humanitarianism" to describe the military's possible involvement in the post–Cold War era was first used by Thomas G. Weiss and Kurt M. Campbell, "Military Humanitarianism" *Survival* 33, no. 5 (September–October 1991): 51–465. See also Robert H. Jackson, "Armed Humanitarianism," *International Journal* 68, no. 4 (1993): 579–606; and Thomas G. Weiss, "Military-Civilian Humanitarianism: The 'Age of Innocence' Is Over," *International Peacekeeping* 2, no. 2 (Summer 1995): 157–174.

13. James F. Hoge, "Editor's Note," *Foreign Affairs* 73, no. 6 (November–December 1994): v.

14. See, for example, Stephen John Stedman, "The New Interventionists," *Foreign Affairs* 72, no. 1 (1992–1993): 1–16; and Barry Posner, "Military Responses to Refugee Disasters," *International Security* 21, no. 1 (Summer 1996): 72–111. The best bibliographic information and its interpretation is found in

Oliver Famsbotham and Tom Woodhouse, *Humanitarian Intervention in Contemporary Conflict* (Cambridge: Polity Press, 1996). See also John Harriss, ed., *The Politics of Humanitarian Intervention* (London: Pinter, 1995); James Mayall, ed., *The New Interventionism: United Nations Experience in Cambodia, Former Yugoslavia, and Somalia* (New York: Cambridge University Press, 1996); Jan Nederveen Pieterse, ed., *World Orders in the Making: The Case of Humanitarian Intervention* (London: Macmillan, 1998); and Chr. Michelsen Institute, *Humanitarian Assistance and Conflict* (Bergern: Chr. Michelsen Institute, 1997).

15. See Michael Ignatieff, "Unarmed Warriors," *New Yorker*, 24 March 1997, 24–71, and *The Warrior's Honor: Ethnic War and the Modern Conscience* (New York: Henry Holt & Co., 1997), esp. 109–163.

16. Leslie H. Gelb, "Quelling the Teacup Wars," *Foreign Affairs* 73, no. 6 (November–December 1994): 5.

17. Quoted by Ken Booth, "Dare Not to Know: International Relations Theory versus the Future," in *International Relations Theory Today*, ed. Ken Booth and Steve Smith (Cambridge: Polity Press, 1995), 348.

18. Ignatieff, *The Warrior's Honor*, 8.

Chapter 1

1. The interested reader is referred to a number of works I coauthored, upon which this section draws: Larry Minear and Thomas G. Weiss, *Mercy under Fire: War and the Global Humanitarian Community* (Boulder, Colo.: Westview Press, 1995), 45–55; Larry Minear and Thomas G. Weiss, *Humanitarian Politics*, Headline Series No. 304 (New York: Foreign Policy Association, 1995), 20–31; and Thomas G. Weiss and Cindy Collins, *Humanitarian Challenges and Intervention: World Politics and the Dilemmas of Help* (Boulder, Colo.: Westview Press, 1996), 39–94.

2. See Jonathan Moore, *The UN and Complex Emergencies* (Geneva: UN Research Institute for Social Development, 1996); Minear and Weiss, *Mercy under Fire*; and Weiss and Collins, *Humanitiran Challenges*.

3. See Human Rights Watch, *The Lost Agenda: Human Rights and U.N. Field Operations* (New York: Human Rights Watch, 1993), and *Human Rights Watch World Report, 1995* (New York: Human Rights Watch, 1994). See also, Paul La-Rose-Edwards, *Human Rights Principles and Practice in United Nations Field Operations* (Ottawa: Department of Foreign Affairs, September 1995); Robert Cohen and Jacques Cuénod, *Improving Institutional Arrangements for the Internally Displaced* (Washington, D.C.: RPG, 1993); and Alice H. Henkin, ed., *Honoring Human Rights and Keeping the Peace: Lessons from El Salvador, Cambodia, and Haiti* (Washington, D.C.: Aspen Institute, 1995).

4. For a discussion, see Frederick C. Cuny, "Dilemmas of Military Involvement in Humanitarian Relief," in *Soldiers, Peacekeepers, and Disasters*, ed. Leon Gordenker and Thomas G. Weiss (London: Macmillan, 1991), 52–81.

5. Cuny, "Dilemmas of Military Involvement," 54.

6. See, for example, an extensive shopping list in "Table 4: Possible Uses of

Military Force for Humanitarian Missions in Complex Emergencies," from U.S. Mission to the United Nations, *Global Humanitarian Emergencies, 1995*, document dated January 1995, 19.

7. Larry Minear and Philippe Guillot, *Soldiers to the Rescue: Humanitarian Lessons from Rwanda* (Paris: OECD, 1996), 163.

8. See John B. Hunt, "OOTW: A Concept in Flux," *Military Review* 4006, no. 5 (September–October 1996): 3–9.

9. See Jarat Chopra, "Back to the Drawing Board," *Bulletin of the Atomic Scientists* 51, no. 2 (March–April 1995): 29–35; "The Space of Peace Maintenance," *Political Geography* 15, nos. 3–4 (March–April 1996): 335–357; and *Peace-Maintenance: The Evolution of International Political Authority* (London: Routledge, forthcoming).

10. Chris Seiple, *The U.S. Military/NGO Relationship in Humanitarian Intervention* (Carlisle, Penn.: U.S. Army War College, 1996), v-vi. See also Robert D. Kaplan, "Fort Leavenworth and the Eclipse of Nationhood," *Atlantic Monthly*, September 1996, 75–90.

11. See Adam Roberts, "Humanitarian War: Military Intervention and Human Rights," *International Affairs* 69 (1993): 429–449.

12. This presentation builds on an argument first made in Thomas G. Weiss, "The United Nations at Fifty: Recent Lessons," *Current History* 94, no. 592 (May 1995): 218–222.

13. UNDP, *Human Development Report, 1994* (New York: Oxford University Press, 1994), 47.

14. Ted Robert Gurr and Will H. Moore, "States versus Peoples: Ethnopolitical Conflict in the 1980s with Risk Assessments for the 1990s," draft paper for the Minorities at Risk Project, University of Maryland, 30 April 1996. See also the more complete document, Ted Robert Gurr, *Minorities at Risk: A Global View of Ethnopolitical Conflicts* (Washington, D.C.: U.S. Institute of Peace Press, 1993). See also Dan Smith, *The State of War and Peace Atlas* (London: Penguin, 1997).

15. Joanna Macrae and Mark Bradbury, *Tackling Transition: A Critical Analysis of Relief—Development Linkages in Situations of Chronic Instability*, Working Paper (New York: UNICEF, 1998), sec. 2.3.1.

16. Inter-Agency Standing Committee, "Working Paper on the Definition of Complex Emergency," document dated December 1994.

17. Detailed calculations have been done by Christer Ahlstrom, *Casualties of Conflict: Report for the World Campaigning for the Protection of Victims of War* (Uppsala: Department of Peace and Research, 1991), 8 and 19. The late Jim Grant made this a battle cry in his later years as UNICEF's executive director. Skeptics point to the campaigns against Native Americans as a possible counter to these "new" civilian casualty trends; civilians also did not fare well during World War II. Nonetheless, the general point is valid: Civilians are increasingly the main victims of wars.

18. Barry Posen, "Military Responses to Refugee Disasters," *International Security* 21, no. 1 (Summer 1996): 108.

19. See Gerald B. Helman and Steven R. Ratner, "Saving Failed States," *Foreign Policy* 89 (Winter 1992–1993): 3–20; and I. William Zartman, ed., *Collapsed*

States: The Disintegration and Restoration of Legitimate Authority (Boulder, Colo.: Lynne Rienner Publishers, 1995).

20. See Jarat Chopra and Thomas G. Weiss, "Sovereignty Is No Longer Sacrosanct: Codifying Humanitarian Intervention," *Ethics and International Affairs* 6 (1992): 95–117. For a series of essays, see Gene M. Lyons and Michael Mastanduno, eds., *Beyond Westphalia? National Sovereignty and Intervention* (Baltimore, Md.: Johns Hopkins University Press, 1995); Paul A. Winters, ed., *Interventionism: Current Controversies* (San Diego: Greenhaven Press, 1995); and Marianne Heiberg, ed., *Subduing Sovereignty: Sovereignty and the Right to Intervene* (London: Pinter, 1994). For a reasoned presentation of some negative and positive arguments in light of international relations theory, see Ernst B. Haas, "Beware the Slippery Slope: Notes Toward the Definition of Justifiable Intervention," in *Emerging Norms of Justified Intervention*, ed. Laura W. Reed and Carl Kaysen (Cambridge, Mass.: American Academy of Arts & Sciences, 1993), 63–87.

21. See Mohammed Ayoob, "The New-Old Disorder in the Third World," in *Collective Security in a Changing World,* ed. Thomas G. Weiss, (Boulder, Colo.: Lynne Rienner Publishers, 1993), 13–30, and *The Third World Security Predicament: State Making, Regional Conflict, and the International System* (Boulder, Colo.: Lynne Rienner Publishers, 1995). See also Kalevi J. Holsti, *The State, War, and the State of War* (Cambridge: Cambridge University Press, 1996); Robert Jackson, *Quasi-States: Sovereignty, International Relations, and the Third World* (Cambridge: Cambridge University Press, 1990); Joel Migdal, *Strong States and Weak Societies: State-Society Relations and State Capabilities in the Third World* (Princeton, N.J.: Princeton University Press, 1988); and Edward E. Rice, *Wars of the Third Kind: Conflict in Underdeveloped Countries* (Berkeley: University of California Press, 1988).

22. See Nigels Rodley, ed., *To Loose the Bonds of Wickedness: International Intervention in Defence of Human Rights* (London: Brassey's, 1992).

23. The United Nations published the third edition of *The Blue Helmets* (New York: United Nations, 1996). The best examples of the growing literature are: William J. Durch, ed., *The Evolution of UN Peacekeeping: Case Studies and Comparative Analysis* (New York: St. Martin's Press, 1993), and *UN Peacekeeping, American Policy, and the Uncivil Wars of the 1990s* (New York: St. Martin's Press, 1996); Paul Diehl, *International Peacekeeping* (Baltimore, Md.: Johns Hopkins University Press, 1993); Mats R. Berdal, *Whither UN Peacekeeping?* Adelphi Paper No. 281 (London: International Institute for Strategic Studies, 1993); and Steven R. Ratner, *The New UN Peacekeeping: Building Peace in Lands of Conflict after the Cold War* (New York: St. Martin's Press, 1995).

24. Boutros Boutros-Ghali, *Supplement to "An Agenda for Peace,"* para. 77, published along with the 1992 *An Agenda for Peace* in *An Agenda for Peace, 1995* (New York: United Nations, 1995). Paragraph numbers are identical to those in the original.

25. For a quick and up-to-date reference about such matters, see http://www.globalpolicy.org.

26. Paul Kennedy, *The Rise and Fall of the Great Powers* (New York: Random House, 1987).

27. Antonio Donini, *The Policies of Mercy: UN Coordination in Afghanistan, Mozambique, and Rwanda* Occasional Paper No. 22, (Providence, R.I.: Watson Institute, 1996), 14.

28. UNDRO was headed by an undersecretary-general. However, Boutros-Ghali had cut dramatically the number of undersecretaries-general as one of his first administrative decisions. Thus, it was not a foregone conclusion that the emergency relief coordinator would occupy the same rank as the disaster relief coordinator.

29. Much of the controversy surrounded the fear of developing countries of a humanitarian "Trojan horse" that would eventually be used to override their sovereignty. For an extended discussion of this controversy, see Mario Bettati, *Le Droit d'Ingérence: Mutation de l'Ordre International* (Paris: Odile Jacob, 1996).

30. Jacques Cuénod, "Coordinating United Nations Humanitarian Assistance," *RPG Focus* (Washington, D.C.: RPG, 1993).

31. Brian Urquhart and Erskine Childers, *A World in Need of Leadership: Tomorrow's United Nations—A Fresh Appraisal* (Uppsala: Hammarskjöld Foundation, 1996).

32. The names of UN bodies and their corresponding acronyms change with confusing rapidity, but this essay uses those in place when events occurred. In 1991, the original Resolution 46/182 called for an emergency relief coordinator, but the first unit was labeled the Department of Humanitarian Affairs, which existed from April 1992 through December 1997. The reform proposals and discussions between July 1997 and the General Assembly's decision in December 1997 referred to the revived Office of the Emergency Relief Coordinator. Following the recommendation of the secretary-general, General Assembly Resolution 52/72 "designated the Emergency Relief Coordinator as the United Nations Humanitarian Assistance Coordinator." This decision produced the rather infelicitous acronym of OUNHAC for his office. In January 1998, at the request of the new undersecretary-general, the Office for the Coordination of Humanitarian Affairs was approved by the secretary-general. The head of this office now uses two titles: undersecretary-general for humanitarian affairs and emergency relief coordinator.

33. See Thomas G. Weiss, "Humanitarian Shell Games: Whither UN Reform?" *Security Dialogue* 29, no. 1 (March 1998): 9–23.

34. See Thomas G. Weiss, ed., *Beyond UN Subcontracting: Task-sharing with Regional Security Arrangements and Service-Providing NGOs* (London: Macmillan, 1997); also published as a special issue of *Third World Quarterly* 18, no. 3 (Summer 1997).

35. See David Shearer, *Private Armies and Military Intervention*, Adelphi Paper No. 316 (Oxford: Oxford University Press, 1998).

36. For an early discussion of the shortcomings of regional action, see S. Neil MacFarlane and Thomas G. Weiss, "Regional Organizations and Regional Security," *Security Studies* 2, no. 1 (Autumn 1992): 6–37. For an extended argument about a "partnership" between the UN and regional organizations, see Alan K. Henrikson, "The Growth of Regional Organizations and the Role of the United Nations," in *Regionalism in World Politics: Regional Organizations and*

World Order, (Oxford: Oxford University Press, 1995), 122–168. For a discussion about the components of accountability in relationship to Russia, see Jarat Chopra and Thomas G. Weiss, "Prospects for Containing Conflict in the Former Second World," *Security Studies* 4, no. 3 (Spring 1995): 552–583; see also, Lena Jonson and Clive Archer, eds., *Peacekeeping and the Role of Russia in Eurasia* (Boulder, Colo.: Westview Press, 1996).

37. See Leon Gordenker and Thomas G. Weiss, "The Collective Security Idea and Changing World Politics," in *Collective Security and Changing World Politics,* ed. Thomas G. Weiss (Boulder, Colo.: Lynne Rienner Publishers, 1993), 3–18.

38. For an outspoken view on this subject, see John Mearsheimer, "The False Promise of International Institutions," *International Security* 19, no. 3 (Winter 1994–1995): 5–49.

39. Marrack Goulding, "The Use of Force by the United Nations," *International Peacekeeping* 3, no. 1 (Spring 1996): 5. This is also a major theme in Adam Roberts, "From San Francisco to Sarajevo: The UN and the Use of Force," *Survival* 37, no. 4 (Winter 1995–1996): 7–28.

40. For a longer discussion, see Thomas G. Weiss, "Humanitarian Action by Nongovernmental Organizations," in the *International Dimensions of Internal Conflict,* ed. Michael E. Brown (Cambridge, Mass.: MIT Press, 1996), 435–459. The emphasis here is on external NGOs, which bring outside resources to the scene of a conflict. Local NGOs are experiencing similar growth, but they are not the focus here. Hence, "NGO" means "international NGO" unless otherwise specified.

41. The term "NGO" refers in this essay to a nonprofit, voluntary, formal, nonviolent, nonpolitical (that is, not primarily interested in promoting candidates for political office) organization whose objective is to promote development and social change. Many private organizations that seek to make profits are excluded, as are organized crime, insurgents, churches in their strictly religious functions, the media, and political parties. Together with NGOs, these other nonstate actors constitute what is usually called "civil society."

42. There is an ever-growing literature produced in the last decade. To cite merely a few key pieces from that time, see Bertrand Schneider, *The Barefoot Revolution: A Report to the Club of Rome* (London: IT Publications, 1988); David Korten, *Getting to the 21st Century: Voluntary Action and the Global Agenda* (West Hartford, Conn.: Kumarian Press, 1990); and Paul Wapner, *Environmental Activism and World Civic Politics* (New York: State University of New York Press, 1996). An annotated bibliography is found in Thomas G. Weiss and Leon Gordenker, eds., *NGOs, the UN, and Global Governance* (Boulder, Colo.: Lynne Rienner Publishers, 1996), 227–240.

43. Union of International Associations, *Handbook of International Organizations* (Brussels: Union of International Associations, 1994).

44. Bill Seary, "The Early History: From the Congress of Vienna to the San Francisco Conference," in *"The Conscience of the World": The Influence of Non-Governmental Organisations in the U.N. System,* ed. Peter Willetts, (London: Hurst, 1996): 15–30.

45. UNDP, *Human Development Report, 1994* (New York: Oxford University Press, 1994).

46. Terje Tvedt, "Development NGOs—Actors in a New International Social System," draft paper for the Centre for Development Studies, University of Bergen, 3 November 1997.

47. Julie Fisher, *The Road from Rio: Sustainable Development and the Nongovernmental Movement in the Third World* (Westport, Conn.: Praeger, 1993).

48. Robin Guthrie, *Civic, Civil, or Servile?* (Geneva: International Standing Conference on Philanthropy, 1994), 7.

49. Andrew S. Natsios, "An NGO Perspective," in *Peacemaking in International Conflict*, ed. I. William Zartman and J. Lewis Rasmussen (Washington, D.C.: United States Institute of Peace Press, 1997): 337–361, 337.

50. Peter J. Spiro, "New Global Potentates: Nongovernmental Organizations and the 'Unregulated' Marketplace," *Cordozo Law Review* 18, no. 3 (December 1996): 957–969.

51. For example, in a recent survey of local NGOs in Bangladesh, Ethiopia, Nicaragua, and Zimbabwe that received support from Norway, over 50 percent had been created since 1980 and 25 percent since 1990. The availability of Norwegian seed money was one of the main explanations for the rapid creation of such local NGOs. See Terje Tvedt, *NGOs in Aid: Some Case Studies* (Bergen: Centre for Development Studies, 1995).

52. See Ian Smillie, *The Alms Bazaar: Altruism under Fire—Non-profit Organizations and International Organizations* (West Hartford, Conn.: Kumarian Press, 1995); Judith Randel and Tony German, eds., *The Reality of Aid, 1997–1998* (London: Earthscan, 1997); and Francesco Mezzalama, *Review of Financial Resources Allocated by the United Nations System to Activities by Non-governmental Organizations* (Geneva: Joint Inspection Unit, 1996).

53. John Borton, *NGOs and Relief Operations: Trends and Policy Implications*, ESCOR Research Study R47774, (London: Overseas Development Institute, 1994), 16.

54. See Mark Duffield and John Prendergast, *Without Troops or Tanks: Humanitarian Intervention in Eritrea and Ethiopia* (Trenton, N.J.: Red Sea Press, 1994).

55. See Jon Bennett, ed., *Meeting Needs: NGO Coordination in Practice* (London: Earthscan, 1995).

56. See, for example, Michael Maren, *The Road to Hell: The Ravaging Effects of Foreign Aid and International Charity* (New York: Free Press, 1997); Alex de Waal and Rakiya Omaar, *Humanitarianism Unbound*, Discussion Paper No. 5 (London: Africa Rights, 1994); David Sogge, ed., *Compassion and Calculation: The Business of Private Foreign Aid* (London: Pluto Press, 1996); and Peter J. Burnell, *Charity, Politics, and the Third World* (New York: Harvester Wheatleaf, 1991).

Chapter 2

1. See, for example, John F. Lehman Jr. and Harvey Sicherman, eds., *The Demilitarization of the Military* (Washington, D.C.: Foreign Policy Research Insti-

tute, 1997). It should be noted that this loss is often more than offset by the testing of logistical and other skills under trying conditions. Many military units (for example, the Scandinavians) get their actual field experience in peacekeeping missions. During the Cold War and right after, even the U.S. military felt that UN missions were a good way to test various logistics and communications systems. Obviously, this has changed as a result of the proliferation of missions in the 1990s.

2. Eventually, it would be useful to establish a baseline for the five cases prior to the humanitarian crises—that is, northern Iraq prior to the Gulf War, Bosnia before the breakup of the former Yugoslavia, Somalia prior to the famine and anarchy, Rwanda before the genocide, and Haiti prior to Aristide. This would adopt the approach of Michael Crenna's edited volume *The True Costs of Conflict: Seven Recent Wars and Their Effects on Society* (New York: New Press, 1994) to gauge what the situation would be like had there been no conflict.

3. Jeffrey Herbst, for instance, has challenged the dogma of sovereignty in Africa in "Responding to State Failure in Africa" *International Security* 21, no. 3 (Winter 1996–1997): 120–144.

4. Charles King, *Ending Civil Wars,* Adelphia Paper No. 308 (Oxford: Oxford University Press, 1997), 12.

5. See Cindy Collins and Thomas G. Weiss, *A Review and Assessment of 1989–1996 Peace Operations Publications,* Occasional Paper No. 28 (Providence, R.I.: Watson Institute, 1997).

6. See Tabyiegen Agnes Aboum, Eshetu Chole, Koste Manibe, Larry Minear, Abdul Mohammed, Jennefer Sebstan, and Thomas G. Weiss, *A Critical Review of Operation Lifeline Sudan: A Report to the Aid Agencies* (Washington, D.C.: RPG, 1991), 55.

7. GAO, "Contingency Operations: DOD's Reported Costs Contain Significant Inaccuracies," Chapter Report, GAO/NSIAD-96–115 (Washington, D.C.: GAO, 17 May 1996).

8. GAO, "Peace Operations: Information on U.S. and UN Activities," Briefing Report, GAO/NSIAD-95–102BR (Washington, D.C.: GAO, 31 February 1995).

9. Philip E. Tetlock and Aaron Belkin, eds., *Conterfactual Thought Experiments in World Politics: Logical, Methodological, and Psychological Perspectives* (Princeton, N.J.: Princeton University Press, 1996).

10. For a persuasive analysis of the failure of outside assistance in Rwanda, see Peter Uvin, *Development, Aid, and Conflict: Reflections from the Case of Rwanda,* Research for Action No. 24 (Helsinki: World Institute for Development Economics Research, 1996). For a more general review, see Judith Randel and Tony German, eds., *The Reality of Aid, 1997–1998* (London: Earthscan, 1997).

11. See Larry Minear, Colin Scott, and Thomas G. Weiss, *Humanitarian Action and Security in Liberia, 1989–1994,* Occasional Paper No. 20 (Providence, R.I.: Watson Institute, 1995); and S. Neil MacFarlane, Larry Minear, and Stephen Shenfield, *Armed Conflict in Georgia: A Case Study in Humanitarian Action and Peacekeeping,* Occasional Paper No. 21 (Providence, R.I.: Watson Institute, 1996).

12. See George Soros, chairman of an Independent Task Force, *American National Interest and the United Nations* (New York; Council on Foreign Relations Press, 1996), esp. 4–6.

13. For discussions, see Michael Pugh, "Humanitarianism and Peacekeeping," *Global Society* 10, no. 3 (1996): 205–224; and F. T. Liu, "Peacekeeping and Humanitarian Assistance," in *Soldiers, Peacekeepers, and Disasters*, ed. Leon Gordenker and Thomas G. Weiss (London: Macmillan, 1991), 33–51.

14. The interested reader is referred to Georgios Kostakos and Dimitris Bourantonis, "Innovations in Peace-keeping: The Case of Albania," and Fatmir Mema, "Did Albania Really Need Operation 'Alba'?" *Security Dialogue* 29, no. 1 (March 1998): 49–58 and 59–62, respectively.

15. This is a major conclusion of a literature review by the Chr. Michelsen Institute, *Humanitarian Assistance and Conflict* (Bergen: Chr. Michelsen Institute, 1997), 17–31.

16. The most controversial analyses are Alex de Waal and Rakiya Omaar, *Humanitarianism Unbound? Current Dilemmas Facing Multi-Mandate Relief Operations in Political Emergencies*, Discussion Paper No. 5 (London: African Rights, 1994), and the same authors' "The Genocide in Rwanda and the International Response," *Current History* 94 (April 1995): 156–161. See also "Rescue—The Paradoxes of Virtue," a special issue of *Social Research* 62, no. 1 (Spring 1995), especially Michael Walzer's "The Politics of Rescue," 53–66; David Rieff, "The Humanitarian Trap," *World Policy Journal* 12, no. 4 (Winter 1994–1995): 1–11; and Amir Pasic and Thomas G. Weiss, "The Politics of Rescue: Yugoslavia's Wars and the Humanitarian Impulse, 1991–1995," *Ethics and International Affairs* 11 (1997): 105–131, with "Commentary" by Andrew Natsios, Morton Winston, Alain Destexhe, and David R. Mapel, 132–149.

17. Richard K. Betts, "The Delusion of Impartial Intervention," *Foreign Affairs* 73, no. 6 (November–December 1994): 20–33.

18. Chester A. Crocker, "All Aid Is Political," *New York Times*, 21 November 1996, A29.

19. See John Prendergast, *Frontline Diplomacy: Humanitarian Aid and Conflict in Africa* (Boulder, Colo.: Lynne Rienner Publishers, 1997). For a more vitriolic treatment, see Michael Maren, *The Road to Hell: The Ravaging Effects of Foreign Aid and International Charity* (New York: Free Press, 1997).

20. See Marrack Goulding, "The Use of Force by the United Nations," *International Peacekeeping* 3, no. 1 (Spring 1996): 1–18.

21. Stanley Hoffmann, "The Politics and Ethics of Military Intervention," *Survival* 37, no. 4 (Winter 1995–1996): 30.

Chapter 3

1. This section relies on Richard I. Lawless, "Iraq: History," in *The Middle East and North Africa, 1997* (London: Europa Publications, 1997), 500–520; Michael M. Gunter, *The Kurds of Iraq: Tragedy and Hope* (New York: St. Martin's

Press, 1992), 119; and Mehrdad Izady, *The Kurds: A Concise Handbook* (Washington, D.C.: Taylor & Francis, 1992).

2. Robert Olson, "The Kurdish Question in the Aftermath of the Gulf War: Geopolitical and Geostrategic Changes in the Middle East," *Third World Quarterly* 13, no. 3 (1992): 475–499.

3. Gunter, *The Kurd of Iraq*, 15.

4. "The cost of the eight year war to the Iraqi economy was estimated by Kamran Mofid to have amounted to $452.6 billion . . . but does not include non-monetary cost elements such as inflationary costs, loss of services and earnings of those who were killed or disabled by the war, depletion of natural resources, loss of potential earnings due to the postponement of development projects, cost of delayed education and training, and the burden on society of those who were disabled." Estimated debt as of 1990: Iraqi government says $42.097 billion, but this is because government considered funds from Gulf states to be grants. However, this belief was not shared by the same states. Therefore, total debt can be estimated at $86 billion, with $35 billion to the West, $11 billion to the Warsaw Pact nations, and $40 billion to other Arab countries. Quoted by Abbas Alnasrawi, "Iraq: Economic Consequences of the 1991 Gulf War and Future Outlook," *Third World Quarterly* 13, no. 2 (1992): 336–337. See Kamran Mofid, *The Economic Consequences of the Gulf War* (London: Routledge, 1990).

5. UNHCR, Centre for Documentation and Research, *Background Paper on Iraqi Refugees and Asylum Seekers* (Geneva: UNHCR, September 1996), at: http://www.unhcr.ch/refworld/country/cdr/cdrirq2.htm. According to document, Middle East Watch cites 50,000 to 100,000 killed, while Committee against Repression and for Democratic Rights in Iraq cites 180,000 to 200,000. DOS, *Report on Iraqi Human Rights Practices, 1996*, (document dated 1 January 1997), at: http://www.state.gov/www/issues/human_rights/1996_hrp_report/iraq.html: According to document, Human Rights Watch cites 70,000 to 100,000 killed. Amnesty International cites 100,000 killed.

6. Lawless, "Iraq," 511.

7. Information and resolutions can be found conveniently in United Nations, *The United Nations and the Iraq-Kuwait Conflict, 1990–1996* (New York: UN Department of Public Information, 1996).

8. Larry Minear, U. B. P. Chelliah, Jeff Crisp, John MacKinlay, and Thomas G. Weiss, *United Nations Coordination of the International Humanitarian Response to the Gulf Crisis, 1990–1992*, Occasional Paper No. 13 (Providence, R.I.: Watson Institute, 1992).

9. Report to the secretary-general on humanitarian needs in Kuwait and Iraq in the immediate postcrisis environment by a mission to the area led by undersecretary-general for Administration and Management Martti Antisaari, dated 20 March 1991, 5.

10. Gregory Quinn, "The Iraq Conflict (1990-), in *The True Costs of Conflict*, ed. Michael Cranna (New York: Saferworld, 1994), 26–27.

11. Alnasrawi, "Iraq," 345–346; and Quinn, "The Iraq Conflict," 26.

12. Quinn, "The Iraq Conflict," 26.

13. See Eric Hoskins, "The Humanitarian Impact of Economic Sanctions and War in Iraq," in *Political Gain and Civilian Pain: The Humanitarian Impacts of Economic Sanctions*, ed. Thomas G. Weiss, David Cortright, George A. Lopez, and Larry Minear (Lanham, Md.: Rowman & Littlefield, 1997), 91–147.

14. See Middle East Watch/Human Rights Watch, *Endless Torment: The 1991 Uprising in Iraq and Its Aftermath* (New York: Middle East Watch/Human Rights Watch, June 1992).

15. Colonel Ahmad Zubaidi, "The Structure of the Iraqi Forces," cited in Faleh Abd al-Jabbar, "Why the Uprisings Failed," *Middle East Report* (May–June 1992), cited in Middle East Watch/Human Rights Watch, *Endless Torment*, 31.

16. Middle East Watch/Human Rights Watch, *Endless Torment*, 30.

17. Middle East Watch/Human Rights Watch, *Endless Torment*, 48–49.

18. Middle East Watch/Human Rights Watch, *Endless Torment*, 60–66.

19. Ranges include: 20,000 Kurds, cited by UN in Eric Hooglund, *Middle East Report* (May–June 1992), cited in Ronald Ofteringer and Ralf Bäcker, "A Republic of Statelessness: Three Years of Humanitarian Intervention in Iraqi Kurdistan," *Middle East Report* (March–June 1994): 41; 150,000 Kurds, cited in Lawless, "Iraq," 514; 25,000–100,000 predominantly in southern Iraq, cited in "Violence Increasing in N. Iraq," *Washington Post*, 4 June 1992, cited in Middle East Watch/Human Rights Watch, *Endless Torment*, 29; 30,000 civilians and rebels and 5,000 soldiers, cited in Greenpeace document "Iraqi Deaths from the Gulf War as of April 1992," cited in Middle East Watch/Human Rights Watch, *Endless Torment*, 29; and 30,000 civilian deaths, cited by demographer at U.S. Census Bureau, cited in "Agency Reinstates Tabulator of Iraqi War Deaths," *New York Times*, 13 April 1992.

20. Franca Brilliant, Frederick C. Cuny, Pat Reed, and Victor Tanner, eds., *Humanitarian Assistance Lessons of Operation Provide Comfort: A Study Prepared for the Office of U.S. Foreign Disaster Assistance and U.S. Army Civil Affairs* (Dallas, Tex.: INTERTECT, 1992).

21. Lawrence Freedman and David Boren, " 'Safe Havens' for Kurds in Post-War Iraq," in *To Loose the Bands of Wickedness: International Intervention in Defence of Human Rights*, ed. Nigel S. Rodley (London: Brassey's, 1992), 43–92.

22. Brilliant et al., *Humanitarian Assistance Lessons*, 43–44.

23. Robert W. Kneller, "The Mortality Experience of Kurdish Refugees Remaining in Turkey," *Disasters* 16, no. 3 (1992): 249.

24. DOS, *Iraqi Human Rights* (Washington, D.C.: DOS, March 1996).

25. Freedman and Boren, "Safe Havens," 51.

26. See John D. H. Porter, Frank L. Van Loock, and Alain Devaux, "Evaluation of the Two Kurdish Refugee Camps in Iran, May 1991: The Value of Cluster Sampling in Processing Priorities and Policy," *Disasters* 17, no. 4 (1993): 341–347.

27. Freedman and Boren, "Safe Havens," 48 and 69.

28. Alnasrawi, "Iraq," 345–346.

29. Larry Minear, Colin Scott, and Thomas G. Weiss, *The News Media, Civil War, and Humanitarian Action* (Boulder, Colo.: Lynne Rienner Publishers, 1996), 50–53.

30. Jane E. Stromseth, "Iraq's Repression of Its Civilian Population: Collective Responses and Continuing Challenges," in *Enforcing Restraint: Collective Intervention in Internal Conflicts,* ed. Lori Fisler Damrosch (New York: Council on Foreign Relations Press, 1993), 97–102.

31. *Operation Provide Comfort Fact Sheet,* at: http://www.incirlik.af.mil/orgs/opc/opcfact.html. The INTERTECT study reveals that as much as 40 percent of the food shipments was packaging. Therefore, the actual usable items of this tonnage were significantly less.

32. *Operations Provide Comfort Fact Sheet.*

33. An OFDA official noted that in one case, 95 percent of the plastic water bottles shattered on impact. See Brilliant et al., *Humanitarian Assistance Lessons,* 25–26 and 31.

34. Brilliant et al., *Humanitarian Assistance Lessons,* 25–26 and 31.

35. Chris Seiple, *The U.S. Military/NGO Relationship in Humanitarian Intervention* (Carlisle, Penn.: U.S. Army War College, 1996), 38–39.

36. Freeman and Boren, "Safe Havens," 56.

37. Seiple, *The U.S. Military/NGO,* 32.

38. Seiple, *The U.S. Military/NGO,* 43.

39. Robert Dirks, "Famine, Hunger Seasons, and Relief-Induced Antagonism," in *African Food Systems in Crisis, Part One: Microperspectives,* ed. Rebecca Huss-Ashmore and Solomon H. Katz (New York: Gordon & Breach, 1989), 295–303.

40. Donald P. Rice, *A New Air Force: Reshaping for the Future,* undated testimony of the secretary of the Air Force during 1992, 20 and 25, cited in Carl Builder, Robert Lempert, Kevin Lewis, Eric Larson, and Milton Weiler, *Report of a Workshop on Expanding U.S. Air Force Noncombat Mission Capabilities* (Santa Monica, Calif.: RAND Corporation, 1993), 4.

41. David keen, "Short-Term Interventions and Long-Term Problems: The Case of the Kurds in Iraq," in *The Politics of Humanitarian Intervention,* ed. John Harriss (New York: Pinter, 1995), 172.

42. Brilliant et al., *Humanitarian Assistance Lessons,* 34.

43. Minear et al., *United Nations Coordination,* 8–10.

44. Gunter, *The Kurds of Iraq,* 82.

45. Minear et al., *United Nations Coordination,* 30.

46. Freedman and Boren, "Safe Havens," 84.

47. Freedman and Boren, "Safe Havens," 51.

48. UNDRO report, from Sheri Laizer, *Martyrs, Traitors, and Patriots: Kurdistan after the Gulf War* (London: Zed Books, 1996), 25.

49. Minear et al., *United Nations Coordination,* 23.

50. Freedman and Boren, "Safe Havens," 53.

51. United Nations, *Blue Helmets: A Review of United Nations Peace-Keeping* (New York: United Nations, 1997), 57.

52. Minear et al., *United Nations Coordination,* 44.

53. Brilliant et al., *Humanitarian Assistance Lessons,* 43–44.

54. The rate itself is also dependent upon the age distribution of the population. Due to varying age distribution, life expectancy at birth is considered a more accurate method of determining the health of a population.

55. Brilliant et al., *Humanitarian Assistance Lessons*, 44; and Freedman and Boren, "Safe Havens," 51.

56. Brilliant et al., *Humanitarian Assistance Lessons*, 43. Three days at peak rate; seven days above rate of five; eleven days above rate of two. INTERTECT report also displays a table that compares this crises to the crises in the Sudan, on the Thai border, and in El Salvador. While in the case of El Salvador the peak rate was lower, the time spent at the emergency level was between three and sixteen times lower for northern Iraq.

57. Brilliant et al., *Humanitarian Assistance Lessons*, 43. While repatriation occurred in a matter of months in northern Iraq, it occurred in a matter of years or even a decade in the other three compared cases in the report.

58. Gunter, *The Kurds of Iraq*, 56.

59. UN Document A/46/612, of 4 November 1991, 2, discussed in Gunter, *The Kurds of Iraq*, 85–86.

60. Brilliant et al., *Humanitarian Assistance Lessons*, 43.

61. Freedman and Boren, "Safe Havens," 76.

62. Freedman and Boren, "Safe Havens," 75.

63. The number of refugees between October and December 1991 was 200,000 (in United Nations, *Blue Helmets*, 58); between October 1991 and January 1992, 300,000. See Keen, "Short-Term Interventions," 170.

64. This is a process similar to that which occurred from 1985 to 1988, when Kurds where forcefully moved from their homes and transported to the center of Iraq, so that Hussein could more completely control the populous. This earlier practice was termed "ethnic cleansing" in Bosnia.

65. Keen, "Short-Term Interventions," 170.

66. Keen, "Short-Term Interventions," 174–176, quote at 175.

67. DOS, *Report on Iraqi Human Rights*.

68. James Ciment, *The Kurds: State and Minority in Turkey, Iraq, and Iran* (New York: Facts on File, 1996), 156.

69. Amnesty International, *Iraq: Human Rights Abuses in Iraqi Kurdistan since 1991*, AI Index: MDE 14/01/95), at: http://www.amnesty.org/ailib/aipub/1995MDE/1.

70. Marzio Babille, "Post-Emergency Epidemiological Survey," *Disasters* 18, no. 1 (1994): 61.

71. DHA, *United Nations Consolidated Inter-Agency Humanitarian Assistance Program to Iraq: Emergency Requirements for the Period October–December, 1996*, document dated 2 October 1996, at: http://www.reliefweb.int/; UNICEF, *Iraq Country Situation Report No. 9* (New York: UNICEF, September 1996). the DHA document estimates that 70,000 refugees went to the Iranian border.

72. UNHCR, *Background Paper*.

73. Henry J. Barkey, "Kurdish Geopolitics," *Current History* 96, no. 606 (January 1997): 2.

74. Keen, "Short-Term Interventions," 172–173.

75. Keen, "Short-Term Interventions," 178.

76. UNICEF, *Emergency Country Profile: Iraq*, at: gopher:/hqfaus01.unicef.org:70/00/.cefdata/emerctyprof95/iraq.

77. Keen, "Short-Term Interventions," 177.
78. GAO, "Peace Operations: Information on U.S. and UN Activities," Briefing Report, GAO/NSAID-95-102BR (Washington, D.C.: GAO, 31 February 1995).
79. Builder et al., *Report*, 22.
80. See Seiple, *The U.S. Military/NGO*, 1–4 and 171–187.
81. Brilliant et al., *Humanitarian Assistance Lessons*, 44.
82. Sadako Ogata, "Role of Humanitarian Action in Peacekeeping Operations," keynote address, Vienna, 5 July 1994, 4.
83. Barry Posen, "Military Responses to Refugee Disasters," *International Security* 21, no. 1 (Summer 1996): 95.

Chapter 4

1. Gerald B. Helman and Steven R. Ratner, "Saving Failed States," *Foreign Policy* 89 (Winter 1992–1993): 3-20.
2. This chapter makes use of Anne Simons, *Networks of Dissolutions: Somalia Undone* (Boulder, Colo.: Westview Press, 1995); Patrick Gilkes, "Somalia: Recent History," in *Africa: South of the Sahara, 1996*, 25th ed. (London: Europa Publications, 1996), 838–845; Miles Smith-Morris, "Somalia: Economy," in *Africa: South of the Sahara*, 845–853; Samuel Makinda, "Politics and Clan Rivalry in Somalia, *Australian Journal of Political Science* 26 (1991): 111–126; *Seeking peace from Chaos: Humanitarian Intervention in Somalia* (Boulder, Colo.: Lynne Rienner Publishers, 1993); I. M. Lewis, "Misunderstanding the Somali Crisis," *Anthropology Today* 9, no. 4 (August 1993): 1–3; Virginia Lung, "Come Back Somalia? Questioning a Collapsed State," *Third World Quarterly* 18, no. 2 (1997): 287–302; and Jarat Chopra, "Achilles' Heel in Somalia: Learning from a Conceptual Failure," *Texas International Law Journal* 31, no. 3 (Summer 1996): 495–526.
3. Simons, *Networks of Dissolution*, 43.
4. Simons, *Networks of Dissolution*, 44.
5. See especially Lung, "Come Back Somalia."
6. Simons, *Networks of Dissolution*, 53.
7. U.S. Department of the Army, *Foreign Military Assistance: Somalia: Army Area Handbooks*, 17 December 1993, at: gopher://gopher.umsi.edu:7000/library/govdocs/armyahbs/aahb3/aahb0227.
8. Simons, *Networks of Dissolution*, 60.
9. Ken Menkhaus, "U.S. Foreign Assistance to Somalia: Phoenix from the Ashes?" *Middle East Policy* 5, no. 1 (January 1997): 126–127.
10. Simons, *Networks of Dissolution*, 125–135.
11. See Michael Maren, *The Road to Hell: The Ravaging Effects of Foreign Aid and International Charity* (New York: Free Press, 1996).
12. Menkhaus, "U.S. Foreign Assistance to Somalia," 135.
13. Menkhaus, "U.S. foreign Assistance to Somalia," 128.
14. U.S. Department of the Army, *Foreign Military Assistance*.
15. Simons, *Networks of Dissolution*, 49; and Makinda, *Seeking Peace*, 19.

16. CDC, "Nutritional Status of Somali Refugees—Eastern Ethiopia, September 1988–May 1989," *Morbidity and Mortality Weekly Report* 38, no. 26 (7 July 1989): 455. Another report also found that 27.6 percent of children were moderately to severely malnourished: Africa Watch Committee, *Somalia: A Government at War with Its Own People* (New York: Africa Watch Committee, 1990).

17. Simons, *Networks of Dissolution*, 70; Gilkes, "Somalia," 840; upper estimate from Africa Watch Committee, *Somalia*.

18. U.S. Department of the Army, *Foreign Military Assistance*, Assistance included 1,200 M16 automatic rifles and two millions rounds of M16 ammunition, 300,000 rounds of 30-caliber ammunition, and 500,000 rounds of 50-caliber ammunition.

19. Stockholm International Peace Research Institute, "Somalia, Military Spending, 1986–95," at: http://www.sipri.se/projects/milex/expenditure/Somalia.html.

20. Gikes, "Somalia," 841.

21. UNHCR, Centre for Documentation and Research, *Background Paper on Somali Refugees and Asylum Seekers* (Geneva: UNHCR, October 1994), at: http://www.unhcr.ch:80//refworld//country/cdr.

22. Gérard Prunier, "Somalia: Civil War, Intervention, and Withdrawal, 1990–1995," from WRITENET (UK), July 1995, at: http://www.unhcr.ch:80/refworld/country/writenet/wrisom.htm,at 1.6. Percentage given here uses RPG figure of 5.1 million preconflict population (RPG, *Lives Lost, Lives Saved: Excess Mortality and the Impact of Health Interventions in the Somalia Emergency* [Washington, D.C.: RPG, November 1994], 35).

23. RPG, *Lives Lost, Lives Saved*, 3.

24. RPG, *Lives Lost, Lives Saved*, 10–13.

25. Patrick S. Moore, Anthony A. Marfin, Lynn E. Quenemoen, Bradford D. Gessner, Y. S. Ayub, Daniel S. Miller, Kevin M. Sullivan, and Michael J. Toole, "Mortality Rates in Displaced and Resident Populations of Central Somalia during 1992 Famine," *The Lancet* 341 (10 April 1993): 935–937.

26. Leslie P. Bosse, Michael J. Toole, and Ray Yip, "Assessments of Mortality, Morbidity, and Nutritional Status in Somalia during the 1991–1992 Famine," *Journal of the American Medical Association* 272, no. 5 (3 August 1994): 372.

27. L. A. Persson, A. S. Adedn, M. M. Ibrahim, M. H. Omar, and S. Wall, "Famine in Somalia," *The Lancet* 341 (5 June 1993): 1478.

28. Moore et al, "Mortality Rates," 937 and 935.

29. Statistics in this paragraph are from RPG, *Lives Lost, Lives Saved*, 24 and 35.

30. William J. Durch, "Introduction to Anarchy: Humanitarian Intervention and 'State-Building' in Somalia," in *UN Peacekeeping, American Politics, and the Uncivil Wars of the 1990s*, ed. William J. Durch (New York: St. Martin's Press, 1996), 316.

31. RPG, *Lives Lost, Lives Saved*, 27.

32. John Sommer, *Hope Restored? Humanitarian Aid in Somalia, 1990–1994* (Washington, D.C.: RPG, 1994), 14.

33. Durch, "Introduction to Anarchy," 316.
34. Andrew S. Natsios, "Humanitarian Relief Intervention in Somalia: The Economics of Chaos," in *Learning from Somalia: The Lessons of Armed Humanitarian Intervention*, ed. Walter S. Clarke and Jeffrey Herbst (Boulder, Colo.: Westview Press, 1997), 88; originally published in *International Peacekeeping* 3, no. 1 (Spring 1996): 68–91.
35. Natsios, "Humanitarian Relief Intervention," 88.
36. Sommer, *Hope Restored*, C1.
37. Sommer, *Hope Restored*, 24.
38. RPG, *Lives Lost, Lives Saved*, 13–14.
39. Jarat Chopra, Åge Eknes, and Toralv Nordbø, *Fighting for Hope in Somalia*, Peacekeeping and Multinational Operations No. 6 (Oslo: Norwegian Institute for International Affairs, 1995), 36.
40. RPG, *Lives Lost, Lives Saved*, 28–31; Sommer, *Hope Restored*, 57.
41. RPG, *Lives Lost, Lives Saved*, 35.
42. See James O. C. Jonah, *Differing State Perspectives on the United Nations in the Post-Cold War World*, Academic Council on the United Nations System (ACUNS) Reports and Papers No. 4 (Providence, R.I.: ACUNS, 1993).
43. Mohammed Sahnoun, *Somalia: The Missed Opportunities* (Washington, D.C.: U.S. Institute of Peace Press, 1994), 13.
44. Makinda, *Seeking Peace*, 67.
45. Chopra et al., *Fighting for Hope*, 36.
46. Chopra, "Achilles' Heel in Somalia," 496.
47. See Robert I. Rotberg and Thomas G. Weiss, eds., *From Massacres to Genocide: The Media, Public Policy, and Humanitarian Crises* (Cambridge, Mass.: World Peace Foundation, 1996), esp. 15–89. See also Nik Gowing, *Media Coverage: Help or Hindrance in Conflict Prevention?* (New York: Carnegie Commission on Preventing Deadly Conflict, 1997); and Warren P. Strobel, *Late-Breaking Foreign Policy: The News Media's Influence on Peace Operations* (Washington, D.C.: U.S. Institute of Peace Press, 1997).
48. Chris Seiple, *The U.S. Military/NGO Relationship in Humanitarian Intervention* (Carlisle, Penn.: U.S. Army War College, 1996), esp. 97–138.
49. Makinda, *Seeking Peace*, 70.
50. These nations were Australia, Belgium, Botswana, Canada, Egypt, France, Germany, Greece, India, Italy, Kuwait, Morocco, New Zealand, Nigeria, Norway, Pakistan, Saudi Arabia, Sweden, Tunisia, Turkey, the United Arab Emirates, the United Kingdom, and Zimbabwe.
51. Walter Clarke, "Failed Visions and Uncertain Mandates in Somalia," in *Learning from Somalia*, ed. Clarke and Herbst, 9.
52. Chopra et al., *Fighting for Hope*, 41.
53. Seiple, *The U.S. Military/NGO*, 121.
54. Gérard Prunier, "The Experience of European Armies in Operation Restore Hope," in *Learning from Somalia*, ed. Clarke and Herbst, 138–139.
55. Jarat Chopra, "The Space of Peace-Maintenance," *Political Geography* 15, no. 335 (1996): 335–357.
56. Richard A. Melanson, *"This Will Not Be Another Vietnam": George Bush*

and the Persian Gulf War, Occasional Paper No. 9 (Providence, R.I.: Watson Institute, 1991).

57. Laura Miller and Charles Moskos, "Humanitarians or Warriors? Race, Gender, and Combat Status in Operation Restore Hope," *Armed Forces and Society* 21, no. 4 (Summer 1995): 615–637.

58. Clement Adibe, *Managing Arms in Peace Processes: Somalia,* Disarmament and Conflict Resolution Project, UNIDIR/95/30 (Geneva: UNIDIR, 1995), 16.

59. Chopra, "Achilles' Heel in Somalia," 45.

60. Chester Crocker, "The Lessons of Somalia: Not Everything Went Wrong," *Foreign Affairs* 74, no. 3 (May–June 1995); 2–8.

61. RPG, *Lives Lost, Lives Saved,* 32.

62. Sommer, *Hope Restored,* 73.

63. United Nations, *Blue Helmets: A Review of United Nations Peace-Keeping* (New York: United Nations, 1997), 296.

64. United Nations, *Blue Helmets,* 297.

65. Chopra et al., *Fighting for Hope,* 74 and 69.

66. Chopra et al., *Fighting for Hope,* 88.

67. Samuel P. Huntington, "New Contingencies, Old Roles," *Joint Forces Quarterly* 2 (Autumn 1992): 338.

68. See Ivo H. Daalder, "Knowing When to Say No: The Development of US Policy for Peacekeeping," in *UN Peacekeeping,* ed. Durch, 35–67.

69. Thomas G. Weiss, "Rekindling Hope in UN Humanitarian Intervention," in *Learning from Somalia,* ed. Clarke and Herbst, 207–228.

70. Gideon Rose, "The Exit Strategy Delusion," *Foreign Affairs* 77, no. 1 (January–February 1998): 58 and 57.

71. Chopra et al., *Fighting for Hope,* 70.

72. Chopra, "Achilles' Heel in Somalia," 495.

73. Gilkes, "Somalia," 844.

74. Chopra, "Achilles' Heel in Somalia," 511.

75. Sommer, *Hope Restored,* C5.

76. Statistics from GAO, *"Peace Operations: Cost of DOD Operations in Somalia,"* Chapter Report, GAO/NSIAD-94-88 (Washington, D.C.: GAO, 1994), 5.

77. Sommer, *Hope Restored,* C5.

78. Gilkes, "Somalia," 844; and Makinda, *Seeking Peace,* 78–79.

79. United Nations, *Blue Helmets,* 27.

80. Phil Gunby, "Extraordinary Epidemiologic, Environmental Health Experience Emerges from Operation Restore Hope," *Journal of the American Medical Association* 269, no. 223 (9 June 1993): 2834.

81. Sommer, *Hope Restored,* 72.

82. See Debarati G. Sapir and Hedwig Deconnick, "The Paradox of Humanitarian Assistance and Military Intervention in Somalia," in *The United Nations and Civil Wars,* ed. Thomas G. Weiss (Boulder, Colo.: Lynne Rienner Publishers, 1995), 151–172, esp. 168.

83. Quoted in Kenneth David Bush, "When Two Anarchies Meet: International Intervention in Somalia," draft prepared for the Parliamentary Centre for Foreign Affairs and Foreign Trade, September 1994.

84. Sommer, *Hope Restored*, 80. Fatmir Mema calculates in Albania that "every soldier in Operation 'Alba' protected less than US[$]17 worth of aid per day. This scale of effort seems a bit ridiculous, and we may conclude that the efforts of some humanitarian agencies were most cost effective" ("Did Albania Really Need Operation 'Alba'?" *Security Dialogue* 29, no. 1 [March 1998]: 61–62).

85. Mema, "Did Albania Really Need Operation 'Alba'?" 56. For an extended argument, see Natsios, "Humanitarian Relief Intervention."

86. Africa Rights, *Operation Restore Hope: A Preliminary Assessment* (London: Africa Rights, May 1993), and *Somalia: Human Rights Abuses by the United Nations Forces* (London: Africa Rights, July 1993).

87. Theo Farrell, "Sliding into War: The Somalia Imbroglio and US Army Peace Operations Doctrine," *International Peacekeeping* 2, no. 2 (Summer 1995): 197.

88. Natsios, "Humanitarian Relief Intervention," 90.

89. RPG, *Lives Lost, Lives Saved*, 35.

90. Sommer, *Hope Restored*, 48.

91. Prunier, "Somalia," at 3.1.

92. Sommer, *Hope Restored*, 3.

93. Barry Posen, "Military Responses to Refugee Disasters," *International Security* 21, no. 1 (Summer 1996): 73.

Chapter 5

1. These and other statistics, unless otherwise noted, are drawn from the UNHCR's annual (since 1993) *Populations of Concern to UNHCR: A Statistical Overview* (Geneva: UNHCR). Donors seek better data about what we call the "casualties of war"—refugees, internally displaced persons, returnees, and war victims—for analysis, as well as for planning, budgeting, fund-raising, and programming. Yet, conceptual and practical problems abound. In the prose of *The State of the World's Refugees, 1995,* in spite of "the constant demands on UNHCR for facts and figures. . . . [it is] difficult to answer such queries with any real degree of accuracy" (see UNHCR, *The State of The World's Refugees, 1995: The Challenge of Solutions* [Oxford: Oxford University Press, 1995], Annex I: "The Problem of Refugee Statistics," 244–246, quote at 244). In April 1995, the Security Council altered the mandates and names for what had been the three separate parts of UNPROFOR—for the Krajina and Slavonia, for Macedonia, and for Bosnia. The troops in Bosnia retained the "UNPROFOR" label, which for the sake of simplicity is what is employed here throughout the analysis.

2. Angela Burke and Gordon Macdonald, "The Former Yugoslavia Conflict (1991–)," in *The True Costs of Conflict: Seven Recent Wars and Their Effects on Society,* ed. Michael Cranna (New York: New Press, 1994), 162.

3. This switch, according to Marrack Goulding, was "very unwise." See his

"The Use of Force by the United Nations," *International Peacekeeping* 3, no. 1 (Spring 1996): 1–18, quote at 10–11.

4. See especially Susan Woodward, *Balkan Tragedy: Chaos and Dissolution after the Cold War* (Washington, D.C.: Brookings Institution, 1995), and "Yugoslavia: Chronology," in *Eastern Europe and the Commonwealth of Independent States* (London: Europa Publications, 1992), 278–285.

5. Woodward, "Yugoslavia," 26.

6. Statistics in this paragraph are from Woodward, "Yugoslavia," 32.

7. John B. Allcock, "Nationalism and Politics in Yugoslavia," in *Eastern Europe and the Commonwealth of Independent States*, 293. A lengthy treatment is found in Tim Judah, *The Serbs: History, Myth, and the Resurrection of Yugoslavia* (New Haven, Conn.: Yale University Press, 1997).

8. David A. Dyker, "The Economy: Yugoslavia," in *Eastern Europe and the Commonwealth of Independent States*, 298.

9. See especially James B. Streinberg, "International Involvement in the Yugoslavia Conflict," in *Enforcing Restraint: Collective Intervention in Internal Conflicts*, ed. Lori Fisler Damrosch (New York: Council on Foreign Relations Press, 1993), 27–76; James Gow and Lawrence Freedman, "Intervention in a Fragmenting State: The Case of the Former Yugoslavia," in *To Loose the Bonds of Wickedness: Collective Intervention in Defence of Human Rights*, ed. Nigel S. Rodley (London: Brassey's, 1992), 93–132.

10. William J. Durch and James A. Schear, "Faultlines: UN Operations in the Former Yugoslavia," in *UN Peacekeeping, American Politics, and the Uncivil Wars of the 1990s*, ed. William J. Durch, ed. (New York: St. Martin's Press, 1996), 208.

11. S. Alex Cunliffe and Michael Pugh, "The UNHCR as Lead Agency in the Former Yugoslavia," *Journal of Humanitarian Assistance*, posted on 1 April 1996 at: http://www-jha.sps.cam.ac.uk/a/a007/htm; published later as Michael Pugh and S. Alex Cunliffe, "The Lead Agency Concept in Humanitarian Assistance," *Security Dialogue* 28, no. 1(March 1997): 17–30.

12. See Thomas G. Weiss, "Collective Spinelessness: U.N. Actions in the Former Yugoslavia," in *The World and Yugoslavia's Wars*, ed. Richard H. Ullman (New York: Council on Foreign Relations Press, 1996), 59–96. See also Thomas Cushman and Stjepan G. Mestrovic, eds., *This Time We Knew: Western Responses to Genocide in Bosnia* (New York: New York University Press, 1997). For firsthand dispatches, see Roy Gutman, *Witness to Genocide* (London: Macmillan, 1993).

13. Branka Magas, "Recent Political History of Yugoslavia," in *Eastern Europe and the Commonwealth of Independent States*, 285–289.

14. See Åge Eknes, "The United Nations Predicament in the Former Yugoslavia," in *The United Nations and Civil Wars*, ed. Thomas G. Weiss (Boulder, Colo.: Lynne Rienner Publishers, 1995), 109–126.

15. See Cunliffe and Pugh, "The UNHCR as Lead Agency"; and Thomas G. Weiss and Amir Pasic, "Reinventing UNHCR: Enterprising Humanitarians in the Former Yugoslavia, 1991–1995," *Global Governance* 3, no. 1 (January–April 1997): 41–58.

16. Larry Minear, Jeffrey Clark, Roberta Cohen, Dennis Gallagher, Iain

Guest, and Thomas G. Weiss, *Humanitarian Action in the Former Yugoslavia: The U.N.'s Role, 1991–1993,* Occasional Paper No. 18, (Providence, R.I.: Watson Institute, 1994), 13.

17. United Nations, *The Blue Helmets: A Review of United Nations Peace-Keeping,* 3rd ed. (New York: United Nations, 1996), 522.

18. Frederick Cuny, *The Bosnian War,* INTERTECT Briefing Book (Dallas, Tex.: INTERTECT, 1992), 72.

19. United Nations, *Blue Helmets,* 524.

20. GAO, "Peace Operations: U.S. Costs in Support of Haiti, Former Yugoslavia, Somalia, and Rwanda," GAO/NSIAS096-38 (Washington, D.C.: GAO, 1996), 15.

21. Durch and Schear, "Faultlines," 250.

22. Durch and Schear, "Faultlines," 239.

23. Durch and Schear, "Faultlines," 228.

24. United Nations, *Blue Helmets,* 523.

25. Julia Devin and Jaleh Dashti-Gibson, "Sanctions in the Former Yugoslavia: Convoluted Goals and Complicated Consequences," in *Political Gain and Civilian Pain: The Humanitarian Impacts of Economic Sanctions,* ed. Thomas G. Weiss, David Cortright, George A. Lopez, and Larry Minear (Lanham, Md.: Rowman & Littlefield, 1997), 149–187.

26. Minear et al., *Humanitarian Action,* 13; and "The Impact of the International Community's Sanctions on the Health of the Population of FR Yugoslavia," *Yugoslav Survey* 1 (1994): 97–111.

27. United Nations, *Blue Helmets,* 525.

28. Rosalyn Higgins, "The New United Nations and Former Yugoslavia," *International Affairs* 69 (1993): 469.

29. As quoted in Minear et al., *Humanitarian Action,* 86.

30. "U.N. Bosnia Commander Wants More Troops, Fewer Resolutions," *New York Times,* 31 December 1993.

31. A moral dilemma is created for all authors writing on the atrocities created by these factions. A question is posed concerning who in these ethnic groups is guilty for these atrocities. The use of an ethnic term such as "Serb," "Croat," or "Muslim" implies the collective guilt of an entire nation: Who was guilty of these atrocities? Factions, the leadership, or simply the rise of collective hatred among the population? When discussing these atrocities, the predominant focus tends to be on the Serbs or the Croats, followed by a brief mention of similar atrocities by Muslims. The actions by the Serbian forces, both by the organized military and the paramilitary militias, stand out as the most egregious and numerous. The discussion becomes a question of degree, but how can one really quantify such data on suffering? Also, such descriptions tend to justify the actions of the Muslim factions by first describing atrocities committed by the Serb factions. All atrocities should be condemned as blatant disregard for the sanctity of human life and the rights of individuals.

32. See Oliver Schuett, "The International War Crimes Tribunal for the Former Yugoslavia and the Dayton Peace Agreement: Peace versus Justice?" *International Peacekeeping* 4, no. 2 (Summer 1997): 91–114.

33. U.S. Committee for Refugees, *World Refugee Survey, 1996* (Washington, D.C.: U.S. Committee for Refugees, 1997), 130; Amnesty International, *Bosnia-Herzegovina: "To Bury My Brothers' Bones,"* Amnesty International Country Report, at : http://www.amnesty.org/ailib/aipub/1996/EUR/46301596.htm.

34. Beverly Allen, "Rape Warfare in Bosnia," *Brown Journal of World Affairs* 3, no. 1 (Winter–Spring 1996): 313–324, and *Rape Warfare: The Hidden Genocide in Bosnia-Herzegovina* (Minneapolis: University of Minnesota Press, 1997).

35. Thomas G. Weiss and Cindy Collins, *Humanitarian Challenges and Intervention: World Politics and the Dilemmas of Help* (Boulder, Colo.: Westview Press, 1996), 83.

36. Minear et al., *Humanitarian Action*, 18.

37. Minear et al., *Humanitarian Action*, 23.

38. David P. Frosythe, "International Criminal Courts: A Political View," *Netherlands Quarterly of Human Rights* 15, no. 1 (1997): 5–19.

39. United Nations, *Blue Helmets*, 524.

40. Statistics in the following three paragraphs are from Minear et al., *Humanitarian Action*, 13–29.

41. Eknes, "The United Nations Predicament," 121.

42. Minear et al., *Humanitarian Action*, 13.

43. See Weiss and Pasic, "Reinventing UNHCR"; and U.S. Mission to the United Nations, *Global Humanitarian Emergencies*, (New York: United Nations, 1993, 1994, 1995, and 1996).

44. Minear et al., *Humanitarian Action*, 14.

45. Minear et al., *Humanitarian Action*, 36.

46. Minear et al., *Humanitarian Action*, 16.

47. Minear et al., *Humanitarian Action*, 42.

48. Minear et al., *Humanitarian Action*, 41.

49. See Thomas G. Weiss, ed., *Beyond UN Subcontracting: Task-sharing with Regional Security Arrangements and Service-Providing NGOs* (London: Macmillan, 1997).

50. See David Owen, *Balkan Odyssey* (New York: Harcourt Brace, 1995).

51. Durch and Schear, "Faultlines," 231.

52. Statistics in the next four paragraphs are drawn from GAO, "Peace Operations: Update on the Situation in the Former Yugoslavia," GAO/NSIAD-95-148BR (Washington, D.C.: GAO, May 1995), 12.

53. Eknes, "The United Nations Predicament," 122.

54. GAO, "Peace Operations: U.S. Costs," 15.

55. Human Rights Watch/Helsinki, " 'Ethnic Cleansing,' Continues in Northern Bosnia," document dated 7 November 1994.

56. United Nations, *Blue Helmets*, 533.

57. Roger Cohen, "Despite Vow, Serbia Is Said to Supply Serbs Fighting in Bosnia," *New York Times*, 12 December 1994.

58. See Human Rights Watch/Helsinki, " 'Safe Areas' in Bihac," document dated 12 May 1994.

59. Stephen Kinzer, "Cease-Fire in Bosnia Starts, and Sides Meet on Details," *New York Times*, 2 January 1995.

60. Burke and Macdonald, "The Former Yugoslavia Conflict," 155–196. The vast majority of journalists and policy accounts use this high figure, which may result from David Rieff's estimates that became almost boilerplate as a result of his publicized *Slaughterhouse: Bosnia and the Failure of the West* (New York: Simon & Schuster, 1995). The lowest and inaccurate estimates are closer to 25,000, with the most likely numbers falling between 75,000 and 100,000. See, for example, the analysis from the former deputy commander in chief of the U.S. European Command, Charles G. Boyd, "Making Peace with the Guilty," *Foreign Affairs* 74, no. 5 (September–October 1995): 22–38.

61. GAO, "Peace Operations: U.S. Costs," 14.

62. Burke and Macdonald, "The Former Yugoslavia Conflict," 163.

63. United Nations, *Blue Helmets*, 558.

64. Amnesty International, *Bosnia-Herzegovina*.

65. See David Shearer, *Private Armies and Military Intervention*, Adelphi Paper No. 316 (Oxford: Oxford University Press, 1998).

66. United Nations, *Blue Helmets*, 559.

67. Durch and Schear, "Faultlines," 246.

68. See Dick Leurdijk, *The United Nations and NATO in Former Yugoslavia, 1991–1996: The Limits of Diplomacy and Force* (The Hague: Netherlands Atlantic Commission, 1996).

69. Michael Mandelbaum, "The Reluctance to Intervene," *Foreign Policy* 95 (Summer 1994): 11.

70. GAO, "Peace Operations: U.S. Costs," 15.

71. Minear et al., *Humanitarian Action*, 32.

72. See Cunliffe and Pugh, "The UNHCR as Lead Agency."

73. See U.S. Mission to the United Nations, *Complex Humanitarian Emergencies, 1996* (New York: United Nations, February 1996), 24.

74. Burke and Macdonald, "The Former Yugoslavia Conflict," 155.

75. United Nations, *Blue Helmets*, 511–563.

76. The first quote comes from a PBS *Frontline* telecast on 14 October 1997, in an episode titled "The Lost American." The second is from an interview I conducted in October 1993.

77. For a discussion, see Sophie Albert, "The Return of Refugees to Bosnia and Herzegovina: Peacebuilding with People," *International Peacekeeping* 4, no. 3 (Autumn 1997): 1–27.

78. Ivo H. Daalder, "Bosnia after SFOR: Options for Continued US Engagement," *Survival* 39, no. 4 (Winter 1997–98): 6.

79. GAO, "Bosnia: Costs Are Uncertain but Seem Likely to Exceed DOD's Estimate," GAO/NSIAD-96-120BR (Washington, D.C.: GAO, March 1996), at: http://webgate.access.gpo.gov/cgi~bin.

80. U.S. Committee for Refugees, *World Refugee Survey*, 129.

81. See Kelly Kate Pease and David P. Forsythe, "Human Rights, Humanitarian Intervention, and World Politics," *Human Rights Quarterly* 15 (1993): 290–314.

82. See "Rescue—The Paradoxes of Virtue," a special issue of *Social Research* 62, no. 1 (Spring 1995), especially Michael Walzer's "The Politics of Rescue,"

53–66. See also David Rieff, "The Humanitarian Trap," *World Policy Journal* 12, no. 4 (Winter 1994–1995): 1–11.

83. See Amir Pasic and Thomas G. Weiss, "The Politics of Rescue: Yugoslavia's Wars and the Humanitarian Impulse," *Ethics and International Affairs* 11 (1997): 105–131, followed by "Commentary" from Andrew S. Natsios, Morton Winston, Alain Destexhe, and David R. Mapel, 133–149.

84. For contrasting views, see Annika S. Hansen, "Political Legitimacy, Confidence-Building, and the Dayton Peace Agreement," *International Peacekeeping* 4, no. 2 (Summer 1997): 74–90; and Chaim Kaufmann, "Possible and Impossible Solutions to Ethnic Wars," *International Security* 20, no. 4 (1996): 136–175.

85. The most controversial analysis is Alex de Waal and Rakiya Omaar, *Humanitarianism Unbound? Current Dilemmas Facing Multi-Mandate Relief Operations in Political Emergencies*, Discussion Paper No. 5. (London: Africa Rights, 1994). There is also a rapidly growing literature on the political dimensions of humanitarian action and peacekeeping. See, for example, Jarat Chopra, "The Space of Peace-Maintenance," *Political Geography* 15, Nos. 3–4 (1996): 335–347; and Antonia Donini, *The Policies of Mercy: UN Coordination in Afghanistan, Mozambique, and Rwanda*, Occasional Paper No. 22. (Providence, R.I.: Watson Institute, 1996).

86. Alain Destexhe, "Foreword," in *Populations in Danger, 1995*, ed. François Jean (London: MSF, 1995), 13–14.

87. Richard K. Betts, "The Delusion of Impartial Intervention," *Foreign Affairs* 73 (November–December 1994): 24.

88. Press release SG/SM/5804, 1 November 1995, 3.

89. As quoted by Tim Weiner, "Clinton's Balkan Envoy Finds Himself Shut Out," *New York Times*, 12 August 1995.

Chapter 6

1. This section relies on Gérard Prunier, *The Rwanda Crisis: History of a Genocide* (New York: Columbia University Press, 1995); Peter Uvin, *Development, Aid, and Conflict: Reflections from the Case of Rwanda*, Research for Action 24 (Helsinki: World Institute for Development Economics Research, 1996); and Glynne Evans, *Responding to Crises in the African Great Lakes*, Adelphi Paper No. 311 (Oxford: Oxford University Press, 1997).

2. Uvin, *Development*, ix.

3. See Benedict Anderson, *Imagined Communities* (London: Verso, 1991); and Thomas J. Biersteker and Cynthia Weber, eds., *State Sovereignty as Social Construct* (Cambridge: Cambridge University Press, 1996).

4. Prunier, *The Rwanda Crisis*, 21.

5. Prunier, *The Rwanda Crisis*, 60.

6. Prunier, *The Rwanda Crisis*, 76.

7. Prunier, *The Rwanda Crisis*, 79.

8. Uvin, *Development*, 15.

9. UNICEF, "Emergency Country Profile: Rwanda," 29 November 1994, at: gopher://hqfaus01.unicef.org:70/00/.cefdata/.emerctyprof95/rwanda.

10. Uvin, *Development*, 19 and 24.

11. Luc Bonneux, "Rwanda: A Case of Demographic Entrapment," *Lancet* 344 (17 December 1994): 1689–1690; Maurice King, "The Population 'Wolf' and Demographic Entrapment in Rwanda," *American Journal of Public Health* 86, no. 7 (July 1996): 1030–1031.

12. UNICEF, "Emergency Country Profile: Rwanda."

13. Bonneux, "Rwanda," 1689.

14. See Janna Karhilo, "Appendix 2C: Case Study on Peacekeeping: Rwanda," in Stockholm International Peace Research Institute (SIPRI), *SIPRI Yearbook, 1995: Armaments, Disarmaments, and International Security* (Oxford: Oxford University Press, 1995), 100–116; J. Matthew Vaccaro, "The Politics of Genocide: Peacekeeping and Disaster," in *UN Peacekeeping, American Politics, and the Uncivil Wars of the 1990s*, ed. William J. Durch (New York: St. Martin's Press, 1996), 367–407.

15. SIPRI, *SIPRI Yearbook, 1995*, 438, in a table on military expenditures, production, and trade.

16. Human Rights Watch/Africa, "Genocide in Rwanda: April–May 1994," *Human Rights Watch Report* 6, no. 4 (May 1994): 3.

17. Karhilo, "Appendix 2C," 100.

18. Human Rights Watch/Africa, "Genocide," 9.

19. Human Rights Watch/Africa, "Genocide," 3.

20. Human Rights Watch/Africa, "Genocide," 8.

21. CDC, "Morbidity and Mortality Surveillance in Rwandan Refugees—Burundi and Zaire, 1994," *Morbidity and Mortality Weekly Report* 45, no. 5 (9 February 1996): 105.

22. United Nations, "Report on the Situation of Human Rights in Rwanda," E/CN.4/1996/68, 29 January 1996: "Unfortunately, there are no statistics to give, if not an accurate idea of numbers, at least an approximate one. The Ministry for the Family and the Promotion of Women recorded 15,700 cases of women raped during the hostilities. This official figure certainly underestimates the true situation for three reasons. The first stems from the fact that it is limited in space and time, since it only covers the period of the massacres in Rwanda. It does not take account of rape which took place after the hostilities in the refugee camp outside the country, particularly of women carried off to the camps as 'loot' and handed over to their tormentors. The second is the result of the reluctance of some women, particularly young girls, to confess or admit that they were raped. The specialists (doctors and psychologists) add a third reason to the foregoing, with reference to the number of pregnancies, which would seem to be between 2,000 and 5,000. According to the statistics, one hundred cases of rape give rise to one pregnancy. If this principle is applied to the lowest figure, it gives at least 250,000 cases of rape and the highest figure would give 500,000, although this figure also seems excessive."

23. See UNICEF, *The State of the World's Children, 1996* (New York: Oxford University Press, 1996).

24. UNICEF, "Emergency Country Profile: Rwanda."

25. United Nations, "Report": "According to an invetigation by the nongovernmental organization 'Emergency Project for Orphans' Care,' 66 percent of the children witnessed the violent death of their parents and that of other family members; 88 percent of the children witnessed the killing of other known persons, carried out by armed militia members; 82 percent of the children were threatened with weapons. Other bodies give even higher figures. According to the latest annual report of UNICEF, 87 percent of children lost their parents while 96 percent were the witnesses of massacres. Many more children, however, met the same fate as their parents."

26. See Thomas G. Weiss and Cindy Collins, *Humanitarian Challenges and Intervention: World Politics and the Dilemmas of Help* (Boulder, Colo.: Westview Press, 1996), 97–134.

27. See Rakiya Omaar and Alex de Waal, *Rwanda: Death, Despair, and Defiance* (London: African Rights, 1994).

28. Quoted by Barbara Crossette, "Why Washington and the World Largely Failed to Act to Head Off Blood Bath," *New York Times,* 25 March 1998, A12.

29. Crossette, "Why Washington," A12.

30. For optimistic views about the future, see Roy May and Gerry Cleaver, "African Peacekeeping: Still Dependent?" *International Peacekeeping* 4, no. 2 (Summer 1997): 1–21; and Jeremy Ginifer, "Emergent African Peace-keeping: Self-Help and External Assistance," in *Humanitarian Force,* ed. Anthony McDermott (Oslo: International Peace Research Institute, 1997), 123–124.

31. Vaccaro, "The Politics of Genocide," 378.

32. Karhilo, "Appendix 2C," 107.

33. Larry Minear and Philippe Guillot, *Soldiers to the Rescue: Humanitarian Lessons from Rwanda* (Paris: OECD, 1996), 77.

34. Minear and Guillot, *Soldiers to the Rescue,* 83.

35. Vaccaro, "The Politics of Genocide," 384.

36. For a discussion of Rwanda in the context of Washington decisionmaking, see Ivo. H. Daalder, "Knowing When to Say No: The Development of US Policy for Peacekeeping," in *Un Peacekeeping,* ed. Durch, 35–67.

37. Mel McNulty, "France's Role in Rwanda and External Military Intervention: A Double Discrediting," *International Peacekeeping* 4, no. 3 (Autumn 1997): 39.

38. See Jarat Chopra and Thomas G. Weiss, "Prospects for Containing Conflict in the Former Second World War," *Security Studies* 4, no. 3 (Spring 1995): 552–583.

39. Vaccaro, "The Politics of Genocide," 384.

40. Minear and Guillot, *Soldiers to the Rescue,* 95.

41. Vaccaro, "The Politics of Genocide," 383.

42. Joint Evaluation of Emergency Assistance to Rwanda, *The International Response to Conflict and Genocide: Lessons from the Rwanda Experience* (Copenhagen: Steering Committee of the Joint Evaluation, 1996), vol. 3, "Humanitarian Aid and Effects," 87–107. See also Linda Melvern, "Genocide behind the Thin Blue Line," *Security Dialogue* 28, no. 3 (September 1997): 333–346; and Astri

Suhrke, "Facing Genocide: The Record of the Belgian Battalion in Rwanda," *Security Dialogue* 29, no. 1 (March 1998): 37–48.

43. Minear and Guillot, *Soldiers to the Rescue,* 101–102.

44. Vaccaro, "The Politics of Genocide," 387.

45. Goma Epidemiology Group, "Public Health Impact of Rwandan Refugee Crisis: What Happened in Goma, Zaire, in July 1994?" *The Lancet* 345 (11 February 1995): 359–361.

46. Chris Seiple, *The U.S. Military/NGO Relationship in Humanitarian Intervention* (Carlisle Barracks, Penn.: U.S. Army War College, 1996), 139.

47. Seiple, *The U.S. Military/NGO,* 139.

48. Goma Epidemiology Group, "Public Health Impact of Rwandan Refugee Crisis," 340.

49. Scott F. Dowell, Alphonse Toko, Claire Sita, Renaud Piarroux, Ann Duerr, and Bradley A. Woodruff, "Health and Nutrition in Centers for Unaccompanied Refugee Children: Experience from the 1994 Rwandan Refugee Crisis," *Journal of the American Medical Association* 273, no. 22 (14 June 1995): 1802.

50. Goma Epidemiology Group, "Public Health Impact of Rwandan Refugee Crisis," 341.

51. CDC, "Morbidity and Mortality," 106.

52. Christophe Paquet and Marcel Van Soest, "Mortality and Malnutrition among Rwandan Refugees in Zaire," *The Lancet* 344 (17 September 1994): 823–824.

53. Dowell et al., "Health and Nutrition," 1805.

54. Vaccaro, "The Politics of Genocide," 388.

55. Minear and Guillot, *Soldiers to the Rescue,* 122.

56. See Edward R. Girardet, ed., *Somalia, Rwanda, and Beyond: The Role of the International Media in Wars and Humanitarian Crises,* Special Report No. 1 (Geneva: Crosslines, 1995).

57. McNulty, "France's Role in Rwanda," 24–44.

58. Minear and Guillot, *Soldiers to the Rescue,* 111.

59. Minear and Guillot, *Soldiers to the Rescue,* 115.

60. Seiple, *The U.S. Military/NGO,* 155.

61. Seiple, *The U.S. Military/NGO,* 144.

62. Seiple, *The U.S. Military/NGO,* 163.

63. Minear and Guillot, *Soldiers to the Rescue,* 130–131.

64. Minear and Guillot, *Soldiers to the Rescue,* 135.

65. A similar experience occurred when the Norwegian Refugee Council's civilian field hospital operated as an integral part of UNAMIR from August 1995 until March 1996 and provided humanitarian medicine to UN soldiers, UN personnel, NGO staff, and the Rwanda population.

66. Minear and Guillot, *Soldiers to the Rescue,* 129.

67. Minear and Guillot, *Soldiers to the Rescue,* 143.

68. Minear and Guillot, *Soldiers to the Rescue,* 63–64.

69. Vaccaro, "The Politics of Genocide," 394.

70. Vaccaro, "The Politics of Genocide," 378.

71. Vaccaro, "The Politics of Genocide," 379.

72. GAO, "Peace Operations: U.S. Costs in Support of Haiti, Former Yugoslavia, Somalia, Rwanda," GAO/NSIAS-96-38 (Washington, D.C.: GAO, 1996), at http://frwebgate.access.gpo.gov/cgi-bin. Except as otherwise noted, data emanate from this source in the following paragraphs.

73. Minear and Guillot, *Soldiers to the Rescue*, 121.

74. Data about the other military contributions are taken from Minear and Guillot, *Soldiers to the Rescue*, 134–139.

75. Minear and Guillot, *Soldiers to the Rescue*, 15.

76. Joint Evaluation of Emergency Assistance to Rwanda, *The International Response*, vol. 3, "Synthesis Report," 34.

77. Joint Evaluation of Emergency Assistance to Rwanda, *The International Response*, vol. 3, 5.

78. United Nations, *Blue Helmets: A Review of United Nations Peace-Keeping*, 3rd ed. (New York: United Nations, 1996), 33.

79. United States European Command Headquarters, After Action Review: Operation Support Hope (Washington, D.C.: DOD, 1994).

80. United Nations, "Report."

81. Joint Evaluation of Emergency Assistance to Rwanda, *The International Response*, vol. 3, "Synthesis Report," 39.

82. Joint Evaluation of Emergency Assistance to Rwanda, *The International Response*, vol. 3, 25.

83. Minear and Guillot, *Soldiers to the Rescue*, 15.

84. Joint Evaluation of Emergency Assistance to Rwanda, *The International Response*, vol. 3, "Humanitarian Aid and Effects," 103. The authors are quite clear earlier on the same page about the hazardous nature of such statistical comparisons: "As a result of the differences in terms of loads carried, aircraft types, routes taken, and uncertainty over the charging basis used by military operators, it is difficult to establish the cost per tonne carried by aircraft."

85. "Clinton's Painful Words of Sorrow and Chagrin," *New York Times*, 26 March 1998, A12.

Chapter 7

1. The following background relies upon Greg Chamberlain, "Haiti: History and Economy," in *South America, Central America, and the Caribbean, 1997* (New York: Europa Publications, 1997), 385–399; Ernest H. Preeg, *The Haitian Dilemma: A Case Study in Demographic, Development, and U.S. Foreign Policy* (Washington, D.C.: Center for Strategic and International Studies, 1996); Robert Maguire, Edwige Balutansky, Jacques Fomerand, Larry Minear, William G. O'Neill, Thomas G. Weiss, and Sarah Zaidi, *Haiti Held Hostage: International Responses to the Quest for Nationhood, 1986–1996*, Occasional Paper No. 23 (Providence, R.I.: Watson Institute, 1996); and David Malone, "Haiti and the International Community: A Case Study," *Survival* 39, no. 2 (Summer 1997): 126–146.

2. Martin Lundahl, "History as an Obstacle to Change: The Case of Haiti,"

Journal of Interamerican Studies and World Affairs 31, nos. 1–2 (Spring–Summer 1989): 2.

3. Maguire et al., *Haiti Held Hostage*, 29–57.

4. Chamberlain, "Haiti," 386.

5. Maguire et al., *Haiti Held Hostage*, 5; Chamberlain, "Haiti," 386.

6. See Robert Maguire, *Demilitarizing Public Order in a Predatory State: The Case of Haiti*, North-South Agenda Papers No. 17 (Coral Gables, Fla.: North-South Center Press, December 1995).

7. Maguire et al., *Haiti Held Hostage*, 7.

8. Justin Morris, "Force and Democracy: UN/US Intervention in Haiti," *International Peacekeeping* 2, no. 3 (Autumn 1995): 393.

9. Patrick Costello, "Haiti: Prospects for Democracy (September 1995)," WRITENET (UK).

10. Bureau of Inter-American Affairs, DOS, "Background Notes: Haiti, September, 1996," at: http://www.state.gov/www/background_notes/haiti_09-96_bgn.html.

11. Domingo E. Acevedo, "The Haitian Crisis and the OAS Response: A Taste of Effectiveness in Protecting Democracy," in *Enforcing Restraint: Collective Intervention in Internal Conflicts*, ed. Lori Fisler Damrosch (New York: Council on Foreign Relations Press; 1993), 126; and Chamberlain, "Haiti," 386.

12. World Bank Group, "Haiti," at: http://www.worldbank.org/html/extdr/offrep/lac/haiti.html.

13. Maguire, *Demilitarizing Public Order*, 25.

14. UNICEF, "Emergency Country Profile: Haiti," at gopher://hqfaus01.unicef.org:70/00/cefdata/emerctyprof95/haiti.

15. Jean Pape and Warren D. Johnson Jr., "AIDS in Haiti: 1982–1992," *Clinical Infectious Diseases* 17, suppl. 2 (1993): S341–345.

16. Maguire et al., *Haiti Held Hostage*; Amnesty International, *On the Horns of a Dilemma: Military Repression or Foreign Invasion*, AI Index: AMR36/33/94; DOS, *Haiti: Country Report on Human Rights*, 24 September 1994, at: gopher://summit.fiu.edu:70/00/State/state.77, and *US State Department Human Rights Report: Haiti*, at: http://library.ccsu.ctstateu.edu/~history/world_history/archives/haiti/haiti059.html; and Commission of Human Rights, UN Economic and Social Council, *Question of the Violation of Human Rights and Fundamental Freedoms in Any Part of the World with Particular Reference to Colonial and Other Dependent Countries and Territories: Situation of Human Rights in Haiti*, E/CN.4/1995/59, 6 February 1995, and *Advisory Services in the Field of Human Rights: Situation of Human Rights in Haiti*, E/CN.4/1996/94, 24 January 1996.

17. Amnesty International, *The Price of Rejection: Human Rights Consequences for Rejected Haitian Asylum-Seekers*, at: http//:www.amnesty.org/ailib/aipub/1994/AMR/5.

18. Bureau of Inter-American Affairs, "Background Notes."

19. For a discussion, see Acevedo, "The Haitian Crisis," 132–133.

20. Morris, "Force and Democracy," 394.

21. See UN Department of Public Information, "United Nations Mission in Haiti (UNMIH)," quoted in United Nations, *The Blue Helmets: A Review of United Nations Peace-Keeping*, 3rd ed. (New York: United Nations, 1996), 613.

22. Maguire, *Demilitarizing Public Order*, 33.
23. Acevedo, "The Haitian Crisis," 135–136.
24. "United Nations Mission in Haiti," at: http://ralph.gmu.edu/cfpa/peace/umih.html.
25. Joaquìn Tacsan, "Searching for OAS-UN Task-sharing Opportunities in Central America and Haiti," *Third World Quarterly* 18, no. 3 (1997): 489–507.
26. Costello, "Haiti," sect. 2.1. Reports from the U.S. Department of State estimate that 3,000 people were killed between September 1991 and early 1994. This chapter accepts the Costello estimate so that total deaths from 1991 to 1994 were well above 3,000. The general inaccuracy and difficulty concerning human rights data should be repeated.
27. Costello, "Haiti," sect. 2.1.
28. For a discussion, see Sarah Zaidi, "Humanitarian Effects of the Coup and Sanctions in Haiti," in *Political Gain and Civilian Pain: The Humanitarian Impacts of Economic Sanctions*, ed. Thomas G. Weiss, David Cortright, George A. Lopez, and Larry Minear (Lanham, Md.: Rowman & Littlefield, 1997), 189–212.
29. Cesar Chelala, "Fighting for Survival," *British Medical Journal* 309 (20–27 August 1994): 526.
30. UNICEF, "Emergency Country Profile."
31. Maguire et al., *Haiti Held Hostage;* 28; and Morris, "Force and Democracy," 395. The controversial document is *Sanctions in Haiti: Crisis in Humanitarian Action* (Cambridge, Mass.): Harvard Center for Population and Development Studies, November 1993).
32. Chelala, "Fighting for Survival," 526.
33. World Bank Group, "Haiti."
34. UNICEF, "Emergency Country Profile."
35. Bureau of Inter-American Affairs, "Background Notes."
36. UNICEF, "Emergency Country Profile."
37. Costello, "Haiti," sect. 2.4.
38. Chelala, "Fighting for Survival," 526.
39. Commission of Human Rights, *Advisory Services*, and Maguire et al., *Haiti Held Hostage*, both use this number.
40. "Health Status of Haitian Migrants—U.S. Naval Base, Guantánamo Bay, Cuba, November 1991–April 1992," *Morbidity and Mortality Weekly Report* 42, no. 7 (26 February 1993): 138–140.
41. UNICEF, "Emergency Country Profile."
42. Costello, "Haiti," sect. 2.3.
43. Amnesty International, *The Price of Rejection.*
44. Maguire et al., *Haiti Held Hostage,* 42.
45. "United Nations Mission in Haiti."
46. Maguire et al., *Haiti Held Hostage,* 23.
47. Maguire et al., *Haiti Held Hostage,* 52 and 47.
48. Commission of Human Rights, *Advisory Services;* and U.S. Committee for Refugees, "Haiti," in *World Refugee Survey, 1996* (Washington, D.C.: U.S. Committee for Refugees, 1996), 194.
49. Malone, "Haiti and the International Community."

50. Commission of Human Rights, *Advisory Services*, 621.
51. Maguire et al., *Haiti Held Hostage*, 36.
52. Amnesty International, *The Price of Rejection*.
53. Amnesty International, *The Price of Rejection*.
54. U.S. Committee for Refugees, "Haiti," 191.
55. See Edwige Balutansky, "Objectivity and the Mainstream U.S. Press," in Maguire et al., *Haiti Held Hostage*, 45; and Larry Minear, Colin Scott, and Thomas G. Weiss, *The News Media, Civil War, and Humanitarian Action* (Boulder, Colo.: Westview Press, 1996), 59–62.
56. Costello, "Haiti," sect. 2.1.
57. Amnesty International, *The Price of Rejection*.
58. Reports include the story of a man forced to consume his own severed ear. Other methods include the *djak*, constraining the body followed by severe beatings, and *halot marosa*, simultaneously bursting both eardrums of the prisoner.
59. Amnesty International, *The Price of Rejection*.
60. See Michael J. Smith, "Humanitarian Intervention: An Overview of the Ethical Issue," *Ethics and International Affairs* 12 (1998): 63–79.
61. Bureau of Inter-American Affairs, "Background Notes."
62. William W. Mendel, "The Haiti Contingency," *Military Review* (January 1994): 48–57.
63. Eric A. Doerrer, "Operational Vignette: Civil Affairs Haiti," *Military Review* (March–April 1996): 73–75 and 77.
64. Doerrer, "Operational Vignette," 77.
65. Melvin E. Shafer, "Attacking through the MIST," *Military Review* (March–April 1996): 76–78.
66. GAO, "Peace Operations: U.S. Costs in Support of Haiti, Former Yugoslavia, Somalia, and Rwanda," Letter Report, GAO/NSIAS-96-38 (Washington, D.C.: GAO, 1996).
67. U.S. Committee for Refugees, "Haiti," 191.
68. David Bentley and Robert Oakley, *Peace Operations: A Comparison of Somalia and Haiti*, Strategic Forum No. 30 (Washington, D.C.: National Defense University, May 1995); and David Bentley, *Operation Uphold Democracy: Military Support for Democracy in Haiti*, Strategic Forum No. 78 (Washington, D.C.: National Defense University, 1996).
69. World Bank Group, "Haiti."
70. U.S. Committee for Refugees, "Haiti," 191.
71. "The Limits of Nation-Building," *New York Times*, 11 December 1997, A34.
72. See, for example, David Rieff, "The Lessons of Bosnia: Morality and Power," *World Policy Journal* 12, no. 1 (Spring 1995): 76–88, and "The Humanitarian Illusion," *New Republic*, 16 March 1998, 27–32.
73. Maguire et al., *Haiti Held Hostage*, 85–86.
74. Boutros Boutros-Ghali, *An Agenda for Peace, 1995* (New York: United Nations, 1995), 26.

Chapter 8

1. Thomas G. Weiss, "A Research Note about Military-Civilian Humanitarianism: More Questions than Answers," *Disasters* 21, no. 2 (June 1997): 95–117. Reproduced with permission.

2. Charles King, *Ending Civil Wars,* Adelphi Paper No. 308 (Oxford: Oxford University Press, 1996), 12.

3. Gideon Rose, "The Exit Strategy Delusion," *Foreign Affairs* 77, no. 1 (January–February 1998): 64.

4. Stanley Hoffmann, "The Politics and Ethics of Military Intervention," *Survival* 37, no. 4 (Winter 1995–1996): 33.

5. Joint Evaluation of Emergency Assistance to Rwanda, *The International Response to Conflict and Genocide: Lessons from the Rwanda Experience* (Copenhagen: Steering Committee of the Joint Evaluation, 1995), "Synthesis Report," 103.

6. Frederick C. Cuny, "Dilemmas of Military Involvement in Humanitarian Relief," in *Soldiers, Peacekeepers, and Disasters,* ed. Leon Gordenker and Thomas G. Weiss (London: Macmillan, 1991), 54.

7. Dick Leurdijk, *The United Nations and NATO in Former Yugoslavia, 1991–1996: The Limits to Diplomacy and Force* (The Hague: Netherlands Atlantic Commission, 1996).

8. Jan Pronk, "Statement in the General Debate in the Second Committee," New York, 14 October 1996, Permanent Mission of the Kingdom of the Netherlands to the United Nations, 3.

9. Joy Olson with Preston Pentony, *U.S. Military Humanitarian and Civic Assistance Programs and Their Application in Central America* (Albuquerque, N.Mex.: Interhemispheric Resource Center, 1995), 8.

10. Mark Duffield, "NGO Relief in War Zones: Toward an Analysis of the New Aid Paradigm," *Third World Quarterly* 18, no. 3 (June 1997): 527–542.

11. Michael Pugh, *From Mission Cringe to Mission Creep? Implications of New Peace Support Operations Doctrine* (Oslo: Institutt for Forsvarsstudier, 1997).

12. Adam Roberts, *Humanitarian Action in War: Aid, Protection, and Impartiality in a Policy Vacuum,* Adelphi Paper No. 305 (Oxford: Oxford University Press, 1996), 84–86.

13. Michael Walzer, *Just and Unjust Wars: A Moral Argument with Historical Illustrations* (New York: Basic Books, 1992), 188. For a symposium on "Twenty Years of Michael Walzer's Just and Unjust Wars," see *Ethics and International Affairs* 11 (1997): 3–98.

14. Thomas G. Weiss, "Overcoming the Somalia Syndrome—'Operation Rekindle Hope?'" *Global Governance* 1, no. 2 (May–August 1995): 171–187, and "Military-Civilian Humanitarianism: 'The Age of Innocence' Is Over," *International Peacekeeping* 2, no. 2 (1995): 157–174.

15. James Ingram, "The Future Architecture for International Humanitarian Assistance," in *Humanitarianism across Borders: Sustaining Civilians in Times of War,* ed. Thomas G. Weiss and Larry Minear (Boulder, Colo.: Lynne Rienner Publishers, 1993), 174–193. This option seems infeasible for a number of rea-

sons. First, there is the implausibility of altering the ICRC's Swiss character. Second, there is the ICRC's unwillingness to budge from its principle of consent, which by definition will be a handicap in enforcement operations. Finally, its ferocious need to maintain autonomy is hardly conducive to being the servant of governments.

16. U.S. Permanent Mission to the United Nations, "Readying the United Nations for the Twenty-First Century: Some 'UN-21' Proposals for Consideration," undated "nonpaper" of July 1995. This theme also appeared in the "Address by Secretary of State Warren Christopher to the 50th Session of the United Nations General Assembly," 25 September 1995.

17. Pronk, "Statement in the General Debate," 7.

18. See Joint Evaluation of Emergency Assistance to Rwanda, *The International Response*, vol. 3, "Humanitarian Aid and Effects," 159–161, and vol. 1, "Synthesis Report," 58.

19. See, for example, Erskine Childers with Brian Urquhart, *Renewing the United Nations System* (Uppsala: Dag Hammarskjöld Foundation, 1994); and Gareth Evans, *Cooperating for Peace* (London: Allen & Unwin, 1993). For criticisms of the disorganized humanitarian system by Frederick C. Cuny, see "Humanitarian Assistance in the Post–Cold War Era," in *Humanitarianism across Borders*, ed. Weiss and Minear, 151–169.

20. Kofi Annan, *Renewing the United Nations: A Programme for Reform* (New York: United Nations, 1997). The reasons behind the rearguard efforts to halt centralization can be found in Thomas G. Weiss, "Humanitarian Shell Games: Whither UN Reform?" *Security Dialogue* 29, no. 1 (March 1998): 9–43.

21. Stephen John Stedman, "Alchemy for a New World Order: Overselling 'Preventive Diplomacy,'" *Foreign Affairs* 74, no. 3 (May–June 1995): 14–20; and Thomas G. Weiss, "The UN's Prevention Pipe Dream," *Berkeley Journal of International Law* 14, no. 2 (1996): 423–437.

22. Michael S. Lund, *Preventive Diplomacy and American Foreign Policy* (Washington, D.C.: U.S. Institute of Peace Press, 1994), 27. See also his *Preventing Violent Conflicts: A Strategy for Preventive Diplomacy* (Washington, D.C.: U.S. Institute of Peace Press, 1996).

23. The most visible of these publications is *Preventing Deadly Conflict* (New York: Carnegie Commission on Preventing Deadly Conflict, 1997).

24. Boutros Boutros-Ghali, *An Agenda for Development, 1995* (New York: United Nations, 1995), under "Recommendations," 99.

25. Thomas Schelling, *Arms and Influence* (New Haven, Conn.: Yale University Press, 1996).

26. Quoted by Michael Ignatieff, *The Warrior's Honor: Ethnic War and the Modern Conscience* (New York: Henry Holt & Co., 1997), 74.

27. The secretary-general, as is to be expected from an international civil servant, tried to make a virtue of this necessity: "While the UNPROFOR Force Commander had estimated an additional troop requirement of approximately 34,000 to obtain deterrence through strength, the Secretary-General stated that it was possible to start implementing the resolution under a 'light-option', with a minimal troop reinforcement of around 7,000" (see http://ralph.gmu.edu/cfpa/peace/unprofor.html).

28. See Alexander L. George and Jane E. Holl, *The Warning-Response Problem and Missed Opportunities in Preventive Diplomacy* (New York: Carnegie Commission on Preventing Deadly Conflict, 1997).

29. Stanley Hoffmann, *The Ethics and Politics of Humanitarian Intervention* Notre Dame, Ind.: University of Notre Dame Press, 1996), 7.

30. For discussions of this phenomenon, see Thomas G. Weiss and Robert I. Rotberg, eds., *From Massacres to Genocide: The Media, Public Policy, and Humanitarian Crises* (Washington, D.C.: Brookings Institution, 1996); Larry Minear, Colin Scott, and Thomas G. Weiss, *The News Media, Civil War, and Humanitarian Action* (Boulder, Colo.: Lynne Rienner Publishers, 1996); Charles C. Moskos and Thomas E. Ricks, *Reporting War When There Is No War* (Chicago: McCormick Tribune Foundation, 1996); Warren P. Strobel, *Late-Breaking Foreign Policy: The News Media's Influence on Peace Operations* (Washington, D.C.: U.S. Institute of Peace Press, 1997); Edward Girardet, ed., *Somalia, Rwanda, and Beyond: The Role of the International Media in Wars and Humanitarian Crises*, Special Report No. 1; (Geneva: Crosslines, 1995); Johanna Neuman, *Lights, Camera, War* (New York: St. Martin's Press, 1996); and Nik Gowing, *Real-Time Television Coverage of Armed Conflicts and Diplomatic Crises* (Cambridge, Mass.: Harvard University Shorenstein Center, 1994), and *Media Coverage: Help or Hindrance in Conflict Prevention?* (New York: Carnegie Commission on Preventing Deadly Conflict, 1997).

31. Andrew J. Goodpaster, *When Diplomacy Is Not Enough: Managing Multinational Military Interventions* (New York: Carnegie Corporation, July 1996), 1.

32. Chris Seiple, *The U.S. Military/NGO Relationship in Humanitarian Intervention* (Carlisle, Penn.: U.S. Army War College, 1996), 129.

33. Task Force on Ethical and Legal Issues in Humanitarian Assistance, *The Mohonk Criteria for Humanitarian Assistance in Complex Emergencies* New York: World Conference on Religion and Peace, 1994), 6.

34. Adam Roberts, "The Road to Hell . . . : A Critique of Humanitarian Intervention," *Harvard International Review* 16, no. 1 (Fall 1993): 13.

35. Jarat Chopra, "The Space of Peace-Maintenance," *Political Geography* 15, nos. 3–4 (March–April 1996): 335–357, and *Peace-Maintenance: The Evolution of International Political Authority* (London: Routledge, forthcoming).

36. Stephen J. Solarz and Michael E. O'Hanlon, "Humanitarian Intervention: When Is Force Justified?" *Washington Quarterly* 20, no. 4 (Autumn 1997): 10–11.

37. Pugh, *From Mission Cringe*, 24.

38. A classic in this field is Mary B. Anderson and Peter Woodrow, *Rising from the Ashes: Development Strategies at Times of Disaster* (Boulder, Colo.: Westview Press, 1989). With specific reference to military operations, see Jeremy Ginifer, ed., "Beyond the Emergency: Development within UN Peace Missions," a special issue of *International Peacekeeping* 3, no. 2 (Summer 1966); republished (London: Frank Cass, 1997).

39. See Judith Randel and Tony German, eds., *The Reality of Aid, 1997–1998* (London: Earthscan, 1997).

40. See Mark Duffield, "Complex Emergencies and the Crisis in Developmentalism," *IDS* [Institute of Development Studies] *Bulletin* 25, no. 4 (October 1994): 37–45.

41. I am grateful to Joanna Macrae and Mark Bradbury for this insight, which results from unpublished work for UNICEF.

42. See Joanne Macrae and John Bolton, "Aid Trends: The State of the Humanitarian System," in International Federation of Red Cross and Red Crescent Societies, *World Disasters Report, 1996* (Oxford: Oxford University Press, 1996), 54–63.

43. Robert Miller, *Aid as Peacemaker: Canadian Development Assistance and Third World Conflict* (Ottawa: Carleton University Press, 1992), 5.

44. See Chaim Kaufmann, "Possible and Impossible Solutions to Ethnic Wars," *International Security* 20, no. 4 (Spring 1996): 136–175.

45. Thomas G. Weiss, "Triage: Humanitarian Interventions in a New Era," *World Policy Journal* 11, no. 1 (Spring 1994): 1–10.

46. UNICEF, *The State of the World's Children, 1993* (New York: Oxford University Press, 1993).

47. See, for example, Boutros-Ghali, *An Agenda for Development, 1995.*

48. Nicholas Stockton, "Defensive Development? Re-examining the Role of the Military in Complex Political Emergencies," *Disasters* 20, no. 2 (June 1996): 144–145.

49. See Umesh Palwankar, ed., *Symposium on Humanitarian Action and Peacekeeping Operations* (Geneva: ICRC, 1994), 102.

50. The transcript is found in "Standoff with Iraq: The Commander in Chief Speaks," *New York Times*, 18 February 1998, A9.

51. This is a fundamental distinction running throughout Thomas G. Weiss, David P. Forsythe, and Roger A. Coate, *The United Nations and Changing World Politics*, 2nd ed. (Boulder, Colo.: Westview Press, 1997). See also, Inis L. Claude Jr., "Peace and Security: Prospective Roles for the Two United Nations," *Global Governance* 2, no. 3 (September–December 1996): 289–298.

52. Stephen M. Walt, "International Relations: One World, Many Theories," *Foreign Policy* 110 (Spring 1998): 30.

53. Robert O. Keohane, "International Institutions: Can Interdependence Work?" *Foreign Policy* 110 (Spring 1998): 83.

54. Boutros Boutros-Ghali, *Supplement to "An Agenda for Peace": Position Paper by the Secretary-General on the Occasion of the Fiftieth Anniversary of the United Nations*, 3 January 1995, document A/50/60, S/1995/1, para. 86.

55. This theme was explored first by Jarat Chopra and Thomas G. Weiss, "Prospects for Containing Conflict in the Former Second World," *Security Studies* 4, no. 3 (Spring 1995): 552–583, esp. 575–583. See also Thomas G. Weiss, ed., *Beyond UN Subcontracting: Task-sharing with Regional Security Arrangements and Service-Providing NGOs* (London: Macmillan, 1997).

56. Alexander George, *Bridging the Gap: Theory and Practice of Foreign Policy* (Washington, D.C.: U.S. Institute of Peace Press, 1993).

57. Philip E. Tetlock and Aaron Belkin, eds., *Counterfactual Thought Experiments in World Politics: Logical, Methodological, and Psychological Perspectives* (Princeton, N.J.: Princeton University Press, 1996).

58. For analyses from one, see Alan James, *The Politics of Peace-Keeping* (London: Chatto & Windus, 1969), and *Peacekeeping in International Politics* (London: Macmillan, 1990).

59. Jarat Chopra and Thomas G. Weiss, "Sovereignty Is No Longer Sacrosanct: Codifying Humanitarian Intervention," *Ethics and International Affairs* 6 (1992): 95–118.

60. David Rieff, "The Humanitarian Illusion," *New Republic*, 16 March 1998, 30.

61. John F. Hutchinson, *Champions of Charity: War and the Rise of the Red Cross* (Boulder: Colo.: Westview Press, 1996).

62. "Introductory Address by Dr. Cornelio Sommaruga," in *Report on the Wolfsberg Humanitarian Forum, 8–10 June 1997* (Geneva: ICRC, 1997), 3.

63. Andrew Natsios, "Commentary," *Ethics and International Affairs* 11 (1997): 133.

64. See, for example, Eric A. Belgrad and Nitza Nachmias, eds., *The Politics of International Humanitarian Aid Operations* (Westport, Conn.: Praeger, 1997).

65. See, for example, Adam Roberts, "Threats to Humanitarian Action: Remedies," in *Report on the Wolfsberg Humanitarian Forum*, 3.

66. Rieff, "The Humanitarian Illusion," 29.

67. See Bernard Kouchner and Mario Bettati, *Le Devoir d'Ingérence* (Paris: Denoël, 1987); Bernard Kouchner, *Le Malheur des Autres* (Paris: Odile Jacob, 1991); and Mario Bettati, *Le Droit d'Ingérence: Mutation de l'Ordere International* (Paris: Odile Jacob, 1997).

68. Larry Minear and Thomas G. Weiss, *Humanitarian Action in Times of War: A Handbook for Practitioners* (Boulder, Colo.: Lynne Rienner Publishers, 1993), 7–41.

69. Ignatieff, *The Warrior's Honor*, 5.

70. Charles William Maynes, " 'Principles' Hegemony," *World Policy Journal* 14, no. 3 (Fall 1997): 36.

71. Mark Duffield, "The Symphony of the Damned: Racial Discourse, Complex Political Emergencies, and Humanitarian Aid," *Disasters* 20, no. 3 (September 1996): 191.

72. Joanna Macrae, "The Death of Humanitarianism? An Anatomy of the Attack," draft paper dated 4 February 1998.

73. Chr. Michelsen Institute, *Humanitarian Assistance and Conflict* (Bergen: Chr. Michelsen Institute, 1997), 3.

74. Myron Wiener, "The Clash of Norms: Dilemmas in Refugee Policies," in *Workshop on the Demography of Forces Migration* (Washington, D.C.: National Academy of Sciences, 1997), 5.

75. See Dan Smith, "Interventionist Dilemmas and Justice," in *Humanitarian Force*, ed. Anthony McDermott (Oslo: International Peace Research Institute, 1997), 13–39, esp. 29–31.

76. Thomas Nagle, *Moral Questions* (Cambridge: Cambridge University Press, 1991), 74.

77. I am grateful to Charles Keely of Georgetown University for this thought.

78. Mary B. Anderson, *Do No Harm: Supporting Local Capacities for Peace through Aid* (Cambridge, Mass.: Collaborative for Development Action, 1996).

79. Edmund Cairns, *A Safer Future: Reducing the Human Cost of War* (Oxford: Oxfam Publications, 1997), 94.

Selected Bibliography of the 1990s

Humanitarian Intervention

The following are up-to-date sources that introduce humanitarian intervention.

Military and Civilian Interactions

Bennett, Jon. *Meeting Needs: NGO Coordination in Practice.* London: Earthscan, 1995.

Berdal, Mats R. *Disarmament and Demobilisation after Civil Wars.* Adelphi Paper No. 303. Oxford: Oxford University Press, 1996.

Builder, Carl, Robert Lempert, Kevin Lewis, Eric Larson, and Milton Weiler. *Report of a Workshop on Expanding U.S. Air Force Noncombat Mission Capabilities.* Santa Monica, Calif.: RAND Corporation, 1993.

Chopra, Jarat. *Peace-Maintenance: The Evolution of International Political Authority.* London: Routledge, forthcoming.

Chopra, Jarat, ed. *The Politics of Peace-Maintenance.* Boulder, Colo.: Lynne Rienner Publishers, 1998.

Chr. Michelsen Institute. *Humanitarian Assistance and Conflict.* Bergen: Chr. Michelsen Institute, 1997.

Collins, Cindy, and Thomas G. Weiss. *A Review and Assessment of 1989–1996 Peace Operations Publication.* Occasional Paper No. 28. Providence, R.I.: Watson Institute, 1997.

de Waal, Alex. *Famine Crimes: Politics and the Disaster Relief Industry in Africa.* Oxford: James Currey, 1997.

de Waal, Alex, and Rakiya Omaar. *Humanitarianism Unbound? Current Dilemma Facing Multi-Mandate Relief Operations in Political Emergencies.* Discussion Paper No. 5. London: African Rights, 1994.

Edwards, Michael, and David Hulme, eds. *Beyond the Magic Bullet: NGO Performance and Accountability in the Post–Cold War World.* West Hartford, Conn.: Kumarian Press, 1996.

Edwards, Michael and David Hulme, eds. *NGOs, States, and Donors: Too Close for Comfort?* London: Macmillan, 1997.
Famsbotham, Oliver, and Tom Woodhouse. *Humanitarian Intervention in Contemporary Conflict.* Cambridge: Polity Press, 1996.
Goodpaster, Andrew J. *When Diplomacy Is Not Enough: Managing Multinational Military Interventions.* New York: Carnegie Corporation, July 1996.
Gordenker, Leon, and Thomas G. Weiss, eds. *Soldiers, Peacekeepers, and Disasters.* London: Macmillan, 1991.
Harriss, John, ed. *The Politics of Humanitarian Intervention.* London: Pinter, 1995.
Heiberg, Marianne, ed. *Subduing Sovereignty: Sovereignty and the Right to Intervene.* London: Pinter, 1994.
Hoffmann, Stanley. *The Ethics and Politics of Humanitarian Intervention.* Notre Dame, Ind.: University of Notre Dame Press, 1996.
Human Rights Watch. *The Lost Agenda: Human Rights and U.N. Field Operations.* New York: Human Rights Watch, 1993.
Ignatieff, Michael. *The Warrior's Honor: Ethnic War and the Modern Conscience.* New York: Henry Holt & Co., 1997.
Lepgold, Joseph, and Thomas G. Weiss, eds. *Collective Conflict Management and Changing World Politics.* Albany: State University of New York Press, 1998.
Loescher, Gil. *Beyond Charity: International Cooperation and the Global Refugee Crisis.* New York: Oxford University Press, 1993.
Lyons, Gene M., and Michael Mastanduno, eds. *Beyond Westphalia? National Sovereignty and International Intervention.* Baltimore, Md.: Johns Hopkins University Press, 1995.
MacKinlay, John, ed. *Peace Support Operations.* Providence, R.I.: Watson Institute, 1996.
McDermott, Anthony, ed. *Humanitarian Force.* Oslo: International Peace Research Institute, 1997.
Minear, Larry, and Thomas G. Weiss. *Humanitarian Action in Times of War: A Handbook for Practitioners.* Boulder, Colo.: Lynne Rienner Publishers, 1993.
Minear, Larry, and Thomas G. Weiss. *Humanitarian Politics.* Headline Series No. 304. New York: Foreign Policy Association, 1995.
Minear, Larry, and Thomas G. Weiss. *Mercy under Fire: War and the Global Humanitarian Community.* Boulder, Colo.: Westview Press, 1995.
Minear, Larry, Colin Scott, and Thomas G. Weiss. *The New Media, Civil War, and Humanitarian Action.* Boulder, Colo.: Lynne Rienner Publishers, 1996.
Moore, Jonathan. *The UN and Complex Emergencies.* Geneva: UN Research Institute for Social Development, 1996.
Natsios, Andrew S. *U.S. Foreign Policy and the Four Horsemen of the Apocalypse: Humanitarian Relief in Complex Emergencies.* Westport, Conn.: Praeger, 1997.
Oakley, Robert B., Michal J. Dziedzic, and Eliot M. Goldberg, eds. *Policing the New World Disorder: Peace Operations and Public Security.* Washington, D.C.: National Defense University, 1998.
Otunnu, Olara A., and Michael W. Doyle, eds. *Peacemaking and Peacekeeping for the New Century.* Lanham, Md.: Rowman & Littlefield, 1998.
Palwankar, Umesh, ed. *Symposium on Humanitarian Action and Peace-keeping Operations.* Geneva: ICRC, 1994.

Pieterse, Jan Nederveen, ed. *World Orders in the Making: The Case of Humanitarian Intervention*. London: Macmillian, forthcoming.

Posen, Barry. "Military Responses to Refugee Disasters." *International Security* 21, no. 1 (Summer 1996): 72–111.

Pugh, Michael. *From Mission Cringe to Mission Creep? Implications of New Peace Support Operations Doctrine*. Oslo: Institutt for Forsvarsstudier, 1997.

Pugh, Michael. "Peacekeeping and Humanitarian Intervention." In *Issues in World Politics*, ed. Brian White, Richard Little, and Michael Smith. New York: St. Martin's Press, 1997, 134–156.

Reed, Laura W., and Carl Kaysen, eds. *Emerging Norms of Justified Intervention*. Cambridge, Mass.: American Academy of Arts & Sciences, 1993.

Roberts, Adam. *Humanitarian Action in War: Aid, Protection, and Impartiality in a Policy Vacuum*. Adelphi Paper No. 305. Oxford: Oxford University Press, 1996.

Rodley, Nigels, ed. *To Loose the Bonds of Wickedness: International Intervention in Defence of Human Rights*. London: Brassey's, 1992.

Rotberg, Robert I., and Thomas G. Weiss, eds. *From Massacres to Genocide: The Media, Public Policy, and Humanitarian Crises*. Washington, D.C.: Brookings Institution, 1996.

Seiple, Chris. *The U.S. Military/NGO Relationship in Humanitarian Intervention*. Carlisle, Penn.: U.S. Army War College, 1996.

Shearer, David. *Private Armies and Military Intervention*. Adelphi Paper No. 316. Oxford: Oxford University Press, 1998.

Smillie, Ina. *The Alms Bazaar: Altruism under Fire—Non-profit Organizations and International Organizations*. West Hartford, Conn.: Kumarian Press, 1995.

Smith, Dan. *The State of War and Peace Atlas*. London: Penguin, 1997.

Strobel, Warren P. *Late-Breaking Foreign Policy: The News Media's Influence on Peace Operations*. Washington, D.C.: U.S. Institute of Peace Press, 1997.

Weiss, Thomas G., ed. *Beyond UN Subcontracting: Task-sharing with Regional Security Arrangements and Service-Providing NGOs*. London: Macmillan, 1998.

Weiss, Thomas, G., and Cindy Collins. *Humanitarian Challenges and Intervention: World Politics and the Dilemmas of Help*. Boulder, Colo.: Westview Press, 1996.

Weiss, Thomas, G., and Leon Gordenker, eds. *NGOs, the UN, and Global Governance*. Boulder, Colo.: Lynne Rienner Publishers, 1996.

Woodhouse, Tom, Robert Bruce, and Malcolm Dando, eds. *Peacekeeping and Peacemaking: Towards Effective Intervention in Post–Cold War Conflicts*. New York: St. Martin's Press, 1998.

Comparisons of Armed Conflicts in the Post–Cold War Era

Ayoob, Mohammed. *The Third World Security Predicament: State Making, Regional Conflict, and the International System*. Boulder, Colo.: Lynne Rienner Publishers, 1995.

Belgrad, Eric, A., and Nitza Nachmias, eds. *The Politics of International Humanitarian Aid Operations*. Westport, Conn.: Praeger, 1997.

Berdal, Mats R. *Whither UN Peacekeeping*: Adelphi Paper No. 281. London: International Institute for Strategic Studies, 1993.

Boutros-Ghali, Boutros. *An Agenda for Peace 1995.* New York: United Nations, 1995.
Brown, Michael E., ed. *The International Dimensions of Internal Conflict.* Cambridge, Mass.: MIT Press, 1996.
Cohen, Roberta, and Francis M. Deng, eds. *The Forsaken People.* Washington, D.C.: Brookings Institution, 1998.
Cohen, Roberta, and Francis M. Deng, eds. *Masses in Flight: The Global Crisis of Internal Displacement.* Washington, D.C.: Brookings Institution, 1998.
Cranna, Michael, ed. *The True Costs of Conflict: Seven Recent Wars and Their Effects on Society.* New York: Free Press, 1994.
Crocker, Chester A., Fen Osler Hampson, and Pamela Aall, eds. *Managing Global Chaos: Sources of and Responses to International Conflict.* Washington, D.C.: U.S. Institute of Peace Press, 1996.
Damrosch, Lori Fisler, ed. *Enforcing Restraint: Collective Intervention in Internal Conflicts.* New York: Council on Foreign Relations Press, 1993.
Deng, Francis M. *Protecting the Dispossessed: A Challenge for the International Community.* Washington, D.C.: Brookings Institution, 1993.
Deng, Francis M., and Roberta Cohen, eds. *Masses in Flight.* Washington, D.C.: Brookings Institution, 1998.
Diehl, Paul. *International Peacekeeping.* Baltimore, Md.: Johns Hopkins University Press, 1993.
Donini, Antonio. *The Policies of Mercy: UN Coordination in Afghanistan, Mozambique, and Rwanda.* Occasional Paper No. 22. Providence, R.I.: Watson Institute, 1996.
Durch, William J., ed. *The Evolution of UN Peacekeeping: Cases Studies and Comparative Analysis.* New York: St. Martin's Press, 1993.
Durch, William J., ed. *UN Peacekeeping, American Policy, and the Uncivil Wars of the 1990s.* New York: St. Martin's Press, 1996.
Girardet, Edward, ed. *Somalia, Rwanda, and Beyond: The Role of the International Media in Wars and Humanitarian Crises.* Special Report No. 1. Geneva: Crosslines, 1995.
Gurr, Ted Robert, and Barbara Harff. *Ethnic Conflict in World Politics.* Boulder, Colo.: Westview Press, 1994.
Hampson, Fen Osler. *Nurturing Peace: Why Peace Settlements Succeed or Fail.* Washington, D.C.: U.S. Institute of Peace Press, 1996.
Henkin, Alice H., ed. *Honoring Human Rights and Keeping the Peace: Lessons from El Salvador, Cambodia, and Haiti.* Washington, D.C.: Aspen Institute, 1995.
Holsti, Kalevi J. *The State, War, and the State of War.* Cambridge: Cambridge University Press, 1996.
Hutchinson, John F. *Champions of Charity: War and the Rise of the Red Cross.* Boulder, Colo.: Westview Press, 1996.
International Federation of Red Cross and Red Crescent Societies. *World Disasters Report, 1998.* Oxford: Oxford University Press, 1998.
Jackson, Robert. *Quasi-States: Sovereignty, International Relations, and the Third World.* Cambridge: Cambridge University Press, 1990.
King, Charles. *Ending Civil Wars.* Adelphi Paper No. 308. Oxford: Oxford University Press, 1997.

Macrae, Joanna, and Anthony Zwi, eds. *War and Hunger: Rethinking International Responses to Complex Emergencies.* London: Zed Books, 1994.
Maren, Michael. *The Road to Hell: The Ravaging Effects of Foreign Aid and International Charity.* New York: Free Press, 1997.
Mayall, James, ed. *The New Interventionism: United Nations Experience in Cambodia, Former Yugoslavia, and Somalia.* New York: Cambridge University Press, 1996.
Prendergast, John. *Frontline Diplomacy: Humanitarian Aid and Conflict in Africa.* Boulder, Colo.: Lynne Rienner Publishers, 1996.
Rice, Edward E. *Wars of the Third Kind: Conflict in Underdeveloped Countries.* Berkeley: University of California Press, 1988.
Sogge, David, ed. *Compassion and Calculation: The Business of Private Foreign Aid.* London: Pluto Press, 1996.
United Nations. *The Blue Helmets: A Review of United Nations Peace-Keeping.* 3rd ed. New York: United Nations, 1996.
UN Department of Humanitarian Affairs. *Humanitarian Report, 1997.* New York: United Nations, 1997.
UN High Commissioner for Refugees. *The State of the World's Refugees, 1997–98: A Humanitarian Agenda.* Oxford: Oxford University Press, 1997.
U.S. Government Accounting Office. "Peace Operations: U.S. Costs in Support of Haiti, Former Yugoslavia, Somalia, and Rwanda." Letter Report, GAO/NSIAS-96-38. Washington, D.C.: GAO, 1996.
U.S. Library of Congress. *United Nations Peace Operations: Case Studies.* Washington, D.C.: Library of Congress, 1995.
Väyrynen, Raimo. *The Age of Humanitarian Emergencies.* Research for Action No. 25. Helsinki: World Institute for Development Economics Research, 1996.
Weiss, Thomas G., ed. *The United Nations and Civil Wars.* Boulder, Colo.: Lynne Rienner Publishers, 1995.
Zartman, I. William, ed. *Collapsed States: The Disintegration and Restoration of Legitimate Authority.* Boulder, Colo.: Lynne Rienner Publishers, 1995.
Zartman, I. William, ed. *Elusive Peace: Negotiating an End to Civil Wars.* Washington, D.C.: Brookings Institution, 1995.

Relevant Country Cases

In addition to country cases in many of the above-mentioned collections, the following sources proved useful in examining the background and costs of outside military involvement in the five cases of humanitarian intervention discussed in this book.

Northern Iraq

Alnasrawi, Abbas. "Iraq: Economic Consequences of the 1991 Gulf War and Future Outlook." *Third World Quarterly* 13, no. 2 (1992): 336–337.
Amnesty International. *Iraq: Human Rights Abuses in Iraqi Kurdistan since 1991.*

AI Index: MDE 14/01.95. At: http://www.amnesty.org/ailib/aipub/1995/MDE/1.

Barkey, Henry J. "Kurdish Geopolitics." *Current History* 96, no. 606 (January 1997): 1–5.

Brilliant, Franca, Frederick C. Cuny, Pat Reed, and Victor Tanner, eds. *Humanitarian Assistance Lessons of Operation Provide Comfort: A Study Prepared for the Office of U.S. Foreign Disaster Assistance and U.S. Army Civil Affairs*. Dallas, Tex.: INTERTECT, 1992.

Ciment, James. *The Kurds: State and Minority in Turkey, Iraq, and Iran*. New York: Facts on File, 1996.

Dirks, Robert. "Famine, Hunger Seasons, and Relief-Induced Antagonism." In *African Food Systems in Crisis: Part One: Microperspectives*, ed. Rebecca Huss-Ashmore and Solomon H. Katz. New York: Gordon & Breach, 1989, 295–303.

Gunter, Michael M. *The Kurds of Iraq: Tragedy and Hope*. New York: St. Martin's Press, 1992.

Hoskins, Eric. "The Humanitarian Impact of Economic Sanctions and War in Iraq." In *Political Gain and Civilian Pain: The Humanitarian Impacts of Economic Sanctions*, ed. Thomas G. Weiss, David Cortright, George A. Lopez, and Larry Minear. Lanham, Md.: Rowman & Littlefield, 1997, 91–147.

Izady, Mehrdad. *The Kurds: A Concise Handbook*. Washington, D.C.: Taylor & Francis, 1992.

Laizer, Sheri. *Martyrs, Traitors, and Patriots: Kurdistan after the Gulf War*. London: Zed Books, 1996.

Middle East Watch/Human Rights Watch. *Endless Torment: The 1991 Uprising in Iraq and Its Aftermath*. New York: Middle East Watch/Human Rights Watch, June 1992.

Minear, Larry, U. B. P. Chelliah, Jeff Crisp, John MacKinlay, and Thomas G. Weiss. *United Nations Coordination of the International Humanitarian Response to the Gulf Crisis, 1900–1992*. Occasional Paper No. 13. Providence, R.I.: Watson Institute, 1992.

Mofid, Kamran. *The Economic Consequences of the Gulf War*. London: Routledge, 1990.

Ofteringer, Ronald, and Ralf Bäcker. "A Republic of Statelessness: Three Years of Humanitarian Intervention in Iraqi Kurdistan." *Middle East Report* March–June 1994): 40–45.

Olson, Robert. "The Kurdish Question in the Aftermath of the Gulf War: Geopolitical and Geostrategic Changes in the Middle East." *Third World Quarterly* 13, no. 3 (1992): 475–499.

Operation Provide Comfort Fact Sheet. At: http://www.incirlik.af.mil/orgs/opc/opcfact.html.

United Nations. *The United Nations and the Iraq-Kuwait Conflict, 1990–1996*. New York: UN Department of Public Information, 1996.

UN Department of Humanitarian Affairs. *United Nations Consolidated Inter-Agency Humanitarian Assistance Program to Iraq: Emergency Requirements for the Period October–December 1996*. 2 October 1996. At: http://www.reliefweb.int/.

UN High Commissioner for Refugees. Centre for Documentation and Research. *Background Paper on Iraqi Refugees and Asylum Seekers.* Geneva: UNHCR, September 1996. At: http://www.unhcr.ch/refworld/country/cdr/cdrirq2.htm.
U.S. Department of State. *Iraqi Human Rights.* Washington, D.C.: State Department, March 1996.
U.S. Department of State. *Report on Iraqi Human Rights Practices, 1996.* 1 January 1997. At: http://www.state.gov/www/issues/human_rights/1996_hrp_report/iraq.html.

Somalia

Adibe, Clement. *Managing Arms in Peace Processes: Somalia.* Disarmament and Conflict Resolution Project, UNIDIR/95/30. Geneva: UNIDIR, 1995.
Africa Rights. *Operation Restore Hope: A Preliminary Assessment.* London: Africa Rights, May 1993.
Africa Rights. *Somalia: Human Rights Abuses by the United Nations Forces.* London: Africa Rights, July 1993.
Chopra, Jarat. "Achilles' Heel in Somalia: Learning from a Conceptual Failure." *Texas International Law Journal* 31, no. 3 (Summer 1996): 495–526.
Chopra, John, Åge Eknes, and Toralv Nordbø. *Fighting for Hope in Somalia.* Peacekeeping and Multinational Operations No. 6. Oslo: Norwegian Institute for International Affairs, 1995.
Clarke, Walter S. *Humanitarian Intervention in Somalia: Bibliography.* Carlisle, Penn.: U.S. Army War College, 1995.
Clarke, Walter S., and Jeffrey Herbst, eds. *Learning from Somalia: The Lessons of Armed Humanitarian Intervention.* Boulder, Colo: Westview Press, 1997.
Crocker, Chester. "The Lessons of Somalia: Not Everything Went Wrong." *Foreign Affairs* 74, no. 3 (May–June 1995): 2–8.
Farrell, Theo. "Sliding into War: The Somalia Imbroglio and US Army Peace Operations Doctrine." *International Peacekeeping* 2, no. 2 (Summer 1995): 194–214.
Jonah, James O. C. *Differing State Perspectives on the United Nations in the Post–Cold War World.* ACUNS Reports and Papers No. 4. Providence, R.I.: ACUNS, 1993.
Makinda, Samuel. "Politics and Clan Rivalry in Somalia." *Australian Journal of Political Science* 26 (1991): 111–126.
Makinda, Samuel. *Seeking Peace from Chaos: Humanitarian Intervention in Somalia.* Boulder, Colo.: Lynne Rienner Publishers, 1993.
Miller, Laura, and Charles Moskos. "Humanitarians or Warriors? Race, Gender, and Combat Status in Operation Restore Hope." *Armed Forces and Society* 21, no. 4 (Summer 1995): 615–637.
Natsios, Andrew. "Food through Force: Humanitarian Intervention and U.S. Policy." *Washington Quarterly* 17, no. 1 (Winter 1994): 129–144.
Natsios, Andrew. "Humanitarian Relief Interventions: The Economics of Chaos." *International Peacekeeping* 3, no. 1 (1996): 68–91.

Patman, Robert G. "The UN Operation in Somalia." In *A Crisis of Expectations: UN Peacekeeping in the 1990s*, ed. Ramesh Thakur and Carlyle A. Thayer. Boulder, Colo.: Westview Press, 1995, 85–104.

Refugee Policy Group. *Lives Lost, Lives Saved: Excess Mortality and the Impact of Health Interventions in the Somalia Emergency.* Washington, D.C.: RPG, November 1994.

Sahnoun, Mohammed. *Somalia: The Missed Opportunities.* Washington, D.C.: U.S. Institute of Peace Press, 1994.

Simons, Anne. *Networks of Dissolution: Somalia Undone.* Boulder, Colo.: Westview Press, 1995.

Sommer, John. *Hope Restored? Humanitarian Aid in Somalia, 1990–1994.* Washington, D.C.: RPG, 1994.

Weiss, Thomas G. "Overcoming the Somalia Syndrome—'Operation Rekindle Hope'?" *Global Governance* 1, no. 2 (May–August 1995): 171–187.

Bosnia

Allen, Beverly. "Rape Warfare in Bosnia." *Brown Journal of World Affairs* 3, no. 1 (Winter–Spring 1996): 313–324.

Caplan, Richard. *Post-Mortem on UNPROFOR.* Centre for Defence Studies No. 33. London: Brassey's, 1996.

Cuny, Frederick C. *The Bosnian Way.* INTERTECT Briefing Book. Dallas, Tex.: INTERTECT, 1992.

Devin, Julia, and Jaleh Dashti-Gibson. "Sanctions in the Former Yugoslavia: Convoluted Goals and Complicated Consequences." In *Political Gain and Civilian Pain: The Humanitarian Impacts of Economic Sanctions*, ed. Thomas G. Weiss, David Cortright, George A. Lopez, and Larry Minear. Lanham, Md.: Rowman & Littlefield, 1997, 149–187.

Lamb, Susan R. "The UN Protection Force in Former Yugoslavia." In *A Crisis in Expectations: UN Peacekeeping in the 1990s*, ed. Ramesh Thakur and Carlyle A. Thayer. Boulder, Colo.: Westview Press, 1995, 65–84.

Leurdijk, Dick. *The United Nations and NATO in Former Yugoslavia, 1991–1996: The Limits to Diplomacy and Force.* The Hague: Netherlands Atlantic Commission, 1996.

Minear, Larry, Jeffrey Clark, Roberta Cohen, Dennis Gallagher, Iain Guest, and Thomas G. Weiss. *Humanitarian Action in the Former Yugoslavia: The U.N.'s Role, 1991–1993.* Occasional Paper No. 18. Providence, R.I.: Watson Institute, 1994.

Owen, David. *Balkan Odyssey.* New York: Harcourt Brace, 1995.

Pasic, Amir, and Thomas G. Weiss. "Humanitarian Recognition in the Former Yugoslavia: The Limits of Non-State Politics." *Security Studies* 7, no. 1 (Autumn 1997): 193–227.

Pasic, Amir, and Thomas G. Weiss. "The Politics of Rescue: Yugoslavia's Wars and the Humanitarian Impulse." *Ethics and International Affairs* 11 (1997): 105–131.

Schuett, Olivier. "The International War Crimes Tribunal for the Former Yugoslavia and the Dayton Peace Agreement: Peace versus Justice?" *International Peacekeeping* 4, no. 2 (Summer 1997): 91–114.

Ullman, Richard H., ed. *The World and Yugoslavia's Wars.* New York: Council on Foreign Relations Press, 1996.

Weiss, Thomas G., and Amir Pasic. "Reinventing UNHCR: Enterprising Humanitarians in the Former Yugoslavia, 1991–1995." *Global Governance* 3, no. 1 (January–April 1997): 41–58.

Woodward, Susan. *Balkan Tragedy: Chaos and Dissolution after the Cold War.* Washington, D.C.: Brookings Institution, 1995.

Rwanda*

Borton, Nan. *Rwanda-Civil Strife/Displaced Persons: Situation Report #7, Fiscal Year (FY) 1995.* Washington, D.C.: OFDA, 28 August 1995.

Evans, Glynne. *Responding to Crises in the African Great Lakes.* Adelphi Paper No. 311. Oxford: Oxford University Press, 1997.

Joint Evaluation of Emergency Assistance to Rwanda, *The International Response to Conflict and Genocide: Lessons from the Rwanda Experience.* 5 vols. Copenhagen: Steering Committee of the Joint Evaluation, 1996.

McNulty, Mel. "France's Role in Rwanda and External Military Intervention: A Double Discrediting." *International Peacekeeping* 4, no. 3 (Autumn 1997): 24–44.

Melvern, Linda. "Genocide behind the Thin Blue Line." *Security Dialogue* 28, no. 3 (September 1997): 333–346.

Minear, Larry, and Philippe Guillot. *Soldiers to the Rescue: Humanitarian Lessons from Rwanda.* Paris: OECD, 1996. Omaar, Rakiya, and Alex de Waal. *Rwanda: Death, Despair, and Destruction.* London: African Rights, 1994.

Prunier, Gérard. *The Rwanda Crisis: History of a Genocide.* New York: Columbia University Press, 1995.

Seybolt, Taylor B. *Coordination in Rwanda: The Humanitarian Response to Genocide and Civil War.* Cambridge, Mass.: Conflict Management Group, 1997.

Uvin, Peter. *Development, Aid, and Conflict: Reflections from the Case of Rwanda.* Research for Action No. 24. Helsinki: World Institute for Development Economics Research, 1996.

Haiti

Amnesty International. *On the Horns of a Dilemma: Military Repression or Foreign Invasion.* AI Index: AMR 36/33/94.

Amnesty International. *The Price of Rejection: Human Rights Consequences for Rejected Haitian Asylum-Seekers.* At: http://www.amnesty.org/ailib/aipub/1994/AMR/5.

Bentley, David. *Operation Uphold Democracy: Military Support for Democracy in*

---

*Unlike other cases, many secondary materials are available in French.

Haiti. Strategic Forum No. 78. Washington, D.C.: National Defense University, 1996.

Bentley, David, and Robert Oakley. *Peace Operations: A Comparison of Somalia and Haiti*. Strategic Forum No. 30. Washington, D.C.: National Defense University, May 1995.

Bureau of Inter-American Affairs. U.S. Department of State. "Background Notes: Haiti, September 1996." At: http://www.state.gov/www/background_notes/haiti_0996_bgn.html.

Chelala, Cesar. "Fighting for Survival." *British Medical Journal* 309 (20–27 August 1994): 526.

Commission of Human Rights. United Nations Economic and Social Council. *Advisory Services in the Field of Human Rights: Situation of Human Rights in Haiti*. E/CN.4/1996/94. 24 January 1996.

Commission of Human Rights. United Nations Economic and Social Council. *Question of the Violation of Human Rights and Fundamental Freedoms in Any Part of the World with Particular Reference to Colonial and Other Dependent Countries and Territories: Situation of Human Rights in Haiti*. E/CN.4/1995/59. 6 February 1995.

Constable, Pamela. "A Fresh Start for Haiti?" *Current History* 96, no. 607 (February 1996): 65–69.

Hall, Donald P. "Stress, Suicide, and Military Service during Operation Uphold Democracy." *Military Medicine* 161, no. 3 (March 1996): 159–162.

Harvard Center for Population and Development Studies. *Sanctions in Haiti: Crisis in Humanitarian Action*. Cambridge, Mass.: Harvard School of Public Health, 1993.

"Health Status of Haitian Migrants—U.S. Naval Base, Guantanamo Bay, Cuba, November 1991–April 1992." *Morbidity and Mortality Weekly Report* 42, no. 7 (26 February 1993): 138–140.

Kumar, Chetan, and Elizabeth Cousens. *Policy Briefing: Peacebuilding in Haiti*. International Peace Academy. At: http://www.ipacademy.inter.net/haiti.htm.

Maguire, Robert. *Demilitarizing Public Order in a Predatory State: The Case of Haiti*. North-South Agenda Papers No. 17. Coral Gables, Fla.: North-South Center Press, December 1995.

Maguire, Robert, Edwige Balutansky, Jacques Fomerand, Larry Minear, William G. O'Neill, Thomas G. Weiss, and Sarah Zaidi. *Haiti Held Hostage: International Responses to the Quest for Nationhood, 1986–1996*. Occasional Paper No. 23. Providence, R.I.: Watson Institute, 1996.

Malone, David. "Haiti and the International Community: A Case Study." *Survival* 39, no. 2 (Summer 1997): 126–146.

Mendiburu, Marcus, and Sarah Meek. *Disarmament and Conflict Resolution Project—Managing Arms in Peace Processes: Haiti*. UNIDIR 96/48. New York and Geneva: United Nations, 1996.

Morris, Justin. "Force and Democracy: UN/US Intervention in Haiti." *International Peacekeeping* 2, no. 3 (Autumn 1995): 391–412.

Oakley, Robert, and Michael Dziedzic. *Sustaining Success in Haiti*. Washington,

D.C.: National Defense University, Institute for National Strategic Studies, 1996.
Pape, Jean, and Warren D. Johnson Jr. "AIDS in Haiti: 1982–1992." *Clinical Infectious Diseases* 17, suppl. 2 (1993): S341–345.
Perusse, Roland I. *Haitian Democracy Restored, 1991–1995.* Lanham, Md.: University Press of America, 1995.
Preeg, Ernest H. *The Haitian Dilemma: A Case Study in Demographic, Development, and U.S. Foreign Policy,* Washington, D.C.: Center for Strategic and International Studies, 1996.
Tacsan, Joaquìn. "Searching for OAS-UN Task-sharing Opportunities in Central America and Haiti." *Third World Quarterly* 18, no. 3 (1997): 489–507.
U.S. Department of State. *Haiti: Country Report on Human Rights.* 24 September 1994. At: gopher://summit.fiu.edu:70/00/State/state.77.
U.S. Department of State. *US State Department Human Rights Report: Haiti.* At: http://library.ccsu.ctstateu.edu/~history/world_history/archives/haiti/haiti059.html.
Zaidi, Sarah. "Humanitarian Effects of the Coup and Sanctions in Haiti." In *Political Gain and Civilian Pain: The Humanitarian Impacts of Economic Sanctions,* ed. Thomas G. Weiss, David Cortright, George A. Lopez, and Larry Minear. Lanham, Md.: Rowman & Littlefield, 1997, 189–212.

Index

Abdic, Fikret, 128
accountability: as area of possible research, 208; ensures that subcontracted mission reflects collective interests, 211, 212
Addis Ababa National Reconciliation Conference of 15 March 1993, 87
Afgoi average daily crude mortality rate, 78
Aga Kahn, Prince Sadruddin, 57
"age of humanitarian emergencies", 1
Aideed, Mohammed Farah, 76, 82; death of, 95; negotiation of a cease-fire between Ali Mahdi and, 81; results of attempt to demonize, 90; war against, 89–88
AIDS pandemic on Haiti, 172
aid workers as logisticians in the war efforts of warlords, 215
air strikes, 112
Akashi, Yasushi, 126
Albania, Operation Alba not cost effective in, 238–39n84
Albright, Madeleine K., 210
Algeria, 212
Amnesty International report on abuses in Iraqi Kurdistan, 62
Anderson, Mary, 219
Anfal campaign, 47
Annan, Kofi, 210

Aristide, Jean-Bertrand; accused of "cronyism," 174; pushed for reforms to eliminate Haitian military, 185; rescinded U.S. Haitian Interdiction Agreement, 181; UN General Assembly resolution supporting return of , 175; winning of election in Haiti by, 173
armed forces in war zones, humanitarian advantages of, 18–19
arms embargo, comments on role of, 195–96
Army Civil Affairs missing from Somalia intervention, 83
Arusha Accords, 142, 143
Aspen Institute, 202
Assembly of the Serb Nation of Bosnia-Herzegovina, 107–8
"assertive multilateralism," xi, 1
atrocities in the former Yugoslavia, justification in the literature of, 241n31
attachés (Haitian group), 170, 180, 182
Australia, costs and services, 157, 161, 237n50
Aziz, Tariq, 210

Bade-Oddur-Baledogle AOR, 88
Bahamas, agreement for voluntary return of refugees from, 191
Baidoa, Somalia, 77, 78, 84, 91

Baker, James, 53
Baledogle, Somalia, 84
Banja Luka, 119, 124 , 128
Bardera, 77, 84
Barre, Mohamed Siad, 73
Barrons, Major Richard, 113
Barzani, Mustafa, 46
Beledweyne, Somalia, 77, 84
Belet-Uen-North AOR, 88
Belgium, 144
Berbera, Somalia, 74, 81
Berlin airlift, significance of, 17, 197
Betts, Richard, 40
Bhatia, Michael, xvi
Biafran War of 1968, 216
Bihac: declaration of safe areas in, 119; defeat by Bosnian-Croat forces, 128; delivery of food to, 121; exclusion zones around, 120; hostilities continued in, 125; unexpected string of victories by Bosnian army in, 122
Biisaasi, 81
Bijeljina, ethnic cleansing at, 122, 124
Bioforce, 151, 153, 154
boat people from Haiti, repatriation of, 171, 189, 191
"body-bag syndrome," impact on UNITAF of, 85
"Boeing people", 171
Booh-Booh, Jacques-Roger, 144
Bosanska Krajiana, reports of ethnic cleansing at, 122
Bosnia: as UN humanitarian failure, 97, 197, 218; early unsupported request for troops in, 204; military costs and benefits across cases (1992–1995), 131, 194; Muslim population in, 107; number of displaced persons within, 115–16
Bosnia and Herzegovina *or* Bosnia-Herzegovina. *See* Bosnia
Bosnian-Croat Federation, 119, 128
Bosnian Muslims: arms embargo of, 122; dissolving of alliance with Croats, 118

Bosnia syndrome, xiii
Boulding, Kenneth, 6
Boutros-Ghali, Boutros, 3, 82
Brcko, increased UN mediation efforts in, 122
Briquemont, Lieutenant General Francis, 113
Bukavu, Zaire, 151, 154
Burundi Tutsi government, Museveni support of, 142
Bush, George, and "new world order" , 1
Butler, Richard, 210

Canada, 157, 161
Caputo, Dante, 176, 183
CARE. *See* Cooperative for Assistance and Relief Everywhere
Carnegie Commission on Preventing Deadly Conflict, 202
Carter, Jimmy, 124, 183
Catholic Relief Services, 11
CDC. *See* Centers for Disease Control
CDR. *See* Coalition pour la defence de la république
Cédras, General Raoul, 174
Centers for Disease Control (CDC) report on Somalia, 77
Chamberlain, Neville, 90
Chechnya, 212
Chelala, Cesar, 177
Chetniks, 101
Cholera victims, burial of, 154
Chopra, Jarat, 206, 82
Christopher, Warren, 201
Church World Action-Rwanda food airlift, 154
Cité Soleil in Port-au-Prince, 172, 180
civilian airlifts to Somalia, financial support for, 80
civilian head of UN operation, 126
civilian leadership, 204
civilian organizations, 8
civilians as main targets in recent complex emergencies, 21, 142–143
"Civil-Military Liaison Centers," 84

Civil-Military Operations Command (CMOC), 155, 186
"clan clientelism," 73
"clinical ethical review teams" approach, 218
Clinton, Bill, 1, 165
CMOC. *See* Civil-Military Operations Command
CMR. *See* crude mortality rate
"CNN effect," 82, 204, 205
Coalition pour la defence de la république (CDR), 142
Cohen, William S., 210
"collective spinelessness," 107, 209
collective state presidency, 103
Combined Logistic Center, 156
Commission of Experts on International Humanitarian Law, 114
Concern NGO, 158
Conference on Security and Cooperation in Europe (CSCE) Crisis Support Office, 105
Conflict Prevention Centre of CSCE, 105
Congressional Black Caucus, 181
"contact group," 121, 122
Cooperative for Assistance and Relief Everywhere (CARE), 11, 79
Costello, Patrick, 178
costs and benefits emphasis, 36–37
Council on Foreign Relations, 202
counterfactual analysis, methodological problems of, 213
criticism of the military, criteria for, 37
Croatia: Army, 111; Defense Council (of Bosnia), 118; Democratic Union, 105; military campaign by, 128
Crocker, Chester A., 41
crude mortality rate (CMR) at peak of Rwanda crisis, 152
CSCE. *See* Conference on Security and Cooperation in Europe
Cuny, Fred, iv, 17, 64, 67, 109
Cyprus, 206

Daalder, Ivo, 133
Dallaire, Romeo, 147
DART. *See* Disaster Response Team
Dayton agreement: as defacto partition of Bosnia, 133; negotiating principles for, 128–29
"Death March" of 1,500 civilians from Srebrenica, 127
de Cuéllar, Javier Pérez , 108
de Lapresle, General Bertrand, 120
Department for International Development (London), 8
Department of Humanitarian Affairs (DHA), 23, 57, 201
Destexhe, Alain, 134–35,
development thinking, crisis in, 207, 208
Dewey, John, 218
DHA. *See* Department of Humanitarian Affairs
disarmament issue faced by UNITAF forces, 85–86
Disaster Assistance Response Team (DART), use in Somalia, 80
Diyabakir forward humanitarian relief center, 54
Doctors without Borders, 215. *See also* Médecins sans Frontiéres
Dominican Republic, 174, 180, 191
Donini, Antonio, 24
Donor Governments, effects of, 8–9
Duffield, Mark, 217
Dulbohante faction, 74
Dutch, in Rwanda, 157, 161
Duvalier regime in Haiti, 170

ECHO. *See* European Community Humanitarian Office
economic sanctions, 111
Ekeus, Rolf, 210
Elément Médical Militaire d'Intervention Rapide (EMMIR), 151, 153, 154
Eliasson, Jan, 25, 93
emergency and development assistance distinctions, 198, 207
emergency relief: coordinator (OUN-

HAC), 226n32, 226n28; most important activities of NGOs, 29
EMMIR. *See* Elément Médical Militaire d'Intervention Rapide
Entebbe, 155, 156
Erbil, bombing of, 61
"ethical realpolitik," 217
Ethnic cleansing and the quandary of protection, 113–15
European Community: Humanitarian Office (ECHO), 9, 117; policy toward breakup of Yugoslavia, 104–5
Executive Outcomes (private security group hired by government for protection), 30
"exit strategy," 196

FAdH. *See* Forces Armées d' Haiti
Food and Agricultural Organization (FAO), 10, 81, 179
food prices, lowered by military intervention, 93
Forces Armées d' Haiti, 170, 182, 183
FRAFBATT. *See* French speaking African Battalion
French Guyana, agreement for voluntary return of refugees from, 191
French-speaking African Battalion, 150
Front Armée du Peuple Haitien, 180, 182
Front Révolutionnaire pour l'Advancement et le Progrés en Haïti (FRAPH). *See* Front Armée du Peuple Haitien

Garde d'Haiti. *See* Forces Armées d' Haiti
Geneva Conventions and Additional Protocols, 148, 208
geopolitics of prevention as an area for future research, 202–4
George, Alexander, 212
Germany, 157, 237n50
Gialalassi, 84, 88
Goma: Canadian delivery of supplies to, 157; deaths in, 152–53; enlargement of airport capability at, 155; Joint Task Force Alpha in, 155; use as logistical and command center by French forces, 151–52
Gorazde: declaration of safe areas in, 119; delivery of food to, 121; NATO decision to use airpower to deter attacks on, 127; percentage of food requirements being met in, 116; Serb ethnic cleansing activities in, 119, 120
Governors Island Agreement, 179–81
Grant, Jim, 208
Greece supplying troops for UNITAF, 237n50
Gulf War and creation of Kurd safe havens, 26

Habyarimana, Major General Juvénal, 140, 144
Haiti: boat people and U.S. foreign policy, 177–78; civilian response to coup, 178–79; cost for operations in, 187; costs and benefits from 1990s intervention, 188, 194, 217–18; country case bibliography, 265–67; decline of foreign aid to, 170–71; democratic elections in, 172; diaspora creation, 171; economic deterioration following ouster of Duvalier regime, 172; factors leading to successful intervention in, 212–13; factors that account for underdevelopment of, 168–69; human rights violations in, 174, 181–82; illegal arms in, 186; National Police, 185; naval blockade, 180; number of killings from 1991 to 1994, 250n26; number of refugees returned to Haiti, 178; UN humanitarian success, 197; US invasion of 1915, 169–70
Hargeysa, Somalia, 75
Hawiye clan, attack on, 75–76
Higgins, Rosalyn, 112
"Hippocratic Oath of Aid", 219

Hoffmann, Stanley, 197, 204
Holbrooke, Richard, 128
HRSs. *See* Humanitarian Relief Sectors
"humanitarian action," 7–8, 244n85
"humanitarian intervention," 43, 96, 189, 191, 219
Humanitarian Relief Sectors, 84
humanitarian "trojan horse," 226n29
Hungary permitted procurement of weapons for Croatian army, 127
Huntington, Samuel, 90
Hutchinson, John, 215
Hutus, 142, 144
HVO. *See* Croatian Army

ICRC. *See* International Committee of the Red Cross
IFOR. *See* Implementation Force
IFRC. *See* International Federation of the Red Cross and Red Crescent Societies
Ignatieff, Michael, 6, 217
Implementation Force (IFOR), 15, 129
incremental application of force, classic argument for, 203
Independent Task Force at the Council on Foreign Relations of 1996, 40
Ingram, James, 201
InterAction, 12
Inter-American Commission on Human Rights, 171
Intergovernmental Organizations, 9–11
Interim Public Security Force, 185
International Committee of the Red Cross (ICRC), 12, 87, 215, 217; in Bosnia, 117; need for revamping, 201; problems in changing, 252n15; in Rwanda, 146; in Somalia, 79
International Civilian Mission in Haiti (MICIVIH), 176, 182
International Criminal Tribunal, 159, 162
International Federation of the Red Cross (IFRC), 57

International Maritime Organization, 57
international relations theory, arguments in light of, 225n20
International Rescue Committee, 11, 147
International War Crimes Tribunal, 115, 127–28
INTERTECT report, 58, 59–60, 67
Intervention: basis for, 182; creation of new problems, 34–35; politics of, 41
Iraq. *See also* Northern Iraq: costs of the eight-year war to the economy, 231n4; foreign debt in 1990, 231n4; military costs and benefits across cases, 194; UN humanitarian success, 197
Irish, contribution in Rwanda, 158
Israel, costs and efforts in Rwanda, 157, 161
Izetbegovic, President Alija (Bosnia), 124
Izmery, Antoine, 180

Japan, costs and efforts in Rwanda, 157, 161
Jean-Rabel (Haiti), massacre of peasants at, 171
Jess, Omar, 76, 84
Joint Evaluation of Emergency Assistance to Rwanda report, 163–65
Joint Task Force, 54, 155, 178
Jonah, James O. C., 81
Jonaissant, Emile, 176

Karadzic, President Radovan, 125, 127–28
Katale, movement of refugees to, 152
Kayibanda, President Grégoire (Rwanda), 140
KDP. *See* Kurdish Democratic Party
Keohane, Robert, 210–11
Kibumba, movement of refugees to, 152
Kigali: Canadian delivery of supplies to, 157; Joint Task Force Bravo in,

155; rebuilding of airport at, 155; Rwanda Patriotic Front control over, 152
King, Charles, 35
Kismaayo, 81, 84, 91
Kismet-Bardera AOR, 88
Kittani, Ismat, 81
Knin, Croatian army capture of, 127
Konjevic Pol, 117
Krajina, capture by Croatian army, 127
Kurdish autonomous region, economic blockade by Bagdad of, 61
Kurdish Democratic Party (KDP), 46, 61, 62
Kurdish refugees, 51; limited UN support for those in Iran, 58; opposition to repatriation, 54–56; in Turkey, 50
Kurdistan, 60–64
Kurds, 45–46, 62, 234n64; Kurdish Iraq uprising of 1991, 48–50; military aid costs in Kurdish refugee resettlement, 58–59
Kuwait, 209, 237n50

Lafontant, Roger, 173–74
Liberia, 212
Lie, Trygve, 204
"low-profile and gap-filling" method, 157
Lund, Michael, 202
Lung, Virginia, 73

McNulty, Mel, 154
Macrae, Joanna, xv, 217
Maguire, Robert, 170
Mahdi, Ali, 76, 95
Malary, Guy, 180
Malval, Robert, 180
Mandelbaum's, Michael, 130
Mandelus, Norelus, 182
"Manifesto Group," 75
Marca Merca Humanitarian Relief Sector, 84
Marehan faction support Barre, 74
"market socialism," 101

Markovic plan, 103
marronage process, 177
Maynes, Bill, 217
Mazowiecki, Tadeus, 115
Médecins sans Frontiéres (MSF), 11, 147; founded as "counter" ICRC, 216; in Rwanda, 146; in Somalia, 79; *See also* Doctors without Borders
media coverage eliciting humanitarian responses, 165
Memisa Dutch NGO, 157
Mercy Corps International, 11
MICIVIH. *See* International Civilian Mission in Haiti
military and civilian interactions: historical overview of, 14–19; selected bibliography, 257–59
military force in complex emergencies, 93, 165, 197, 199, 205, 206, 208; costs and benefits across cases, 194; functions in humanitarian arena, 14
Military Information Support Team, 186
military intervention. *See* military force in complex emergencies
military logistics, 197
military operations under post–cold war UN auspices, 19–30; sub-contracting for security and services, 26–30
Military Professional Resources, Inc., assistance and training of Croatians by, 127
Milosevic, Slobodan, 104, 122
Minear, Larry, 216
"mission creep," xii, 199
Mladic, Ratko, 125, 127–28
MNF. *See* Multinational Force
Mogadishu, 76, 77, 81, 83, 88–89, 126
Mohonk Criteria for Humanitarian Assistance in Complex Emergencies, 205
mooryan (roving Somali militias), 76

Morgan, General Mohamed Siad, 76, 84
Morillon, French General Philippe, 118
MSF. *See* Médecins sans Frontiéres
Mugunga, movement of refugees to, 152
multilateral military operations, 1, 41, 200
Multinational Force (MNF), 182, 185–190
Munigi, movement of refugees to, 152
Museveni, Yoweri, 140, 142
Muslim-Croat alliance. *See* Bosnian Muslims

Nagle, Thomas, 218
Namphy, Henri (Haiti), 171
National Security Service, 73
"nation building," 86, 206
Native Americans, campaigns against, 224n17
NATO (North Atlantic Treaty Organization), 99, 112, 116, 122, 130
Natsios, Andrew, 215
New Zealand, costs and services of, 157, 161, 237n50
NGOs (nongovernmental organizations), 28–29, 36, 57, 146, 227n40, 227n41
no-fly zone, use of, 63, 112
Northern Iraq: abuses by government authorities in Kurdistan, 62; harassment of police in Zakho, 56; military costs and civilian benefits, 65, 66, 217; number of refugees between October and December 1991, 234n63; refugee repatriation much more rapid than elsewhere, 234n57; selected relevant country case bibliography of the 1990s, 261–63; *See also* Iraq
North Mogadishu, 91
Norwegian support and services, 237n50, 247n65, 228n51

Ntaryamira, President Cyprien (Burundi), 144
Nunn, Senator Sam, 183

OFDA. *See* Office of Foreign Disaster Assistance
Office for the Coordination of Humanitarian Affairs, 9, 25–26
Office of Emergency Operations in Africa, success of, 25
Office of Foreign Disaster Assistance (OFDA), 54, 93, 117
Ogata, Sadako, 68, 132, 147
Operation Alba, 238–39n84
Operation Continue Hope, cost of, 91
Operation Deny Flight, 133
Operation Desert Shield, 47
Operation Express Care, 53
Operation Interns for Hope, 157
Operation Lifeline, 120–21
Operation Maritime Guard, 111
Operation Passage, 157
Operation Provide Comfort, 43–45, 54, 63; costs of, 64; humanitarian effects from, 59–60; success of, 64, 67, 68
Operation Provide Relief, 80, 91
Operation Restore Democracy. *See* Multinational Force
Operation Restore Hope. *See* Unified Task Force [U.S.]
Operation Scotch, 157
Operation Sharp Fence, 111
Operation Sharp Guard, 111
Operation Southern Watch, 63, 64
Operation Storm, 98
Operation Support Hope (OSH), 137, 154–56, 161
Opération Turquoise, 137, 149–54, 161, 163
Operation Vigilant Warrior, 64
Orasje, increased UN mediation efforts in, 122
Organization for Economic Cooperation and Development, 36
Organization of American States and Haitian coup, 175:

OSH. *See* Operation Support Hope
OUNHAC. *See* Emergency Relief Coordinator
Outside Military Forces as peacekeepers and enforcers, 12–14
Owen-Stoltenberg plan, 118
Oxfam, 11, 219

Pakistan, 89, 237n50
Pan American Health Organization, 179
Pascal-Trouillot, Ertha, 171, 174
Patriotic Union of Kurdistan (PUK), 61, 62
PDD (Presidential Decision Directive) 25, 149, 156
peace dividend, xiv
peacekeeping, 88–89, 113
peace support operations, 206
Pellnas, Swedish General Bo, 121–22
"people of concern", 33–34
politics and humanitarianism, 214
politics of fragmentation, 221n04
politics of rescue, 40, 134
Posen, Barry, 68, 96
poverty in humanitarian emergencies, 208
Powell, Colin, 110, 183, 185
Preeval, René, 189, 190
Presidential Decision Directive 25, 90
preventive diplomacy, 202
"preventive protection" as UN strategy, 114–15
Prijedor, Serbian ethnic cleansing activities in, 119, 124
principles articulation and application, 217, 218
private organizations as external civilian actors, 11–12
Pronk, Jan, 198, 201
Protocol of Washington, 175
"Providence Principles", 216–17
psychological operations (PSYOP), 184, 186–87
Pugh, Michael, 199, 206
'pure humanitarians', 217

Quick Reaction Force, 187

Raboteau (Haiti), killings in, 182
rape. *See* sexual violence
Rapid Deployment Force in Turkey, 56–57
Red Cross movement, 12
Refugee Policy Group, report on Somali from, 77
refugees: number that went to the Iranian border, 234n71; repatriation in northern Iraq, 234n57; in Serbia and Montenegro, 111–12; in Serbian/Croatian warfare, 105–6
Richardson, UN Ambassador Bill, 210
Rieff, David, 191, 215
Roberts, Adam, 199, 205–6, 214–15
Robinson, Randall, 181
Rosenau, James, 2
Roth, Kenneth, 148
Ruhengeri, invasion of, 152
Rules of Engagement (ROEs), request for an expansion of, 147
Rwanda: bibliography of the 1990s, 265; ethnic groups in, 139; foreign aid in, 165; military action in, 160, 194, 218; OAU neutral military observer group in, 143; outside assistance in, 229n10; Patriotic Front 1990 invasion of, 141–42; precrisis population, 153; refugee flows from, 144, 146; Tutsi expatriate community in Uganda, 140; Tutsi massacre in 1963, 140; UN humanitarian success, 197

"safe areas," 120
"safe haven policy," 118–30, 181
Sahnoun, Mohammed, 81, 82, 93;
sanctions, 111, 176–77, 192
Sarajevo, 108–9, 119
Save the Children, 11, 79
Schelling, Thomas, 203
"scientific socialism" policy, 73
Security Council: approval for intervention, 211; Resolution 46/182, 226n32; Resolution 660, 47, 48. called from unconditional with-

drawal from Kuwait, 47; Resolution 661, 61. authorized Chapter VII economic sanctions, 47; Resolution 662, 48; Resolution 678, 52; Resolution 687, 47, 48, 61, 209, 210; Resolution 688, 52; Resolution 733, 81; Resolution 743, 106; Resolution 749, 81, 97; Resolution 751, 81; Resolution 758 and 761 and 764, 108; Resolution 771 and 776, 109; Resolution 780, 115; Resolution 781, 112; Resolution 787, 111; Resolution 794, 69, 83; Resolution 814, 71; Resolution 824, 119; Resolution 837, 89; Resolution 841, embargo of Haiti, 176; Resolution 912 & 918, 148; Resolution 940, authorized creation of U.S.-led Multinational Force, 182; Resolution 929, 137; Resolution 955, 159; Resolution 998, 126
Seiple, Chris, 67, 85
Serbs: attack on NATO forces, 120; Autonomous Region of Krajina, 105; in Bosnia, 108; execution of military-age men, 127; hostage-taking of UN soldiers, 125; seizure of humanitarian personnel including UNPROFOR soldiers, 123; violations of no-fly zone, 122
"service packages," criticism regarding UNCHR use of, 158
sexual violence: disappearances and rapes, 124; pregnancies per rapes, estimate number of, 245n22; in Rwanda, 146; by Serbs against the Muslim population, 114; as a weapon of war and nationalist policy, 114
Shiites: refugees in Saudi Arabia, 51; uprising in Iraq, 48–50
Sierra Leone, 212
"silent" emergencies, 208
Silopi forward humanitarian relief center, 54
situational ethics, requirement for, 217

situational morality, 218
Slovenia, ten-day war with Yugoslavia, 104
Smith, Rupert, 125
Smith Jr., Admiral Leighton W., 120
Solarz, Stephen, 206
"solidarity humanitarians," 217
Somalia, xiii, 3, 71, 90; bibliography of the 1990s, 263–64; famine in, 77; military action in, 92, 194, 218; political organizations, 75, 76. *See also* Somali Salvation Democratic Front; Red Crescent, 79; refugees in, 236n16; Salvation Democratic Front (SSDF), 74, 76; "Somaliazation" as a favored epithet, 71; U.S. military assistance to, 236n18; UN humanitarian failure in, 197
Somaliland, Republic of, 95
Sommaruga, Cornelio, 214–15
Sommer, John, 93
Srebrenica: creation of safe area in, 118; delivery of food to, 121; elimination of safe area, 126–27; ethnic cleansing in, 114; percentage of food requirements being met in, 116; Serb attacks in, 116
SSDF. *See* Somali Salvation Democratic Front
Stabilization Force (SFOR), hidden protection issues, 15
Stedman, Stephen, 202
Steering Committee for Humanitarian Response, 12
Stockton, Nicholas, 208
"strategic overstretch" by the UN, 23
Stromseth, Jane, 52
Sudan, 234n56
Sulaimaniya, 61, 63
surface-to-air missiles, 123

Talabani, Jalal, 46
Territorial Defense Forces, 102
Tharoor, Shashi, 130
Tito, Josip Broz, 101
"tontons macoutes", 170
Transitional National Council, 87

Travnik, 122, 125
Tudjman, Franjo (Croatia), 124–25
Turkey: attacks against northern Iraq, 61; supplying troops for UNITAF, 237n50
Tutsis, 139, 144
Tuzla: declaration of safe areas in, 119; increased UN mediation efforts in, 122; Serbian shelling of, 125; Serbian withdrawal of weapons but not troops from, 120; war preparations continued in, 125

UNAMIR. *See* UN Assistance Mission in Rwanda
UN Assistance Mission in Rwanda (UNAMIR), 137, 143, 147–49; costs of, 161; created havens for potential victims, 149; expansion of, 148; UNAMIR II, 158–9
UN Children's Fund (UNICEF), 9, 57, 58, 81, 179, 201; assistance in the former Yugoslavia, 116; efforts to provide Kurds with safe water, 64; history and functions of, 10; withdrawal from Somalia to Kenya, 78
UN coordination, 24, 201
UN credibility, 203
UN Development Programme (UNDP), 9, 10–11, 57, 81, 179
UN direction of civilian and military forces, 132
UN Disaster Relief Office (UNDRO), 9–10, 23, 226n28
UNDP. *See* UN Development Programme
UNDRO. *See* UN Disaster Relief Office
UN forces in Bosnia, 123
UNGCI. *See* UN Guards Contingent in Iraq
UN Guards Contingent in Iraq (UNGCI), 56, 57
UNHCR. *See* UN High Commissioner for Refugees
UN High Commissioner for Refugees (UNHCR), 9, 25, 57–58, 81, 108, 158, 179, 201; aid to Serbs, 117; assistance in the former Yugoslavia, 116; relief efforts among Kurds, 56; history and functions of, 10; saving lives, 115
UN humanitarian activities, 132, 179
UNICEF. *See* UN Children's Fund
Unified Task Force [U.S.](UNITAF, Operation Restore Hope), 82–87; beginnings, 69, 71; cost of, 91; deployment, 84; nations supplying troops for, 237n50
UNIKOM. *See* UN Iraq-Kuwait Observer Mission
UN inspectors, 123, 210
UN Institute for Disarmament Research, 86
UN intelligence-gathering capacity, 202–3
UN Iraq-Kuwait Observer Mission (UNIKOM), 48, 64
UNITAF. *See* Unified Task Force [U.S.].
United Somali Congress, 75, 76
United Somali Front & United Somali Party, 76
United States Agency for International Development, 8
UNMIH. *See* UN Mission in Haiti
UN military operations, 13–14, 97–98, 137, 159
UN Mission in Haiti: costs, 187; deaths, 189; initial deployment of, 180; Multinational Force (U.S.-led) replaced by, 183, 187; U.S. forces withdrawal from, 191
UN Observers, 143, 172
UN Operation in Somalia Areas of Responsibility, 88
UN Operation in Somalia I [UNOSOM I], 69, 81–82, 91
UN Operation in Somalia II [UNOSOM II], 71, 87–91
UNOSOM. *See* UN Operation in Somalia
UNPAs. *See* UN Protected Areas
UN peacekeepers, 13, 14; in Bosnia, 107; final departure from Haiti of, 191; in the former Yugoslavia, 130

UN Preventive Deployment Force in Macedonia, 125
UNPROFOR. *See* UN Protection Force
UN Protected Areas(UNPAs), 97, 128
UN Protection Force (UNPROFOR), 97, 110, 113, 120, 218; in Bosnia, 125; Chapter VII operation, 99; costs to the United Nations, 99; in Croatia, 108; decision to station only in areas controlled by Muslims and Croats, 110; deployment of at request of six Yugoslavia republics, 106; direct costs, 132; extension to Bosnia-Herzegovina, 108; in Yugoslavia, 111
UNREO. *See* UN Rwanda Emergency Office
UN Resolution. *See* Security Council Resolution
UN Rwanda Emergency Office (UNREO), 155, 159
UN Security Council. *See* Security Council
"UN Self-Protection Force", 113
UN soldiers, 113, 125
UN Special Commission, 210
UN's "perceived failures," 197
UN sub-contracting for security and services under UN auspices, 26–30
USAID costs, 161, 187
U.S. Army Civil Affairs units effectiveness, 186
U.S. expenditures in the former Yugoslavia, 133
U.S. Haitian Interdiction Agreement, 171, 181
U.S. Institute of Peace, 202
U.S. Refugee Act distinctions between economic and political refugees, 171
USC. *See* United Somali Congress
USS *Harlan County* debacle, 180
Ustashe, 100–101
Uvin, Peter, 139

Uwilingiyimara, Agathe, 144

Vance, Cyrus, 106
Vance-Owen plan, 118, 121
Väyrynen, Raimo, 1
"Vidovdan" Constitution, 100
Vincent, Father Jean-Marie, 182
Vojvodina Serbian majority, 103
Volkswagen Stiftung, 202

Walzer, Michael, 200
war criminals, 115, 147
"wars of national debilitation," 4
Weapons Exclusion Zones in Bosnia, 118–30
Western Somali Liberation Front, 73
WFP. *See* World Food Programme
WHO. *See* World Health Organization
Wiener, Myron, 217
Woodward, Susan, 102
World Food Programme (WFP), 9, 57, 58, 81, 179, 201; food airlift, 154; in the former Yugoslavia, 116; in Goma, 154; history and functions of, 10; in Somalia, 78, 80
World Health Organization (WHO), 57, 58, 116
World Vision, 11, 79

xeer (conflict resolution mechanisms in Somalia), 72

Yugoslavia: inflation within, 103; National Army, 102, 112; Red Cross, 112

Zakho transit camps, 54, 56
Zepa: declaration of safe areas in, 119; delivery of food to, 121; percentage of food requirements being met in, 116; Serbian capture of, 127; UN commander in Bosnia empowered to set up exclusion zones around, 120
Zone Humanitaire Sure (ZHS), 151

About the Author

Thomas G. Weiss is Distinguished Professor of Political Science at the Graduate School and University Center of the City University of New York. As research professor at Brown University's Thomas J. Watson Jr. Institute for International Studies (1990–1998), he held a number of administrative assignments (director of the Global Security Program, associate dean of the faculty, associate director), was executive director of the Academic Council on the UN System, and codirected the Humanitarianism and War Project. Previously he held several UN posts (at the UN Conference on Trade and Development, the UN Commission for Namibia, the UN Institute for Training and Research, and the International Labour Organisation) and was executive director of the International Peace Academy. He is on the editorial boards of *Global Governance* and *Third World Quarterly*.

His most recent books include: *Collective Conflict Management and Changing World Politics* (Albany: State University of New York Press, 1998), edited with Joseph Lepgold; *Beyond UN Subcontracting: Tasksharing with Regional Security Arrangements and Service-Providing NGOs* (London: Macmillan, 1998), edited; *The United Nations and Changing World Politics,* 2nd ed. (Boulder, Colo.: Westview Press, 1997), with David P. Forsythe and Roger A. Coate; and *Political Gain and Civilian Pain: The Humanitarian Impacts of Economic Sanctions* (Lanham, Md.: Rowman & Littlefield, 1997), edited with David Cortright, George A. Lopez, and Larry Minear.